Stalin's Secret War

MODERN WAR STUDIES

Stalin's Secret War

Soviet Counterintelligence against the Nazis, 1941–1945

Robert W. Stephan

Published by the University Press of Kansas (Lawrence, Kansas 66049), which was organized by the Kansas Board of Regents and is operated and funded by Emporia State University, Fort Hays State University, Kansas State University, Pittsburg State University, the University of Kansas, and Wichita State University

Maps on pages 23 and 33 courtesy of *When Titans Clashed: How the Red Army Stopped Hitler* by David M. Glantz, University Press of Kansas, 1995

Library of Congress Cataloging-in-Publication Data
Stephan, Robert W., 1951–
Stalin's secret war : Soviet counterintelligence against the Nazis, 1941–1945 / Robert W. Stephan.
p. cm. — (Modern war studies)
Includes bibliographical references and index.
ISBN 0-7006-1279-3 (cloth : alk. paper)
1. World War, 1939–1945—Military intelligence—Soviet Union. 2. Military intelligence—Soviet Union. 3. World War, 1939–1945—Deception—Soviet Union. 4. Military intelligence—Germany—History—20th century. I. Title. II. Series.
D810.S7S8516 2003
940.54'8647—dc22 2003015862

British Library Cataloguing-in-Publication Data is available.

Printed in the United States of America

10 9 8 7 6 5 4 3 2 1

The paper used in this publication meets the minimum requirements of the American National Standard for Permanence of Paper for Printed Library Materials Z39.48-1984.

To Astrid

The USSR is the country of the lie, the absolute lie, the integral lie. Stalin and his subjects are always lying, at every moment, under every circumstance, and by dint of lying they no longer even realize that they are lying. Where everything lies, nothing lies. The USSR is nothing but a lie based on fact. In the four words those initials stand for, there are no fewer than four lies.

Boris Souvarine, 1937

CONTENTS

A photo gallery follows chapter 4.

ILLUSTRATIONS

Appendix Charts

ACKNOWLEDGMENTS

A project of this size is virtually never accomplished without the help of others, including colleagues, friends, and family members. I owe an extraordinary debt of gratitude to David Thomas, adjunct professor at the Institute of World Politics in Washington, D.C., not only for allowing me to make use of his extensive files and expertise over almost two decades but also for his unflagging support, never-ending encouragement, valuable advice, and insightful comments on the manuscript. Over the last ten years Kerry Hines of Fairfax, Virginia, whose deep understanding of Soviet and Russian military history (as well as German) is outstanding, provided countless hours of intellectual stimulation and guidance on numerous issues not only relating to German military decision making and Soviet counterintelligence support to military deception operations but also on German, and Soviet and Russian, military history in general. Kerry brought his considerable analytic talents to bear on the project, and his comments on the draft manuscript were greatly appreciated and, above all, on the mark. Bob Lavery of Clifton, Virginia, a former Marine platoon commander in Vietnam, as well as a former Cincinnati police officer who is an avid student of military history, in my view, is one of the best counterintelligence officers currently serving in the Central Intelligence Agency and possibly the U.S. government. Bob's highly constructive and detailed comments on the draft manuscript would be ignored at the writer's peril. Errors of fact are, of course, my own.

As this book grew out of my dissertation, I would like to extend my thanks to the dissertation committee. I especially wish to thank Muriel Atkin of George Washington University not only for her support of the dissertation but also for her guidance, understanding, and patience throughout that long process. She is an exceptional professor with an unrivaled sense of humor and the ability to impart a great deal of enthusiasm for Russian and Soviet history, as well as the study of history in general. Her students were and continue to be privileged to have her. I also owe significant gratitude to John Dziak of the Institute of World Politics and to the late Raymond Rocca, formerly Deputy Chief of the Counterintelligence Staff at the Central Intelligence Agency. Their highly informative and often oversubscribed courses on the Soviet Intelligence and Security Services, which they both taught in the 1980s at, respectively, George Washington University and the Defense Intelligence School (now the Joint Military Intelligence College), stimulated my long-standing interest in Soviet intelligence and counterintelligence operations. That interest has never waned, and I am eternally grateful for the high quality of instruction I received.

This book could not have been produced without the excellent support (and, of course, patience) of editor-in-chief Mike Briggs and his efficient and pleasant staff at the University Press of Kansas. Mike's ability to keep authors on track is no mean feat and the University Press of Kansas is lucky to have him. Likewise, the comments on the draft manuscript made by John Ferris of the Department of History, University of Calgary, and Colonel (Ret) David Glantz, the preeminent scholar of the Eastern Front writing in English today (and arguably in the world), were extremely helpful. The staff of the National Archives in College Park, Maryland, particularly Robin Cookson and Larry Macdonald, greatly assisted in navigating the arcane mysteries of retrieving declassified U.S. government intelligence documents.

Above all, I am indebted to my wife of twenty-eight years, Astrid, for her limitless patience, unwavering devotion, and willingness to drop everything to fix yet another one of those innumerable "disasters" inflicted on technologically illiterate authors by that bane of modern existence, the "computer." Without her this book would never have been written.

Lastly, because I am a U.S. government employee and a member of the intelligence community, my employer had to review this book to determine whether any current U.S. classified information has been used (it has not). As I am a serving officer of the Central Intelligence Agency, my employer has a sensible prohibition on unofficial contact with Russian intelligence and counterintelligence officers (SVR, GRU, FSB), which would be required to gain access to the information contained in operational files. Because of this restriction I was not allowed to travel to Russia for this project. The opinions expressed are my own and do not represent the official position of the U.S. government.

Stalin's Secret War

INTRODUCTION

We know the result. By the end of April 1945 the Red Army had, in four long bloody years and at a horrific cost, ejected the Nazis from the USSR, destroyed the Wehrmacht as an organized fighting force, and occupied virtually all of the Reich's eastern territories as well as almost half of Germany proper. Soviet military deception operations contributed enormously to that victory. In every major battle against the Red Army — Moscow, Stalingrad, Kursk, Belorussia, and the Vistula-Oder operation — the Germans underestimated the Red Army's reserves and recuperative capacity with terrible consequences.[1] One of the major threats to effective deception is good reliable intelligence from well-placed human sources. This book details how Soviet State Security defeated German agent operations in Russia, prevented them from acquiring "well-placed human sources," and misled German intelligence. State Security's ruthlessness, brutality, and inefficiency did not stop it from forging counterintelligence into a strategic weapon that ensured the Nazi intelligence services would not recover from their mistakes. The defeat of Hitler's spies was a key element in the success of Soviet military deception. For without knowledge of true Soviet intentions that only a reliable and bona fide human or high-level technical intelligence source could provide, the Germans were severely and consistently handicapped throughout the entire war in the East.

From 1941 to 1945 the secret services of Hitler's Germany and Stalin's Russia waged the most intense and brutal intelligence and counterintelligence war in modern history. No quarter was asked, and none was given. Both services captured, doubled, shot, tortured, deported, or imprisoned tens of thousands of agents (in addition to millions of "non-agents"), the overwhelming majority of whom were Soviet citizens. The Germans decisively lost the intelligence war in Russia, and although their performance in the USSR was far better than in the West, it was not good enough. Stalin's Chekists, by no means infallible as Soviet triumphalist literature would have us believe, not only terrorized the Soviet population into cooperating with the "security organs" but conducted highly sophisticated double-agent operations as well (i.e., operations in which an agent is "authorized" by a counterintelligence service to commit espionage), a specialty in which the Bolsheviks have traditionally excelled.[2] By mid-1944 double-agent operations and draconian rear-area security regimes — combined with Soviet military deception operations — caused German military intelligence to underestimate Soviet troop strength by 1.2 million men in the Belorussian offensive in the summer of that year. This unprecedented fiasco substantially contributed to the destruction of the German Army Group Center, some 350,000 men (a disaster worse than Stalingrad and arguably worse than the German miscalculation of Allied intentions regarding the Normandy landings).[3] Combat counterintelligence matters and can become an extraordinary force multiplier when elevated to the level of a strategic weapon, as it was with the British Twenty Committee and its rough Soviet equivalent.

The study of combat counterintelligence on the Eastern Front has largely been ignored in the West because of inaccessibility of archival and documentary material for more than the last fifty years. To date, the Russians have published no equivalent that meets the historiographic standards of the *History of British Intelligence in the Second World War*.[4] The archives of the Federal Security Service (FSB, the current Russian internal counterintelligence service) and the SVR (the current Russian Foreign Intelligence Service) and the GRU (Russian Military Intelligence) remain closed to researchers, and the Russians have no systematic document declassification system such as that in the United States.[5] This accounts to some extent for the disjointed, albeit at times highly valuable but no doubt incomplete, disclosures made to Western historians and journalists by former Russian intelligence officers who have been authorized piecemeal access to selected operational files.[6] It also gives the Russian intelligence and counterintelligence services a huge advantage in making sure that they carefully manage the publicity (or leaking) of information so that they can exact influence on how their side of the story is told and protect individual officers from any future repercussions of disclosing classified information — no small threat in a society notorious for changes in the political wind (the show trials and subsequent purges in the 1930s, for example) and arbitrary and historically brutal punishments for imagined crimes against the state as well as the Communist Party.[7] Parceling out disclosures also enables the Russian services, even sixty years after the events, to protect sources and methods and, most important, to protect the country's past and present political and intelligence service leadership from uncomfortable and no doubt highly embarrassing disclosures.

One major exception was the unprecedented cooperation by the SVR that former CIA officer David Murphy received on his highly praised book *Battleground Berlin: CIA vs. the KGB in the Cold War*, a history of the CIA's Berlin Operations Base from the end of the war through the Berlin Airlift and the establishment of the Berlin Wall.[8] Murphy collaborated with retired KGB lieutenant general Sergei A. Kondrashev in an extraordinarily productive effort to tell a vitally important part of Cold War intelligence history. As both officers were retired, they had the approval of their respective services for the project.

But even with the cooperation of the SVR, Murphy could not gain direct unrestricted access to already declassified SVR documents much as any researcher would be able to delve into the hundreds of thousands of pages of declassified U.S. intelligence services' documents housed in the National Archives in College Park, Maryland (of course, not all are operational files). Kondrashev — who was on good terms with the SVR — managed to obtain 87 photocopies of original documents and 250 file abstracts. Murphy, who speaks fluent Russian and had access to previously classified CIA documents, was able to put the Soviet documentation into its proper perspective.[9] While there should be more of these kinds of efforts, neither the SVR nor the FSB or GRU is likely in the near future to routinely support these kinds of useful and necessary projects.

The lack of a publicly available archive that contains declassified Soviet security and intelligence service documents on their operations contrasts sharply with the practice in the United States. The CIA recently declassified 400,000 Office of Strategic Services (OSS) documents as well as thousands of pages of documents related to Nazi war crimes. The National Security Agency declassified hundreds of thousands of World War II intercepted messages. These massive collections of documents have been indexed and made available to all researchers in the National Archives, including virtually the entire World War II record of OSS X-2 (counterintelligence). Neither the SVR nor the FSB or GRU — despite all the publicity of recent years — has even come close to matching this effort. Undoubtedly both organizations and their predecessors have a great deal to hide. During World War II the USSR came within a few weeks of total collapse, and more Soviet citizens died because of military incompetence, calculated indifference to high casualty rates, and outright murder directly or indirectly at the hands of the secret police than were exterminated by the Germans.

In a country where there is no long-standing tradition of the public's right to know, the FSB, SVR, and GRU do not feel compelled to open up their World War II operational histories, warts and all, to the public. This "genetically ingrained" culture of secrecy stifles the serious study of intelligence and counterintelligence by Russian academics and historians. With few documents to work from — at least as measured by Western standards — no critical independent study of the operations of Russia's intelligence and security organizations can take hold in that country. While the discipline of "intelligence studies" in the West has flourished in numerous academic institutions over the last two decades, its acceptance and support in Russia has a long way to go despite the tens of thousands of books and articles published on the intelligence and security services over the last fifty-odd years by the Russian as well as the Soviet print media.[10]

This is not to say that the Russians have made no progress. For example, since the fall of the USSR, a six-volume history of the Russian Foreign Intelligence Service has been published, as well as a documentary history of the headquarters staffs of the VCheka through the KGB.[11] A substantial compendium of declassified security service documents covering the period from November 1938 through 31 December 1941 has also been released.[12] In 1999 the FSB, along with the Moscow State Archive, published an impressive photo album, accompanied by narrative detailing the history of State Security.[13]

In July 1997 Latvian archival researcher Indulis Zalite obtained a 1977 *History of Soviet State Security Organs,* which was classified top secret and published under the auspices of an editorial board comprising such luminaries as Lieutenant General V. M. Chebrikov who later headed the KGB from 1982 to 1988. The history was used for training senior KGB officers. With Zalite's assistance, the document made its way to the West, is still classified top secret in Russia, and is now available in Russian on the Harvard University website for its "Joint Cold War History Project."[14] Colonel D. P. Tarasov, chief of the military counterintelligence section in World War II that coordinated double-agent "feed material" with the General Staff, published his memoirs in 1997, albeit highly sanitized from a classified publication cited as a footnote in the World War II section of the top secret *History of the State Security Organs.*[15] Collectively this material provides important and authoritative insights on "fatherland counterintelligence" during the Great Patriotic War, as the Russians call it. However, it does not divulge a great deal of detail on specific operations, exactly how they were run, or provide "lessons learned." The discipline of "intelligence studies" in Russia has not yet reached the same status of those of military history and military science.

Nevertheless, when Russian documents, memoirs, and histories are combined with a myriad of other sources, enough data are available to put together a detailed outline of one of the most important and as yet untold stories of World War II: how the Soviets duped German intelligence by shutting down its ability to conduct good-quality agent operations in Russia and the impact of that defeat on military operations. When Russian and Soviet documentary and secondary sources are melded with British, American, and German ones, a solid picture of why the Germans "botched" the intelligence war so badly can be pieced together. When sources on the intelligence and security services of both sides are combined with the Western scholarly literature analyzing military and deception operations — much of which relies on Soviet as well as German archival material — the magnitude of the failure of Fremde Heere Ost (FHO, the German military intelligence organization in the East) becomes even worse. For the estimates of Soviet intentions and troop strength that FHO provided at critical junctures to OKH (Oberkommado des Heeres, the High Command of the Army, the organization largely responsible for running the war in the

USSR) turned out to be seriously flawed. A good argument can be made, although not a hermetically sealed one, that Soviet military deception and the supporting counterintelligence operations had a direct and significant negative impact on OKH operational decision making. The Russians need to make public the details of their agent operations and the impact those operations had on the senior officers in OKH in order to gain a more accurate operational picture of the effectiveness of their counterintelligence beyond the standard, largely uncritical glorification of wartime Chekist exploits. Without this data, judgments on whether OKH decision making would have been altered had the intelligence picture been different are tentative.

The National Archives in College Park, Maryland, contains a large number of declassified documents from many U.S. and Allied intelligence organizations. U.S. Army Counterintelligence Corps (CIC) debriefings of Abwehr officers are generally found in Record Groups 319, 332, and 338. The records of the Combined Services Detailed Interrogation Center (CSDIC) and the London Counterintelligence War Room (Record Group 165) also contain interrogation reports of Abwehr officers who served in the East. OSS records (Record Group 226) add some documents on Soviet operations against the Germans. The captured microfilmed documents of OKH and FHO (Record Group 242, microfilm rolls T-77 and T-78) provide researchers with voluminous and unfiltered original documentation on the estimates of FHO and the military operations of OKH as well as hundreds of tactical reports from German and captured Soviet agents. In addition, Allied counterintelligence teams and historians assigned to U.S. forces in Europe after the war produced several studies covering Soviet and German counterintelligence operations and were based on captured documents and interrogations of German intelligence officers. Scattered throughout this body of material are Allied as well as German studies of the mission organization and functions of the Soviet intelligence services. This solid body of archival material is supplemented by the memoirs of German intelligence officers and Western analyses of German, and to some extent Soviet, wartime intelligence operations. Many of the records in the National Archives have been exploited previously and used in various books and articles over the years.[16] However, to this writer's knowledge, no one has attempted to dedicate his work solely to the scope and magnitude of the Soviet counterintelligence effort against the Germans, and no one has used Soviet material to paint a more detailed and comprehensive picture of the counterintelligence war in the East.

This book by no means pretends to be the definitive work on Soviet counterintelligence operations in World War II. There are still too many maddening gaps in our understanding of exactly how the Soviets defeated German intelligence. A Soviet equivalent to John Masterman's *The Double Cross System*, which was the joint MI 5/MI 6's postwar report on the success of its "doubling" of all German agents in Britain, has yet to be published.[17] The description by former chief of the Fourth Directorate of State Security Lieutenant General P. A. Sudoplatov of Operation Monastery (see chapter 6), one of the most successful Soviet double-agent operations of the war, raises more questions than it answers. However, Sudoplatov's account contains much more information than the 1977 top secret history of Soviet State Security. His description still remains one of the best sources, albeit an imperfect one, on the specifics of Operation Monastery.

Many of the records of the German military human intelligence collection (HUMINT) in the East (known as Stab Walli I and later as Leitstelle I Ost) were either captured by the Russians or destroyed during the German retreat. Colorful biographies of Soviet State Security officers such as those often seen in British and U.S. intelligence literature are nonexistent even though prominent Western scholars such as Michael Parrish, Robert Conquest, and Amy Knight have made tremendous strides in unearthing biographic details of hundreds of Soviet intelligence and counterintelligence officers as well as in analyzing the internal politics of the internecine warfare within the Soviet security services.[18] Information on the Soviet counterintelligence training process and whether that training was effective remains secret. Operations of the Soviet radio counterintelligence service, which was responsible for hunting down German agent transmitters, have barely been mentioned. The Russians have not even made public the details of the organizations that conducted "radio games." Even the detailed declassified organizational history of the staffs of the VCheka through the KGB, which from 1917 to roughly 1990 included unprecedented but necessary minutiae on the number of officers assigned to various directorates, skipped details of this entity. Radio games were the primary means State Security used to pass misleading information to the Germans. It is astounding why such basic information on what appears to be a Soviet success story, and would seem to enhance a tarnished Chekist image, remains secret almost sixty years after the events.

The Russians continue to hide three critical components of their counterintelligence story: whether they penetrated any German military intelligence or counterintelligence organization in the East that would have given State Security sustained detailed information on German countrywide agent deployments, as well as German counterintelligence operations; whether they broke any high-level German military or intelligence codes; and their involvement in passing misleading information to Abwehr agent Richard Kauder's (alias Klatt, German code name "Max") organization in Sofia and later in Budapest. German agent deployments behind Soviet lines enjoyed an almost 90 percent failure rate.[19] Even given the oppressive security measures in the Red Army's rear, 90 percent is a high rate of failure and suggests that the Russians recruited an agent or agents who might have been staff officers of German military intelligence with access to agent deployments. Reasons for Russian silence on this issue are unknown at this point. With the capture of so many Enigma machines and German code clerks, it strains credulity to think that the Russians did not break at least some high-level German codes. Lastly, the Russians have never officially or fully explained their involvement in the complex "Klatt Affair" (see chapter 6). German intelligence relied heavily on reports from Klatt's organization, and the Russians knew it.[20] Despite recent Russian revelations that a postwar Soviet analysis of fewer than one-third of Klatt's 1,856 intercepted messages analyzed proved "not even coming close to the truth," there were ample opportunities for the Russians to pass controlled information to the Germans through Klatt, and for Klatt to attribute that information to his organization's alleged "agents" inside Russia.[21]

The primary goals of this book are to stimulate further research on combat counterintelligence in general, lay out the current state of research on the Soviet equivalent of the British Twenty Committee, and induce the Russians to publish a declassified credible history of their operations against the Germans that meets Western historiographic standards. For nowhere else in the annals of modern history can we study the impact of counterintelligence on military operations more thoroughly than in World War II. Records for the wars in Korea, Vietnam, and the Soviet War in Afghanistan — all relatively long wars involving reasonably large military formations — are still largely classified. Counterintelligence and intelligence records of Japan's long war in China (late 1930s to 1945) suffer from a lack of researchers with the necessary language skills and access to archival records. Enough information, however, has become public that allows us to establish the parameters of the Soviet operational counterintelligence effort in World War II. This book is intended not only to add to our understanding of the "shadow war" in the East but also to complement David Glantz's unrivaled *Soviet Deception in the Second World War,* his 1987 article in the journal *Intelligence and National Security* entitled "The Red Mask: The Nature and Legacy of Soviet Military Deception in the Second World War," Dr. David Thomas's article cited above on the mistakes of FHO, and portions of David Kahn's classic *Hitler's Spies.*[22]

By focusing on the operational counterintelligence aspects of the war, and even more specifically on Soviet double-agent operations and their impact on FHO, I have purposely left out discussions on Kremlin politics, the internal political struggles within the Soviet security services, details of the "whys and wherefores" of the reorganizations of the various Soviet Security organizations, and generally how State Security functioned as a political institution during the war. These issues have been covered most notably by Amy Knight and Michael

Parrish. I also have not delved into Soviet partisan operations largely because they were a German counterintelligence problem and, although Soviet counterintelligence was responsible for their security and used them operationally, little information is available on how they were specifically employed against German intelligence and counterintelligence targets. They did, however, consume a good deal of the effort of German military counterintelligence. Another area not treated extensively is the German use of various ethnic groups to fight the Bolsheviks. These groups were often either destined for concentration camps once liberated or so heavily penetrated by State Security that they ceased to be an effective intelligence threat. I have also only included enough material on German and Soviet atrocities so that the reader can understand the hostile operational environment in which both Soviet and German agents worked.

I have elected to organize the book by function rather than chronologically because the data do not allow for a smooth chronological presentation and because many Soviet double-agent operations ran for months and even years. However, chapter 1, which is chronologically organized, provides the reader who is unfamiliar with the war in the East with a brief but detailed introduction to the major campaigns and a feel for the brutality of the Russo-German conflict. I have purposely inundated the reader with numerous statistics largely to convey the unprecedented savagery of the war of extermination waged by both sides. Chapter 1 serves primarily as background to the counterintelligence war and places chapter 2 (an overview of the "secret war") in a military-operational context. For chapter 1, I have relied primarily on the works of such prominent well-regarded authors as David Glantz, John Erickson, Richard Overy, Albert Seaton, Anthony Beevor, Earl Ziemke, Mikhail Heller, Gerhard Weinberg, Omar Bartov, and John Keegan, as well as volume 4 of the ten-part series published under the auspices of the Research Institute for Military History in Potsdam and entitled *Germany in the Second World War.*[23] The historical study conducted under the direction of the U.S. Army Office of the Chief of Military History in 1955 entitled *The German Campaign in Russia: Planning and Operations (1940–1942)* still remains a valuable source.[24] These works all used Soviet and German records and, to date, collectively represent some of the best scholarship on the Eastern Front.

Chapter 2 provides a general overview of the secret war in the East and enables the reader to gain an understanding of German and Soviet concepts of counterintelligence. To comprehend the magnitude of the intelligence and counterintelligence problems faced by the Abwehr, SD, and FHO, chapters 3 and 4, respectively, discuss in detail the defensive and offensive aspects of the

Soviet counterintelligence system. Chapter 3 describes Soviet defensive counterintelligence operations, a significant component in making life miserable for German agents operating behind Soviet lines as well as for the Soviet populace as a whole. Chapter 4 gives a basic introduction to Russian offensive counterintelligence operations (double agents and recruitment of enemy intelligence officers). Together chapters 3 and 4 lay the groundwork for understanding chapter 5, which enumerates the problems within the German intelligence organizations. To enable the reader to appreciate how the Soviets forged their counterintelligence operations into a strategic weapon and how it all worked together, chapters 6 and 7 recount three major Soviet "radio games." Chapter 6 describes in detail Operation Monastery, a major Soviet radio game that had a significant impact on FHO estimates. That chapter also discusses the complex and controversial case of Richard Kauders (aka Klatt, code name "Max") whose information the Germans considered reliable even though he was a swindler and probably served as a channel for Soviet-controlled information at least some of the time. Chapter 7 describes Operation Berezino, an offshoot of Monastery in which the Soviets misled the Germans about the existence of a Lieutenant Colonel Scherhorn's group of soldiers allegedly trapped behind Russian lines. Chapter 7 also includes details of State Security's attempts to destroy Operation Zeppelin, an effort by Sicherheitsdienst Ausland (often referred to as SD Amt VI — the foreign intelligence service of the SS) to infiltrate masses of Soviet POWs behind Russian lines. Both Berezino and Zeppelin involved extensive use of radio playbacks. Chapter 8 concludes with an assessment of Soviet wartime counterintelligence. There are several appendixes for chronologies and two detailed appendixes on the organization of Soviet and German intelligence.

Notes on Terminology

Any study of the intelligence and security services of the USSR and Nazi Germany requires an understanding of the terms and abbreviations used to describe concepts of operations, organizations, modus operandi, and the nomenclature of both sides' intelligence and counterintelligence services, as well as their armed forces. Some understanding of U.S. terms is also necessary. The "alphabet soup" that characterizes much of the source material for this book cannot be avoided. To aid the nonspecialist reader in navigating through the dizzying array of abbreviations and terms I have divided the glossary into Russian, German, and U.S. sections. I have also elected to place the glossary before the main narrative rather than as an appendix with the hope that this will enable the reader to better understand the narrative without having to constantly refer to an appendix in the back of the book. Although organizational detail often interrupts narrative, it is crucial to understanding operations. Therefore Appendixes A and E provide the reader with flowcharts and organizational descriptions of the Soviet and German services.

Because language dictates the way we think, it plays an important role in the organization and development of a concept of operations. *Razvedka,* the Russian word for intelligence, can also mean reconnaissance. Therefore *kontrrazvedka* (counterintelligence) means both counterintelligence (commonly understood in English as basically the collection, analysis, and exploitation of information concerning an intelligence and security service) as well as "counter-reconnaissance," a concept that in the West could be roughly associated with military operational security (OPSEC).[25] What is remarkable about the Soviet concept is that Russian has no exact translation for the English word *counterespionage,* which, in English, tends to denote the investigative aspects of spycatching. The Soviets, however, did have components dedicated to conducting counterespionage investigations. Although the Russian words precede the existence of the Soviet Union, the totalitarian nature of Soviet ideology, with the security services acting as the sword and shield of the Communist Party of the Soviet Union (CPSU), makes these words easily adaptable to an all-consuming obsession with counterintelligence. Similarly, *maskirovka* is the Soviet umbrella term for a wide array of deceptive practices. The term is difficult to translate as it incorporates elements of what is commonly referred to in English as strategic deception, currently termed *perception management* in the United States, as well as the military practices of camouflage and concealment. Again, there is no exact English equivalent for this concept.[26]

The *Soviet Military Encyclopedia* defines counterintelligence simply as "the activity carried out by special organs of the state with the aim of combating the intelligence activities of other states."[27] The definition goes on to pay the requisite homage to combating "espionage, saboteurs, ideological saboteurs, terrorists, and other subversive activities of capitalist states." A top secret 1972 Soviet counterintelligence glossary defines *counterintelligence* in more detail but in much the same way. The glossary, more blunt than the *Soviet Military Encyclopedia,* defines the term as "one of the weapons of the political authority of the state."[28] This all-embracing concept of counterintelligence and security supported by a totalitarian ideology enabled the security organs to permeate every facet of Soviet society for almost seventy-five years. No industrialized society in the world before the end of World War II could boast such a comprehensive and brutal apparatus for the repression of the populace. The philosophical underpinning of the concept also enabled the Soviets to more easily acquire a strategic view of counterintelligence — an orientation the Nazi services lacked.

The German words governing intelligence and counterintelligence — *Nachrichten* (information or intelligence), *Aufklaerung* (reconnaissance), *Gegenspionage* (counterespionage), *Spionageabwehr* (again a strong connotation of counterespionage), and *Abwehr* (warding off or, loosely translated, protection or defense) — no doubt contributed to the fragmentation of the Nazi intelligence and counterintelligence system. The Nazi approach to counterintelligence was, both conceptually and in practice, more precise but far less cohesive than that of the Soviets. The internecine warfare waged by the *Reichssicherheitshauptamt* (Reich Security Main Officer or RSHA, the umbrella organization for SS intelligence and counterintelligence) and the Abwehr (German military intelligence) substantially reduced their effectiveness.[29] The Germans also lack a precise translation for the English concept of counterintelligence. To the extent that language imposed limits on conceptualization, the decentralization of the Nazi intelligence and security services significantly contributed to the Nazis' defeat.

The meaning and connotation of the English word *counterintelligence,* therefore, lies somewhere between the all-encompassing Soviet concept and the fragmented German one. The various English definitions of *counterintelligence* are too numerous to list here; basically the term is defined as identifying, detecting, assessing, countering, penetrating, neutralizing, and exploiting the information collected on foreign intelligence and counterintelligence activities targeted against the United States and its allies.[30] The U.S. concept has never contained the idea that the counterintelligence agencies are a political weapon of the state. The English word *counterespionage* tends to connote activities such as the investigation of individuals suspected of espionage. Nevertheless, despite the varying definitions, all services conduct offensive and defensive counterintelligence operations in peacetime and in wartime. Those operations roughly break down into the following categories:

- Protecting military operations and vital civilian industries from enemy intelligence (defensive).
- Detecting and neutralizing enemy agents (defensive).
- Recruiting enemy intelligence officers (offensive).
- Establishing reliable mechanisms for the passage of controlled information (which could be deceptive, misleading, or true), often accomplished through the use of double agents (offensive) (see below for the definition of a double agent).
- Influencing or controlling the enemy intelligence system (offensive).

To achieve these goals, intelligence and security services engage in a wide variety of mutually supportive activities:

– Apprehending enemy agents and convincing them to work for the other side.
– Ensuring that controlled information is properly passed over captured agents' radios without alerting the enemy service (these activities are called "radio playbacks" in English, *radio igry* [radio games] in Russian, and *Funkspiele* in German [which also translates as radio games].
– Collecting and analyzing information on the methods of operation, organization, and mission of the enemy intelligence service.
– Overseeing the security of military operations.
– Running informant networks inside the armed forces as well as in society at large in order to ferret out sedition, potential espionage, and sabotage by enemy agents and to provide early warning of suspicious activity.
– Recruiting or capturing and debriefing enemy intelligence officers in order to obtain exploitable information such as identities of enemy agents, identities of enemy intelligence officers, locations of intelligence facilities, and how the enemy service operates.

The term *agent* bears explaining. An agent is seldom a staff officer (employee) of an intelligence service unless he or she has been recruited by, or volunteered his or her services to, the other side. The contemporary connotation of the word often implies a well-trained, well-placed spy who is passing secrets to another intelligence service. In much of the source material evaluated for this book, an agent could be anyone from a "line crosser" with little or no training who was given simple tasks, to saboteurs, to members of reconnaissance teams commanded by intelligence officers, to individuals who were given six months of training and then parachuted behind enemy lines often equipped with a radio to report on the movements of enemy troops or to penetrate enemy intelligence organizations. The Soviet counterintelligence glossary defines numerous types of agents and apparently has a separate word for informant (*osvedomitel'*, page 195 in the Soviet glossary), which may not have been used as much by the outbreak of World War II. However, the preferred Soviet term for what in the U.S. lexicon would commonly be called an informant is "agent of the organs of state security."[31] The definition is too complex to explore here, but the thrust of this term is heavily weighted toward the recruitment and handling of Soviet citizens. I have tried to differentiate as much as possible between informants and agents.

The term *double agent* probably ranks as one of the most misunderstood and misused terms currently in use. Experienced counterintelligence officers of every major service have never used the term *double agent* to refer to a staff officer of an intelligence organization who is clandestinely working for the other side. The definition of a double agent can become complicated but, for ease of understanding, it is an agent who commits "authorized espionage." In other words, the individual or agent passing controlled information (often but not necessarily classified) is authorized to do so by the sponsoring counterintelligence service or component.

The terms *radio playback, radio igra,* and *Funkspiel* all refer to the same process of transmitting controlled information over a captured agent's radio so that the agent's parent service does not know its agent has been doubled. For stylistic purposes, these terms have tended to be used in this book interchangeably. However, it is important to note that the terms *radio igra* and *Funkspiel* possess a slightly different connotation than the English term *radio playback.* Since the German and Russian terms contain the word *game,* the implication is that a strategy is inherent in the process. The English *playback,* although it can have a strategic meaning, does not immediately connote a process linked to a wider strategy. It tends to conjure up the tactical image of a counterintelligence service ensuring that the turned agent perform his or her duties without alerting the parent service that the agent is under control.

The terms *State Security* and *Soviet counterintelligence* have been used interchangeably for stylistic reasons as well, as have the terms *Soviet* and *Russian.* For German organizations on the Eastern Front, I have often used the terms *German military intelligence* and *Abwehr* for the same organization when, in reality, the majority of the German military intelligence organizations in the East were subordinate to Fremde Heere Ost (or Foreign Armies East), the intelligence staff of German Army High Command (Oberkommando des Heeres, or OKH) which de facto ran the war against Russia. The abbreviations FAK/FAT (Frontaufklaerungskommando and Frontaufklaerungstruppen) for German mobile intelligence and counterintelligence units have been used throughout for brevity even though, technically, those terms did not come into existence until 1944. Until then, those units were referred to as Abwehrtruppen and Abwehrkommandos. On a final note, to maintain consistency I have used the Library of Congress transliteration system for Russian terms and names.

RUSSIAN AND SOVIET TERMS AND ABBREVIATIONS

Cheka	See also VCheka. Cheka is the English phonetic rendition of the Russian abbreviation ChK which translates as Extraordinary Commission, the shortened term for VCheka, the first Soviet intelligence and security organization established in 1917.
Chekisty	Name given to employees of the Soviet intelligence and counterintelligence organizations.

Front	Name given to a Soviet military formation roughly equivalent to a U.S. Army Group.
FSB	Federal'naia Sluzhba Bezopasnosti (Federal Security Service); the current Russian internal counterintelligence service.
GKO	Gosudarstvennii Komitet Oborony (State Defense Committee).
GPU	Gosudartsvennoe Politicheskoe Upravlenie (State Political Administration); predecessor to the NKGB (1922–1923).
GRU	Glavnoe Razvedyvatel'noe Upravlenie (Main Intelligence Directorate of the Soviet General Staff).
GUKR	Glavnoe Upravlenie Kontrrazvedki (Main Directorate for Counterintelligence); formal name given to Soviet military counterintelligence in 1943 after its subordination to the People's Commissariat of Defense.
GUGB	Glavnoe Upravlenie Gosudarstvennoi Bezopasnosti (Main Administration for State Security); subordinate to the NKVD.
INU	Innostrannoe Upravlenie (Foreign Directorate); element of the GUGB/NKGB responsible for targeting foreigners for recruitment both inside and outside the USSR, and forerunner of the First Chief Directorate of the KGB.
KGB	Komitet Gosudarstvennoi Bezopasnosti (Committee for State Security) (1954–1991).
KI	Komitet Informatsii (Committee for Information) (1947–1951).
Kontrrazvedka	Usually translated as counterintelligence.
KRU	Kontrrazvedyvatel'noe Upravlenie (Counterintelligence Directorate). Subordinate to the GUGB/NKGB, the KRU was responsible for nonmilitary counterintelligence within the USSR. It eventually evolved into the Second Chief Directorate of the KGB.
MGB	Ministerstvo Gosudartsvennoi Bezopasnosti (Ministry of State Security); immediate forerunner of the KGB.
MVD	Ministerstvo Vnutrennikh Del (Ministry of Internal Affairs).
NKGB	Narodnyi Komissariat Gosudarstvennoi Bezopasnosti (People's Commissariat for State Security).
NKO	Narodnyi Komissariat Oborony (People's Commissariat of Defense).

NKVD — Narodnyi Komissariat Vnutrennikh Del (People's Commissariat for Internal Affairs).

NKVMF — Narodnyi Kommissariat Voyenno-morskovo Flota (People's Commissariat for the Navy).

Maskirovka — Loosely translated as deception. The concept incorporates all aspects of military deception. The closest U.S. military concept is often referred to as perception management.

OGPU — Ob"edinennoe Gosudarstvennoe Politicheskoe Upravlenie (Combined State Political Administration) (1923–1924).

OKR — Otdel' Kontrrazvedki (Department of Counterintelligence) (often used for subordinate Smersh units).

OO — Osobye Otdeli (Special Departments); generally refers to the Directorate for Special Departments (GUOO/UOO), the name for Soviet military counterintelligence that is often referred to as OO/NKVD.

Radio igra — Radio game. Soviet counterintelligence term for using the radio, usually of a captured or "turned" agent of a foreign intelligence service, to pass controlled information to the enemy.

Razvedka — Intelligence or reconnaissance.

Smersh — Smert' Spionam (Death to Spies); name given to Soviet military counterintelligence from April 1943 to the end of the war, often referred to as GUKR-NKO-Smersh.

Stavka — Supreme Command of the Soviet Armed Forces, subordinate directly to the GKO.

SVR — Sluzhba Vneshnei Razvedki (current name for the Russian Foreign Intelligence Service); formerly the First Chief Directorate of the KGB.

VCheka — Vserossiiskaia Chrezvychainaia Komissiia po bor'be Kontrrevoliutsiei Spekuliatsiei, Sabotazhem i Prestupleniiami po Dolzhnosti (All-Russian Extraordinary Commission for Combating Counterrevolution, Speculation, Sabotage, and Crimes in Office) (1917–1922).

GERMAN TERMS AND ABBREVIATIONS

Abteilung — Section or department.

Abwehr — German Military Intelligence and Counterintelligence Organization.

Abwehrstelle (Ast)	Literally, Abwehr Station. Abwehr component one step below a Leitstelle (loosely, Leading Control Station). For example, Abwehrstelle (Ast) Vienna.
Amt	Literal translation is office; was used to denote various "directorates" within the SS's Reich Security Main Office (see below). The term is widely used within a multitude of German bureaucracies.
Aufklaerung	Often translated as reconnaissance but can also mean intelligence.
FA	Frontaufklaerung (literally, Front Reconnaissance); the German military term for small mobile frontline units, divided into Frontaufklaerungstruppen (FATs) that were subordinate to Frontaufklaerungskommandos (FAKs), which conducted intelligence, counterintelligence, and sabotage operations.
FAK/FAT	See FA above.
FHO	Fremde Heere Ost (Foreign Armies East); the German Army High Command's (OKH) intelligence organization on the Eastern Front, headed by General Reinhard Gehlen.
Gegenabwehr	Usually translated as counterintelligence.
Gegenspionage	Counterespionage.
Gestapo	Geheime Staatspolizei (Secret State Police); also referred to as Amt IV (Office IV) of the Reich Security Main Office — the umbrella organization for SS intelligence and counter-intelligence.
GFP	Geheime Feldpolizei (Secret Field Police); part of the German army's military police organization.
KO	Kriegsorganisation; subordinate directly to Abwehr headquarters, the KO was responsible for collecting military intelligence from German embassies abroad.
Leitstelle (I, II, and III Ost)	Loosely translated as Leading Control Station; German military intelligence (I), sabotage (II), and counterintelligence (III) (same as Stab Walli; see below).
Luftmeldekopf Suedost	Literally, Air Reporting Post Southeast; the official name for Richard Kauder's (alias Klatt) organization in Sofia subordinate to Ast Vienna.

Nachrichten	Translated literally as information but can also mean intelligence.
OKH	Oberkommando des Heeres (High Command of the German Army); the organization largely responsible for running the war in the East.
OKW	Oberkommando der Wehrmacht (High Command of the German Armed Forces).
RSHA	Reichssicherheitshauptamt (Reich Security Main Office); the SS organization responsible for intelligence, counterintelligence, and certain police functions.
SD	Sicherheitsdienst (Security Service); subordinate to the RSHA of the SS, the SD had both an internal and external mission. SD/Ausland (also known as Amt VI), headed by Walter Schellenberg, was the foreign intelligence organization of the SS. SD/Inland, headed by Otto Ohlendorf, was responsible for running informant networks inside Germany.
Stab Walli I, III	Staff Walli I, III. Name given to the German military intelligence and counterintelligence staff of OKH/FHO; nominally subordinate to the Abwehr in Berlin.

U.S. AND BRITISH TERMS AND ABBREVIATIONS

CIC	U.S. Army Counterintelligence Corps.
CPSU	Communist Party of the Soviet Union.
Deception	Measures designed to mislead the enemy by manipulation, distortion, and falsification of evidence to induce the enemy to react in a matter prejudicial to the enemy's interests.
Double agent	An agent who is "authorized" to commit espionage.
Enigma	Code name for the German cipher machine that was in widespread use by the armed forces, the SS, the Abwehr, and even the German state railways.
Feed material	Controlled information, classified or unclassified, true or misleading, passed to the enemy service usually by a double agent or via a radio playback.
GSUSA	General Staff United States Army.
HUMINT	Human intelligence; can be acquired clandestinely, semi-clandestinely, or overtly.

MI5	British Security Service (BSS); responsible for counterintelligence within Britain.
MISC	Military Intelligence Service Center.
OSS	U.S. Office of Strategic Services (wartime forerunner of the CIA).
Perception management	A contemporary U.S. military term meaning actions to convey and/or deny selected information and indicators to foreign audiences in order to influence their emotions, motives, and objective reasoning as well as to intelligence systems and leaders at all levels in order to influence official estimates, ultimately resulting in foreign behaviors and official actions favorable to the originator's objectives. In various ways, perception management combines truth projection, operations security, cover and deception, and psychological operations.
Radio playback	Using an agent's radio to pass controlled information (feed material) to the enemy.
SIS	British Secret Intelligence Service (MI6); responsible for foreign intelligence operations.
Twenty Committee (XX)	Also known as the Double Cross Committee; the wartime British intelligence committee consisting of representatives from several organizations (including SIS and MI5) to coordinate the operations of, and feed material to be passed by, British-controlled German agents.
ULTRA	Code name the British assigned to the information derived from decrypting German enciphered communications from the Enigma machine.
X-2	Counterintelligence element of the OSS.

"The World Will Hold Its Breath": Barbarossa, 22 June 1941

The Red Army cannot be defeated with operational successes because they simply do not know when they are defeated.

General Franz Halder, Chief of the German Army High Command, 26 July 1941

At 0330 hours on Sunday morning, 22 June 1941, the "world held its breath" as the Nazis began their bloody 1,200 mile march into European Russia, only hours after the last freight trains delivered the final load of raw materials to Germany, the last vestiges of the Nazi-Soviet Pact signed in 1939. The German Army High Command (OKH) allocated 75 percent of the existing German army field strength to Barbarossa. The invasion force comprised 3,050,000 German troops divided into 148 divisions, 19 of which were panzer divisions. Finland and Romania added another 650,000-plus troops. Support for this enormous force included 3,648 tanks out of a total stock of 5,694 available in June 1941, 7,184 artillery pieces, 600,000 motor vehicles, and 625,000 horses. Half the entire invasion force — 77 infantry divisions — relied on horse-drawn wagons for provisions from the railheads. The Luftwaffe provided 2,770 aircraft — 65 percent of its total first-line strength of 4,300.[1]

The strength of the Soviet armed forces in the summer of 1941 totaled 5.7 million men. Of those, roughly 3 million, divided into 170 divisions, were deployed in the Western military districts. Of the 13,288 aircraft assigned to Soviet military districts, the majority — 7,133 — were deployed in the West. By the outbreak of the war the Red Army could boast a total of 24,000 tanks (14,000–15,000 stationed in the Western military districts) and more than 67,000 artillery pieces and heavy mortars — 34,695 of which were also deployed in the

Western military districts. Despite these huge numbers, the Soviet armed forces lacked a good infrastructure to support this massive force. It desperately needed trucks, radios, and prime movers for artillery (farm tractors were often used to pull artillery pieces). Even the newest tanks did not carry radios, and in the air force only squadron commanders' aircraft were equipped with radios. Of the enormous quantity of booty the Germans captured in 1941, only 150 radios were seized. To add to the Soviet military logistical problems, the seizure of Bessarabia, eastern Poland, and the Baltic states complicated railroad supply as those countries used a different railroad gauge than that used by the USSR. Supplies had to be off-loaded at the old borders and transferred to different cars.[2]

Surprise does not begin to describe the reason for the ensuing disaster inflicted on the Soviet army and air force. The German attack caught the Russians in the middle of a long-term mobilization plan and by no means on full alert.[3] Within eight days the Germans encircled more than 400,000 troops of the Soviet Western *Front*. It ceased to exist as an organized force. The Luftwaffe destroyed 1,200 Soviet aircraft on the first morning of the invasion, 2,000 by 24 June, and a total of 8,000 within the first week.[4] German commandos, often dressed in Soviet uniforms, sabotaged communications facilities, bridges, ammunition dumps, anything to hamper resupply, reinforcement, and command and control.[5] Confusion reigned supreme. German Army Group Center intercepted desperate Russian radio signals asking, "We are being fired on what shall we do?" To which the reply came, "You must be insane, and why is your signal not in code?"[6] The Politburo, in a futile attempt to minimize hostilities, ordered the Red Army at 0715 hours on 22 June to keep out of Germany and restricted air activity to a limit of ninety miles within enemy territory.[7]

By 3 July Army Group Center had advanced 285 miles, elements of Army Group North 200 miles, and Army Group South 120 miles (see map).[8] Army Group Center captured another 300,000 prisoners in the first two weeks of July as it seized the cities Orsha and Smolensk.[9] The economic chaos wreaked by the German onslaught was so bad that the bread ration for the average Soviet plummeted to anywhere from 300 to 1,200 grams of bread a day, depending on a person's position and type of work. Housewives received the lowest ration, and military industrial workers the highest.[10] General Franz Halder declared in his diary on 3 July 1941, with little equivocation, that "it is thus probably no overstatement to say that the Russian campaign has been won in the space of two weeks."[11] On 8 August the Wehrmacht was 60 miles from Leningrad, 200 miles from Moscow, and in the south only 50 miles from the Dnepr River.[12] By early December 1941 German forward observers could see the steeples of the Kremlin — the Sixth Panzer Division was only 9 miles from Moscow and 15 miles from the Kremlin. Soviet losses stood between 4 million and 5 million

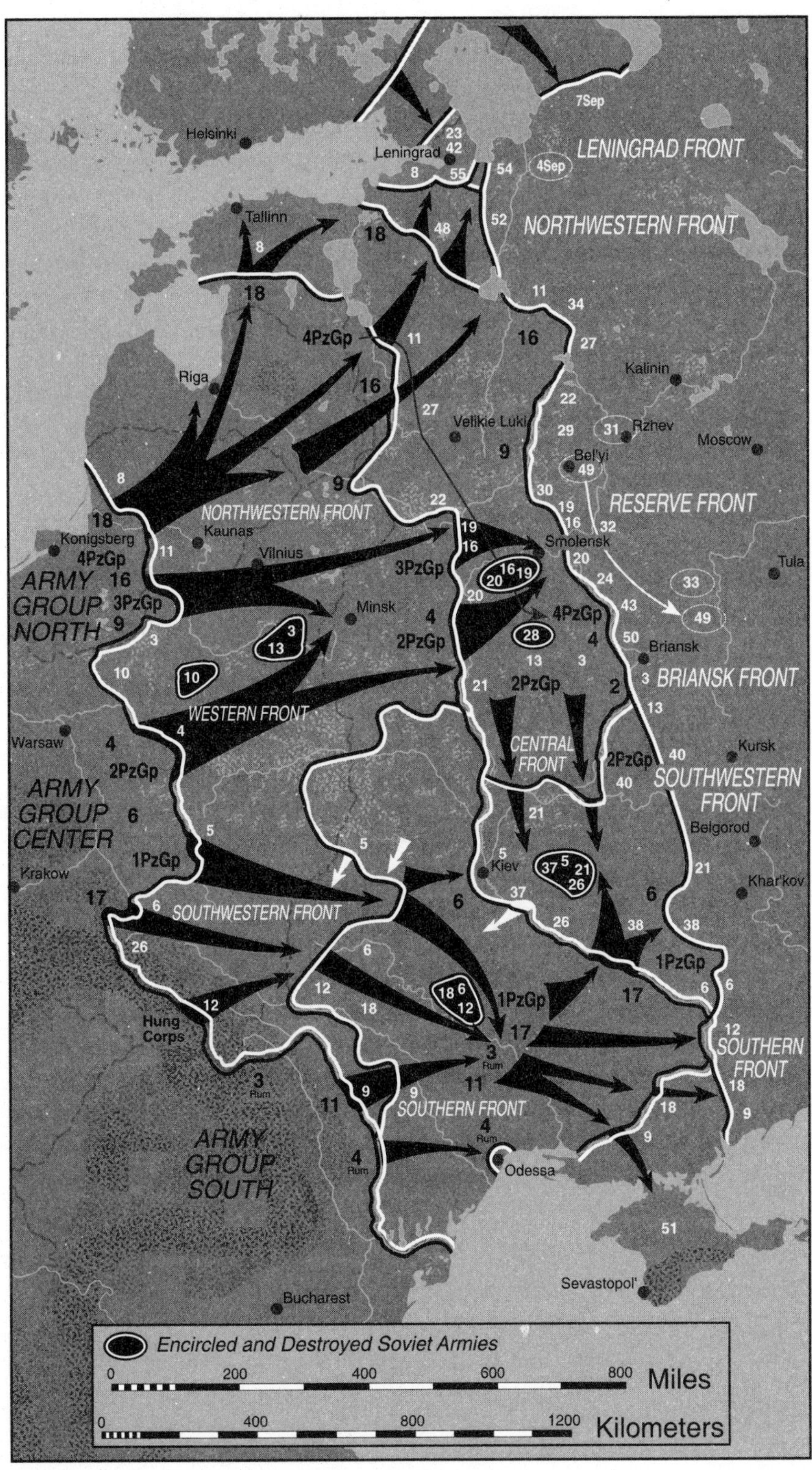

Operation Barbarossa, 22 June 1941–30 September 1941

troops killed, captured, wounded, or missing in action.[13] The Blitzkrieg destroyed or captured 101,000 guns and mortars, 17,900 aircraft, and 20,500 tanks, and deprived the Soviet Union of 40 percent of its population and 35 percent of its productive capacity.[14] Virtually the entire Red Army in the west had to be replaced twice in six months. All that stood between the Germans and Moscow were 90,000 Soviet troops and the highly competent Soviet general G. K. Zhukov.[15] On 1 December German Field Marshal Walter von Brauchitsch, chief of OKH, declared that the Red Army had no large reserve formations and was a spent force.[16]

However, the Wehrmacht itself also came close to becoming spent as the initial German victories came at a heavy price. By 13 July the Wehrmacht had suffered 213,300 casualties.[17] Official reports for 26 November 1941 show that almost one-third of the initial German invasion force was killed, captured, wounded, or missing in action, and that less than half the force was replaced.[18] German pre-invasion estimates of their own casualties had called for 475,000 killed, captured, or wounded by October, which would exhaust the army's trained reserves.[19] By 26 November 743,112 Germans had been killed, captured, and wounded or were missing in action, and the army was short 340,000 replacements.[20] Infantry companies were reduced to 25 to 30 percent of their strength and first lieutenants were commanding battalions.[21] Of more than 500,000 vehicles, only one-third were fully serviceable. Many panzer divisions were reduced to 35 percent of the original tank strength.[22] On 1 November OKH assessed the 136 divisions on the Eastern Front as equivalent to no more than 83 full-strength divisions, and 17 panzer divisions had been reduced to the effectiveness of only 6.[23] The Eighteenth Panzer Division, which was assigned to Army Group Center, began the campaign with 200 tanks. By 24 July, not least because of encounters with the superior Soviet T-34 tanks, the division was left with only 12 tanks.[24] Even after having received a meager 50 replacement machines, by 9 November it had only 14 tanks left and ten days later all were put out of action because of lack of fuel.[25] Only 1 German tank in 10 had survived the muddy season, and many could not move through snow because of their narrow tracks.[26] Even as early in the campaign as late July, the effectiveness of the motor transport of Army Group Center was reduced by 50 percent because of poor roads and mechanical breakdowns.[27] By late November, of the 500,000 trucks that began the campaign, 150,000 were lost and another 275,000 needed repair. According to General Franz Halder, armored divisions required six months for rehabilitation.[28] Losses of men and equipment could not be replaced fast enough because of inadequate railroads.[29] At least one high-ranking German officer — Colonel General Fritz Fromm, chief of the Reserve Army and land-force armaments — thought that the logistical problems were so critical and the troops so tired that it was time to make peace proposals.[30]

At 0300 hours on Friday, 5 December 1941, in weather thirteen degrees below zero Fahrenheit and snow a meter deep, Zhukov, reinforced by troops from the Soviet Far East, made von Brauchitsch eat his words.[31] Zhukov unleashed his "spent force" of 1.1 million troops, 7,562 guns, and 774 tanks on an exhausted and shocked Army Group Center.[32] Exhaustion as a result of intense combat and appalling weather conditions became such a serious problem that it was not uncommon for orders to be checked for accuracy to avoid a total breakdown of command and control.[33] Field Marshal Fedor von Bock — commander of Army Group Center — remarked that "our troops run away whenever a Russian tank appears."[34] Within five weeks the Germans were pushed back 200 miles in several sectors.[35] At the conclusion of the Soviet offensive (consisting of several counterattacks along the entire German front), which lasted from December 1941 until April 1942, Army Group Center lost 256,000 men, an additional 350,000 troops to sickness, 55,000 motor vehicles, 1,800 tanks, and 10,000 machine guns.[36] Halder reported to Hitler on 21 April 1942 that the German army along the entire Eastern Front was deficient by some 625,000 troops, 1,900 guns, 7,000 antitank guns, and 14,000 machine guns.[37] Soviet losses were also heavy, and Stalin failed to completely destroy the German army. However, he eliminated the direct threat to Moscow and bought valuable time.[38]

The OKH expectation of obliterating the ability of the Red Army to fight as an organized force in European Russia in nine to seventeen weeks and pushing the Soviet armed forces across the Don, Volga, and Severnaia Dvina rivers, degenerated into a long, bloody slogging match that lasted four years.[39] By early July 1941, just two weeks after the invasion, Hitler and Halder considered the war against the USSR basically won.[40] By the end of August doubt crept into at least one OKH survey, which noted that operations might be necessary in 1942 to totally destroy Russian resistance.[41] OKH knew that the objective of destroying the bulk of the Red Army in western Russia so that it could not retreat in strength to the heartland of the USSR had not been achieved. In June 1941 the Blitzkrieg was undefeated. In 1938 the Germans annexed Austria with minimal losses, seized the rump of Czechoslovakia in March 1939, and seized half of Poland in September of the same year. The Nazis overran France, Denmark, Norway, and the Low Countries in 1940, and the Balkans in the spring of 1941. These quick victories implied good intelligence. The Blitzkrieg's unparalleled success in the first few months of the campaign in Russia reinforced OKH estimates that its war against Bolshevism would be a short one. What went wrong?

To this day, historians of every stripe continue to debate this complex question. Hitler's war with his generals still holds extraordinary fascination, and German military decisions are subjected to what often seems to be microscopic examination. Therefore discussion of the merits of this or that military decision need not be repeated here. However, one aspect of the failure of the German armed forces to achieve victory over the Russians that has not been sufficiently explored is why German military intelligence continually underestimated the Russian military strength during the entire war. In a nutshell, the Germans planned for a short war. They collected intelligence accordingly. Information on the Soviet order of battle close to the border was good. With no agents that could report from the heartland of the Soviet Union or in positions to provide information on actual Soviet plans and intentions, FHO was prone to serious miscalculations. In fact, a month before the invasion FHO assessed that "in the event of an attack from the west, it is improbable that the main weight of Soviet forces would be withdrawn into the interior of the country." The chief of FHO at the time, Lieutenant Colonel Eberhard Kinzel, believed that the Russians were too dependent on the major war industries in the Ukraine, Moscow, and Leningrad, that they lacked the capability for rapid maneuver or coordinated strategy, and that their command and control procedures were "ponderous."[42] The Germans never recovered from the initial mistake and paid the price. Soviet State Security ensured that the price was high. Though the German intelligence failure will be discussed in more detail in chapter 5, below is a brief preview of the initial miscalculations of Russia's strength.

FHO knew that, in general terms, about 1 million Russian civilians could be converted to two divisions at wartime strength. With 190 million people in the USSR, FHO believed that the Soviet armed forces could generate a total of 370 "large formations."[43] On 20 June 1941 FHO assessed the total Red Army strength at 179 rifle divisions, 33 cavalry divisions, 10 armored divisions, 42 armored or motorized-mechanized brigades, and 7 to 8 paratroop brigades.[44] On the fifty-first day of the campaign Halder realized that FHO had underestimated the speed with which the Soviets could mobilize. The Germans increased their estimates of Soviet formations to 360, although not all may have been "combat-ready."[45] Two weeks later Hitler told Mussolini that the Abwehr had failed for the first time since the "beginning of the conflict."[46] In August the Germans assessed that the Red Amy had the "fighting value" of about 60 to 65 divisions and 10 armored divisions, with 40 divisions being organized in the rear with "inadequate leadership, arms, and equipment."[47] By the fall of 1941 FHO had identified 390 divisions but forecasted that the Russians were no longer capable of large-scale attacks or of establishing a "continuous defensive front."[48]

German intelligence not only underestimated the Soviet order of battle, it underestimated the resilience and recuperative capacity of the USSR.[49] The impression that OKH had of the Soviet war machine changed little from 1940, and assessed the Soviet military's major problems — lack of a competent senior officer corps, a shortage of modern weapons, and poor troop training and equipment — as requiring years to correct.[50] Because of the high losses of officers and technicians, the Germans believed that the Russians would not be able to restore the combat effectiveness of their formations in European Russia. However, OKH was surprised that the Soviets could mount such an effective defense despite horrific losses.[51] The Germans expected that with the time gained through stubborn Russian resistance the Red Army might be able to create new units and mount counterattacks.[52] This is essentially what the Russians did. OKH knew that the Soviets would use all their reserves to halt the occupation of the USSR's industrial centers in Moscow, Leningrad, and the Ukraine, and as early as the end of July German SIGINT (signals intelligence) identified twenty-eight divisions deployed in the area around Moscow, many of which were headed for the front.[53]

The Germans were under no illusions that the Russians would defend Moscow and could bring up reinforcements. The actual transfer of Soviet divisions from the Far East was well known and was mentioned in several German intelligence reports.[54] However, FHO believed that, even with the USSR's inexhaustible supply of reserves, it could not field a combat-ready army. Halder was also aware that the Soviet transportation infrastructure was good enough to move troops from the Trans-Caucasus and the Far East to the defense of Moscow. Despite the exhaustion of German troops and the depletion of equipment, Halder believed that one more attack would bring a decisive victory.[55] Red Army counterattacks on Army Group Center in mid-November were designed to relieve pressure on Moscow. As late as 4 December FHO assessed the Russian forces facing Army Group Center as not being able to mount a "large-scale attack" without "significant reinforcements."[56] Zhukov proved them wrong.

The mass slaughter and destruction of men and machines took place in a climate arguably barely fit for human habitation. Major General Hans von Greiffenberg, the chief of staff of Army Group Center when the invasion began, called the Russian climate a "series of natural disasters."[57] Weather wreaked havoc on men and machines. In Russian winters — where temperatures reached thirty to forty degrees below zero Fahrenheit — goggles froze to the face in minutes, firing pins on rifles snapped, entrenching tools were useless on the hard ground, trigger fingers froze to gun metal, oil and grease solidified in the recoiling systems of artillery pieces, artillery pieces froze to the ground and had to be pulled out by tractors or abandoned, and the cold rendered telescopic sites useless. Mines were unreliable. Oil became virtual tar. Fires had to be lit under vehicles to keep the oil warm and enable them to start. Small arms often froze solid. Only one in five German tank guns could fire. The only weapon to retain some degree of efficiency was the grenade.[58] The Russian winter of 1941–1942 was one of the worst on record up to that time. In the area northwest of Moscow the mean temperature was thirty-two degrees below zero for the month of January 1942. On the twenty-sixth of that month the thermometer dropped to sixty-three degrees below zero Fahrenheit in the same area — the lowest temperature recorded during the Russian campaign.[59]

German troops — unprepared for winter weather in December 1941 — seldom had changes of clothes and fought a continuing battle with lice, respiratory diseases, typhus, skin infections, influenza, spotted fever (which claimed 36,434 victims in early 1942), intestinal inflammations, frostbite, and slow-healing wounds. Hot food was practically nonexistent for frontline troops, and food that did arrive was often frozen.[60] German army standard-issue jackboots retained the damp and were discarded when possible in favor of Russian felt boots. Snow fell horizontally in obliterating white blankets. Sentries had to be changed every fifteen minutes as the snow and wind pierced the face like a "thousand frozen needles." Efforts to tear away frozen goggles from the face, and fingers from triggers, resulted in flesh being ripped from the skin. Jackboots were intended to be lined with paper and straw — rare commodities in a Russian winter.[61] The wounded froze to death on ambulance trains, which often had no heat.[62] One German panzer division lost almost 70 percent of its tanks, because it had sought shelter and later learned that mice had eaten through the electric lines on its tanks.[63] Tanks had no heating systems for their crews.[64]

If the Russian winter destroyed armies, the *rasputitsa* [seas of mud] halted operations.[65] Mud, sometimes more than a meter deep, immobilized entire divisions. Road surfaces vanished completely. Seventeen percent of the 2.5 million horses that served the German army on the Eastern Front died of heart failure while towing guns or vehicles through the mud. Some German formations lost 60 percent of the vehicles to the unrelenting mud.[66] Jackboots were sucked off the wearer's feet, horses drowned in potholes, and foxholes collapsed. If one could move at all, mobility was reduced to two kilometers an hour.[67] Even the Russians — whose tanks could move with less difficulty in the mud than German tanks — respected its effects so much that they seldom launched major attacks during muddy seasons. The muddy season in October 1941 was more severe than any the Germans had experienced in World War I or the remaining years of World War II. It halted the advance of an entire German army. Only horse-drawn vehicles could move. The season lasted a whole month, costing the Germans valuable time. The German armed forces never recovered from their mistakes in the early stages of the war against the USSR, even though, as time went on, the Germans managed to adapt to winter weather and the mud.[68]

Capturing the Caucasus oil fields and controlling the economic resources of the Volga River region dominated German strategy in much of 1942. The ambitious plan, code-named Operation Blau, called for German troops to move forward over difficult terrain to points 800 kilometers beyond the farthest German spearheads at Rostov.[69] This plan was all the more ambitious as there were only 2,847,000 German troops in the East in the summer of 1942, and they were plagued with shortages of tanks, motor vehicles, horses, ammunition, and fuel. Company strengths were reduced from 180 troops to 80, and infantry divisions were reorganized on the basis of 7 battalions instead of 9. Of the 5,663 tanks available on the Eastern Front on 1 July 1942, only 3,741 were ready for combat operations.

Stalin's and Hitler's mistakes aside, neither the German nor the Soviet armed forces possessed enough of an advantage during the next six months to decisively affect the outcome of the war in the East. The war degenerated into a World War I–type "slugfest" in which neither side had enough strength to win.[70] The Soviets, well aware that the Germans were planning attacks as soon as the ground dried, launched a series of spoiling attacks. The Eastern Front seesawed back and forth. The Germans — assisted by a well-executed deception plan code-named Operation Kreml — deceived Stalin into thinking that the main German thrust in the summer of 1942 would be against Moscow. The plan worked. Stalin underestimated German strength in the south, and the subsequent disaster at the second battle for Khar'kov in May 1942 cost the Soviets roughly 277,190 men out of total strength of 765,300 and 1,240 tanks.[71] By late August 1942 the Germans were near the outskirts of Grozny, and Bavarian mountain troops had raised the swastika on the peak of Mt. Elbrus (the highest point in the Caucasus) and were already engaging Soviet troops in and around Stalingrad.[72] However, by mid-September 1942 Operation Blau had run out of steam, not the least a result of severe fuel and transport shortages.[73]

In November 1942 the Soviets launched Operations Uranus and Mars in tandem to gain the strategic initiative. Uranus, the well-known operation to destroy German forces at Stalingrad, succeeded well beyond Soviet expectations. Mars — designed by Zhukov to destroy Army Group Center — failed miserably.[74] Contrary to Zhukov's officially argued line that the Mars offensive was a diversion to draw off German forces in the south so that Uranus could succeed, recent scholarship shows the Stavka planned for Mars to be as significant as the Stalingrad offensive, if not more so, and might not have been a diversion. Only 200 kilometers from Moscow in November 1942, Army Group Center still represented a real threat. Both offensives employed similar numbers of troops and were designed to envelop Army Group Center and Paulus's Sixth Army at Stalingrad, respectively.[75] Nevertheless, Zhukov's argument cannot be entirely discounted. Sudoplatov stated that in one of the most successful operations of the war a Soviet double agent passed disinformation to the effect that the Soviets would attack not at Stalingrad but near Rzhev and in the North Caucasus, and that Zhukov at the time never knew that the Germans were anticipating the Russian attack.[76]

The Soviets suffered a monumental setback when Operation Mars failed. On 25 November 1942, in dense fog, snow falling an inch an hour, low clouds, and visibility reduced to twenty meters, Zhukov launched 668,000 men and 2,000 tanks against Army Group Center's Rzhev salient.[77] The Germans were ready and in one day's fighting decimated three Soviet rifle divisions. Within three weeks the Soviets lost 335,000 men — killed, wounded, or missing in action — and 1,600 tanks.[78] Fighting was so fierce that, according to German Ninth Army records, the Red Army lost 300 tanks in a four-kilometer-wide sector within forty-eight hours from 12 to 14 December 1942. It was one of the worst defeats inflicted on Soviet troops since the initial invasion and explains in part why it took so long for the Red Army to beat back the Nazi invaders.[79] Zhukov called off the offensive on 24 December.[80]

Operation Uranus, launched on 19 November 1942 by 1 million Soviet troops, 14,000 heavy guns, almost 1,000 tanks, and 1,350 aircraft, encircled the 300,000 men of Paulus's Sixth Army and half the 4th Panzer Army within two days, and isolated the Germans in a pocket thirty miles across from east to west and twenty-five miles from north to south.[81] The offensive represented the beginning of the end of the battle for Stalingrad, which had been raging almost since September 1942.[82] A detailed operational history of the epic battle and the pros and cons of Soviet and German strategy and tactics, troop movements, and the attempts to rescue the embattled Sixth Army need not be retold here; however, a few insights into the nature of one of the most important battles of World War II further illustrate the ferocity of the Soviet-German War.

In October, for example, elements of the 24th Panzer Division fought over one house for fifteen days with mortars, grenades, machine guns, and bayonets. By the third day fifty-four German corpses were strewn about the cellars, staircases, and landings.[83] According to the memoirs of Soviet lieutenant general V. I. Chuikov, commander of the city's defenses, on 14 October the Luftwaffe flew 2,000 sorties, and the "roar was so deafening one could not hear separate explosions." On that same day sixty-one men in General Chuikov's headquarters were killed.[84] The Red Air Force shot down 488 Luftwaffe transports and killed 1,000 crewmen, staving off the ill-fated effort to resupply the encircled Sixth Army by air. In minus-thirty-degree weather the Germans were subjected to relentless bombardment by artillery, rockets, and aircraft.[85] On Sunday, 10 January, the Soviets opened up their final attack on the Stalingrad pocket (Operation Kol'tso) with a 7,000-gun barrage that lasted for an hour and a half. One German general, in a letter to his wife, called it a "rather unpeaceful Sunday."[86] So intense was the Soviet bombardment of the Stalingrad pocket that from 10 January to 2 February 1943, for example, the Soviet Don *Front* alone expended 911,000 artillery shells of all calibers, almost 1 million mortar rounds, and 24 million machine gun and rifle rounds.[87]

In early December the Sixth Army had only 100 tanks left, and by early January most were unserviceable.[88] By 23 December the Sixth Army had lost 28,000 men dead, many from no apparent cause other than shrinkage of the heart as a result of loss of fatty tissue brought on by malnourishment, exhaustion, and exposure.[89] From early December 1942 to 10 January 1943 German troops had consumed 39,000 horses, and toward the end of the siege German troop rations plummeted to below concentration camp levels — a minimum of two ounces of bread and half an ounce of sugar per day, supplemented by rats, mice, horsemeat, and, on occasion, cannibalism.[90] By mid-January 20,000 German wounded, most uncared for, sought shelter in the ruins of the city along with an equal number of freezing, starving, sick, unarmed stragglers. When Soviet troops finally closed in, almost 100,000 Germans had retreated from the outlying steppes into the city, and conditions in some of the tunnels where wounded Germans were housed were so horrific that even some Russian military doctors were appalled.[91]

When the remaining 108,000 starving, freezing, and filthy German troops of Paulus's Sixth Army, including the field marshal himself and twenty-four generals, surrendered to the Soviets on 2 February 1943, Germany's bid for world power, as well as any ability to link up with the Japanese troops marching westward, was destroyed.[92] The Soviet victory also had the added benefit of destroying the Nazi plan to eradicate or deport the entire population of the city.[93] In hindsight the Soviet victory set the USSR on the road to becoming a world power. However, victory for the Russians did not come cheap. In the seventy-six days of the Stalingrad campaign, Soviet killed, captured, wounded, and missing in action totaled 485,777 men out of 1,143,500.[94] Despite indescribable conditions, German resistance had been fierce. For example, from 10 to 13 January the Don *Front* alone lost 26,000 men and more than half its tank strength assaulting an already severely weakened Sixth Army.[95] By the end of 1942 Soviet military losses climbed to 11 million killed, captured, wounded, or missing in action.[96]

To capitalize on their Stalingrad victory the Soviets envisioned three successive offensives that would destroy German Army Group Center and an offensive to destroy the two German Army Groups in the south. However, the success of the offensives against Army Group Center was predicated on the ability of the Southwestern and Voronezh *fronts* to reach the Dnepr River. The ambitious plan called for the seizure of Smolensk in the north and for Soviet troops to be approaching the Dnepr River by mid-March.[97] However, Field Marshal Erich von Manstein, then commander of Army Group Don, launched an offensive on 20 February 1943 that in the next twenty-six days demolished four Soviet armies and recaptured Khar'kov.[98] Von Kluge's Army Group Center also managed to stop the Soviet onslaught. Despite Manstein's victories, however, the Germans barely staved off disaster.[99]

The Soviet offensive pushed back Axis troops 500 miles from Stalingrad and even further from Grozny. On 1 April 1943 the German army in the East totaled only 2,732,000 men and was short 470,000. On 23 January 1943 the Wehrmacht had only 495 tanks fit for battle along the entire Eastern Front, although by 1 April this may have increased to 1,336. Panzer divisions existed in name only. Some had only twenty or thirty serviceable tanks. The invincible force which two years before had almost obliterated the entire Soviet armed forces in a few short months was now an out-of-date force relying on obsolescent equipment. The Red Army facing the Germans totaled 5,792,000 troops supported by 6,000 tanks of recent vintage and 20,000 artillery pieces.[100] The longest "lull" of the war in the East ensued. Both German and Soviet forces worked feverishly to reorganize, reequip, and resupply their spent forces over the long "muddy season" and began planning on how best to deal with the bulge at Kursk, a legacy of the Soviet 1942–1943 winter campaigns. The better part of two Soviet fronts in the Kursk salient — which incorporated an area half the size of England — now stood in danger of being completely encircled by the Germans.[101]

The Battle of Kursk, which the Germans code-named Operation Zitadelle (Citadel) and which raged from 5 to 12 July 1943, arguably stands as the greatest battle of World War II. If Stalingrad can be viewed as a huge psychological turning point in the war for both sides, Kursk sealed the fate of the German armed forces in the East. Numerous articles and books by historians in both the East and the West have documented virtually every facet of this monumental battle, including the details of troop movements, and the pros and cons of the German and Soviet operational military decisions. As with Stalingrad, the details need not be repeated here. However, to continually drive home the brutality and scale of combat on the Eastern Front, a few insights below convey the nature of the losses on both sides.

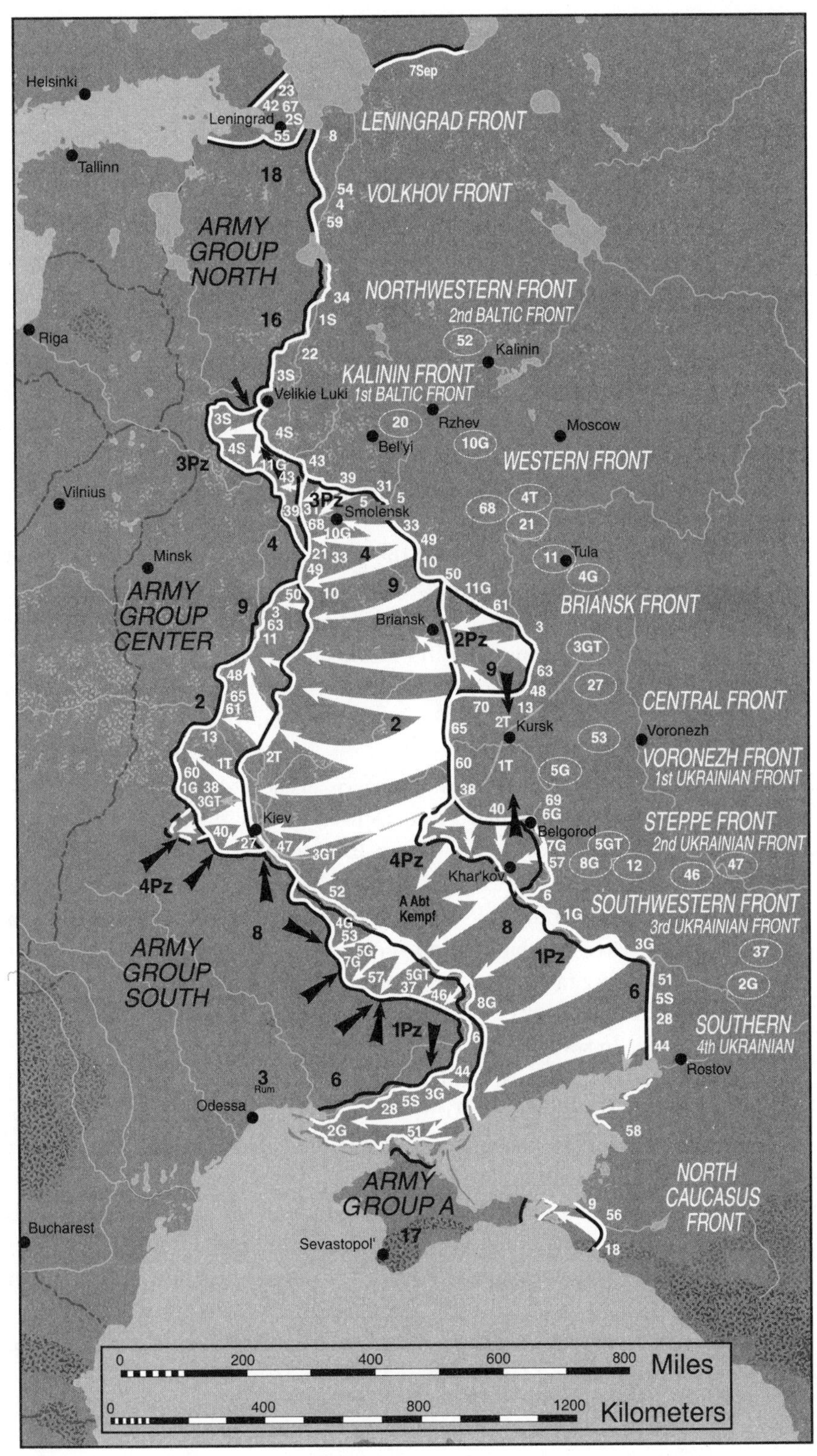

Summer-fall campaign, June–December 1943

Stalin finally decided, with some reluctance, that in the face of large-scale concentrations of German forces to cut off the Soviet armies in the Kursk bulge, he would absorb the shock of the German attack and, once spent, the Red Army would counterattack. Soviet preparations were massive. If Soviet fortifications in the salient were to be stretched out in one line, they would have covered the distance from Moscow to Irkutsk.[102] Red Army engineers laid 500,000 mines on the Central Front alone; in critical sectors the density reached 5,100 mines per mile of front.[103] This means that within the area of responsibility of just the Sixth Guards Army, engineers laid roughly 163,200 antitank and antipersonnel mines. Even artillery shells were buried with remote control devices to act as additional mines. On the Voronezh *Front* alone, 500 miles of antitank obstacles were built.[104] Three hundred thousand civilians were pressed into service to build fortifications,[105] and streams were dammed up to be opened on German tanks.[106]

The 1.3 million combat troops of the Central and Voronezh *fronts* in and around the salient had at their disposal almost 20,000 guns and mortars, more than 6,000 antitank guns, 920 Katyusha M-13 rocket batteries, and almost 3,500 tanks and self-propelled guns in position. The Stavka reserve, the Steppe Front, comprised almost another 500,000 troops, 8,500 guns and mortars, and an additional 1,639 tanks and self-propelled guns.[107] The Red Air Force supported this effort with 2,500 aircraft.[108]

For the attack on the Kursk salient the Germans fielded 435,000 troops, 3,155 tanks, and 10,000 guns organized into 50 divisions, augmented by 2,000 aircraft.[109] In the early morning hours of 5 July detailed foreknowledge of the German attack prompted the Soviets to unleash a preemptive artillery barrage disrupting the German timetable.[110] Nevertheless, the German offensive began only a few hours late. Attacking the northern part of the salient, General Walter Model's Ninth Army ran into stiff Soviet resistance. German tank losses were heavy and Model lost almost 10,000 men in two days. In one day the Germans lost 586 tanks.[111] In seven days of fighting the Ninth Army managed to penetrate only twelve kilometers into Soviet defenses. In the south Colonel General Hermann Hoth's Fourth Panzer Army advanced thirty-five kilometers, but the Germans could not close the encirclement as they could not break the Soviet defense in depth.[112]

In and around the town of Prokhorovka, located south of Kursk, in high winds and rain, elements of the Fourth Panzer Army and the Voronezh *Front* fought one of the largest tank battles in history. From 11 to 12 July 1,800 German and Soviet tanks pounded each other. In the area where the heaviest tank fighting took place, the front was only three miles wide and four miles deep. Fighting was so close that burning tanks rammed one another. Aircraft on both sides served as flying artillery. In two days the Germans lost 400 tanks.[113] After one week of fighting the Russians had dealt the Wehrmacht a decisive defeat. The Germans lost roughly 50,000 troops, killed, captured, wounded, or missing in action, and almost 2,000 tanks and assault guns were damaged or destroyed.[114] The Soviets destroyed 1,400 German aircraft, 5,000 trucks, and more than 1,000 guns. Companies were reduced to 40 men. In one case the Nineteenth Panzer Division was down to as few as 17 "patched-up" machines.[115] Soviet losses at this stage totaled 177,847 killed, captured, or missing in action and 1,614 tanks totally destroyed. A total of 323 German tanks were destroyed.[116] For the first time the Soviet armed forces halted a German strategic offensive before it could break through its frontline defenses and conclusively ended any real prospect for a German victory in the East.[117]

The massive sophisticated Soviet counterattacks (Operations Kutuzov and Rumianstev), launched from 12 July to 23 August 1943, caught the Germans by surprise. The goal was to smash German troop concentrations around Orel and Bryansk, unhinge Army Group Center, and capture Belgorod and Khar'kov.[118] By 28 August Soviet forces, despite stiff German resistance, captured all four cities. The counterattack had been remarkably successful but at a tremendous cost. Out of a total of 2,431,000 troops (not all directly committed to combat), Soviet losses (dead, captured, missing in action, sick, and wounded) climbed to 715,456, out of which 183,140 were considered irrevocable (killed, captured, died of wounds, missing in action, or nonreturned POWs). Of almost 6,500 tanks and self-propelled assault guns committed to both offensives, the Germans destroyed or damaged beyond repair 50 percent of Soviet tank strength. The Germans lost slightly more than 800 tanks and assault guns of those committed.[119] Some Soviet divisions were reduced to 2,000 men. The Fifth Guards Tank Army, out of an original tank strength of 500, now had 50. From July through August Soviet forces had fired off 42,105,000 shells, and only half had been replaced.[120]

Nevertheless, despite these heavy losses, the Soviet High Command had learned considerable lessons since 1941.[121] Concentrating on increasing the output of artillery and armor paid dividends; for example, the Eleventh Guards Army in its assault on Orel in July 1943 used 3,000 guns and heavy mortars, almost twice the number used by armies in the Stalingrad operation, and three times the number used in the devastating Moscow offensive in December 1941.[122] The Russians had shown their mastery of mobile and combined arms warfare in their counterattacks at Kursk.[123] However, the Germans noticed a decline in the quality of Soviet infantry, which, because of the emphasis on technical branches of the combat arms, received the lowest-quality recruits, the least-competent officers, and very little training. Yet low quality does not equal ineffectiveness in all areas. The men in the Soviet infantry continued to be expert scroungers, as the Soviet logistical system became overwhelmed by rapid advances over long distances.[124]

For much of the war the front in and around Leningrad remained stable. As early as August 1941 Hitler had decided to lay siege to the city by cutting it off from its supply lines and forcing the city's surrender through artillery and air bombardment as well as starvation. German troops halted only seven miles from the city center. It was the first time the Blitzkrieg had failed.[125] By the end of August 1941, 636,000 Leningraders had been evacuated. The city was turned into a fortress. Hitler abruptly halted the German offensive against the city in late September 1941 as troops moved south for the assault on Moscow. The Germans began to dig in for a long siege that lasted for most of the war. In the winter of 1941–1942 — by far the worst for Leningraders — food supplies ran out. Soldiers and workers received only eight ounces of bread a day; everyone else received four. People ate anything in sight, stole food and ration cards from the dead and dying, and made soup out of glue and leather. The death rate soared to as high as 5,000 a day. Cannibalism became punishable by death. However, despite this gruesome toll, the city managed to turn out 1,000 guns and mortars for the defense of Moscow. From July to December 1941 Leningraders produced 3 million shells, 1,100 tanks and combat vehicles, and 10,000 mortars.[126]

The heroic efforts of the Red Army under impossible conditions that resulted in travel over Lake Lagoda becoming a vital supply route did not prevent the death of almost 30 percent of the city's population in a few short months. Of the 2.5 million Leningraders in the city in the winter of 1941–1942, 1 million died. Hitler's plan to wipe Leningrad from the face of the earth failed.[127] By mid-1943 Soviet forces had pushed the Army Group North back to Velikie Lyuki. The Soviet and German forces immediately facing each other numbered about the same (710,000 for Army Group North and 734,000 for the Red Army), and the Soviets possessed almost half a million more men in reserve. Army Group North had only 40 tanks fit for combat. The Russians could field 209 tanks with 843 in reserve. However, not until 1944 did the Soviets make substantial breakthroughs against Army Group North.[128]

This is not to say that the fighting in and around Leningrad did not have important consequences despite the relative stability of the front for much of the war. When the Wehrmacht failed to capture the city in late 1941, the Germans reinforced Army Group North with sixteen divisions and two brigades. Seven of those divisions were culled from Army Group Center. This severely weakened the main German attack on Moscow, since at the time almost 32 percent of German forces north of the Pripat' Marshes were tied down in combat related to the siege of Leningrad.[129] The Soviet offensive at Tikhvin in November 1941 and the Red Army's victory over Army Group North in early 1944 paved the way for the outstanding successes of Zhukov's Moscow offensive in December 1941 and Operation Bagration (Belorussian offensives) in the summer of 1944.[130]

From 1941 to 1945, in the slaughter in and around Leningrad, the Red Army lost 3,964,193 soldiers, killed, captured, wounded, missing in action, or sick. That translates into roughly 14 percent of the almost 30 million total Red Army losses during the war. Of those losses, between 1.6 and 2 million Russian soldiers died. As David Glantz points out in his newly published book on the battle for Leningrad, the cost in lives of defending this single Soviet city was almost six times greater than the total number of deaths the United States suffered during the entire war. This does not include the additional 1 million Soviet civilians who perished during the siege. In short, despite untold human suffering and staggering losses, both sides knew that the war would not be won in the north. But the battle for Leningrad played a substantial role in the outcome of the war.[131]

By the end of 1943 the Red Army had cleared large portions of the Ukraine and the whole of the Northern Caucasus of German troops and had cut off a fair size of Romanian-German formation in the Crimea. The Soviets capitalized on the momentum of their counterattacks at Kursk and by the end of the year had forced the Germans out of Gomel' (the southern flank of Army Group Center) and Smolensk. In the north the Soviets severed the boundary between Army Group Center and Army Group North at Nevel, which the Russians could not completely exploit until the summer of 1944. The northern flank of Army Group Center remained dangerously exposed.[132] Despite heavy losses, German counterattacks blunted the Soviet attacks and limited the situation to dangerous rather than catastrophic. The Soviets finally had reached the Dnepr. The battle for the Dnepr line had begun.[133]

Although the Soviets experienced difficulties in replenishing their rifle divisions at the beginning of 1944, the Red Army — in a series of offensives from January to mid-May 1944 — freed almost all Soviet territory in the south and, in the process, shattered the better part of four German armies. Soviet attacks against Army Group North were not as successful as those in the south. Nevertheless, the Germans were pushed back to the west of Luga, and on 26 February Leningrad was declared officially free. In a few short months the Soviet war machine — despite seven distinct offensives against Army Group Center in the same period that made few significant gains and cost 200,000 casualties — wiped sixteen German divisions off the map and reduced another sixty to "bare bones" strength. Soviet forces were poised to strike Romania, and the Germans occupied Hungary to prevent its defection. For the Germans, the situation on the Eastern Front became disastrous. Army Group Center, which was now a huge 650-mile salient pointed east, became a catastrophe waiting to happen.[134]

German losses in the East had been appalling. The Wehrmacht had entered Russia with a force totaling almost 3,050,000. By November 1943 the number of German troops had plunged to 2,026,000, not including allies. From November 1942 to October 1943 the Nazis lost 1,686,000 troops, of which only 1,260,000 were replaced. Of those losses 900,000 were permanently lost (killed, died of wounds, missing in action, or nonreturned POWs). Only one-third of the total 2,300 German tanks on the entire Eastern Front were battleworthy. This force faced a Soviet army numbering upward of 6.5 million men, 90,000 guns and mortars, 5,600 tank and assault guns, and 8,800 aircraft. The Germans still held 5 million Soviet prisoners of war.[135]

Operation Bagration — a catastrophe for the Germans far worse than Stalingrad — took somewhat less than two months in two successive offensives and resulted in the decimation of Army Group Center and the isolation of Army Group North. A separate offensive dealt Army Group North Ukraine a severe blow.[136] Bagration was presaged by partisan attacks against Army Group Center's key transportation points, and air strikes. The Soviets followed up with a massive offensive involving 2,331,700 men and more than 5,800 tanks and self-propelled artillery guns, 6,000 combat aircraft (including long-range bombers), and 32,600 guns and mortars (almost 320 barrels to the mile). This massive force destroyed the premier German Army Group on the Eastern Front.[137] The German line now had a gap 250 miles wide and 100 miles deep.[138] German losses from 22 June through 29 August 1944 soared to 450,000 men, almost 50 percent of Army Group Center's strength at the onset of Bagration. Another 100,000 German troops were lost elsewhere on the Eastern Front in the same period.[139]

Soviet losses totaled 765,815 troops with 178,507 of those considered permanent. Red Army material losses were also significant. Almost 3,000 tanks and self-propelled guns and 2,500 artillery pieces had been knocked out of action.[140] These losses do not include Soviet casualties in the June 1944 war with Finland or those lost in other offensives against the Germans in the summer of 1944. By the end of the summer of 1944 the Soviet army had pushed back the once invincible Wehrmacht 350 miles to within the borders of Hitler's Reich and to within 200 miles of Berlin.[141]

July and August 1944 were some of the worst months of the war for the Nazis. In addition to having Army Group Center destroyed, Army Group North isolated, and Army Group North Ukraine severely mauled, Hitler barely survived an assassination attempt on 20 July. The popular field marshal Erwin Rommel was wounded when an Allied aircraft strafed his car, General George Patton's Third Army was driving through France at a rapid rate, and the Allies had broken out of Normandy. By 29 August Army Group South Ukraine, consisting of two Romanian armies as well as the German Sixth Army, had lost 400,000 men out of a combined total of 905,000 (of which 405,000 troops were Romanian). By 1 September Bucharest and the Polesti oil fields passed to Soviet control, and Romania had changed sides. The antifascist coup in Romania on 23 August effectively opened the way for the rapid advance of the Red Army into Hungary and threatened the collapse of the entire German southeastern theater of operations. One whole Romanian army surrendered to the Russians and began almost immediately to fight the Germans. Soviet forces had cleared Bulgaria by late September, and Bulgaria now joined the Russians. In the north the Red Army cleared Estonia of German troops. Hungary remained the only German Ally in the East.[142] In the months from September through December 1944 Soviet troops fought their way through the Balkans and parts of Hungary, and regained the territory lost to Finland in 1940.

Even with substantial Soviet superiority in men and material, the Soviet High Command recognized that it would take careful planning to destroy the seven understrength German armies remaining in the East.[143] That careful planning paid off. From January to April 1945, in a series of offensives from the Baltics to the Carpathians, Soviet forces advanced to within thirty-six miles of Berlin and were poised to strike Vienna.[144] In one of the most successful operations of the war (Vistula-Oder), the Red Army pushed the Wehrmacht back from the Vistula to the Oder River in three weeks. Soviet forces were nothing short of overwhelming. Their superiority was so great that the average density in infantry formations was one rifle division per 3.7 kilometers, and sixty-four tanks and twelve guns per kilometer over a 300-mile front. Half of all Soviet armor in the West was committed to the Vistula-Oder operation. Fighting in and around Budapest became almost as fierce as the fighting at Stalingrad.[145] Weather and supply problems slowed the Soviet advance somewhat; the Red Army inflicted another 660,000 casualties on the Wehrmacht. German troop strength dwindled to just below 2 million with more than 550,000 of these troops totally isolated in East Prussia and no threat to the Russians. Of the 6.5 million Soviet troops facing the Germans — of which 1,030,494 had been transferred to the Red Army from the GULAG — more than 2.5 million of them were headed straight for Berlin.[146]

In addition to those 2.5 million troops (including 485 battalions of combat engineers), the Soviets amassed 6,250 tanks and self-propelled guns, 41,600 artillery pieces and mortars, and 7,500 combat aircraft for the final assault on the nerve center of Nazism. On the main attack corridors Soviet artillery density was 400 guns per mile.[147] Facing this overwhelming force were approximately 1 million German troops with 1,500 tanks and 9,300 assault guns and mortars.[148] The details of the "Last Battle" have been told elsewhere, so only a brief summary follows.[149]

The Soviet attack began on 16 April. By 23 April the Third Guards Tank Army (GTA) had taken up positions along the Teltow Canal in the southern suburbs of Berlin. To obliterate the well dug-in Germans, the Third GTA concentrated an unimaginable 650 guns per kilometer for the assault. On 24 April Berlin was finally encircled, and a massive hour-long bombardment that began at 0620 hours signaled the beginning of the city's final death throes. On 26 April another 464,000 Soviet troops, supported by 12,700 guns, 1,500 tanks, and 21,000 Katyusha multiple rockets, attacked Berlin from the north.[150] The thousand-year Reich lay in ruins.

Hitler and his wife committed suicide on 30 April 1945; Berlin surrendered on 2 May; and Soviet troops raced to the Elbe to join the advancing British, French, and American forces. Germany finally surrendered on 7 May 1945.[151] Taking Berlin cost the Red Army 352,475 casualties, of which only 78,291 were permanent.[152] The last major battle of the Russo-German conflict cost Stalin's army some of the fewest permanent losses of the war. Despite the triumph of the USSR over the Nazis, its subsequent subjugation of Eastern Europe, and the USSR's elevation to superpower status, the "disastrous victory" had resulted in 35 million dead Soviet citizens and a country that had not seen such destruction since the Mongol invasion.

Mikhail Heller and Aleksandr Nekrich, both insightful historians of the USSR, argued that Russian history died on 7 November 1917 and that the history of "Homo Sovieticus" (New Soviet Man) began on that same date; they called it "year zero." With Lenin's and Stalin's notorious secret police in the vanguard, the machinery of repression murdered and enslaved millions of Soviets from 1917 to shortly after the end of World War II, and sustained a seventy-three-year hideous and cynical experiment in reengineering the collective memory of an entire nation.[153] The year 1941 holds a strong second place for the honor of being dubbed "year zero." Arguably the Great Patriotic War — the Russians' term — was the worst catastrophe in Russian history since the Mongol invasion in the 1200s, which some historians have contended retarded the development of the Russian state for 150 to 200 years.[154] In hindsight the Great Patriotic War was certainly the worst disaster since Ivan the Terrible's reign of terror from 1565 to 1572.[155]

In the six months after Operation Barbarossa began on 22 June 1941 the Soviet state and army teetered on the brink of total collapse. The Red Army finally dealt the Nazis a significant defeat before Moscow in early December

1941; then, in early 1943, it wiped Field Marshal von Paulus's Sixth Army off the face of the earth at Stalingrad, obliterated Hitler's Panzers at Kursk in July 1943, destroyed German Army Group Center in 1944, and finally took Berlin in May 1945. However, the cost of the earlier victories (as well as the defeats) had been so high that even as late as the summer of 1943 Stalin actually attempted to make a separate deal with the Nazis, although nothing concrete ever materialized. Stalin had assessed that the German army in mid-1943 still had considerable punch, that the probability of the Americans and the British opening a second front in Europe in 1943 was extremely low, and that the Soviet army would not be able to beat the Germans back to Berlin alone.[156] In fact, the German army was still only 290 miles from Moscow even as late as May 1944.[157] For Stalin to have considered a separate peace even after the disastrous German defeats at Stalingrad and Kursk testifies to the monumental human and material losses suffered by the USSR, as well as to the dictator's political ruthlessness and cynicism.

During the war millions of Soviet citizens were killed, wounded, or maimed in combat; murdered, tortured, or starved to death in POW camps; or deported to slave labor and concentration camps by both the Nazi and the Soviet secret police. Virtually the entire population of the USSR, and especially Soviets located in the areas west of Moscow, were affected by the Nazi quest to eradicate and enslave Slavic "sub-humans" or by Stalin's obsession with eliminating all real or imagined enemies of the state.[158] Despite the superpower status that accrued to the USSR after the war, Russia today, like the Soviet Union before it, has never fully recovered — demographically, psychologically, or materially — from this cataclysm despite almost sixty years of relative peace.[159]

The butcher's bill for the unprecedented war of extermination waged by the Nazis and the Bolsheviks from 1941 to 1945 numbs the mind. Soviet military losses, including those killed, captured, wounded, or missing in action, totaled almost 30 million. Of those, almost 11.3 million died, if one assumes that the majority of the roughly 4.5 million Soviet soldiers reported as captured or missing in action also perished. The German army was essentially ordered to let Soviet POWs starve to death.[160] Soviet soldiers, therefore, accounted for about 47 percent of the total number of military deaths in World War II.[161] Or, looked at from another perspective, of the 34,476,700 men who donned some type of a Soviet uniform during the war, almost 33 percent died. At any given time the Soviet field army fighting the Germans numbered somewhere between 5 million and 6.5 million men.[162] In purely statistical terms this means that the entire Soviet field army fighting the Nazis was replaced at least twice from 1941 to 1945, or almost five times if one uses the total figures for soldiers killed, captured, wounded, and missing in action.

Recent scholarship estimates Soviet civilian deaths as ranging somewhere between 17 million and 24 million.[163] In other words, the well-prepared Nazi war of annihilation, combined with Stalin's unbridled ruthlessness, resulted in anywhere from 28.3 million to 35.3 million dead Soviet citizens, when the 11.3 million Soviet military deaths (if one believes that the majority of the 4.5 million Soviet soldiers captured or missing in action died) are included. This equates to more than ten dead Soviet citizens for every meter of ground between Moscow and Berlin.[164] In addition, Plan Ost — developed well before the invasion — called for the Nazis to deport 31 million people from Poland and European Russia and to resettle the area with ethnic Germans over a thirty-year period.[165] The number of Soviet dead fulfilled Plan Ost's quota twenty-six years ahead of schedule. Depending on whether one accepts the "lower" end of this horrific scale or the higher, the USSR suffered a little under or a little over half the total number of 60 million deaths in all of World War II.[166] By 1945, out of a Soviet population of 194.1 million before the war, upward of 18 percent had died.[167] Had this catastrophe taken place in the United States, it would have meant that by the end of the war 27 percent of Americans would have been killed out of a population of 132,164,000 in 1940.[168] By comparison, of the roughly 12 million Americans who served in the armed forces in World War II, about 400,000 died. Had the numbers been the same for the U.S. military as they had been for the Soviets, about 2,160,000 U.S. troops would have perished. Soviet material losses were equally catastrophic. Citing official Soviet figures, Heller and Nekrich state that 71,710 towns, cities, and villages, 32,000 industrial enterprises, and 65,000 kilometers of railroad were totally or partially destroyed. Twenty-five million people became homeless. Inflation was rampant, and prices of some foodstuffs doubled or tripled.[169] These grisly figures continue to defy the imagination even half a century after the war's end.

The Wehrmacht did not fare much better. Of the 13,448,000 German troops killed, captured, wounded, or missing in action in World War II (75 percent of the total mobilized, or 46 percent of the entire male population of Austria and Germany in 1939) almost 7 million were lost on the Eastern Front.[170] Of those, anywhere from 2.3 million to 3.5 million died, depending on how one calculates the number of dead in the figures for those missing in action or who died in captivity.[171] Germany's major allies — Hungary, Italy, Romania, and Finland — added another 1,725,000 killed, captured, wounded, or missing in action to the human cost of the war.[172] Material losses for the Germans on the Eastern Front alone totaled 48,000 tanks, 167,000 artillery pieces, and 77,000 aircraft.[173] This means that from the beginning of the invasion, the number of German troops was replaced a bit more than roughly two times, tanks thirteen times, artillery twenty times, and aircraft almost twenty-eight times.

Seven million Germans died. This equates to approximately 6 percent of the total prewar population of Germany. Of all male Germans born in 1924, 25 percent were killed and another 30 percent wounded. In many of Germany's major cities, more than 90 percent of German houses were uninhabitable. German cities were covered by 400 million cubic feet of rubble, which is equivalent to a 100-square-mile area covered to a height of several feet in rubble. Twenty million Germans were homeless, and the average basic ration was no more than 1,000 calories per day. In some areas it was reduced to 400 calories a day, less than the ration in the Bergen-Belsen concentration camp. Germany had not seen such devastation since the Thirty Years War 300 years before.[174] During the last few months 2 million German women were raped by the Red Army, and the population of East Prussia, which had stood at 2.2 million in 1940, was reduced to 193,000 by May 1945.[175] If 1917 is year zero for the Russians, Germans referred to the end of the war as *Die Stunde Null,* or "zero hour."

At any given time between 6 to 9 million Nazi and Soviet troops were engaged in unremitting combat for three years, ten months, and sixteen days on a front never less that 2,400 miles long and, at most, one that stretched to 3,060 miles in late 1942. The battlefields were spread in depth and breadth from the Arctic Ocean to the Caucasus and from the Caspian Sea to the Elbe River. The land area of operations approximated that of the entire continental United States east of the Mississippi River. By the summer of 1942, with German forces approaching the Caspian Sea, the Nazis held 1,926,000 square kilometers of Soviet territory. No other theater of the war experienced such non-stop combat for the better part of four years between such large forces over such a huge area.[176]

The German invasion stimulated a second industrial revolution in Russia since, from August to October 1941, 80 percent of the Russian war industry was on the move eastward. The Nazi advance, as rapid as it was, was not quick enough to totally destroy the Soviet war industry. In the first three months of the war the Soviet railway system, while transporting 2.5 million troops westward, transported 1,523 factories to the East. One heavy-machine tools factory was stripped down in five days (including 10,000-ton presses) and loaded onto wagons under German bombing, while its 2,500 technicians marched twenty miles to the nearest railhead for the trip eastward. The Khar'kov tank works turned out its first 25 T-34 tanks in just less than 10 weeks after having been evacuated from Khar'kov.[177] In the winter months Soviet industry managed to produce 4,500 tanks, 3,000 aircraft, 14,000 guns, and 50,000 mortars.[178] The Soviet armed forces dealt the Wehrmacht a severe blow. After the battle for Moscow and the subsequent Soviet counterattacks, the Germans never regained the strategic initiative.[179]

In the midst of this endless carnage the Nazi and Soviet security and intelligence services were pitted against each other in a four-year-long intelligence and counterintelligence war of unprecedented breadth and scope. While Hitler's and Stalin's secret police exterminated, tortured, deported, enslaved, and starved to death untold millions of soldiers and civilians, the German and Soviet services also conducted a ruthless clandestine human intelligence (HUMINT) war on a massive scale. The Soviets won the "invisible war" not because they were more efficient but because they were able, under impossible conditions, to effectively exploit German mistakes in numerous instances and reduce the Nazi ability to exploit Soviet ones. To quote Frederick the Great in the Seven Years War: "It is not enough to kill Russians, you have to knock them down."[180]

The Soviet State Security apparatus decisively thwarted the Germans' ability to recruit agents within the higher levels of the CPSU, the armed forces, and the security and intelligence services. Colonel Hermann Baun, commander of all Abwehr clandestine human operations targeted against Russia during the war, said in his postwar interrogation that virtually none of his operations was successful. This was a staggering admission considering the bloody history of Soviet repression that drove millions into the hands of the Germans in the initial phase of the war.[181] That the Germans never had a reliable human intelligence source (or a significant technical one such as Ultra) that could, for one thing, tell them the Stavka's true military intentions or, for another, give them information on any Soviet agents working at the senior levels of their own intelligence and security services became two of the most important factors in the success of Soviet military deception, which the Russians employed to great effect in virtually every operation during the war.

The "Invisible Front"

We look upon the Soviet government as if it were any other government — but it isn't. Because it is essentially a counterintelligence apparatus. It was conceived in 1903 by Lenin as an operation in counterintelligence against the Czarist regime, and it has remained a conspiracy ever since . . . the government is there. It's a front, it performs certain functions. But when a major change takes place, it is within the context of the intelligence apparatus which is identical with the Communist Party.

Issac Don Levine, 23 May 1960

The character of Smersh is independent of war and peace.

U.S. Army Counterintelligence Corps Report, 24 March 1947

In a war of such immense barbarity, gross incompetence and miscalculations on both sides, and Nazi arrogance, the question arises as to why combat counterintelligence matters at all. It matters because if intelligence services are the "eyes, ears, and noses" of states and their armies, and counterintelligence and security services are the "immune system," the absence of counterintelligence substantially increases the "risk of death." Without an effective immune system, the "senses" of the army cannot function well, if at all. If an intelligence service can be rendered "deaf and dumb" as well as blind, by extension, the effectiveness of the state and its army becomes severely threatened. For example, poor intelligence and mediocre counterintelligence, aided by numerous subversive high-level anti-Hitler sympathizers within the Abwehr, no doubt accelerated the German defeat in both the East and the West.[1] The abysmal failure of German intelligence was not offset by some significant German counterintelligence successes such as the joint Gestapo/Abwehr "roll up" of the extensive European-wide Soviet intelligence network commonly referred to as the Rote Kapelle, or Red Orchestra.[2] Soviet State Security, in the early stages of the war, withstood exceptional strain but recovered largely because it reestablished its battered informant networks and was able to prevent the Germans from penetrating deep into the Soviet rear, as well as the higher levels of the Party, the army, and the security services.[3]

State Security's recovery cannot be totally explained by German arrogance and unpreparedness. The Soviet concept of counterintelligence defeated the Germans. The Abwehr and the SD had little idea what they were up against. If the USSR was said to have been "a conspiracy disguised as a state," one Western scholar of the Soviet intelligence security services refined the idea and coined the USSR "a counterintelligence state."[4] The concept, in brief, means that the Soviet Union — whose existence spanned almost a quarter of a century by 1941 — was designed from top to bottom at its inception to catch, manipulate, kill, or imprison "spies," "traitors," and dissidents of every stripe, real or imagined, to keep the Communist Party in power. In other words, the Soviets understood and had been practicing deception at every level for twenty-five years with the intelligence and security services in the forefront. This, of course, does not include the time the Bolshevik Party spent honing its "conspiratorial" skills while evading the Okhrana, the Tsarist Secret Police, before it took power in 1917.[5]

If used effectively and under the right conditions, counterintelligence can be more than just a force multiplier.[6] The Soviets linked counterintelligence and security to, and coordinated it with, military deception operations early in the war, Stalingrad (1942) and Kursk (1943) being the primary examples. It became even more effective toward the latter part of the war, culminating in the highly successful deception (or, more precisely, perception management) effort incorporated into Operation Bagration in June 1944, which destroyed German Army Group Center.[7] The Soviets forged counterintelligence — albeit ruthlessly and certainly not efficiently — into a formidable strategic weapon.[8] Although the British did the same thing, that is, marry counterintelligence operations to strategic deception, it took them somewhat longer for the concept to mature, culminating in the finely tuned strategic deception operation that kept several Nazi divisions tied down in Pas de Calais, thereby ensuring the success of the Normandy landings in June 1944.[9]

During the war the British Twenty Committee ran roughly thirty-nine double agents, about fifteen involving radio playbacks. The Twenty Committee, with the help of Ultra (the British code name for material gleaned from breaking high-level German Enigma ciphers), and the doubling of every Abwehr agent in England as well as some others located elsewhere, saved thousands of Allied lives in part because the British fed the Germans enough of the right kind of information so that the Germans believed that the invasion of "Fortress Europe" would take place at Pas de Calais and that the Normandy landings were a diversion. The deception was, of course, backed up by the actual movement of troops, construction of dummy tanks, aircraft, and artillery pieces, as well as the transmission of dummy radio messages and even the issuance of insignias for a phantom army. The Germans, therefore, did not move their armored divisions from Pas de Calais to Normandy.[10] Had the Germans defeated the Allies on the beaches, it would have been a disaster for the Allied forces in the West as well as the Russians. The Germans might have transferred large numbers of their troops to the Eastern Front, increasing the chances of possibly fighting the Russians to a stalemate or significantly prolonging the Red Army from entering Germany proper. The British also deceived the Germans earlier in the war in a similar — albeit less elaborate — way as to whether the Allies would invade Sicily and, on occasion, misdirected German bombing campaigns.[11]

Although no Russian or Soviet publications have detailed the existence of a Soviet equivalent of a "Twenty Committee," solid circumstantial evidence strongly indicates that one existed. According to recently published declassified Soviet counterintelligence documents, General L. F. Raikhman, who was a major and deputy chief of the Second Directorate (counterintelligence) of the NKVD in the beginning of the war and who held the same position in the NKGB, was heavily involved in double-agent operations, and was identified as being responsible for liaison with the Operations Directorate of the General Staff in early 1943. The Second Directorate of the NKVD had 227 officers assigned to its staff in Moscow to cover the entire country.[12] Raikhman's rise from a major of State Security in 1941 to a general in 1945 while assigned to the same position as deputy chief of the internal counterintelligence directorate, however, suggests that, in addition to being well connected, he either supervised or was heavily involved in some highly successful counterintelligence operations.[13] Raikhman was involved in the notorious Katyn Forest massacre of 15,000 Polish officers as well as the deportation of Volga Germans from Saratov in August 1941. He headed the GULAG at one point in his career.[14] In short, to quote the eminent scholar of the Great Purges Robert Conquest, Raikhman (among others) was, by the middle of the war, a "highly decorated and richly uniformed thug, despite his substantial involvement in radio games and double agents against the Germans.[15]

In 1979 a Soviet history of military counterintelligence revealed that one Vladimir Yakovlevich Baryshnikov headed a small office that directed and coordinated offensive military counterintelligence operations (read double-agent operations).[16] Baryshnikov had been chief of the first section of the first department of the Second Directorate of the NKVD.[17] This section basically was responsible for the "security of the areas and people liberated from the German occupation and conducting counterintelligence operations in those areas."[18] In 1997 retired KGB colonel D. P. Tarasov, who during the war was assigned to closely coordinate all disinformation (read controlled information) passed by

Soviet military counterintelligence through radio games, published an unclassified memoir of his experiences, much of it, but not all, fictionalized to protect sources. His book vaguely identified the then captain of State Security Baryshnikov as having three deputies, all of whom were involved in directing radio playbacks.[19] Baryshnikov had been transferred to Smersh.

Tarasov further revealed that the then major of State Security P. P. Timofeev was Baryshnikov's boss.[20] At the beginning of the war Timofeev headed the first department of the Second Directorate of the NKVD.[21] Although the specific name of this department is elusive, the department had six sections all of whose functions related to rooting out German agents and conducting counterintelligence operations.[22] Timofeev had also been transferred to military counterintelligence.[23] Unfortunately Tarasov does not specifically identify the component responsible for conducting radio playbacks. Even an examination of the detailed organizational breakdown of the headquarters components of the Directorate of Special Departments (Osobye Otdely or OOs) of the NKVD (military counterintelligence) in May 1942, in Appendix A, does not readily reveal an element designed specifically for the coordination of double-agent operations.[24] However, a history of the Soviet State Security organs published in 1999 shows that the third department of Smersh handled both searches for enemy agents and radio playbacks.[25] The 1977 top secret history of State Security only identifies Smersh's third department as one for "combating parachutists."[26] German documents identify the function (usually as counterespionage, for example) but often do not identify the specific nomenclature.[27]

A close reading of Tarasov's book, combined with an analysis of newly released Soviet documents, clearly shows that the first department of the Second Directorate of the NKVD, along with Timofeev and Baryshnikov, were transferred to Smersh in 1943.[28] Timofeev eventually won the Order of the Mark of Honor Smersh.[29] Tarasov goes on to say that out of Timofeev's department an entity within Smersh was set up to penetrate German intelligence and counterintelligence organizations.[30] According to Tarasov, the transfer of Timofeev's department to Smersh along with Baryshnikov's section greatly sped up the coordination of radio games with the General Staff.[31] Meetings to coordinate the text of radio game messages were held in various People's Commissariat of Defense buildings and a building on Kirov Street in Moscow belonging to the Stavka.[32]

Other sources, albeit in not as much detail, repeatedly emphasize the close coordination with the General Staff and counterintelligence elements.[33] General Sudoplatov, former chief of the NKVD/NKGB's Fourth Directorate (Terror and Sabotage behind Enemy Lines), mentioned several times in his memoirs that he closely coordinated disinformation with Colonel General F. F. Kuznetsov (head of the GRU — Soviet military intelligence — from 1943 to 1949).[34] Given that figures such as L. P. Beria (the notorious head of the NKVD) and V. S. Abakumov, who later headed Smersh, held prominent positions either on the State Defense Committee or on the Stavka (Supreme High Command), and that these organizations had staffs, it seems logical that the overall coordination of Soviet deception operations resided somewhere in those entities as well as on the General Staff. In some cases Beria and Stalin took a strong personal interest in or controlled some of the more important operations.[35]

To control the disinformation that was passed over the 183 radio playbacks that the Soviets conducted during the war, as well as disinformation passed through other channels, a centralized planning organization or clearinghouse certainly would have been needed.[36] To add further credence to an overall organization within the Soviet hierarchy that coordinated deception operations, Walter Schellenberg, chief of the SS's foreign intelligence service (Sicherheitsdienst Ausland, or SD Ausland) told his Allied interrogators after the war that, as a result of monitoring the communications of an SD agent strongly suspected of passing disinformation to the Germans, the SD concluded that there was a central office in Moscow engaged in "large scale deception work."[37] The Germans ran radio playbacks as well, but on a far smaller scale. One declassified U.S. Army Counterintelligence Corps (CIC) document indicated that German military counterintelligence had at any one time about thirty-five *Funkspiele* in operation.[38]

This begs the question: If the Soviets destroyed the effectiveness of German intelligence, why employ deception at all as it was not needed? The answer is that all commanders want battlefield predictability to eliminate the "fog of war" and leave no doubt that they can win. Sowing confusion within the enemy's intelligence service and, by extension, its military operational decision-making process — often a goal of military deception operations — might increase the chances that one will win. Soviet military deception may not have been as precise or efficient as that of the British, but it often "got the job done" in a more demanding and brutal operational environment.[39] Further, the "counterintelligence state's" never-ending desire and fundamental need to uncover and destroy "enemies of the state" would hardly allow an admission that the Nazi intelligence services were rendered ineffective. An omnipresent enemy requires deception to be employed at every level without letup, especially if the enemy is viewed as wily, resourceful (but not too resourceful), dangerous, and a threat to the existence of the state.

The intelligence-counterintelligence war in the East bore no resemblance to the world of James Bond or to the operations conducted during the Cold War. It was waged over a greater area, involved tens of thousands of agents, and was far more brutal than the one conducted between the Germans and the Western Allies.[40] In the beginning of the war "counterintelligence" almost resulted in a Soviet defeat as hundreds of thousands of Soviet soldiers surrendered, and millions welcomed the Nazis initially as liberators largely because of the murders, purges, and deportations that the NKVD carried out on an unimaginable scale in the prewar years.[41] But the terror eradicated any threat to Stalin's reign. The "immune system" had turned on itself. However, by the end of November 1941, the Soviet army still held, in no small part because of the NKVD blocking detachments (NKVD troops assigned basically to shoot retreating Soviets of the regular army).[42] Had the Nazis not consigned their "colonial subhumans" to firing squads, torture, the gas chambers, and slave labor, and instead molded them into a real cohesive effective fighting force, the outcome of the war in the East might have been far different. Soviet intelligence possessed excellent sources accurately predicting the German invasion in June 1941, but Stalin chose not to heed the warning. The "brain" ignored the rest of the body.[43]

Stalin's security services waged a two-front war: one against the Germans and one against Soviet citizens. The Soviet counterintelligence services recruited millions of citizens to spy on one another, and Soviet foreign intelligence recruited numerous foreign intelligence officers from its legal and illegal residencies abroad.[44] Real or imagined threats to Stalin's reign, as well as to the country as a whole, continued to be mercilessly eliminated. Draconian measures enforced "political" discipline throughout the entire society and the armed forces, and elevated the concept of rear-area security to a "mini-holocaust" in its own right. The NKVD/NKGB and Smersh deported, murdered, consigned to labor camps, or tortured millions of Soviet citizens (and later Eastern Europeans) who had the misfortune of having been under German occupation, a POW, living near the front lines, or a member of an ethnic group perceived as a threat to the Soviet State.[45]

A by-product of this thinly disguised orgy of terror was to severely impair the German intelligence and security services' senses by making the USSR an exceedingly hostile operating environment for German (as well as other foreign) agents.[46] Insatiable, unrelenting suspicion made it hard for German spies to collect high-quality information on Soviet forces. Under those conditions, a German agent — even if the majority were Soviets captured by the Germans, trained, and sent behind Soviet lines — no doubt had a hard time existing for long in the "counterintelligence state." The Germans' lack of good HUMINT substantially increased the odds that Soviet double-agent operations, radio games, and military deception would be successful.[47]

This demanding operational environment required of both sides agent deployments on nothing short of a massive scale. One comprehensive postwar study of Soviet agent deployments — which was dubbed Project Cleopatra and was based on extensive analysis of German records — characterized the intelligence and counterintelligence war in the East as "bringing the concept of total war into espionage operations."[48] Although no official figures of the total number of agents deployed during the Soviet-German war have been published by either the Germans or the Russians, Allied debriefings of German counterintelligence officers provide a glimpse of the magnitude of the war on "the invisible front." According to Colonel Heinrich Schmalschlaeger, commander of all German military counterintelligence units (Abwehr III) in the East, the Soviets committed more than 130,000 trained agents and many times that number of poorly trained ones against German targets over four years of war and a 2,000-mile front. In fact, Schmalschlaeger told his debriefers that the number of applicants wishing to become Soviet agents was so large that many of the 500 Soviet espionage schools identified by the Germans were forced to temporarily cancel all further applications.[49] The number of captured Soviet agents became so high that German interrogators could not process them.[50]

Another German counterintelligence officer placed the number of overall Soviet agent commitments at 10,000 new agents every three months.[51] That would add up roughly to 150,000 agents for four years of war. Project Cleopatra's analysis of the detailed information collected and analyzed by German counterintelligence organizations, including 550 transcripts of agent interrogation reports, estimated that the Soviets may have committed more than 300,000 agents, most of whom were not trained but just given low-level intelligence assignments. German records of captured agents revealed that the Soviets trained only about one in three agents. Implied or real coercion motivated almost 90 percent of Soviet agents. Only 10 percent were volunteers.[52]

No comparable figures for German agent deployments have been published or made available. A study of German military intelligence on the Eastern Front produced in 1954 by Generalmajor Rudolph Langhaeuser, placed Abwehr agent deployments at roughly 500 to 800 agents behind Soviet lines at any one time for the period from 1942 to 1944.[53] Two Abwehr officers — Colonel Baron Rudolph-Christian von Gersdorff and Gerhard Sayffaerth — both of whom served on the Eastern Front in intelligence posts and were interviewed in the early 1970s by David Kahn for his book on the Abwehr entitled *Hitler's Spies,* stated that it was not unusual for Army Group Center alone to deploy as many as 8 to 10 agents a day.[54] A Russian account of the intelligence war between the Germans and the Soviets stated that the Germans trained 7,500 agents and 2,500 saboteurs and radio operators in 1942.[55] This means that the best estimate for German agent deployments when rounded off to the nearest thousand and multiplied by 45 months of war, ranged between 36,000 and 44,000.

Most of the agents dispatched by both sides were Soviet citizens employed as line crossers or parachute agents given the task of short-term tactical intelligence or sabotage missions. Their training generally ranged from one day to six weeks, and the majority did not receive radio training. The Germans recruited almost all their agents from among Soviet POWs. In addition to employing Soviet citizens as agents, the Soviets also dispatched some German POWs on intelligence missions behind German lines.[56] When adding a total of 130,000 to 150,000 trained agents for the Russians, and 36,000 to 44,000 for the Germans, agent deployments over the course of the war for both sides ranged between 166,000 and 194,000, with deployments averaging 41,500 to 48,000 per year. These numbers are, of course, only estimates and fluctuated across the length of the front depending on numerous factors, such as the overall military situation; the availability of aircraft, airfields, instructors, radios, and facilities in which to train agents; and agent attrition rates. Until the Russians formally declassify and make available to researchers captured Abwehr I and Abwehr II (sabotage) records, as well as the requisite Soviet intelligence and counterintelligence documents, the above figures will have to remain estimates. Nevertheless, they are a solid indicator of the extraordinary scope of the "invisible front" in the East.

Conducting agent operations in the Soviet Union proved difficult at best for the Germans. Frontiers were closely guarded. The border zone, which extended to a depth of 100 kilometers, was riddled with NKVD guard posts and checkpoints, and every citizen within the zone was expected to inform the nearest border guard post of any stranger he or she met. The extensive informant network, immense distances, poor roads, and inability to travel by air, train, car, or bus without arousing suspicion hampered the ability of agents to effectively operate inside Russia for an extended period. Nuances of language, dress, and customs compounded the physical difficulties of avoiding detection while traveling inside the USSR. Radio communication was difficult because a powerful transmitter was needed to send messages over long distances. Often Soviet radio counterintelligence could easily detect the signal. All these factors greatly limited the ability of the German intelligence services to operate in the USSR.[57] Despite the extensive border security, German intelligence in the border area was good; however, overall intelligence on the USSR, especially intelligence on the mobilization system prior to the war, was poor.[58]

Soviet counterintelligence killed, captured, or neutralized the overwhelming majority of German agents. As one German officer put it, "If the losses were not over 90 percent we were satisfied. If we could reduce them to 60 percent, that was the acme of success."[59] Of approximately 150 agent groups (three to ten men each) deployed by one German intelligence unit from October 1942 to September 1943, all but 2 fell into Soviet hands.[60] In 1944 a German evaluation of 159 agents operating against the Russians revealed only 51 as being "very valuable to usable."[61] The captured enemy document section of Leitstelle III Ost (German military counterintelligence in the East) closed down by 1944 because of a lack of material.[62] Therefore the Germans were forced to rely predominantly on the analysis of signals intelligence, aerial reconnaissance, and POW interrogations.[63] Other than the 183 radio games Tarasov mentioned, which would have involved the doubling (or turning) of considerably more German agents than just those radio operators, no figures are available on exactly how many German agents the Russians doubled.

Schmalschlaeger stated in his postwar debriefing that of the 130,000 trained agents deployed by the Russians, German military counterintelligence units identified 50,000 of those agents, put another 20,000 of them out of action, and identified almost 3,000 Soviet intelligence and counterintelligence officers. German military counterintelligence in the USSR (FAK/FAT units starting with the number 3; see Appendix E) suffered 30 percent casualties out of 1,000 men.[64] Under combat conditions, and in the face of an unrelenting torrent of Soviet agents of all types, Schmalschlaeger accomplished an impressive feat with few resources. Nevertheless, it was not good enough. The Germans still could not identify, neutralize, or put out of action the remaining 60,000 or more Soviet agents. Even more devastating is the fact that, given scarce counterintelligence resources, the Germans probably could have done little against the 50,000 identified Soviet agents. Identification is a necessary first step in catching spies, but for counterintelligence to be effective it cannot be the only measure.[65] "Immune systems" cannot be "voyeurs."

The effectiveness of Soviet counterintelligence against the German agents was summed up by Colonel Hermann Baun, commander of the majority of German clandestine collection operations against Russia (Leitstelle I, Ost), when he admitted to his U.S. Army interrogator that virtually none of his operations was successful.[66] The Soviets achieved this degree of success despite having lost, from the late 1930s to the beginning of the 1940s, more than 20,000 intelligence and counterintelligence officers. Another 6,000 military counterintelligence officers were killed from 1941 to 1944.[67] Even after having sustained such high casualty rates, one Soviet military counterintelligence unit was still able to train 70 agents a month.[68] Sudoplatov claimed in his memoirs that his Fourth Directorate alone, which was responsible for sabotage and guerrilla operations behind German lines, dispatched almost 14,000 agents and State Security officers into German-occupied territory during the war.[69]

The overriding impression conveyed by examining the official documentation and evaluating the anecdotal evidence on the intelligence war in the East is one in which the ruthless exploitation of human life on an unprecedented scale was the norm. The primary method of accomplishing the mission was to drop or infiltrate as many agents as possible behind enemy lines in the right place and hope that some might get through. Thousands of agents on both sides were routinely captured, tortured, shot, or doubled.[70] Schmalschlaeger was amazed at the Soviet indifference to agent casualties. After a heavy snowfall the Soviets would drop agents without parachutes to avoid detection, having ordered them to shoot their comrades if one of them was injured on landing. According to interrogations of captured Soviet agents, the order was often carried out.[71] It was not uncommon for intelligence and counterintelligence officers to command combat units because no other officer was left.[72] During the war at least 12,000 "operational workers," and members of "special units of State Security" lost their lives in battle or in combat with the German intelligence and security services.[73]

The intelligence war in the East from 1941 to 1945 dwarfs in scale, scope, and intensity any clandestine war in modern history between major powers. The totalitarian nature of Stalin's Russia, the ability of the Soviet foreign intelligence service (NKGB) to recruit intelligence officers worldwide, and the belated Nazi recognition that human intelligence sources at the higher levels of the CPSU, the Soviet armed forces, the NKVD/NKGB, and the Soviet government were desperately needed but never acquired, all combined both to directly and indirectly enhance the success of the major Soviet military deception operations of the war. The Germans never had detailed knowledge of the Stavka's true intentions. Soviet counterintelligence throughout the war made sure the status quo did not change.

"Death to Spies": Defensive Counterintelligence Operations

It is more likely that an Arab with a burnoose can walk through Berlin undetected than a foreign agent through Russia.

General Ernst August Koestring, German Military Attaché to Moscow, 1941

Stalin once remarked to British Air Chief Marshal Tedder — Eisenhower's Deputy Supreme Commander — that there was no hope of surprise if enemy agents were permitted to infiltrate effectively, and that the identification and repression of the enemy's espionage apparatus in the rear areas was as essential a part of the preparations for an attack as the accumulation of the necessary supplies.[1] Stalin's remarks were, if anything, grossly understated. The three pillars of Soviet defensive counterintelligence and security operations consisted of the "recruitment" of large numbers of informants; the use of security troops to man checkpoints, apprehend spies, physically guard sensitive facilities, and constantly check documents; and the use of terror and deportation to eradicate real or imagined threats to the regime or the security of the state. These activities served the dual function of catching German agents and enforcing the political reliability of the population. As one FHO document matter-of-factly put it:

> In Russia, one can never distinguish quite clearly between police spying for the protection of the regime and combat [*sic*] of foreign activities. In wartime especially, every Soviet citizen is encouraged to be on guard against both these sources of danger. Security and counterintelligence work go hand in hand, and a great amount of energy is devoted to both activities."[2]

After almost a quarter of a century the unrelenting obsession with spies and the limitless number of activities that could be construed as a threat to the interchangeable trio of Stalin, the Communist Party, and the state transformed Soviet society into one enormous GULAG covering one-sixth of the world's surface. One high-level Soviet official decreed that every citizen of the USSR must be an employee of the NKVD.[3] Informants blanketed every level of society, the Party, the army, even the police. In 1952, according to a statement made by the then chief of the Ministry of State Security (MGB), S. D. Igant'ev, there were 10 million informants in the USSR at that time.[4] During the war there may have been considerably more, possibly as many as 22 million (see below). Such an environment spelled disaster for a German intelligence effort that never seriously attempted to conduct strategic intelligence against the USSR.[5] Colonel Hans Piekenbrock — chief of Abwehr I (largely clandestine HUMINT collection) at the beginning of the war and later captured by the Russians, further elaborated on the intelligence fiasco in the East. He told his captors that, shortly after the invasion, the Germans showed little or no interest in reports from agents because POWs and captured documents gave OKH a "complete picture of the enemy forces."[6] One prominent Western historian of the war in the East pointed out that in the days when the German General Staff was at the height of its power five to ten years of intelligence preparation would have been considered necessary before any worthwhile operational planning could be started.[7]

When the major elements of the Soviet counterintelligence system — informants, rear-area security, and terror — resulted in the imprisonment of the entire country, it would have been difficult for the Germans, even after ten years of planning, to acquire reliable agents with access to Soviet plans and intentions. Since 1917 foreign powers, including the British, the Japanese, and even the Poles, had a difficult time spying against the USSR largely because of the overall effectiveness of the internal organs of State Security.[8] However, the Germans in the pre-Barbarossa period were arguably in the best position to acquire strategic intelligence on Stalin's Russia. They had a sustained political, diplomatic, and military relationship with Russia for almost fifteen years after the end of World War I and had good bases in the Baltics to use as a springboard for intelligence collection. The Nazis did not rise to the occasion. Arrogance permeated OKH's planning process. Hitler also banned aggressive intelligence collection against Russia after the Nazi-Soviet Pact in 1939.[9] Canaris's Abwehr, already a hotbed of anti-Hitler sentiment, could ill afford to reduce its clandestine collection efforts against Russia. The hostile operating environment in the USSR and Nazi arrogance aside, Hitler's ban on aggressive intelligence operations against Russia reduced the time that that Abwehr needed to acquire agents inside Russia. By the time Barbarossa started it was too late.

Arrests of German Agents

Virtually all components of the Soviet intelligence and security services — except the GRU (Soviet Military Intelligence), the INU of the NKGB (foreign intelligence; see Appendix A), and those organizations responsible for offensive counterintelligence (double agents, radio playbacks, and recruitment of intelligence officers) and some minor support functions — were dedicated to defensive counterintelligence and security duties.[10] Although no specific numbers are available, it would be safe to estimate that well over three-quarters of the resources of the Soviet intelligence and security services were devoted to internal security and defensive counterintelligence duties.[11]

According to Michael Parrish's well-documented study entitled *The Lesser Terror: Soviet State Security, 1939–1953*, retired Colonel of the Judiciary A. Liskin, who published an article in March 1993 in *Schit I Mech* [Sword and shield], stated that from 1941 to 1945 the security organs questioned nearly 7 million people and arrested 2 million.[12] According to one recent history, citing a report to the State Defense Committee (GKO) from 22 June 1941 to October 1941, NKVD troops and military counterintelligence detained 657,364 servicemen who retreated or left their units. Of those, 1,505 spies and 308 saboteurs were exposed.[13] Neither original German intelligence records nor postwar Allied counterintelligence debriefings of German officers reflect any figures on how many German agents were arrested, charged, shot, or sentenced to labor camps for political crimes or reasons other than working for German intelligence. It is highly possible that such precise figures do not exist, as it would have been difficult for the Germans to know under what specific charges their agents had actually been arrested, as well as the disposition of the cases. Given the ruthlessness of the Soviet regime, it would have hardly mattered whether there were bona fide German agents in the masses of individuals destined for the firing squads or labor camps, as any real German agents would have been rendered ineffective anyway.[14]

However, the 1977 top secret history of the Soviet State Security organs sheds at least some official light on the number of German agents "neutralized" by State Security. Citing "Works of the Higher KGB School, 1971" (no. 2, page 51), the history mentions that military counterintelligence together with NKVD troops "neutralized more than 4,000 spies, diversionaries, and terrorists" in 1941, and in 1942 the Special Departments (military counterintelligence) exposed 7,000 enemy agents in the "active army."[15] Using several documents in the KGB Central Archive as sources, the history states that, in 1943, military counterintelligence along with the "territorial and transportation" State Security organs detained 20,000 "fascist spies, saboteurs (diversionaries), and terrorists in the front and rear."[16] Again citing "Works of the Higher KGB School, 1971" (no. 2, page 55), the top secret history goes on to state that "altogether during the war military counterintelligence organs neutralized more than 30,000 spies, approximately 3,500 saboteurs, and more than 6,000 agent-terrorists."[17] Although these figures, no doubt, include people who were falsely arrested, and then tortured, deported, shot, or doubled, nevertheless they correlate, at least on paper, with German assessments of their own failure rates. If the roughly 44,000 agents estimated to have been deployed by the Germans are basically correct, theoretically Soviet military counterintelligence alone rendered 39,500 of them useless.

The Informant System

Of the three interlocking functions required to hold the Soviet defensive counterintelligence system together — informants, rear-area security, and terror and deportation — the informant system, backed up by coercion real or implied, was the linchpin.[18] The Bolsheviks designed the informant system primarily as a tool to keep the population in check and to detect any signs of unrest or dissatisfaction with the regime.[19] Without people at all levels of society willing (or unwilling) to spy on their friends, neighbors, coworkers, and colleagues, the "counterintelligence state" cannot function. Turning in your neighbor or coworker was made easy. For example, in 1943, after Khar'kov was retaken by Soviet forces, special red boxes were hung in the streets so that anyone could drop in a report on individuals who had "collaborated with the Germans."[20] The informant network was so pervasive that it extended even to such organizations as NKVD troops as well as to Soviet military intelligence.[21] Saturating Soviet society with millions of informants made it difficult for foreign agents to penetrate Soviet organizations.[22]

Massive internal spying places extraordinary pressure on an agent to behave inconspicuously to avoid detection. Lack of attention to the minutest detail can spell disaster. Using the wrong type of soap, stitching buttons improperly, wearing the wrong type of underwear, using different kinds of staples on documents, and countless other mundane compromises might result in an agent being caught, interrogated, tortured, and shot.[23] In close quarters, such as when a Soviet citizen captured by the Germans was trained and dropped behind Soviet lines to infiltrate Soviet military units, mastery of such details became a matter of life and death. Soviet counterintelligence officers instructed their informants to report even the most minor indications of disaffection such as increased interest in enemy propaganda leaflets.[24]

German intelligence officers debriefed after the war and Allied evaluation of captured German documents were unequivocal in their assessments that the informant system significantly reduced the ability of the Germans to penetrate Soviet organizations, although no specific cases were mentioned.

One U.S. Army Counterintelligence Corps (CIC) document stated, "the decisive weapon of Smersh is and has been an extensive net of informants and agents." The same document went on to say that those "who had managed to infiltrate the Red Army during the Soviet retreat soon got caught in the closely knit Smersh network" and that "a similar fate awaited those in 1943 who later attempted to spy against the Red Army." One major study of the Soviet intelligence services indicated that "the large number of informants used makes the penetration of enemy agents very difficult and also constitutes an important counterintelligence measure against the enemy's secret service."[25]

Schmalschlaeger stated in his debriefing that "in the spring of 1942 the defensive activities of the Soviet intelligence services had reached their peak." The objective of "combining all efforts to protect the Soviet Union from secret attacks," a phrase frequently found in Soviet orders, had been accomplished. These measures tended to make the task of sending out German agents, especially those assigned to long-range missions, increasingly difficult. Included in this assessment of Soviet security measures were Soviet spy campaigns, which heightened the population's awareness of German espionage activity.[26]

Estimates for the number of informants in the USSR during the war vary, and no official figures have been published. Even the classified History of the Soviet State Security Organs does not mention a figure. However, according to one major U.S. Army study of wartime Soviet intelligence and counterintelligence — much of it based on German sources — at least 12 percent of the armed forces worked as informants for military counterintelligence.[27] Based on this figure, of the 17 million members of the armed forces, approximately 2 million informants worked for Smersh alone. Other estimates, one of which was based on a Soviet order captured by the Germans, placed the number of informants in the military at one-ninth of the total number of troops in the armed forces, and still another German study placed the number at one-fifth. In other words, the best available figures range between 1,540,000 and 3,400,000.[28]

Although no figures are available for the total number of informants during the war in the Soviet population at large, every citizen was required by law to report treason or "counterrevolutionary crimes," or face six months to ten years of imprisonment.[29] The Germans had much less information on how the informant system worked outside than within the Soviet armed forces.[30] Unclassified accounts of Soviet counterintelligence operations do not mention the role of the informant system, even though this kind of activity was considered noble in Soviet society.[31] Nevertheless, the general principles used in recruiting and handling informants in the armed forces, with some minor modifications, applied equally to the Soviet population.[32]

At the beginning of the war the Soviet population stood at roughly 200 million people.[33] Given the climate of "paranoia" that existed in Stalin's USSR, it would not have been inconceivable for the percentage of informants among the civilian population to have rivaled that of the armed forces. Using the 12 percent figure for the armed forces, Soviet counterintelligence may have employed almost 22 million civilian informants or, alternatively, at the higher end of the scale, almost 40 million, if one were to use a figure of one-fifth the population.[34] Though 40 million informants might not have been inconceivable in Stalin's wartime USSR, the paperwork burden alone (see below) surely would have strained a security service already operating under highly stressful combat conditions.

Almost every function performed by Smersh (and the civilian KRU as well) required the recruitment of informants.[35] As only one Smersh officer was assigned to a battalion (about 1,000 to 1,500 men), the primary method used to accomplish the wide array of duties was the use of informants.[36] German translations of Soviet military counterintelligence orders show that Smersh was charged not only with the "discovery and prevention of counterrevolutionary tendencies" and the exposure of "Russian traitors who collaborated with the enemy" but also with such tasks as observation and elimination of all defects that might lower preparedness of the Red Army; elimination of low morale and cowardice; prevention of desertion, self-inflicted wounds, laxity in discipline, and sabotage; and determination of defects of the leadership of the troops.[37] It was also charged with overseeing Soviet military operational security.[38]

Transportation and territorial organs of State Security recruited informants who worked in railroad junctions, train stations, power stations, river boat stations, rest homes, medical-screening facilities, restaurants, hotels, and postal facilities, generally in any areas where German agents might be likely to appear. Although the primary job of these informants was to be on the lookout for German agents, suspicious behavior on the part of any Soviet citizen would be subjected to intense scrutiny. Added to this were the informants recruited among such diverse groups as collective and state farmers, workers in isolated industrial enterprises, herdsmen, foresters, road-repair workers, and railway workers by the chiefs of "hunter battalions" (more on these militia-like formations below) whose primary function was also to be on the lookout for German agents. Redundancy might not be efficient, but its effect was to blanket the USSR with human sensors by mobilizing hundreds of millions of "eyes and ears" and training those "eyes and ears" to pick up the slightest anomaly, real or perceived.[39]

Organization and Size of the Informant Networks

Out of an estimated 2 million informants in the Soviet armed forces, 250,000 potentially served as resident agents. Applying the same principle to Soviet nonmilitary counterintelligence organizations, out of a possible 22 million informants, approximately 1.4 million civilians may also have been resident agents. According to a captured Soviet military counterintelligence officer, Smersh coerced almost half of all informants into working for it. Using the above figures, this would mean that Soviet State Security coerced at least 13 million of Stalin's subjects (2 million military and 11 million civilians) into informing on their fellow citizens.[40] The 1977 top secret History of the Soviet State Security Organs chillingly, but matter-of-factly, states that in October 1942 the Special Departments of the Stalingrad Front created 1,144 *rezidenturas* [informant networks headed by a resident] and by 1 November 1942 increased the number to 4,339.[41] That represents a massive 300 percent plus increase in the internal spying of one Soviet front in one month. No data exist on the effectiveness of an informant who had been coerced or exactly what criteria the individual had to meet to be considered a full-fledged informant.

The Soviets used four types of informants: secret agents, residents, reserve residents, and informers. Secret agents were highly qualified agents who infiltrated dissident groups by posing as members; a resident controlled informants; a reserve resident was to take over the duties of the resident if the resident became a casualty or was transferred; and an informer was the lowest type of agent in the chain and informed on his or her colleagues. Residents generally did not recruit informants but only collected reports from them and passed original copies every five days to the Smersh officer. Residents were required to write reports twice a month on all they saw and heard. A Smersh officer, however, had to meet personally with those military officers who were informants.[42]

A battalion-level Smersh officer not only recruited his own informants to spy on the battalion staff but also recruited "resident agents," that is, informants who were required to recruit an additional six to eight informants (see chart). Residents generally had to be politically dependable; often they were members of the Communist Party and occupied jobs that enabled them to come into regular contact with as many soldiers as possible.[43] Typical jobs included company and platoon commanders, mechanics, cooks, clerks, first sergeants, and deputy chiefs of staff of chemical and medical units. Each resident was appointed a deputy in case the resident became a casualty.[44] Military counterintelligence officers could recruit their informants virtually anywhere, but OO officers often used medical facilities as well as other facilities in rear areas. Special Depart-

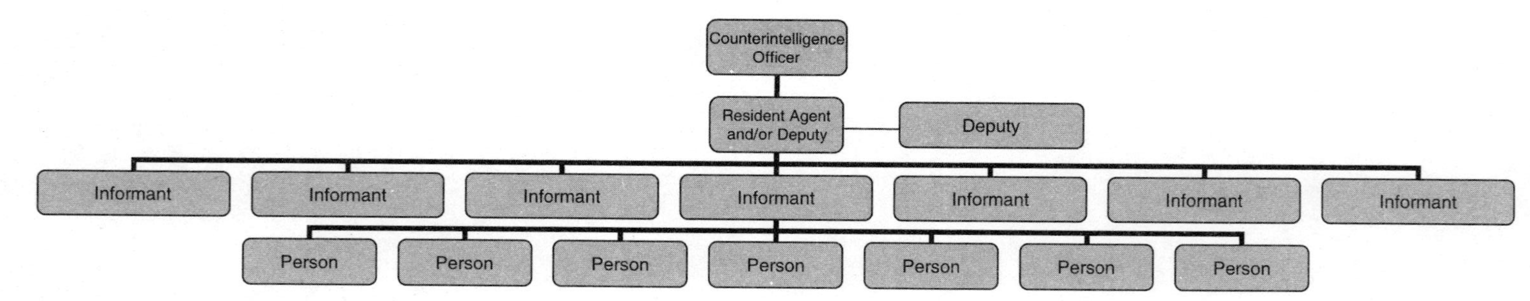

Organization of a Soviet Informant Network

ment officers gave particular attention to recruiting informants in those units or areas where German agents would most likely be encountered such as infiltration points, document inspections posts, headquarters, combat security units, reserve formations, supply points, and railroad stations.[45]

Each informant signed a "voluntary" secrecy pledge, wrote out his autobiography, swore to report any cases of anti-Soviet activity, and received a code name.[46] An informant was responsible for watching approximately six to eight men. Soviet counterintelligence regulations required the presence of at least one informant even in patrols as small as three men. In some cases informants who performed exceptionally well were designated "patriotic agents"; they were authorized to take "immediate corrective action" should there have been indications of desertion or lowering of morale.[47]

Secrecy dominated Smersh informant nets. Each resident agent knew only the Smersh officer who recruited him. Resident agents did not know one another as resident agents. Each informant only knew and reported to one specific resident.[48] Informant coverage extended from a lowly rifle squad to the Internal Troops and the Border Guards all the way to the Soviet General Staff.[49] In addition, each net checked on the other net unbeknownst to one another.[50]

An informant in civilian life often continued his service to State Security in the military. NKVD officers served on every draft board and forwarded all available information on inductees to the nearest Smersh unit.[51] At the same time the NKVD representative gave the Smersh unit a list of informers already placed within the group of new draftees. This process provided Smersh with a steady stream of experienced informants. When the informant was discharged, a report on his activities while in the army was forwarded to the NKVD/NKGB.[52]

The Nazi invasion, however, temporarily interrupted the transfer, recontact, and recruitment of informants. Since the German army overran vast expanses of the USSR and captured millions of Soviet troops, informants had to be replaced and trained on a huge scale. The Special Departments themselves were plagued with shortages of officers and lack of training and experience. New recruits who had been informants for the civilian counterintelligence services were not always instructed to contact military counterintelligence on their entry into the armed forces. In 1941–1942 military counterintelligence concentrated primarily on replacing its shattered networks. As the war dragged on Smersh placed much more emphasis on ridding its networks of "turncoats and disinformers." From 1941 to 1944 the informant network doubled in size.[53]

One Smersh document, dated 1944, demonstrated exactly how some units of a Soviet rifle division had been literally smothered with internal spies.[54] The document identified 11 resident agents serving among the members of the 838th Signal Company (about 400 to 500 men) of the 389th Rifle Division. As resident agents each recruited six to eight informants, the number of informants in the signal company could have been as high as 88, or roughly 1 in 5 men. The same document showed that in a reconnaissance company of 62 men, 6 residents, and more than 40 men, may have been informants.[55] In December 1944 informers comprised almost 25 percent of the 363rd Penal Company. Even an engineer unit totaling only 132 men had 7 resident agents and therefore 32 informants.[56] The desire of the "counterintelligence state" to turn every citizen into a spy never abated.

Smersh officer meetings with their residents took place at intervals of once every one to two weeks.[57] Meetings were clandestine; all informant reports had to be in writing; and informers were required to submit reports every five days. During combat, meetings between residents and informants occurred after the battle.[58] Smersh officers were required to submit a daily report to division headquarters detailing the number of scheduled meetings, how many meetings were held, numbers and types of agents recruited, and numbers of individuals who potentially could be recruited as informants or residents.[59] Although no figures on the number of reports per month written by the OOs are available, by 1943 the U.S. Army CIC in Europe generated 150,000 reports a month and was handling about 50,000 informants; by 1945 it had expanded to 5,000 officers worldwide.[60] The paperwork Smersh generated must have been enormous.

The informant networks served as the "eyes and ears" of Smersh.[61] During the war various groups of individuals routinely came under more scrutiny than others. Smersh officers interrogated all Soviet soldiers who escaped German captivity and fought their way back to Soviet lines, who had relatives in German-occupied territory, and Soviet agents who returned from their missions behind German lines.[62] If no evidence against these groups of people was discovered, they were returned to their units and placed under close surveillance by informants for a period afterward.[63]

Smersh also worked closely with its civilian counterparts, although the division of labor between it and the KRU of the NKGB sometimes became blurred. German interrogations of captured Soviet agents show that there was considerable confusion in and around garrison towns about whether surveillance of civilians was the responsibility of the KRU or of Smersh.[64] For example, although it was the responsibility of the KRU to prevent enemy agents hiding in the civilian population from penetrating Red Army facilities, installations, and units, Smersh often tried to double enemy agents uncovered near military installations.[65] Soviet field orders actually encouraged close cooperation among counterintelligence organizations. At least one Soviet order chastised NKVD units for not passing information on civilians to Smersh.[66]

The informant network also extended to the partisans and to the families of Smersh officers. OO/NKGB (responsible for counterintelligence within the guerrilla movement) and Smersh exchanged information on security threats and cooperated in arrests, much of this information, no doubt, having been generated by informants.[67] OO/NKGB used its informants to seek out all individuals who either sympathized or collaborated with the Germans. These names were then forwarded to Smersh or to the NKGB.[68] Smersh headquarters even had a "subsection for observation of families of officers of the GUKR."[69]

Informants served as the backbone of the state's repressive machinery. The system was highly redundant and no doubt inefficient by Western standards, as it diverted vital resources, created a climate of fear, and destroyed the lives of millions of innocent people.[70] However, inefficiency does not necessarily equate to ineffectiveness. The informant system — along with the threat of swift and brutal punishments — was nevertheless effective in keeping the Soviet armed forces and the population in check, and in limiting the effectiveness of German clandestine collection operations. Although spies cannot be caught without the help of informants, Soviet counterintelligence officers responsible for administering the system also depended on the physical controls imposed by rear-area security units to catch German agents.

Rear-Area Security

Soviet rear-area security operations bolstered the effectiveness of the informant networks by controlling the ability of Soviet soldiers and civilians, as well as German agents, to freely move about behind Russian lines.[71] Such security operations ranged from two- or three-man checkpoints manned by the Internal Troops, rear-area security regiments, or Border Guards to making extensive, periodic sweeps of the rear area to hunt down German spies. Soviet counterintelligence conducted these defensive operations in coordination with military and civilian agencies. The process consisted of four elements: imposing physical control over the rear area by evacuating civilians and setting up checkpoints; randomly checking documents of all individuals and generally observing, or actively looking for and reporting, suspicious behavior; arresting presumed German agents as a result of receiving tips on suspicious activities and individuals from informants, double agents, radio intercepts, captured documents, or arrested German agents who confessed; and the investigation and interrogation of apprehended persons.[72]

Sealing the Rear

To make it extremely difficult for enemy agents to operate behind Soviet lines, the Red Army and Soviet counterintelligence established several interlocking prohibited zones extending to 50 kilometers behind the front line.[73] To a depth of approximately 5 to 7 kilometers, the Red Army established a "prohibited area" to prevent enemy-agent infiltration into the front line from the rear. NKVD rear-area security units controlled the next two security zones to a depth of 50 kilometers. Thus an NKVD security regiment usually covered a sector 120 kilometers long and 50 kilometers deep. After that, NKVD Internal Troops took over. Coverage could be so extensive that NKVD rear-area security units even watched swamp areas at night for parachute agents.[74]

NKVD rear-area security troops, often commanded by Smersh officers, set up document checkpoints, listening posts along likely routes of infiltration for German agents, and conducted searches for enemy agents based on information gleaned from every imaginable source. Captured documents were especially valuable in exposing German agents.[75] In addition to NKVD rear-area security troops, almost 328,000 politically reliable citizens were organized into 1,700 "hunter battalions," which protected such vital installations as industrial enterprises, electric power stations, and railroad facilities. They also patrolled populated areas; battalion commanders were actually allowed to recruit informants among collective farmers, herdsmen, foresters, and railway workers to report on suspicious activity.[76]

The commander of a Soviet *front* had at his disposal five to six regiments of "security troops" (about two divisions) who were subordinate to the Chief of Security Troops of the Rear Area (see Appendix A). A regiment consisted of about 1,650 men. These regiments were made up of Border Guards and NKVD troops; the commanders were NKVD officers; and Smersh officers often had operational control over the disposition of these units. Smersh units at the *front* also had a dedicated guard company of 100 men. The infamous blocking detachments that machine-gunned retreating Soviet troops were from NKVD troops and Border Guards. Other missions for these regiments included searching for and apprehending German agents, evacuating civilians from areas behind the front, maintaining checkpoints, and preventing desertion.[77] Entry into the zones protected by rear-area security units required various degrees of identification. The Soviets set up a highly complex and sophisticated identification system.

The War of Documents

For the most part the NKVD evacuated the civilian population from the "prohibited zone" closest to the front and subjected those remaining to extensive security regulations.[78] Only those civilians remained whose activities were judged essential to military operations, and they were subjected to tight security controls. Three-man checkpoints and roving patrols scrutinized documents, pay books, and identification papers of both military personnel (to prevent desertion and to catch German agents in Soviet uniforms) and civilians. Strict controls on the movement of military personnel and constant examination of documents made it more difficult for German agents to operate behind Soviet lines.[79] Soviet soldiers, especially commissioned officers, were required to carry five to ten different documents on their person. Soldiers, for example, carried leave orders, discharge papers (if applicable), a pay book, a military identification book, and military orders. Civilians carried a photo identification card, a work pass, and a temporary work pass (if applicable), and those who needed to have a weapon carried a weapons pass. Truck drivers needed a bill of lading, travel orders, registration certificates, and a title.[80]

A 1942 Soviet directive ordered security units to immediately issue passes and identity papers to all persons who had business or resided within 100 kilometers of the front.[81] The order further decreed that all unauthorized persons were to be evacuated to the rear within five days and that all persons lacking proper identity documents, or coming from enemy territory, were to be arrested and turned over to the NKVD.[82] According to a 1943 FHO study, all individuals living in the sector between a divisional headquarters and the front line had to carry a special pass issued by the respective divisional headquarters.[83] Unless given permission by the local military commander, strangers were prohibited from taking up residence in any town or village occupied by military personnel.[84] Unauthorized residents had to be reported to the NKVD. Civilians also had to have the proper passes in order to move between towns and villages. In addition, civilians needed a special permit to be exempted from nighttime curfews and were evacuated from towns and villages housing military staffs.[85] Three-man roving patrols randomly inspected documents along roads and other transportation routes.[86]

The NKVD placed heavy emphasis on document inspection. Checkpoints dotted main roads every six to seven kilometers and the slightest lack of confidence in one's behavior or a minor mistake was enough to arouse the suspicion of the well-trained guards.[87] At various intervals Soviet security forces introduced new passes or supplemented old passes by issuing additional pages or rubber stamps to the old documents.[88] The Soviets further complicated German operational planning by placing distinct but inconspicuous markings on documents, randomly alternating those markings, and by using a special type of paper (and sometimes alternating the paper) for various documents. For example, a dot would be placed before the signing official's name one week and *behind* the name the next week.[89] However, even routine Soviet document production made it difficult for the Germans to equip their agents with documentation that could withstand Soviet scrutiny. The Soviets stapled documents with a kind of rusting wire not available in Germany and printed some of the documents on wallpaper that was not available outside the USSR, which might have been a Russian improvisation because of lack of other materials.[90]

As of 1 April 1943 Abwehr 1G, the section responsible for procuring and issuing forged papers, secret writing systems, cameras, codes, and microdots to agents, distributed a total of 400,000 Soviet documents of more than 140 different types to German intelligence units on the Eastern Front with specific instructions on how the agents should fill out the documents.[91] These documents included armed forces identification cards, "unfit for military service cards," travel orders, military group travel orders, partisan identification cards, Communist Party membership books, military pay books, service records and civilian internal passports, driver's licenses, employment cards, service records, six kinds of hospital discharge certificates, deferment certificates for workers employed in the war industry, birth certificates, and more than sixteen different kinds of officer identity cards, distinct from the four basic types of officers' personal identity cards.[92] Even with this amount of original Soviet documentation in Abwehr 1G's possession, the need for more original documentation continued to increase during the war.[93]

The Abwehr's possession of large numbers of original Soviet documents did not defeat the ability of Soviet counterintelligence to detect German alterations of those documents. For example, a Soviet order issued by Colonel Andrianov, chief of Smersh of the 46th Army, instructed Smersh officers to pay attention to rubber stamps and seals on documents. The order explained how to do so in detail: "when the rubber stamp is cut, it leaves a blank space into which a number can be inserted; however, this manipulation can be detected by examining differences in the ink impression; clear, crisp ink impressions which are sharp and round serve as indications that the Germans stamped the documents, as ours are more oval and fainter."[94]

The scrutiny did not stop with the examination of rubber stamps. Soviet counterintelligence also instructed their field units on how to look for forgeries and alterations of Communist Party membership books.

> Field units were told that German espionage agencies have issued two editions of forged Party membership books. In the first edition the lines forming the upper section of the frame on the pages for membership contribution amounts are heavily underscored. No such underscoring is given in the genuine books. The loop over the letter *i* in the word *Chlenski* [membership] is given as two dots. The forgery is most apparent from the disparity between the serial number of the Party book and the years shown for the contribution payments. In the genuine Party books, up to number 3,800,000 contribution years are given in print for the period from 1935 to 1943. In cards above 3,800,000, an empty space is left for the specific date of the contribution to be inserted in writing. Several Party books have been found that show a serial number below 3,800,000 but give an empty space for the contribution year; thus they are obviously forged. In various forged membership books, the signature of the holder is in ordinary black ink, but it should be signed with the same black ink used for the remaining text. In genuine books the stamp imprints are always black, whereas in forgeries they are sometimes violet.[95]

The document went on to say that even though the quality of the forgeries increased, they could still be detected by a hyphen between the months of June and July in the line provided for the signature of the Party secretary.

In fact, the 1977 classified history of State Security credits the Document Technical Service — the entity responsible for developing the indicators for uncovering anomalies in German agent documentation — with playing a large role in exposing German agents. NKVD Instruction Number 66, issued on 20 February 1942, laid out in handbook form the items that characterized anomalies in German agent documentation as well as cover stories and clothing. Military counterintelligence units memorized checklists for examining all facets of an individual's documentation. NKO of the USSR Order Number 330, dated 7 October 1941, established a letter system for army documents that changed every ten to fifteen days. Any communication with agents was further obstructed by intense censorship of all mail, radio direction finding, and telephone monitoring.[96]

Detecting Suspicious Persons

Soviet counterintelligence did more than scrutinize documents in its relentless search for agents. Counterintelligence officers also examined the uniforms of suspected persons. For example, the Germans sometimes sewed shoulder tabs down to the sleeves of uniforms issued to their agents; however, on genuine Soviet uniforms the tabs hung from the collar and only touched the sleeve.[97] A detail as insignificant as uncovered buttons on the underwear issued to

German agents could generate Soviet suspicion, as Soviet officers wore covered buttons on their underwear.[98] German agents were generally issued a Nagan revolver with twenty cartridges, whereas the Soviet military actually issued its troops twenty-one cartridges for three loadings.[99]

State Security uncovered other Abwehr "signatures" that revealed the existence of potential German agents. For example, the Soviets tested the speech of suspected German agents to determine if they actually came from the regions claimed on their documents.[100] One Soviet history also noted that German agents trained at the Abwehr school in Poltava consistently received 3,000 rubles in 30-ruble notes. According to this history, military counterintelligence caught many German agents as a result of the Germans not having paid attention to such minutiae. Soviet counterintelligence, for example, caught one German agent because he carried on him a bar of German ersatz soap.[101]

Operations were designed to simultaneously apprehend deserters as well as enemy agents.[102] Smersh officers commanded search parties that sealed off particular areas and checked the identification papers of every civilian and military member in those areas. Individuals not having the proper identification were sent to divisional Smersh sections where their names were checked against a list of known deserters, German agents, and draft evaders.[103] If an individual was suspected of being a German agent, the case was forwarded to an army-level or *front*-level Smersh unit. Draft evaders and deserters who were apprehended during such operations were transferred to the divisional judge advocate for court-martial, execution, or sentencing to a penal battalion.[104]

The number of persons of interest to the NKVD/NKGB and Smersh encompassed an extraordinarily wide range of groups. These included, but were not necessarily limited to, former POWs, soldiers who had escaped German encirclements, members of the military whose homes and families were located in German-occupied areas, the entire population in those areas occupied by the Red Army, female members and employees of the armed forces, vagrant and adolescent children, all persons in possession of enemy propaganda material, all Soviet agents returning from enemy territory, and all members of the Red Army who were drafted from western Belorussia, the Ukraine, Bessarabia, and the Baltic states. The NKVD/NKGB even extended their list to include "rumormongers" and "persons who have joined the ranks under doubtful circumstances."[105] In the first forty-five days of the war, the OOs of the Southwestern Front "uncovered 287 German agents by screening Soviets who had escaped German POW camps."[106]

One Soviet commander, Colonel Korolev, of the OO/NKVD (military counterintelligence) of the Nineteenth Army, went so far as to issue an order requiring the purging of all individuals from headquarters staffs who had escaped areas either surrounded or occupied by the Germans, the investigation of all troops who had returned from German captivity, and the surveillance of all troops from Ukraine, Bessarabia, and the Baltic states.[107]

According to one Soviet history, the Germans took children twelve to fifteen years of age from orphanages in occupied territories and trained them in sabotage operations. They would then infiltrate these children behind Soviet lines with orders, for example, to throw explosives disguised as coal into steam engines and coal storage bunkers. The Germans apparently established a special school in Kassel, Germany, specifically for the training of juveniles. One Soviet intelligence officer (probably posing as a German citizen), who made the acquaintance of the deputy commander of the school, won him over, and, as a consequence, Soviet counterintelligence knew in advance the details of all the juvenile agent deployments from that school.[108] The Germans even used individuals posing as beggars and mentally deranged people as covers for their agents.[109] Virtually anyone living or fighting from Moscow west was subjected to intense unrelenting scrutiny.

The Search for Fascist Agents

The NKVD ruthlessly enforced its decree Number 001552, dated 10 December 1940, which stated that relatives of all captured German parachute agents were to be arrested and sentenced by the "Special Commission of the NKVD to five years banishment."[110] Even relatives of NKVD officers were not immune from punishment. For example, the Germans captured a senior NKVD officer who was a member of the Supreme Soviet and in charge of the fortifications for the city of Leningrad. He was carrying documents regarding the fortifications at the time of his capture. When the NKVD learned about his capture, it fired his three sisters, all of whom worked for the NKVD, and evicted them from their apartments. One of the sisters was even exiled to Ufa, Siberia, where she eventually died of tuberculosis.[111]

Soviet counterintelligence agencies circulated indexes of suspected individuals, including the names, pictures, and descriptions of possible German agents.[112] The Soviets disseminated these lists so frequently that, from June 1941 to June 1942, one unit distributed almost 200 copies each of 30 different lists, each containing the names of 50 suspected German agents.[113]

FHO assessed Soviet interrogations as "most exhaustive and thorough," thereby making it "most difficult to mislead expert investigators."[114] The NKVD/NKGB issued voluminous detailed directives on what specific questions to ask suspects. Reports on the interrogations of Soviet citizens and Red Army personnel returning from German-occupied areas had to include such items as a detailed personal history and character evaluation of the subject, descriptions of the subject's experiences behind German lines, and a statement on how the subject conducted himself in battle.[115] Soviet counterintelligence officers delved into even more detail regarding the mission, organization, modus operandi, and training the Germans provided, if the individual was also suspected of working for one of the German intelligence services.[116]

Further questions included asking the subject about the circumstances surrounding his joining the German Intelligence Service, the locations of German training facilities, biographic data on German intelligence and counterintelligence officers and their agents, the kind of equipment the Germans issued, security measures at German facilities, German methods for evaluating intelligence reports, German procedures for investigating suspected Soviet agents, and the overall German military situation.[117] A wartime Smersh interpreter who later fled to the West, one N. Sinervirsky, described Smersh interrogators as a "gallery of fanatics and alcoholics in a chamber of horrors."[118]

German military counterintelligence officers Major Johannes Gaenzer (Walli-III) and Captains Helmut Daemerau (FAT 326) and Kurt Koehler (FAK 304) told their U.S. Army CIC debriefers after the war that "they were greatly handicapped by an express order from Admiral Canaris forbidding physical pressure as an aid in interrogation." All three officers said that the "Russians generally fear pain but not death, so that '*verschaerfte Methoden*' [literally, intensified methods] would probably have led to greater successes." The three German officers said that several severe courts-martial were meted out for mistreatment of suspected agents under interrogation.[119]

However, German-employed Soviet-citizen agents, when given positions of authority, often mistreated their compatriots. It was not uncommon for German officers to turn a blind eye when these Soviets "softened up" captured agents before turning them over.[120] A common German test for agent bona fides before full recruitment was to have prospective agents (who were usually POWs) murder one of their comrades.[121] The theory behind this rather brutal test was if a Soviet POW was willing to cold-bloodedly kill one of his comrades, it would be a deterrent to the prospective agent who was thinking about turning himself in to Soviet counterintelligence on landing behind Russian lines. Relentless and highly suspicious Soviet interrogators would eventually uncover the agent's crime.

State Security used the information derived from interrogations of German agents to conduct searches for more agents, to protect installations from potential sabotage and agent infiltration, and to improve the operational security of Soviet-agent operations. Any intelligence information on the German armed forces was forwarded to the appropriate agencies.[122] A 23 May 1942 order issued by the notorious chief of the NKVD, Lavrenti Beria, outlined the procedures for the disposition of cases. This order included the statement that "enemy agents whose guilt has been established and who cannot be used to further advantage are to be shot."[123]

Like any good security service, State Security recruited informants and agents among POWs and detainees. During the war State Security identified more than 2,000 enemy intelligence and counterintelligence officers. Among the prisoners were two former chiefs of Abwehr I, Colonels Georg Hansen and Hans Piekenbrock; former chief of Abwehr III, Lieutenant General Bamler; numerous prominent SD Ausland officers; former military attachés; and Abwehr liaison officers who were assigned to the various German army groups and corps (1c's).[124] In short, the Soviets gradually acquired extensive knowledge of the German intelligence services from some excellent sources. Given State Security's infamous interrogation methods, undoubtedly most of the prisoners gave up a substantial amount of relevant and highly useful information.

Official details of how the Soviets actually detected, arrested, and interrogated an agent and then disposed of the case are sparse, for many reasons; however, four main reasons stand out: (1) the continued Russian penchant for secrecy remains strong, and no operational files have been declassified and made available to researchers; (2) there is no evidence that the Germans recruited and ran in-place Soviet counterintelligence staff officers, and therefore the Germans had little or no information on the disposition of many of their cases; (3) as the Germans were largely on the defensive after December 1941, opportunities for the seizure of NKVD/NKGB or Smersh documents were reduced, and the fluidity of combat operations no doubt hampered the ability of the Germans to exploit all the available Soviet documentation seized; and (4) many of the documents were destroyed during the war. However, during the initial advance, FAKs and FATs captured so much material that the evaluation of it was not completed until shortly before the end of the war. Walli III, which received only the most important documents, registered more than 3,000 documents. The FAKs also seized, in the autumn of 1941, the complete files of the Soviet Nineteenth Army.[125]

Though not meeting Western historiographic standards, Soviet unofficial histories provide some insight into how Soviet counterintelligence actually caught German agents. For example, on 16 January 1942 Mikhail Ivanovich Kononov, a bookkeeper at the State Bank in Pskov, reported to NKVD Lieutenant Roshchin that a Colonel Kruglov of the Quartermaster Service had visited the bank.[126] Kononov explained that he had recognized Kruglov by the name of Andrei Blazhko, a former White Army officer, but concealed this knowledge from Kruglov. Roshchin passed Kononov's information to higher headquarters, and Kononov was further interviewed by Senior-Lieutenant of State Security Vdovichenko. Kononov told Vdovichenko that he and Kruglov-Blazhko had been born in the same village in the Sumy region, had graduated high school together in 1915, had attended the same noncommissioned officer (NCO) school in Tiflis, and had served in the same regiment during World War I.[127]

Kononov went on to explain that during the civil war he and Kruglov-Blazhko fought on different sides. Kruglov-Blazhko had been promoted to captain in the White Army and had fled abroad with General Wrangel's troops in 1920. Many years later Kononov had accidentally met Kruglov-Blazhko's father in the Sumy market. The father had told Kononov that Kruglov-Blazhko was living in Germany and studying at some academy.[128]

Vdovichenko reported his findings to the front-level OO, which noted that Kruglov-Blazhko's name had appeared in a notebook previously seized from another suspected German agent. Further OO investigation revealed that a Colonel Aleksandr Petrovich Kruglov — who was born in 1896, had no Party affiliation, and served as a quartermaster in one of the armies of the Southwestern Front — was listed as missing in action in September 1941. Aleksandr Kruglov's colleagues at his former unit stated during interviews that they believed Aleksandr Kruglov was dead. OO officers also showed pictures of Kruglov-Blazhko to Colonel Kruglov's family; however, the family displayed no interest in the photographs.[129] The OOs also assessed it as too dangerous to interview Kruglov-Blazhko's relatives and friends, as they were all living in German-occupied territory.

Military counterintelligence then discovered that Kruglov-Blazhko claimed to have escaped German encirclement with a group of enlisted men and commanders from the 297th Rifle Division. After hiding for three weeks in the village of Moshchnyy while recovering from an illness, he reportedly had made his way back to Soviet lines and was subsequently sent to a collection point in Pskov. From this collection point Kruglov-Blazhko was assigned as quartermaster to a different unit. As it was common practice for Soviet soldiers to ask to be returned to their original units, the OOs noted that Kruglov-Blazhko had accepted the first assignment given to him and had not volunteered to go back to his former regiment.[130]

An interview with Kruglov-Blazhko's landlady revealed that Kruglov-Blazhko had given her a cover story, had become intimate with her, and that Kruglov-Blazhko's real intention was eventually to have her work as a German agent. The local OO wanted to arrest Kruglov-Blazhko; however, he was summoned to Moscow under a pretext and arrested there. The local OO was later informed that Kruglov-Blazhko had been an important Abwehr agent who had used the documents of the real Colonel Aleksandr Kruglov to infiltrate the Soviet army in order to uncover the "operational and strategic plans of the Soviet High Command." According to OO headquarters in Moscow, the real Kruglov had been captured and tortured by the Gestapo.[131]

Soviet counterintelligence went to even more extraordinary lengths to root out German agents. For example, in late 1941 the OOs dispatched behind German lines a sergeant, a junior lieutenant of state security, and one "informant," identified as senior Border Guard NCO Ivan Chayka. Their mission was to bring out a wounded soldier who could verify that Quartermaster Third-Rank Goldin actually had surrendered to the Germans.[132] OO interviews with Goldin's colleagues who had escaped encirclement could not accurately determine whether Goldin had indeed surrendered.[133] His colleagues had noted that Goldin had led a reserved life and would only occasionally venture into Voronezh. He would wash in the city bath, sit on a bench not far from the ticket office of the railroad station, and read the first volume of Tolstoy's *War and Peace* for an hour; he then would return to headquarters by trolley.

Chayka and one of the state security officers (the other had been killed) finally returned with the wounded soldier. Soviet military counterintelligence then arrested Goldin on 1 December 1941.[134] He was interrogated by State Security Lieutenant Kazanov. During the interrogation, Goldin related the following story.

When he was captured he "volunteered" to become a German agent under the threat of being turned over to the Gestapo and shot as a Jew. The commander of FAK-107, Major Furman, instructed Goldin to make his way back to Soviet lines, regain his old position, and summarize or copy all documents from the General Staff and the People's Commissariat of Defense, if possible.[135] Furman further instructed Goldin to pass the information to a courier on the 14th and 24th of each month between 1000 to 1200 hours. Meetings were to take place near the ticket office of the Voronezh railroad station. In order for the courier to recognize Goldin, Furman told Goldin to hold a copy of *War and Peace* so that individuals near him could read the title.[136]

Goldin also claimed under interrogation that he never passed any documents to the Abwehr and that he went to Voronezh only once to tell the courier that he had changed his mind about working for the Germans; however, no one met him at the station. Goldin finally admitted that he would work for whatever side was winning. According to this Soviet account, Goldin was "sent to a military court and prosecuted to the fullest extent of Soviet law."[137]

Soviet counterintelligence often thwarted acts of sabotage. For example, the Soviet armed forces extensively used railroads to transport troops, equipment, supplies, and ammunition. In May 1942 State Security arrested four German agents whose mission was to blow up the railroad line from Yelets to Yefremov in Tula *oblast'* (south of Moscow).[138] As a result of their interrogations, Soviet security troops interdicted several additional German sabotage missions.[139] In the summer of 1944 FAK 204 dispatched twenty-eight agents behind Soviet lines into the Ukraine disguised as members of a Soviet mining brigade. Their mission was to blow up bridges, warehouses, and roads. Those who surrendered on landing greatly aided Soviet counterintelligence in capturing the remaining saboteurs.[140]

Abwehr II analyses of their own operations also bear out the low success rate of sabotage missions. One report showed that FAK 202 carried out 59 missions in a six-month period in 1942, of which only 11 were successful. Of the 11 "successful missions," 9 were based solely on agent statements. Another summary of Abwehr II operations on the Eastern Front for 1942 showed that of 502 operations, 302 were successful. However, this 60 percent success rate for 1942 must be qualified. The Germans divided Abwehr II operations into three categories: guerrilla warfare, sabotage, and sedition. The Abwehr II summary for all of 1942 indicates that only 29 percent of sabotage missions executed were successful (38 out of a total of 132). One reason for poor sabotage mission success was the intense security surrounding sensitive installations in the Soviet rear. For example, in addition to intensive physical security around a particular installation, armed guards equipped with dogs patrolled inside the plants with ratios of employees to guards sometimes reaching 2 to 1. One electric power plant in Krivoy Rog employed 1,000 workers and 500 guards, in addition to saturating the plant with informants.[141]

German intelligence faced not just a well-integrated system to catch foreign agents. It confronted a system designed to seal off the Soviet Union from the outside world and to reengineer the thought process of every Soviet citizen in order to eliminate all threats to the regime, real or imagined. A key element in this process was the use of, or implied threat to use, terror and deportation or both. Therefore no discussion of Soviet counterintelligence would be complete without a brief summary of the ability of the NKVD/NKGB to terrorize the Soviet population by executing, deporting, relocating, or sending to labor camps millions of Soviet citizens.

Terror Incorporated

From Lenin's overthrow of the tsarist regime in 1917 through Stalin's reign, the Soviet Union consistently inflicted state-sponsored terror on its own citizens. By the time Stalin took power in the mid-1920s, mass arrests, murders, and deportations were not uncommon. Just as the Bolsheviks began to consolidate their power, Stalin ordered that the peasants be collectivized. As a result, millions more died. At least 6 million perished in the Great Famine of 1932–1933.[142] The Great Purges of the mid-1930s to the early 1940s followed and wreaked more havoc on the Soviet population and the military, as well as on the security services.[143]

The carnage did not end there. A "Lesser Terror" continued from 1939 to 1953. To quote Michael Parrish: "During the period 1939–1953, terror was just as pervasive as it had been during the previous three years, but it was less publicized, claimed fewer victims among those in the top leadership and had a larger percentage of victims who were either foreigners or minority nationalities of the USSR."[144] Stalin's orgies of murder prompted one British official to dub him "Genghis Khan with a telephone."[145] The eminent historian of the Great Purges Robert Conquest likened the mass slaughter to the "ceremonies of some barbarian cult."[146]

The figures for the total number killed during the Great Purges are still debated but range anywhere from a low but officially documented figure of 700,000 to Robert Conquest's figure of 5 million.[147] Both the leadership of the army and of the Party were destroyed. The NKVD's workload was so great that it employed 3,000 interrogators for Moscow alone and possibly as many as 123,680 nationwide.[148] Execution quotas were given to the NKVD.[149] Torture was commonplace and officially sanctioned.[150] One estimate by dissident and émigré researchers placed the number of military officers murdered at as high as 80,000 (including political officers) out of an officer corps of 130,000.[151] Nor were the Chekisty immune to Stalin's terror. Roughly 23,000 Chekisty died in the late 1930s.[152] No doubt many of them were executed as a result of Beria "cleaning house" when he became head of the NKVD in 1938.[153] Of the 122 top leaders of the security services, only 21 survived the purges.[154]

The purges clearly affected the functioning of the Soviet State Security organs. The 1977 classified history unequivocally states that the former chiefs of the NKVD, Yagoda and Yezhov, as well as "other criminal persons" who led State Security organs, "inflicted irreparable harm on Chekist cadres."[155] The purges decimated the leadership and the officers of the Foreign Department of the NKVD (GUGB/INU) and the GRU, and induced numerous defections.[156] While paying the requisite tribute to the success of the security organs in combating foreign intelligence services during the late 1930s, the history also acknowledged that many experienced senior officers of the State Security services, including those who served directly under the Cheka's founder, Felix Dzerzhinskii, were purged and that the ensuing lack of experience negatively affected the security organs' operations up to the outbreak of the war.[157] By mid-1939 sergeants were investigating cases that in 1937 would have been assigned to majors.[158]

The Soviet use of terror and violence can be broken down into three broad, overlapping categories: punishments meted out to Soviet soldiers and their relatives for infractions of military rules and regulations, such as desertion, and engaging in espionage or "anti-Soviet activities"; mass deportations and relocations; and mass murder. The use of terror and violence to punish and often execute Soviet troops as well as civilians for offenses ranging from desertion and espionage to stealing bread is well documented, as are the mass deportations and relocations of millions of ethnic minorities.[159] Mass deportations and relocations are activities not normally associated with traditional defensive counterintelligence operations. However, because of the magnitude of these operations, that they were carried out by a combination of State Security officers and internal security troops, and because of their potential effect on German agent operations, they are fixtures of the operational environment in which German clandestine HUMINT operations took place.

Harsh punishments meted out to individuals or groups of individuals for offenses such as desertion, having the wrong documents, cowardice, and so on, were integral to the ability of the Soviet counterintelligence to thwart German agent activity and helped to maintain discipline within the armed forces. Therefore the disaster that struck the USSR in June 1941 required, at least by Soviet calculations, brutal solutions. With the Soviet army on the verge of total collapse, NKVD "blocking detachments" machine-gunned retreating Soviet troops to stiffen resolve.[160] That Stalin had cowed his subjects through the wanton murder, deportation, and imprisonment over the ten-plus years prior to the Nazi invasion undoubtedly induced millions of Soviet soldiers and civilians to accept the Germans as liberators or to accept their fate by dying for the motherland.

On 25 July 1941 the NKVD rounded up 1,000 deserters and shot most of them.[161] On 27 July the death sentence was imposed on at least 9 senior Soviet generals, ostensibly for their part in allowing the Soviet Army to disintegrate so rapidly.[162] Colonel Korolev, chief of the OO of the 19th Army located near Smolensk, rounded up another 1,000 deserters and ordered 7 of them executed outright; a further 23 were ordered shot by a military tribunal.[163] A 1947 U.S. Army CIC document, based on debriefings of former Abwehr officers and translations of a few Soviet documents, stated that Soviet military counterintelligence saved the Red Army from collapse, and that by 1942 Soviet security measures had reduced desertion to a minimum.[164] It went on to state that German agents who had been infiltrated into the Red Army during the retreat "soon got caught" by Soviet security measures.[165]

The use of terror and violence made the operational environment in the Soviet rear considerably more hostile than it otherwise would have been. The groups of individuals the Germans used as agents — deserters, POWs, Soviet citizens living in occupied areas or Soviet soldiers caught in them, and members of various ethnic minorities — heightened the interest of Soviet counterintelligence. That these groups of people knew that they were destined to be shot or deported to labor camps solely because they had spent time in German-occupied areas induced many of them to give themselves up on their arrival behind Soviet lines in the vain hope of possibly saving their lives. Families of captured Soviet agents were to be arrested and exiled for a period of five years.[166] At Stalingrad the NKVD executed about 13,500 Soviet soldiers, more than an entire division of troops, for all kinds of offenses.[167] In 1945 alone Soviet military tribunals condemned 135,056 officers and men for "counterrevolutionary crimes," including 273 senior officers.[168]

Punishment for merely having been captured was brutal. On 27 December 1941 the State Defense Committee formally established NKVD Special Camps for former POWs and escapees from German-occupied areas. It had a headquarters staff of about 30 people.[169] As of 1 October 1944, of the 354,952 officers and men of the Red Army who had spent time in German-occupied areas, 2,182 enlisted men, NCOs, and warrant officers, and 16,200 officers were consigned to penal battalions.[170] In July 1944 one Soviet pilot with nine enemy "kills" to his credit was shot down, captured by the Germans, and sent to a camp on the Baltic coast. The resourceful pilot and nine other Soviet POWs managed to escape by hijacking a German bomber back to Soviet lines. Senior Lieutenant Deviataev, the mastermind of the escape, was sent to the GULAG for his trouble. He spent twelve years there and was released in 1957, having been awarded Hero of the Soviet Union.[171]

Soviet counterintelligence organizations, such as NKVD rear-area security and Interior Troops, committed mass murder on a wide scale. In 1941 and 1942 the NKVD murdered thousands of inmates of various prison camps, including Lvov (Lemberg), Rovno, Kiev, Khar'kov, Orel, Tallin, Smolensk, Minsk, and many others.[172] On 25 June 1941 the NKVD killed 3,000 people in the process of suppressing an uprising in Lvov.[173] No precise figures are available for the actual number of bona fide German agents caught in such mass killings; however, the ability of the Soviet services to carry out this kind of activity undoubtedly made life even more hazardous for German agents.

During the war the NKVD relocated or deported to labor camps millions of Soviet citizens and civilians from occupied territories. From 1939 to 1941, 1,060,000 Poles were sent either to Siberia or to labor camps.[174] In August 1941 the Soviet government abolished the Volga Autonomous Republic and deported the 600,000 people living there, two-thirds of whom were ethnic Germans. To ensure that as many Nazi sympathizers as possible were caught, the NKVD employed such brutal tactics as dropping a battalion of its own paratroopers dressed in German uniforms near population centers and massacring the inhabitants who showed any sympathy for the Germans.[175] Along with the Volga Germans the NKVD deported another 200,000 Balts (4 percent of the 5 million inhabitants of Latvia, Estonia, and Lithuania).[176]

Hundreds of thousands of Soviet citizens who had lived under German occupation also were considered a threat to the regime. From 1943 to 1944 — after the German retreat — the NKVD deported almost 1 million people from the Caucasus region alone.[177] Deportations of Crimean Tatars soon followed.[178] One Western analyst of the Soviet security services described the scale of some of these operations:[179] "On 7 March 1944, almost 220,000 NKVD, NKGB and Smersh officers and men began the deportation of 500,000 Chechens and Ingushes. On 8 March, 337,103 Balkars were added to the list. From 18 to 20 May, more than 180,000 Crimean Tatars were expelled, and in June 1944 the NKVD deported 33,000 Armenians, Greeks and Bulgarians. All were deported under inhuman conditions rivaling the Nazi transportation of the Jews to extermination camps. Beria recommended, and Stalin approved, 413 NKVD officers for awards."[180] By 1944 at least one estimate placed the population of the GULAG at 5 million, including former Soviet prisoners of the Germans.[181]

Some Western researchers have asserted that various non-Slavic peoples in the USSR were sympathetic to the Germans. Clearly many members of various minority groups collaborated with the Germans — some, no doubt, unwillingly — and surely the Germans launched special operations to induce some members of those groups to conduct guerrilla warfare.[182] For example, in December 1941 Hitler ordered the establishment of "national legions" consisting of non-Russian Soviet prisoners. In total, these legions consisted of somewhat more than 500,000 troops, 80 percent of whom were later sent to the West. About 10 to 15 percent of the members of these units deserted, and many joined Western resistance groups fighting against the Germans.[183] There are no figures for the exact number of bona fide German agents who belonged to Soviet, non-Slavic minority groups.

However, the scale of "collaboration" — depending on how one measures collaboration — by Soviet minority groups was small in comparison with the number of Slavs who either worked for German-occupation authorities, volunteered their services to German intelligence, or actually wanted to overthrow the Soviet regime.[184] For example, out of a population of 134,000 Kalmyks who lived in the Soviet Union in 1939, only 5,000 might have collaborated with the Germans, although they were not necessarily German agents. According to one source, estimates of German collaborators among the Crimean Tatars range from 12,000 to 20,000 out of a population of 250,000.[185] The total number of auxiliary troops (Hilfswillige or Hiwis) — many of whom were Slavs — who served the German army and the occupation authorities, totaled nearly 1 million.[186] Many of these individuals were destined for labor camps or firing squads after liberation.

The overall effectiveness of terror as a tool of Soviet counterintelligence to apprehend and deter actual German clandestine agent activity is decidedly mixed. One Soviet historian even admitted that the struggle with the Nazi intelligence services would have been more effective had the organs of State Security in the prewar years not been preoccupied with repression.[187] Terror and deportation were — at least until the early 1950s — the primary methods the Soviet counterintelligence organs used to sustain the security of the regime and to keep the Soviet population in check. The severe punishments the Soviets meted out to individuals who had worked for the Germans, combined with brutal German-occupation policies, probably convinced a significant number of German agents to increase their chances of survival by surrendering to Soviet counterintelligence authorities. However, the terror unleashed by Stalin's secret police prior to and during the war undoubtedly played no small role in driving hundreds of thousands of Soviets to surrender to the Germans or desert.[188] Therefore the Soviet counterintelligence organs, under Stalin's direction, bear a significant responsibility for initially providing the Germans with a substantial pool of potential agent candidates.

No figures are available on the number of agents the Germans actually employed who were killed or caught up in mass murders and deportations. Once the Germans deployed their agents behind Soviet lines, terror served, at a minimum, to increase the already hostile operational environment. When Soviet forces liberated German-occupied areas, massive numbers of individuals who had collaborated with the Germans were shot, arrested, or deported.[189] These types of operations clearly affected the Germans' ability to sustain those agents that were ordered to stay behind (agents commonly referred to as "stay-behinds") to collect and report intelligence information on Soviet forces during the German retreat.[190] Although terror was not the decisive weapon that defeated the Abwehr, it nevertheless negatively affected the Germans' ability to sustain agent deployments.

Defeat of the Abwehr

The activities of the "internal organs of State Security" — to use a well-known "Sovietism" — complemented Soviet offensive counterintelligence operations (employing double agents and recruiting enemy and allied intelligence officers) in addition to ensuring the security of the regime. By reducing German agent mission-success rates to between 10 and 20 percent, Soviet counterintelligence effectively denied the Germans long-term strategic access to the Soviet rear area and also severely limited the effectiveness of German tactical agent deployments. Therefore, while Soviet double agents and radio games fed the Germans and OKH misleading information (these operations will be discussed in the next three chapters), Soviet security units — greatly aided by the informant system — sealed off the rear area of the Soviet army to reduce the capability of German agents to report accurate and timely intelligence. As the war went on, the effectiveness of German aerial reconnaissance was reduced both by better Soviet *maskirovka* [deception] and shortages of aircraft.[191] POWs were reduced to a trickle by 1944, thereby shutting off another major source of German intelligence.[192] The Soviets blinded two-thirds of the German intelligence capability. With no high-level Soviet ciphers broken and no bona fide agents with access to strategic intelligence or counterintelligence, German signals intelligence could not make up for the loss of photo-reconnaissance and clandestinely acquired human intelligence (HUMINT).[193]

Even though German spying against Russia gradually increased over time, the Abwehr was not fully engaged — Soviet claims aside — until December 1940, only six months prior to the invasion.[194] The 1977 classified history of the State Security organs, citing a *Voprossi Istorii* article in 1965, claimed that Soviet counterintelligence captured 1,500 German agents in 1940 and the first quarter of 1941.[195] The classified history goes on to say — this time citing volume 1 of the *History of the Great Patriotic War of the USSR* — that, by the second quarter of 1941, 24 to 30 times more agents were captured in the western part of the USSR than in the second quarter of 1940.[196] Although no figures of captured German agents were given for the fourth quarter, if a rough average of 300 German agents were captured per quarter (for five quarters), the number of German agents supposedly apprehended by Soviet counterintelligence for the second quarter of 1941 would range somewhere between 7,200 and 9,000.[197]

Neither the Abwehr nor the SD were capable of supporting such large numbers of agents at that time, despite Soviet claims that Piekenbrock told them that a "massive number of agents were infiltrated into the USSR on the eve of war." The Abwehr was instructed only to "observe changes in the Soviet forces on the frontier," as the war, according to Jodl, would be short and was virtually already won.[198] The mobilization of an entire Soviet state to ferret out spies, saboteurs, wreckers, traitors, and numerous other categories of suspects in every "nook and cranny" of Soviet society — along with the Nazis' own inhuman treatment of Stalin's subjects — destroyed the ability of German intelligence to recover from initial mistakes.[199]

The totalitarian system of repression denied German agents the ability to survive for long periods behind Soviet lines. Although missions were often tactical in nature and of short duration (usually three to fifteen days), 80 to 90 percent failure rates in German agent deployments were not uncommon.[200] Examples include the following:

– From October 1942 to September 1943 FAK 104 dispatched 150 groups of agents numbering 3 to 10 people each. Only some members of two groups returned, and the Germans deemed the military information they had collected worthless.[201]
– Schmalschlaeger stated that out of every 100 agents, only 10 would return and that Leitstelle III Ost did not send agents behind Soviet lines because the Soviet intelligence service was impenetrable. From the beginning of 1944 Leitstelle III Ost ceased using double agents except in partisan-held areas because of the unreliability of potential double-agent candidates.[202]
– An Abwehr III report dated 3 September 1941 stated that, of the several waves of agents sent to the USSR prior to the outbreak of the war with orders to find locations of Soviet intelligence installations, only one had returned.[203]
– A 1944 analysis of Abwehr I Ost agents revealed a far-flung agent network consisting of 159 sources, most of whom were not operating on Soviet territory. On 22 October 1944 German Naval intelligence reviewed the accuracy of 192 intelligence reports and concluded that only 15 reports had been accurate and judged the remainder as consisting of rumor and disinformation. The study went on to state that "instead of clarifying the situation when received, the reports caused the greatest possible confusion."[204]

German agent deployments during the war were so unsuccessful that FHO officers accepted a 20 percent accuracy rate in agents' reports as indicative of success.[205] In 1943 SD/Ausland had inserted nineteen agent groups (a total of 115 agents) into the rear of the Red Army. The Soviets liquidated fifteen groups before they could accomplish their mission; the remaining four groups were either caught or later surrendered.[206] One German assessment of the effectiveness of the Soviet services bluntly stated that "German intelligence operations have been seriously impaired by the interception or liquidation of our agents."[207]

Captain Heinrich Sojoun, a former Abwehr officer who directed German radio-equipped agents behind Soviet lines, remarked that the agents were so afraid of being caught and punished by the Soviet security services that they often gave themselves up to Soviet authorities as soon as possible after arrival in Soviet territory.[208] Schmalschlaeger and several others stated in their postwar debriefings that the Germans' brutal treatment of the Soviet population, and the fact that the Soviet armed forces began to go on the offensive in late 1942, reduced the number of potential agents willing to work for the Germans, which contributed to the abysmal survival rate of German agents behind Soviet lines.[209]

However, low success rates of German agent deployments tend to corroborate Soviet claims of arresting large numbers of German agents throughout the war. For example, one "unofficial" Soviet history of military counterintelligence claimed that 10,500 German agents were uncovered in 1942 alone. If each of the three major German army groups had averaged deployments of 10 agents a day (or 30 for every day), such an average would total about 10,950 agents a year. If the Germans considered a success rate of 10 to 20 percent routine, at least some Soviet arrest figures for the number of actual German agents arrested or "neutralized" might not be completely exaggerated.[210] Another history of Soviet military counterintelligence claimed that during the last six months of 1941 alone, 1,850 enemy agents and 50 sabotage-reconnaissance groups were destroyed.[211] F. F. Sergeev claimed in his book, *Tainye Operatsii Natsistskoi Razvedkoi,* that, from January to November 1942, 170 Abwehr agents "were rendered harmless" in the Caucasus. He went on to state that "several thousands" of Hitler's spies, including 1,750 parachutists, were also rendered harmless during the course of the war.[212]

By the time the Germans realized the necessity for clandestinely acquired strategic intelligence from the higher levels of the Soviet government, from the CPSU, from the military, and from the intelligence and security services, it was too late.[213] After the invasion of the USSR, when most of the German-run agents were Soviet citizens, one German document, dated 1943, stated that "numerous full- or part-time Russian organizations and activities render any deployment of our agents most difficult."[214] One Soviet history declared that the Germans did not "penetrate the ranks of Soviet counterintelligence during the war."[215] A German assessment of Soviet successes indicated that "the Russian counterespionage service" had been able to secure, in numerous instances, advance notice of German intelligence operations that enabled Soviet counterintelligence to apprehend German agents. The document went on to give an example in which Soviet counterintelligence possessed a list of 681 German agents.[216]

Draconian Soviet defensive counterintelligence efforts virtually guaranteed that the Germans would not recover from their original mistake of devaluing the importance of clandestinely acquired strategic intelligence on the USSR.[217] That devaluation contributed to the magnitude of the Nazi defeat. In the best of circumstances it would have been difficult for the Abwehr and the SD to conduct effective clandestine operations inside the USSR.[218] With no agents having access to actual Soviet plans and intentions before the invasion, and little or no real prospects for acquiring them later in the war, the German ability to uncover Soviet military deception above the tactical level remained almost nonexistent. If the Germans had been running a high-level penetration of Soviet counterintelligence, German agent operations might have been much more successful than the documentary record indicates. Once the Soviets recovered from the initial shock of the invasion, they resumed their attack on the German intelligence services with the same ferocity with which they hunted down real or imagined spies on Soviet territory. They threw thousands of double agents at every level against the entire German intelligence establishment. Many were caught, but many more were not. The ultimate effect was to severely weaken the ability of German intelligence to effectively support the High Command. By and large the strategy worked.

Soviet Offensive Counterintelligence Operations

The Soviet Union is a state with a maximum centralization of executive power and below average intelligence.

Generalmajor Hoffman von Waldau, Chief Operations Department, Luftwaffe General Staff, July 1941

The Soviet armed forces conducted 50 major strategic operations and more than 140 *front*-level (army group) offensive operations.[1] The *front* operations ranged from 500 kilometers long to 650 kilometers deep and involved between 300,000 and 25 million men.[2] They used deception with varying degrees of success in almost every one of those operations.[3] Deception measures included, but were not limited to, generating false or misleading radio traffic, moving troops at night, camouflaging and concealing troops, equipment, and positions, maintaining radio silence, simulating troop movements and activities, and conducting false maneuvers.[4]

The Soviets deceived the Germans on the scale and scope of Soviet attacks in almost every operation, even when the general location of the main attack was known.[5] Such success strongly indicates that during World War II Soviet intelligence on all levels functioned effectively.[6] For intelligence to succeed on that level over a sustained period, good counterintelligence is a prerequisite. Soviet State Security provided it. That the Russians by and large shut down any meaningful German clandestine collection against the Soviet Union substantially enhanced the effectiveness of Soviet military deception operations. A German intelligence document stated that "it is obvious that Russian counterespionage operations have made valuable contributions to the cause of the Red Army and the Red Fleet" and that "German intelligence operations have been seriously impaired by interception and liquidation of their agents."[7]

The German failure to accurately assess the scope and magnitude of major Soviet offensives, such as those at Moscow in 1941, Stalingrad in the winter of 1942 to 1943, Belorussia in 1944, and the Vistula-Oder operation in 1945, attest to — among other things — the poor to mediocre analytical and operational performance of the Abwehr, FHO, and the SD.[8] Without the unique offensive and defensive operational capabilities of Soviet counterintelligence, the Germans would have had much less difficulty in interpreting the real direction, scope, and magnitude of Soviet military offensives. Although the Germans' ability to uncover Soviet deception operations arguably might not have affected the outcome of the war, it might have resulted in a longer conflict with corresponding higher casualty rates.[9]

As the war progressed German intelligence experienced increasing difficulty in obtaining a precise picture of overall Soviet force dispositions as operational defeats mounted, despite being able to acquire generally accurate tactical signals throughout the war.[10] The rapid advance of Soviet armies diminished Luftwaffe aerial reconnaissance capabilities, decreased the number of POWs, deserters, and line-crossers, and thereby reduced the amount of intelligence gleaned from interrogations and clandestine agent operations.[11] The decline in the overall German intelligence effort increased the likelihood that Russian military deception would work.

General Reinhard Gehlen, chief of FHO, said in his memoirs that, by late 1942, it was no easy task to see through Soviet deception measures and that Soviet agents were instructed to play down Soviet military capabilities if they were captured and interrogated by the Germans.[12] Gehlen and FHO were formally aware of Soviet deception techniques on the tactical and operational level; however, FHO lacked an understanding of the Soviets' ability to deceive the Germans on a strategic level. One U.S. postwar analysis of German documents stated that "no broad knowledge of Russian principles guiding such operations enters into the description" and characterized the lack of an appreciation for the principles guiding Soviet counterintelligence as "surprising."[13]

The cumulative effect of good Soviet intelligence and counterintelligence, which in turn greatly enhanced the success of Soviet military deception measures, reduced the capability of the Abwehr and FHO to make sense of contradictory and confusing information. Soviet counterintelligence contributed to keeping the German intelligence services off-balance, perpetually confused, and paralyzed by ambiguity, and rendered thousands of German agent deployments ineffective.[14] With few, if any, reliable agents either before the war or during it, German intelligence missed numerous significant Soviet military developments.

For example, the Germans were surprised by the introduction of the Soviet medium T-34 and heavy KV-1 tanks in the initial stages of the war, and the deployment of Katyusha multiple rocket launchers in late 1941.[15]

German intelligence failures regarding Soviet aircraft production and the ability of the USSR to mobilize strategic reserves are also well documented.[16] The Germans rightly judged in May 1941 that the Soviet air force was in the process of reequipping itself with new aircraft. However, German air intelligence had no knowledge that the Soviets had already produced 2,739 modern aircraft nor that the front-line strength of the Red Air Force was 50 percent higher than expected.[17] By 1944 Soviet deception measures confounded the Germans to such an extent that it was not uncommon for the Germans to miss as much as 50 percent of Soviet strength. The Soviets learned that this afforded them, to quote Glantz, a "huge if not decisive advantage." From 1941 to 1943 the Germans could identify newly deployed Soviet divisions within twenty-four hours of arrival at front-line positions. By early 1944 it took two to three days, and by late 1944 it took three to four days.[18]

The Soviet ability to effectively integrate and centralize offensive and defensive counterintelligence operations significantly contributed to the German defeat in the East. Though cooperation of organizations responsible for offensive and defensive counterintelligence among Western services is common, in the Soviet context the two were inseparable. This enabled NKVD rear-area security units to apprehend thousands of German agents more quickly (defensive), thereby enhancing the ability of the Soviets to turn many of those agents against the Germans (offensive). In most Western armies, rear-area security units consist of regular troops detailed to rear-area security duties to augment the military police.[19] In contrast to the Soviet practice, these types of units in Allied militaries were not directly subordinate either to the military counterintelligence components or the civilian security service. Also, that Abwehr and SD bureaucratic infighting severely damaged German effectiveness is well documented.

Soviet offensive counterintelligence consisted of four basic types of operations: (1) running double agents to disrupt the Germans' clandestine collection effort and to obtain information on its modus operandi; (2) conducting double-agent operations for the purpose of establishing a clandestine channel for the passage of deceptive, misleading, or even true information (this often involved turning the enemy agent and using his radio to transmit the controlled information) to the enemy service; (3) penetrating the German intelligence services (as well as some Allied services) by recruiting German (or Allied) intelligence officers and by sabotaging German intelligence facilities; and (4) kidnapping or assassinating Nazi intelligence officers and agents.

Although sabotage, kidnapping, and assassination are generally not considered counterintelligence activities by Western services, during World War II Soviet counterintelligence officers, as well as agents in the employ of Soviet counterintelligence organizations, sabotaged Abwehr, SD, and Gestapo facilities, and kidnapped and assassinated many German intelligence officers and agents.[20] Offensive counterintelligence operations can also be conducted to mislead or deceive the enemy about the plans, capabilities, intentions, and operations of one's own intelligence service. For example, the Soviets used double-agent operations to supply the Germans with misleading information on the progress of German intelligence missions in Soviet territory, Soviet security measures, locations of Soviet intelligence personnel and schools, and the general capabilities of the Soviet services.[21]

The amount of resources the Soviet services devoted to their offensive against German intelligence and counterintelligence is hard to measure, as no official Soviet or Russian figures are available. Nevertheless, some inferences can be drawn concerning the number of Soviet agents assigned to counterintelligence missions. Smersh units assigned to Soviet army-level formations and above, the KRU, OO/NKGB, counterintelligence elements of partisan units, and the Fourth Directorate of the NKGB all carried out offensive counterintelligence operations and were the primary organizations responsible for them. By the summer of 1944 Leitstelle III Ost maintained a card index containing biographical data on 20,000 trained Soviet agents. Not all the names in the index were Soviet agents with counterintelligence missions. German counterintelligence officers viewed the index as useful only in a minimum of cases. Identified agents would disappear or reappear under totally different names. Information was forwarded to Abwehr III headquarters in Berlin, which would check it with its holdings and then forward the results of those checks to Leitstelle III Ost. The procedure was considered a nuisance. In addition, German counterintelligence officers realized that, in the face of 10,000 new Soviet agents deployed every three months, the Leitstelle III Ost index card holdings for 20,000 trained Soviet agents covering the whole Eastern Front was far from complete.[22]

Though the index had its limitations, the Germans kept detailed records on the numbers of captured Soviet agents and on Soviet agent deployments. German analyses of captured Soviet agents categorized those agents by age, gender, service, mission, party affiliation, and when and where those agents were captured. One percent were estimated to have been engaged in counterintelligence missions. Not all Soviet agents employed by Soviet counterintelligence were double agents. Some agents were only given the task of identifying German intelligence officers and places where they congregated, locating facilities, acting as couriers and cut-outs, or identifying Soviets working for the German-occupation authorities. One Walli III document broke down Soviet agent deployments for January 1944 even further, to include ethnicity, occupation, Party status, how and where they were caught, and which German organization caught them (GFP, SD, Abwehr, Feldgendarmerie — military police, regular army, etc.). In these statistics, out of 419 Soviet agents caught, the Germans assessed 70 as having some kind of counterintelligence mission. Leitstelle III Ost also plotted Soviet agent commitments on detailed maps of the rear of the German army. According to Schmalschlaeger, the analysis of Soviet agent deployments was successfully used to predict some Soviet offensives (the more agents deployed in a certain area, the more likely an offensive was to take place there).[23]

In 1947 Schmalschlaeger told his U.S. Army CIC debriefers that German counterintelligence analyses estimated that Smersh accounted for 12 percent of the total number of 130,000 trained agents deployed in the German army's rear area during the war.[24] This would indicate that Smersh dispatched approximately 15,600 agents. According to another CIC report, 30 percent of all Soviet counterintelligence agents uncovered during the war had been assigned to special camps for deserters.[25] Schmalschlaeger stated that partisans accounted for 38 percent of Soviet agent deployments, some of whom had counterintelligence missions.[26] Sudoplatov claimed that the Fourth Directorate of the NKGB dispatched between 7,000 and 10,000 agents of all types, some of whom were also assigned to counterintelligence missions.[27] One FHO document, dated October 1943, stated that 10 percent of the agents assigned to counterintelligence missions were deployed by the KRU.[28]

Soviet counterintelligence, in coordination with components of the Soviet General Staff, provided Soviet deception planners with channels (double agents) to pass misleading information. By virtue of their functions, Soviet State Security organs were also responsible for acquiring detailed knowledge of how the German intelligence system processed and disseminated clandestinely acquired information, and for obtaining information on the contents of the intelligence reports and analyses on Soviet forces that FHO was forwarding to OKH.

Armed with details of the enemy intelligence dissemination and processing system, planners can make educated judgments on whether the controlled information being passed through enemy intelligence channels has a reasonable chance of coming to the attention of the right office or individual. Knowledge of the contents of FHO intelligence reports, if obtained quickly, would also show how the Germans viewed the disposition of Soviet forces at any given time. Although there is no documented indication that the Soviets possessed detailed knowledge of the contents of FHO reports, given the Germans' extensive use of Soviet citizens as agents, interpreters, instructors in agent training schools, and employees of the German intelligence services in general during the course of the war, by no means can the likelihood be ruled out. This knowledge, in turn, would better enable the Soviets to monitor the effect of their deception efforts on the Germans.

Successful decryptions of high-grade German ciphers would also have been invaluable in monitoring the effect of any deception operations. The Soviet and Russian governments have never acknowledged that high-level German cipher systems were broken, even though there is strong circumstantial evidence that the Soviets might have done so. The Red Army captured several Enigma machines (the name for the German cryptographic equipment) at Stalingrad, complete with user manuals, plain and cipher texts of messages, and tables of key settings. Thereafter, according to John Erickson, Soviet operational and strategic assessments greatly improved. Yuriy Modin, a retired senior KGB officer who handled high-level Soviet penetrations of British intelligence, stated in his book that the Soviet troops at Stalingrad captured twenty-six partially destroyed Enigma machines. Even though German prisoners revealed the cipher that had been used on the machines, Soviet technicians could only decode a few batches of messages and never succeeded in finding the general key for the Enigma system.[29]

FHO and Abwehr records, as well as Soviet anecdotal evidence, make no mention of Soviet counterintelligence having had detailed knowledge about the processing and dissemination system of German intelligence.[30] However, much of it could have been obtained by interrogations of captured intelligence officers, the seizure of documents, and information provided by any agents inside the SD, the Abwehr, and FHO. Former German intelligence officers who served on the Eastern front had the impression that the Soviets generally had accurate information about the Abwehr and the SD.[31] They also noted that the primary goal of Soviet offensive counterintelligence was not to acquire order-of-battle information on the German intelligence services but to disrupt their work by subverting, misleading, and turning German intelligence officers and agents into Soviet collaborators.[32]

Double-Agent Operations

In the absence of any reliable official disclosures by the Russians that the Soviet services had high-level penetrations of German intelligence or counterintelligence with access to agent operations in the East, double-agent operations — including radio games — provided Stalin and his generals with the most effective offensive counterintelligence weapon against the Abwehr and the SD, and ultimately OKH. Double agents, especially if they had a functioning radio, served as channels for the rapid transmission of Soviet-controlled information. The ceaseless quest to identify, find, arrest, interrogate, torture, shoot, imprison, or "turn" German agents ensured a substantial supply of German agents willing to turn on their controllers.

How many German agents became Soviet-controlled agents can only be estimated. The former executive officer of Leitstelle I Ost, one Captain Auffermann, stated that "of 100 agents whom we send in, 60 perhaps abandon their mission, and simply disappear, 20 will surrender to the Russians and tell them all about their mission, and 20 will work." This would indicate that roughly 20 percent (8,800) of the estimated 44,000 German agents deployed against the Soviets during the war might have had the potential to work for Soviet counterintelligence.[33] This figure would not include those agents — previously unknown to the Germans — dispatched by the Soviets to infiltrate all levels of German intelligence.

The Soviets obtained their sources for double-agent operations in a variety of ways. The three most common methods were (1) to apprehend German agents and coerce them into working for Soviet counterintelligence; (2) to dispatch an agent behind German lines under the guise of a refugee, deserter, or agent on an actual mission and instruct the individual either to volunteer his services to the Germans or, when questioned by the Germans, to offer to work for them; and (3) to fully "recruit," vet, and train those German agents who volunteered their services to State Security.[34] Because many German agents were Soviet citizens, they turned themselves in to Soviet counterintelligence immediately on deployment behind Soviet lines.[35] Other methods included contacting Soviets in the occupied areas who were working for the Germans and coercing them into cooperating, and instructing agents, who were to stay behind when Soviet forces retreated, to ostensibly volunteer their services to the Germans. Despite Soviet suspicions of even those double agents who were directed to work for the Germans, some received medals for their accomplishments.[36]

The following examples, derived from translations of German documents and Soviet accounts, illustrate how the Soviets conducted double-agent operations. Although they represent only a small cross-section of thousands of cases, they show the variety of methods Soviet counterintelligence used to recruit double agents. Collectively they demonstrate, albeit incompletely, the Soviet ability to transmit disinformation through double agents, and to effectively plan, initiate, and sustain double-agent operations under extraordinary, stressful conditions.

At least one Soviet double-agent operation, involving a Baltic-German journalist named Ivar Lissner, may have affected the Luftwaffe's estimate of the

Red Air Force.[37] Lissner, an Abwehr principal agent (an agent who recruits other agents but is not a staff officer of the service), established in 1940 numerous contacts with émigré Russian opponents of the Soviet regime in Harbin (now Shengyang), China.[38] He soon made contact with the leader of the Russian Fascists in Harbin, Konstantin Rodzaievsky. Rodzaievsky supposedly dispatched his agents into Siberia and some, ostensibly, infiltrated the Red Army's Far East Command.[39] In exchange for intelligence on Japan and its armed forces, Rodzaevsky gave Lissner intelligence on the Soviet Union.[40]

Probably through NKVD penetrations of Rodzaievsky's network, Soviet counterintelligence began passing controlled information to Rodzaievksy's agents in 1941, and Rodzaievsky, in turn, passed it along to Lissner, who then forwarded it to August Ponschab, the German consul general in Harbin.[41] The composition and complexity of the material, which dealt with a wide variety of military, diplomatic, and political issues and included statements by senior Soviet and foreign leaders, strongly suggest that a small committee, under Beria, assembled the information for passage to the Germans.[42] The Soviets apparently designed the material to convince the Germans not to invade the USSR.[43] It was, of course, ignored, and there is no evidence that the Germans subjected Ponschab's information to individual or collective analysis.[44] In June 1943 the Japanese arrested Lissner on suspicion of espionage, interrogated him under torture, and finally released him after the war.[45]

The Soviets had suspicions that their operation failed because the Germans had penetrated the Soviet Consulate in Harbin, and therefore a German source had tipped off the Abwehr that the material being passed to Lissner was controlled by the NKVD. After the war an NKVD commission visited the former assistant to the German consul in Harbin, Georg Korter, who was being held in a camp near Sverdlovsk. Although the commission wanted to know who the German source was in the Soviet Consulate, the interrogation went nowhere, as the Germans had no source. The Soviets apparently did not believe Korter and did not release him until 1955. August Ponschab, the German consul in Harbin, was released by the Soviets in 1953.[46]

It may be too harsh to claim that the Lissner operation failed because one of the original Soviet objectives — to convince the Germans not to invade the USSR — was not met.[47] Another Soviet objective — which was to pass to the Germans misleading information on the Soviet air force — was met. According to one German biographer of Admiral Canaris, Canaris stated that Lissner was the sole source of comprehensive reports on Asiatic Russia and the Manchurian-Russian frontier, and that he also provided detailed material on the Soviet aircraft industry.[48] Canaris further elaborated that Lissner produced the only documentation of the Soviet air force order-of-battle in the Far East, including details of its reserves.[49] At least one Abwehr officer who was interrogated after the war stated that Lissner's information was considered good by the Luftwaffe Fuehrungsstab (German Air Force High Command) and OKH.[50] Although a detailed analysis of the Luftwaffe's data resulting in the underestimation of the Soviet air force does not specifically mention Lissner as an air intelligence source, Canaris's statements on Lissner's importance show that the Abwehr factored Lissner's information into its estimates.[51]

Other Soviet double-agent operations were primarily directed at the German intelligence services. For example, Abwehr II (sabotage) dropped Lieutenant L. L. Puchov behind Soviet lines in August 1943.[52] Soviet counterintelligence subsequently caught him and convinced him to work for them as a double agent; however, the Germans later uncovered Puchov's activity. While this operation is essentially a Soviet failure (although, according to Puchov's statements, the Soviets had foreknowledge of his initial deployment), this example is representative of the kind of double-agent operation conducted by the Soviets throughout the war; many, of course, were more successful than this one.

There is no information in the available documentation on how Puchov came to the attention of the Abwehr or why he was in Riga in 1943.[53] However, Abwehr II decided to recruit him, sent him to an agent training camp at Priedaine, and gave him the cover name of Leonid Petrov. On 21 August 1943 Abwehr II dispatched Puchov on a sabotage mission from the German airfield at Pleskau and dropped him behind Soviet lines along with his partner, one "agent Bruchanov." According to statements Puchov later provided in October 1943 to FAT 311 in a camp near Pskov after his return from Soviet lines, he strained his knee on landing and Bruchanov broke his leg.[54] After two days they arrived at the village of Sonki and were given housing by the president of the village council.[55]

That night the secretary of the local Party committee demanded to see Puchov's papers and, while looking at them, remarked that "he knew all about this" and instructed the pair to remain until morning. The next morning NKVD officers arrived and quickly concluded that Puchov and Bruchanov were sent by the Germans. The NKVD officers confiscated their explosives and transported the two men to the local NKVD militia office.[56] There, a militiaman asked for their names. When Puchov (still using the alias Petrov) answered that he was Petrov and the other was Bruchanov, the militiaman replied "correct." Puchov was under the distinct impression that the Soviets had been expecting them.[57]

During the subsequent interrogation an NKVD officer asked Puchov specific questions about his mission, the location of his training camp, and the names of other German agents.[58] When Puchov could not give the exact location of the German intelligence facility in Riga, the NKVD officer accused Puchov of being a poor spy. When Puchov stated that all he wanted to do was return home, the NKVD officer accused him of wanting to blow up Soviet railroads and told him that he was nothing but a traitor.[59]

On 6 September 1943 a board of three counterintelligence officers gave Puchov a choice: either return to the Germans as a double agent or be shot as a traitor. The officers knew Puchov's entire case, including his real name. They even knew details of his family and strongly implied that, if he did not cooperate, his family, including his parents, would suffer.[60] Puchov agreed to cooperate, was photographed, and was given orders to gain access to the "German counterespionage staff," and to report on the number of people and the exact location of the offices. Puchov was also to return to the school at Priedaine, approach those willing to work for Soviet counterintelligence, and tell them that if they reported directly on their arrival behind Soviet lines they would not be shot.[61]

Soviet counterintelligence gave Puchov false papers and, on 9 October 1943, infiltrated him behind German lines. FAT 311 caught him almost immediately.[62] Specialist Riech, who was in charge of the investigation, employed the services of a trusted Soviet-born agent, Nina Nesterova, to elicit from Puchov whether he was working for the Soviets.[63] Riech introduced Puchov to Nesterova and told Puchov separately that Nesterova could not be trusted. After becoming acquainted over a two-day period, Puchov tried to carry out his mission for Soviet counterintelligence by telling Nesterova his cover name, and telling her to contact Soviet counterintelligence and inform them he was on his way to Riga, as instructed.[64] There is no further information on the disposition of the case. Since the Germans could no longer trust Puchov, he was probably shot.

Other Soviet double-agent operations achieved substantial success. In the autumn of 1942 Soviet military counterintelligence dispatched Ivan Semenovich Savchuk, a young military doctor, on a one-year mission behind German lines under the guise of a deserter.[65] The Soviet officer handling the case instructed him to have German intelligence recruit him for agent training. The Germans did not initially believe Savchuk's story and sent him back behind Soviet lines with instructions to volunteer his services to the Soviets and to return in five to seven days. Under Soviet direction, Savchuk was reinfiltrated behind German lines.[66]

The Germans again sent him back behind Soviet lines, this time accompanied by another agent.[67] The Soviets arrested them both on arrival, subsequently gave them an opportunity to escape (a plan Savchuk had worked out with Soviet counterintelligence prior to this mission), and did not interfere with their trek back to German lines. They crossed over at a predetermined point that only Savchuk knew. Savchuk's fellow agent thanked him for saving his life.[68]

Savchuk thus gained the trust of the Germans and was soon acting as an interpreter for German intelligence officers screening Soviet POWs for potential agent candidates.[69] He began to fill out false information on genuine captured Soviet documents for issuance to German-trained agents being dispatched behind Soviet lines. By the time the operation ended, Savchuk had given Soviet military counterintelligence detailed information on eighty agents and thirty Abwehr staff officers, and had successfully returned to Soviet lines.[70] He had communicated that information through various Soviet agents working behind German lines. One of the agents was the proprietor of an apartment building and another was a relative of his living near Kremenchug. Savchuk even used an agent dispatched by the Germans behind Soviet lines — who was actually working for the Soviets — to inform Soviet counterintelligence of Abwehr activities.[71]

The Soviets also used individuals who resided in German-occupied territory to render German agent deployments ineffective. For example, sixty-year-old Khariton Plakasyuk, who spoke fluent German, gained the Germans' trust through his position as a quartermaster in the local Gebietskommisariat [regional commissariat].[72] Eventually he was able to predict the number of German agents and their deployment schedules through analysis of food rations drawn by a neighboring Abwehr unit that was located near an airfield.[73] On instructions from Soviet counterintelligence, Plakasyuk then guided Soviet partisans to an unidentified airfield which they destroyed in order to hamper German agent deployments. The partisans also killed a number of German agents during the attack.[74]

Among the primary targets for Soviet offensive counterintelligence operations were the approximately sixty major German agent training facilities identified by Soviet counterintelligence during the course of the war.[75] Of the 345 agents whom State Security dropped behind German lines from 1 October 1943 to 1 May 1944, 57 penetrated German intelligence schools and other establishments, and brought back valuable information.[76] Many Soviet agents inside these camps inflicted serious damage on German agent operations.[77] One Smersh report to the State Defense Committee, dated 22 July 1943, briefly detailed the exploits of one Smersh officer code-named "Severov." Severov identified 93 German intelligence officers and 133 agents who were going to be deployed behind Soviet lines. Severov, although not a radio operator himself, was used in the elaborate radio game "Zagodka," which lasted from June 1943 to September 1944.[78] Severov also provided numerous other documents, including exemplars of German agent documentation and eighteen photographs of German intelligence officers and agents.[79]

Because German security measures and compartmentalization were severely lacking, agents ostensibly in the employ of the Germans and actually working for the Soviets identified thousands of bona fide German agents and reported their names, targets, infiltration routes, drop locations, and scheduled deployment dates and times. Troops of FAKs/FATs I, II, and III were often billeted close to one another. If caught, German agents could easily reveal the identities and locations of many of the personnel and agents of all three units.[80] Once behind Soviet lines, Soviet rear-area security units apprehended them, extracted names of other German agents from them, or, depending on the situation, killed them immediately.[81]

Soviet counterintelligence seriously reduced the effectiveness of numerous Abwehr training schools by concentrating on uncovering the identities and targets of German agents and by convincing them to work for the Soviets prior to their deployments.[82] In 1943 one Soviet agent infiltrated the "Saturn" intelligence training school, became an instructor, and, according to Soviet sources, provided Soviet counterintelligence with detailed information on hundreds of German agents, many of whom surrendered on arrival behind Soviet lines.[83] Another Soviet agent infiltrated the agent training school at Grossraum (near Koenigsberg, also known as Kaliningrad), convinced 10 German agents to work for the Soviets, and gave Soviet military counterintelligence complete information on 142 Abwehr officers, employees, and agents. Another agent penetrated the "Brussard" Abwehr training school and ultimately convinced 42 German agents to give themselves up once behind Soviet lines.[84]

One Soviet history, which described several double-agent operations, attributed the first major Soviet counterintelligence victory over the Abwehr to the penetration of German agent training schools.[85] For example, Lieutenant Nikolai Rakhov was wounded in July 1941, captured by the Germans, placed in the POW camp at Bobryusk, and later released by the Germans to spend the remainder of the war with his wife, who lived in an area occupied by the Germans. The Germans released Rakhov because his wife's aunt — who had heard about Rakhov's internment — convinced the German commandant that Rakhov's wife had been the victim of Soviet power; her father had been sent to Siberia because he was a kulak. The Germans not only released him but gave him a pass to move about freely. Rakhov had second thoughts, returned to Soviet lines on his own, and was recruited by military counterintelligence to infiltrate the Abwehr training school at Poltava. On his arrival behind German lines, the Gestapo apprehended him and turned him over to the Abwehr. Rakhov allowed himself to be recruited by the Abwehr, was given eight days of agent training at Poltava, and was dispatched behind Soviet lines in February 1942.[86]

Soviet counterintelligence suspected Rakhov's mission to be a German test to determine whether Rakhov was actually working for the Soviets.[87] The Germans assigned him a narrowly defined mission with the idea that, if Rakhov would return with substantially better information than expected, he was probably a Soviet double agent. The Soviets therefore tailored their information on troop morale and numbers of tanks and artillery pieces for Rakhov by giving him just enough to fulfill his mission.[88] It took Rakhov three days to give Soviet counterintelligence a complete report on his training at Poltava. Rakhov returned to German lines, was debriefed, and was then given a pass to stay with his wife as the Abwehr had previously promised.[89]

The Gestapo arrested Rakhov again, threw him in prison, and brutally interrogated him. Five weeks after his arrest, the Gestapo staged a conversation within earshot of Rakhov's cell in which two individuals were talking about escaping.[90] When asked about escaping at the next interrogation session, Rakhov reported the conversation to the Gestapo. Thus Rakhov had passed the reliability test, and the Abwehr sent him through an intensive one-month agent training course.[91] The primary purpose of the course was to prevent the Soviets from blowing up the Grozny oil fields by killing Soviet demolition teams during the German offensive.[92] Although Rakhov was not dispatched, the group the Germans deployed to carry out the mission was immediately arrested by Soviet military counterintelligence on arrival in the Soviet rear.[93]

In June 1942 the Germans dropped Rakhov and a partner near Khar'kov. Rakhov feigned food poisoning and told his partner that he would stay with his aunt for a few days to recover.[94] The NKVD apprehended him and turned him over to military counterintelligence.[95] Rakhov told his interrogator that the Germans were planning an offensive toward Stalingrad and that FAK 101 planned to drop 200 agents near Tambov, Saratov, Stalingrad, Krasnodar, and Stavropol.[96] Rakhov was told to return to German lines and tell the Abwehr that his partner had been killed. Soviet counterintelligence subsequently arrested 110 agents in July 1942, largely based on the detailed information Rakhov provided. German counterintelligence later pieced together from several sources the fact that Rakhov had been working for the Soviets. He was finally arrested and shot by the Gestapo.[97]

Some Soviet double agents became instructors in Abwehr training schools. For example, the Germans captured one Lieutenant Voinov, gave him agent training, and sent him behind Soviet lines, where, on arrival, he volunteered his services to Soviet counterintelligence.[98] Voinov managed to spend seven months (much of that time as an instructor) at the premier Abwehr training school at Sulejowek (near Warsaw), which was headquarters for Abwehr I operations in the East (Walli I). His detailed information on agent names (including photographs), codes, deployment schedules, and targets resulted in the Soviets apprehending 112 German agents.[99]

From July to December 1942 Lieutenants Rakhov and Voinov, both Soviet double agents whose primary mission was to penetrate German agent training schools, provided Soviet counterintelligence with information that led to the neutralization of more than 200 Abwehr agents.[100] M. A. Belousov, a former Soviet counterintelligence officer himself, attributes the Abwehr's cessation of large-scale agent airdrops to the efforts of Rakhov and Voinov. According to Belousov, it was the first major victory over the Abwehr by Soviet counterintelligence.[101]

Debriefings of former Abwehr officers confirm Soviet successes in penetrating agent training schools. Colonel Schmalschlaeger told U.S. Army CIC officers in January 1947 that the Soviets possessed extraordinary detail on Leitstelle I Ost training schools.[102] Soviet counterintelligence knew the locations of individual barracks, and the names of the faculty in at least three major Leitstelle I Ost training schools.[103] In addition, Schmalschlaeger said that Soviet counterintelligence collected detailed information on German intelligence units located at Dno, Valk, Yelya, Smolensk, Orsha, Poltava, Taganrog, Rostov, and the SD post located at Khar'kov.[104] An FHO document, acknowledging the successes of Soviet counterintelligence, stated that "Russian counterespionage has also been the cause of large-scale desertions from agent training camps."[105]

State Security infiltrated German rear-area security units as well. For example, the Germans recruited locals to serve in the Ordnungsdienst, auxiliary police units that became heavily involved in combating partisans.[106] A lieutenant in Soviet counterintelligence, who posed as a former Red Army captain, was trained in 1943 at the Ordnungsdienst officers' school in Minsk.[107] His mission was to effect the defection of his unit to the Soviets. By 1944 over 50 percent of his 200-man unit had defected to the partisans.[108] The other 50 percent were so demoralized that the Germans disbanded the unit and sent the remaining members to work in Germany. The lieutenant escaped back to Soviet lines.[109] Although German rear-area security units were heavily infiltrated by the Russians, the main focus of Soviet offensive counterintelligence operations was the Abwehr, FHO, and SD/Ausland.

Radio Games

Soviet State Security, primarily military counterintelligence, conducted at least 183 radio games during World War II against the German intelligence services.[110] These figures, recently provided by retired KGB colonel D. P. Tarasov in his book, *Bol'shaia Igra* [The Big Game], published in Moscow in 1997, are more than double those previously given by the former head of Soviet military counterintelligence (Third Chief Directorate of the KGB) General Georgii Tsinev. Tsinev stated in 1978 that, from the end of 1941 to March 1943, Soviet military counterintelligence was operating 80 radio games for the express purpose of passing disinformation to the Germans.[111] Even the 1977 top secret history of State Security echoes Tsinev's figures.[112] Tarasov, however, did say that the Soviets had 56 radio playbacks in operation by the end of 1942 and 96 by the end of June 1943.[113] The radio games involved at least 400 German agents.[114]

Although his exact position during the war has not been made public even more than sixty years after the events, Tarasov spent thirteen years in military counterintelligence (1939 to 1952). According to his memoirs, he was, at least after the reorganization of Soviet intelligence in 1943, in charge of the "radiogram" section in Smersh consisting of eight people whose job was to transmit disinformation to the Germans.[115] Tarasov was awarded the Order of Lenin first and second degrees for his work during the war, as well as seventeen other medals during his more than thirty-five-year career in State Security. If Stalin's best weapon for passing controlled information to German intelligence was radio games, Tarasov's decorations attest to their effectiveness. His account currently stands as one of the more authoritative ones on Soviet radio playbacks, albeit an incomplete one, and one that was, for security reasons, heavily sanitized by Western standards. Although his account has considerable detail on how radio games were run — including texts of some of the actual messages sent by controlled Soviet agents (most are tactical in nature) — it lacks detail on their impact on military operations. Tarasov may not have known what the precise overall impact was on Soviet military operations, or he may not have been allowed to disclose it. Nevertheless, Tarasov's account of his experiences is generally borne out by German documents.

The three major radio games, Operation Monastery, Operation Berezino, and the series of operations that defeated Operation Zeppelin — and involved several radio games — will be discussed later because of their complexity, the fact that the Soviets ran them over the course of two to three years, and because Soviet and German documentation is available in enough detail to link these operational counterintelligence successes to military operations. However, enough information is available on other Soviet radio games to illustrate how they worked.

As Tarasov points out, these operations were complex and required considerable expertise to conduct. However, because his account is sanitized, Allied debriefings of German intelligence officers who served in the East provide a better understanding of the complexities inherent in such an arcane art. Radio-playback operations, because of their complexity and importance, required a high level of security, compartmentalization, and coordination with the Soviet General Staff. Their success depended primarily on the reliability and skill of the agent operating the radio. To protect the security of the operation, counterintelligence officers conducting these operations needed detailed knowledge of the intricacies and idiosyncrasies of securely operating an agent radio to avoid detection by the enemy service, as well as good agent-handling skills.[116]

Counterintelligence officers on both sides not only needed reliable agents but also had to be completely knowledgeable of the radio agent's detailed instructions on the timing, frequency, and method of transmission. The reliability of the agent was crucial because many times both sides trained their radio operators to transmit a prearranged code — which only that radio agent and his controller knew — to signal danger.[117] Soviet and German handling officers had to be able to determine that a prospective radio-equipped double-agent candidate followed procedures that would not alert the agent's parent service to the fact that he might be working for the opposing side. Knowledge of such minutiae was necessary in order to ensure that the passage of misleading information was perceived as reliable by the enemy.[118]

For example, in early June 1943 Abwehr II dropped a group of twelve Soviet nationals, who had been trained near Riga, 2,500 miles behind Soviet lines.[119] Although the group successfully landed behind Soviet lines, it did not establish radio communications with its German controllers until late June. Abwehr III Lieutenant-Colonel Rasehorn's counterespionage unit then began a routine but detailed analysis of the radio transmissions. Rasehorn's radio-counterespionage experts analyzed, over a period of months, such minutiae as the differences between the original radio operator's rate of transmission exhibited in training and those exhibited on this particular mission; the number of dits after the numbers 4, 5, and 6 to compare them with those of the original operator; the amount of time the operator paused between transmissions; and whether the operator was transmitting on the proper frequencies at the proper times. After several months of such detailed analysis, the Germans concluded, by October 1943, that the group's radio transmissions exhibited several anomalies, such as not following proper transmission procedures, observing peculiarities in the operator's transmission of the numbers 4, 5, and 6, and occasionally pausing for a minute between transmissions. Therefore Abwehr III concluded that "after a thorough and prolonged check" the traffic was more than likely under Soviet direction.[120]

The above example, although a Soviet failure, demonstrates the attention to detail required to establish a bona fide channel for passing controlled material to the enemy service. Given the combat conditions on the Eastern Front and the fluidity of military operations, complexities of this nature no doubt placed extraordinary pressure on counterintelligence officers to constantly verify that the radio-equipped agent was transmitting identically to his previously established pattern. As Soviet counterintelligence officers would have to assume a fair degree of competence on the part of Abwehr III's radio counterintelligence service, the slightest mistake could reveal that the transmitter was under enemy control.

Such a mistake would increase the risk of rendering ineffective any misleading or deceptive information passed over that transmitter after its bona fides were determined to be suspect. However, if the Germans had trained an originally Soviet-controlled agent, who after his training was dropped behind Soviet lines, Soviet counterintelligence officers would be less concerned with the technical aspects of transmitting messages. The radio agent would theoretically be reliable, continue to transmit as he normally would, and the operation would be less vulnerable to compromise through painstaking traffic analysis.

The Germans captured Soviet radio specialist Panin in 1941, eventually recruited him (his true motivation was to return to Soviet-held territory), trained him, and dispatched him behind Soviet lines.[121] On arrival, he turned himself in to Soviet authorities. Soviet counterintelligence debriefed him in detail on his agent training and decided to use him in a radio playback. Panin volunteered to actually operate the radio. Under Soviet direction, Panin informed the Germans that his group had been scattered on landing, that he did not know where the others were, that he was in an old woman's house in Volokolamsk, and that he had collected some information of interest. Soviet counterintelligence, in coordination with the General Staff, passed a considerable amount of military information over Panin's radio which German intelligence subsequently verified. Panin received the Iron Cross for his valued information. Finally, he requested replacements when his radio batteries began to run low. A courier delivered them and was duly arrested while in the process of returning to German lines. The Soviets continued the operation for a short while after that and then terminated it, probably because the Germans either suspected it was under Soviet control as a result of the arrest of the courier or because the operation had outlived its usefulness.

Some Soviet radio games were conducted more for political security reasons than for military ones. For example, Archbishop Ratmirov headed an ostensibly anti-Soviet clerical organization in Kalinin that was actually supported by the Russian Orthodox Church in Moscow.[122] Soviet counterintelligence initiated "Operation Courier" when Ratmirov was transferred from Kalinin to Samara (Kuibyshev) after Soviet troops liberated Kalinin. In Samara, Ratmirov wanted to establish branches of his organization in German-occupied territory and eventually form all of them into one unified Orthodox Church.

Ratmirov dispatched two priests, Ivan Mikheev and Vassili Ivanov — who were, unbeknownst to Ratmirov, actually Soviet counterintelligence officers — to carry messages to the head of the Pskov Monastery, who was working for the Germans. Both officers had worked with Ratmirov in Kalinin and were well known to the Germans. Therefore their presence did not raise German suspicions. Mikheev and Ivanov operated freely among anti-Soviet religious communities and, partially because of their efforts, the Germans deployed two radio-equipped agents to Samara in 1943 to set up an agent network. Soviet counterintelligence recruited both radio agents, passed misleading information on the transportation of raw materials and ammunition from Siberia to the front, and, in the process, thwarted the establishment of an anti-Soviet religious organization. Mikheev and Ivanov both received gold watches and a medal for their efforts from the Soviet government.

State Security, in coordination with the General Staff, made transmitting disinformation a priority.[123] Coordination with the General Staff was so close that messages were transmitted only after the General Staff approved the time and text. The Stavka received regular updates on the progress of radio games as well as the content of the messages.[124] Sudoplatov, in his book, *Special Tasks,* stated that GRU Colonel-General Kuznetsov supervised the preparation of military disinformation to the Germans.[125]

Soviet sources state unequivocally that radio games contributed to the Soviet victories at Kursk, Stalingrad, and the Belorussian offensive in 1944 (code-named Operation Bagration).[126] One history opined that the information transmitted in these types of counterintelligence operations basically satisfied the Germans and deterred them from trying to establish parallel agent networks.[127] Tarasov said that State Security often maintained the enemy's confidence in its agents and that therefore many aggressive German intelligence units became complacent and reduced their activity.[128]

Of course, it is often difficult to verify the claims in detail since, to date, the Russians have not declassified much of the actual disinformation passed to the Germans so that it can be compared to German intelligence estimates. A careful reading of Tarasov shows, however, that some of the information passed by Soviet radio-equipped double agents was low-level tactical information designed to complement Soviet military deception operations and to deceive the Germans on the actual status of their agents. In other words, it would be exceedingly difficult with no records from Abwehr I in the East to measure the effect of such seemingly low-level tactical messages on the impact of German military operations as a whole.[129]

Nevertheless, the magnitude of the German defeat in the East, the well-known abysmal record of Abwehr I, FHO's lack of recognition that the Soviets were capable of strategic deception, and the historical Soviet success with double-agent operations add up to more than a strong circumstantial case but less than 100 percent certainty that radio games badly hobbled German intelligence. Soviet anecdotal evidence strongly indicates — and German documentary evidence confirms — that intelligence information obtained from Soviet-controlled radio games (as well as from double agents) was factored into FHO estimates.[130] At one point Soviet agents became so brazen that some Soviet counterintelligence officers instructed their agents to contact them by using the radio facilities at German agent training camps.[131]

There is not much information on Soviet radio games prior to mid-1942. No doubt this was owing to the dire military situation and the lack of experienced counterintelligence officers. Nevertheless, the Special Departments of the Northwest Front conducted one of the first radio playbacks in September 1941. The military Chekists captured ten German agents during this operation.[132] Tarasov detailed one State Security attempt to draw a group of twenty-two German agents (two of whom were radio operators), equipped with forged documents, further into the Soviet rear. The group, in addition to collecting information on Soviet troop movements, was also given the task of intercepting Soviet military communications. In early 1942 the Germans infiltrated this group using horse-drawn carriages into areas in the Orlovskaia *oblast'*. State Security quickly captured them and proposed using one radio operator to transmit disinformation to the Germans about the fate of the group, and to lure more agents and supplies onto Soviet territory. NKVD guards were even dressed in the exact German uniforms the group used. The attempt failed. The Germans ignored the first transmission. It was sent twenty days after the agents were captured, and the Germans probably wrote off the mission as under Soviet control and a failure.[133] From 1 May to 1 August 1942, Soviet counterintelligence, in coordination with the General Staff, passed to German intelligence misleading information on 255 rifle divisions, 3 tank armies, 6 tank corps, 53 tank brigades, 80 artillery regiments, 6 cavalry divisions, and 3 army-level headquarters.[134]

Prior to the German offensive at Kursk in 1943, the Soviets employed more than nine radio games.[135] Nine transmitters were located in and around the cities of Livna, Yelets, Shchigra, Kastornoye, and Tambov.[136] It was a massive effort. All German agent groups captured by State Security in and around the Kursk bulge were used to transmit disinformation. Transmitters confirmed each other's information and then went off the air under various non-alerting pretexts so that the Nazis could not validate all the information and would not suspect that their information was Soviet-controlled. The Soviets employed transmitters as far away as Moscow, Saratov, and Penz to cleverly corroborate information provided by the controlled radio transmitters in the Kursk area of operations.[137] This masked the true nature of the Soviet counterattack, and its scope surprised the Germans. FHO failed to detect the magnitude of the deadly Soviet counterattack.[138]

Tarasov and the classified *History of State Security* elaborate somewhat on the above general description of radio games during the Kursk offensive and counteroffensive. The initial phase of Operation Opyt' ran from May through June 1943. Three German agents were captured in May. They were equipped with 120,000 rubles, topographical maps of the operations area, and forged Red Army officer documents. Their missions ranged from gathering information on Soviet troop movements and the conditions of roads and bridges to collecting information on the families of Red Amy commanders. Opyt' was part of the overall deception plan for the Kursk counteroffensive.[139] Messages were transmitted every two to three days.[140] The disinformation reinforced the idea that the Soviets were planning to go on the defensive as the agents reported on such matters as shipments of barbed wire, the digging of antitank ditches, and the construction of bunkers. In Opyt' the Soviets tried to keep to a minimum their reporting on troop movements.[141] A scaled-down version of Opyt' continued to the end of 1944.[142]

These operations were not the only ones conducted in 1943. For example, Operation Podryvniki, conducted against the SD for more than a year on the territory of the Volgoda oblast', resulted in the arrest of more than twenty-two German agents and five shipments of ammunition, explosives, and other supplies. Podryvniki, like many other radio games, was not conducted in a vacuum. Hundreds of German agents were lured into the USSR to resupply existing groups and, in turn, were doubled by the Russians. These operations were interdependent, centrally controlled and managed, and continued throughout the war. Podryvniki was initiated as a result of another operation, and it spawned yet more radio playbacks.[143]

According to S. Ostryakov, who, in 1979, wrote probably the "best" unclassified history of Soviet military counterintelligence up to that time, Soviet disinformation consisted, at least in part, of creating the perception in the Germans' minds that the Soviet forces would not attack in the vicinity of Stalingrad. On 28 October and 12 November 1942 Gehlen assessed that the Soviets did not have enough strength to carry out an offensive. On 19 November 1942, 1,143,500 Soviet troops attacked Paulus's Sixth Army.[144] Tarasov is strangely mute on the role of specific radio games in one of the most important offensives of the war, as is the 1977 classified *History of Soviet State Security*.

Red Army counterintelligence radio games — in concert with military deception — contributed significantly to the success of the Soviet Korsun'-

Shevchenkovskii offensive in late January–early February 1944. FHO could not pin down the timing and the exact location of the attack. On 5 February the Soviets transmitted information to the Germans that the First and Second Ukrainian Fronts were preparing for an attack in the general direction of Vapnyarka. The Germans halted their counterattack, and that bought valuable time for the Soviets to bring up their reserves. By the time the offensive was over, the Soviets had killed, captured, or wounded 73,000 Germans, and the Germans who escaped lost much of their equipment. Stalin promoted General I. S. Konev, commander of the Second Ukrainian Front, to Marshal of the Soviet Union and made Lieutenant General P. A. Rotmistrov (commander of the Fifth Guards Tank Army) the first Marshal of Tank Troops.[145]

Operation Bagration, the massive Soviet offensive in the summer of 1944 that destroyed German Army Group Center and resulted in the loss of more than 350,000 German troops, was arguably the single largest German intelligence failure of the war. Gehlen underestimated not only the main thrust of the Soviet offensive but also underestimated Soviet strength by more than 1.2 million men.[146] Ostryakov, in his account, stated that Smersh caught dozens of German agents in the areas around Vitebsk, Orsha, Mogliev, and Minsk. Taking advantage of the increased agent activity, the Soviets doubled a number of them and, in concert with Soviet military deception operations, used those German agents to enhance German perceptions that the main attack would come further south. Gehlen and OKH believed it, and, as a result, the Germans suffered their worst military disaster of the war.[147]

The Russians did not let up. Operation Priyateli ran from June 1944 to May 1945 and destroyed German agent operations in Romania and Bulgaria through the creation of an imaginary insurgent group. State Security arrested 179 insurgents, including their leader, and obtained information on U.S. and British policy in the region.[148] Soviet counterintelligence used twenty-four radio transmitters located throughout the USSR to convince OKH and FHO that there would be no winter offensive in East Prussia and Poland in early 1945. Again the Germans were fooled.[149] During January 1945 six new radio playbacks were initiated, and in February and April an additional eight. Up to the end of the war, however, German communications were proclaiming impending victory.[150]

Recruiting Intelligence Officers

A number of German and Allied intelligence officers clandestinely passed to the Soviets large quantities of classified information on a wide variety of subjects.[151] Collectively that information contributed greatly to Soviet knowledge of the German war effort, specifically of anti-Soviet activity conducted by resistance groups and of Allied and German agent operations outside and sometimes inside the USSR. It is less clear how much specific information these penetrations — to use intelligence jargon — had on German agent operations in the East.

Although Soviet penetrations of the British and U.S. intelligence services and the German services in Germany are well documented, speculation continues as to whether any German staff officers in FHO, the Abwehr Asts and Nests in the East, Leitstellen I, II, and III, the higher levels of SD/Ausland, or the Gestapo worked for Soviet intelligence.[152] This is more than an academic question as the lackluster performance by German intelligence — specifically by Colonel Baun's Leitstelle I Ost — would suggest that one or more Germans with access to agent deployments worked for Russian counterintelligence. Even sixty years after the events, the Russians are strangely silent on this issue. Three reasons come to mind: the individuals are still alive, they became penetrations of the postwar German intelligence services, or the Russians could be covering up the fact that if they did indeed reveal such a success story, it might raise embarrassing questions about whether that agent identified real German spies in the Party, the army, or the security services. However, it is possible that the Russians obtained all their information from double agents, agents who were Soviet citizens but worked for German intelligence in such capacities as cooks, clerks, or translators, captured German intelligence officers, or cipher breaks.

That most German operations behind Soviet lines ended in disaster or produced meager results strongly argues that the Soviets had a source, or several sources — possibly staff officers in the Abwehr or the SD assigned to the Eastern Front — with access to detailed information on agent deployments. A solid circumstantial case exists. A German evaluation of the successes of the Soviet intelligence services acknowledged that the Soviets had, in numerous instances, advance warning of German agent deployments and that the Soviets used this valuable information to counter those deployments.[153] Lieutenant Colonel Hermann Baun was accused after the war by some of his former agents of being a Soviet spy.[154] Baun had extensive experience in Russia, his record of success was almost nil, and he was originally born in Odessa.[155] Therefore the allegations that some of his former agents leveled were not, on their face, without merit. The subsequent U.S. Army CIC investigation found no solid evidence as of 1950 to substantiate the charges. CIC believed at the time that the allegations were made for personal reasons.[156] After the war Baun went on to work for Reinhard Gehlen, when the latter became chief of the newly created Bundesnachrichtendienst (Federal Intelligence Service).[157]

Walter Schellenberg, chief of SD/Ausland (Amt VI), fueled speculation that Heinrich Mueller, chief of the Gestapo, was a Soviet agent prior to his disappearance after the war by stating that Mueller had established contact with the Soviet secret service.[158] Vitaly Chernyavsky, who claims to have spent fifteen years in Soviet intelligence, was assigned to the German desk in the "Foreign Department of the NKVD" in March 1944.[159] He stated that he would have known about Mueller's working for Soviet intelligence, denied that this was true, and likewise denied that Mueller was in contact with Soviet intelligence in 1943 or 1944.[160] William Hood, a former counterintelligence officer with OSS and the CIA, stated in his book, *Mole,* that a Smersh operative recruited a high-ranking Gestapo officer in Danzig and that V. S. Abakumov (chief of Smersh) supervised the maneuvering of the agent to subsequently sound out and recruit Mueller.[161] Hood did not provide any concrete evidence that Mueller was actually recruited by Soviet intelligence. However, he astutely noted that "Abakumov must have had remarkable insights into the Nazi high command to realize that Mueller could be convinced that the millennial Reich was doomed and that he was enough of an opportunist to make a deal."[162] The recently declassified CIA Counterintelligence Staff Study completed in 1977 on "Le Affair Mueller" strongly indicates that he fled to the Russians near the end of the war. Former State Security officer Major Peter Deriabin, who defected in 1954 and who had served in Smersh, the Kremlin Bodyguards, and in Vienna as a counterintelligence officer with the MGB's Austro-German Department (MGB being the immediate forerunner of the KGB), stated in a 1971 memorandum for the CIA that in 1952, while in Moscow, he had read portions of Mueller's interrogations, heard that Mueller had been recruited, and even named Mueller's Soviet interrogators.[163] Even if Mueller were to have been a Soviet agent, he might not have had sustained access to agent deployments in the East.[164]

Reinhard Gehlen caused a considerable sensation in the early 1970s by claiming that Martin Bormann — Hitler's personal secretary and *Reichsleiter* of the Nazi Party — had been a Soviet agent, fled to the USSR after the war, and eventually died there.[165] According to Gehlen's memoirs, he and Admiral Canaris had suspicions that Bormann was a Soviet agent, that he was running a radio transmitter network and was using it to send coded messages to Moscow. Gehlen claims that when OKW radio intercept monitors reported the existence of the radio transmitter network, Canaris demanded an investigation.[166] However, Canaris's discreet initial inquiries only revealed that Hitler himself had apparently been informed previously of the transmitters and authorized them. Although Gehlen is sketchy on details, it is clear from his memoirs that he and Canaris believed that Bormann wanted to succeed Hitler so badly that he was capable of extraordinary intrigue and probably not above committing treason for personal gain. In short, according to Gehlen, although he and Canaris did not believe that the transmissions were legitimate, they decided not to risk launching an independent investigation.[167] Gehlen further claimed that after the war he received two reports from behind the Iron Curtain indicating that Bormann was alive and well in the USSR and that he had been a Soviet agent. Bormann's body was eventually discovered in Berlin in 1972, and the case was officially declared closed by a German judge on 24 September 1973.[168]

Although Gehlen was wrong about Bormann having fled to the USSR, and he did not provide any more evidence of Bormann's treason, Gehlen and Canaris were not the only ones who believed Bormann had been in the employ of the Soviets. Otto Ohlendorf, chief of SD/Inland, told his American interrogators before he was executed at Nuremberg that Bormann was a Soviet agent.[169] In 1953 British authorities in Germany arrested Werner Naumann, deputy to Reich Propaganda Minister Joseph Goebbels. Under interrogation, Naumann also stated that Bormann was working for the Soviets.[170] Wilhelm Flicke, a former radio counterespionage officer within the Abwehr whose task was to monitor Soviet agent communications between Berlin and Moscow, identified at least one transmitter operating from "Bormann's Party Ministry."[171] Schellenberg also had his doubts about Bormann.[172]

The circumstantial nature of the evidence alleging that Bormann and Mueller were actual Soviet agents bears repeating, because it serves as an indicator that at least some prominent German officers believed that the higher levels of the Nazi Party were penetrated by the Soviets and that these agents were "passing rapid and detailed" information on top-level German military decisions in the East.[173] General Franz Halder, Chief of OKH from 1938 to 1942, once commented that he believed that "nearly all the plans of the High Command were revealed to the Russians as soon as they were drawn up — even before they got to my desk." Halder went on to elaborate that this continued right up until the end of the war.[174]

Whether Bormann or Mueller or both were Soviet agents might never be resolved. What is clear, however, is that the Soviets had extensive penetrations of the German government, the High Command, and the Abwehr in Germany. The Gestapo itself was penetrated. Many of these agents were members of the far-flung Soviet illegals network known as the Red Orchestra, or Rote Kapelle. ("Illegals" are generally defined as Soviet intelligence officers posing as non-Soviets and having no contact with an official Soviet establishment.) Although the Germans caught and/or doubled many members of the network, at least one Western author claims that NKVD files show that of the roughly 400 members of the Red Orchestra the Gestapo arrested only about 130.[175]

The Allied and German intelligence officers who became Soviet agents but did not serve on the Eastern Front were recruited and handled by Soviet intelligence officers assigned to the INU (Foreign Intelligence of the GUGB/NKGB) and, in some cases, the GRU and the Fourth Directorate of the NKGB.[176] These sources supplied the Soviets with substantial quantities of information about the German armed forces, the politics of the Third Reich, the Nazi war effort, postwar Allied policy toward Germany, and the overall German ability to prosecute the war.[177] Collectively they also provided the Soviets valuable counterintelligence information that included extensive data on German intelligence and counterintelligence missions, organizations, and activities in the West, data on anti-Soviet resistance movements, and counterintelligence information on British and Allied intelligence organizations and agents.[178]

These types of Soviet sources might not have had direct sustained access to details of German agent operations in the USSR. However, brief descriptions of the classified information they were known to have given the Soviets demonstrate their extraordinary access. Because of the wide variety of information available to German and Allied intelligence officers working for the Soviets — and who were serving outside the USSR — it is plausible that at least some of them could have given the Soviets highly useful information on German operations in the East.

For example, Yuri Modin, the NKGB headquarters desk officer during the war for the "Cambridge Five" (Kim Philby, Anthony Blunt, John Cairncross, Guy Burgess, and Donald Maclean — all long-term Soviet penetrations of British intelligence and the British government) in his book, *My Five Cambridge Friends,* as well as British author Nigel West in his recent book, *The Crown Jewels* (detailing exactly what information the "Cambridge Five" passed to the Soviets) illustrate how Soviet penetrations of British intelligence aided the war effort against Germany.[179]

During his employment with the British government's Code and Cipher School at Bletchley Park, John Cairncross passed Soviet intelligence a series of Ultra intercepts concerning German plans for Operation Citadel (German code name for the attack on the Kursk salient in 1943), which Modin claimed saved the lives of "tens of thousands of Soviet soldiers."[180]

Cairncross provided Soviet intelligence with documents concerning the thickness of Tiger tank armor. The Germans were convinced that Soviet cannons could not penetrate the armor. Cairncross's information enabled Soviet engineers to design and subsequently manufacture armor-piercing shells capable of destroying the Tiger tanks.[181]

Before the battle of Kursk in 1943 Cairncross furnished the Soviets with intercepted texts of German intelligence reports, which accurately gave the exact locations, strengths, and identifications of all Soviet units in the region.[182] This enabled Soviet commanders to move their forces at the last minute and outmaneuver the Germans. Cairncross also gave the Soviets a detailed list of all the Luftwaffe bases in the region. The Soviet air force carried out surprise attacks, destroying almost 500 German aircraft.[183]

Cairncross passed the Soviets good "order-of-battle" type information on German military counterintelligence stations in the Baltics, Finland, the Ukraine, and Poland.[184]

Kim Philby passed so much information on British agents that Soviet counterintelligence possessed nearly a complete list of British agents operating worldwide, including those operating in the USSR. He also passed along to the Soviets intercepts of Abwehr communications.[185]

Anthony Blunt, who worked in MI5 (British counterintelligence) during the war, kept the Soviets abreast of the details of many MI5 operations against the Soviet Embassy in London as well as against the British Communist Party, including specific details of MI5 surveillance targets and capabilities.[186] Blunt included details of the mission, organization, and functions of MI5 as well as names of its agents abroad and the names of British agents in the various resistance movements. Blunt also passed the Soviets copies of the contents of the diplomatic pouches (which MI5 opened and resealed) of exiled governments. This gave Soviet counterintelligence detailed information on anti-Soviet resistance movements that was later used to crush them.[187]

Although Soviet intelligence had no direct contact with Leo Long who worked in the War Office in charge of a section dealing with German troop movements, Blunt recruited him in the 1930s.[188] Through Blunt, Long passed the Soviets Ultra intercepts. The information frequently complemented that passed on by Kim Philby.[189] A review of Blunt's file by former KGB colonel Oleg Gordievsky indicates that Blunt received numerous compliments from the Soviet General Staff on the quality of his information.[190]

In August 1941 Abwehr IIIF in Brussels (Ast Belgien) initiated an investigation based on intercepts of Soviet agent communications in Belgium.[191] The investigation, which was taken over by the Gestapo and SD in 1942, uncovered an extensive, well-placed network of Soviet agents all over Europe.[192] Many of the agents were eventually caught, and the Gestapo turned some of them against the Soviets. On 2 May 1945 Gestapo officer Heinz Pannwitz (real name Heinz Paulson), who played a significant role in uncovering the Rote Kapelle, surrendered to Soviet forces and was duly flown to Moscow and interviewed by chief of Smersh Viktor Abakumov. His Soviet interrogators, including Abakumov, refused to believe that the Germans could double Soviet agent nets. The Soviets believed that the Germans had a penetration of the NKVD/NKGB at the highest level. The Soviets sentenced Pannwitz to twenty-five years in a labor camp but allowed him to return to the West in 1954. Despite some suspicions on the part of Eugen Steimle (who was Pannwitz's former boss in the RSHA) that Pannwitz may have been working for Soviet intelligence after his return from the USSR, Pannwitz worked for the West German intelligence services from time to time.[193] Manfred Roeder, the presiding officer at the trials of many of the Rote Kapelle agents, stated that German counterintelligence estimated that the network in Germany alone cost the German armed forces the loss of an additional 200,000 men.[194]

The Rote Kapelle performed reasonably well in obtaining vital information from highly placed sources in Germany.[195] However, details of exactly how these well-placed sources contributed to the German intelligence service defeat in the East are sketchy at best. For example, strong circumstantial evidence suggests that Major General Hans Oster, a career Abwehr officer who eventually rose to become its chief of staff (*Abteilung* Z), wittingly or unwittingly passed compromising information to the Soviets. Because of his position and long service in the Abwehr, Oster had extraordinary access to a wide variety of sources of information and was well known to have provided Germany's enemies with vital information if it furthered the anti-Nazi cause.[196] Before he became chief of staff of intelligence for Army Group Center, Colonel Baron Rudolph von Gersdorff and several other officers in the German armed forces were working for Rudolph Roessler's Lucy ring in Switzerland.[197] It is not clear how much, if any, information on agent operations was passed to the Russians by these two well-placed sources.

In 1941 Soviet intelligence solidified the recruitment of Harro Schulze-Boysen (Soviet code name "Starshina"); he was an air intelligence officer who held several positions during his career. He became head of a group of Soviet agents (commonly referred to as the Schulze-Boysen group). Schulze-Boysen had been passing information to the Soviets since at least 1936. He was transferred at one point to the Attaché Group of the Luftwaffe and was on such good terms with the group chief, that he was considered the group chief's right-hand man. Schulze-Boysen had access to target maps for the Luftwaffe's bomber force, and to all reports from German air attachés worldwide. In addition, information obtained from his wide circle of contacts on the Luftwaffe staff gave Soviet intelligence extraordinary insight into the Luftwaffe's plans and intentions.[198] The Schulze-Boysen group continually provided Moscow with specific and detailed information on the plans, intentions, and capabilities of the

German armed forces. Information often reached Soviet intelligence in the USSR within twenty-four hours.[199]

In one message to Moscow Schulze-Boysen stated that the Germans had lost confidence in a quick victory by late 1941; in another he gave the precise whereabouts of Hitler's headquarters on the Eastern Front; in another message he told the Soviets that Canaris had recruited a French officer on de Gaulle's staff; and in still another message he gave the Soviets the names of members of the entire Free French espionage network in France. Schulze-Boysen also told Moscow that the Germans could decipher a greater part of British telegrams to the U.S. government, and that the Germans had uncovered the entire British agent network in the Balkans.[200] Some of the information Schulze-Boysen gave to the Soviets included information on German intelligence activities in Spain, drawings of new Luftwaffe equipment, tables of arms production, information about the precise routes of Allied convoys sailing from Iceland to north Russian ports before they even sailed, and the facts that the new Messerschmidt fighter could reach speeds of up to 375 miles per hour and that the Germans planned to use Russian anticommunist formations on the Eastern Front.[201]

Schulze-Boysen was so important to Soviet intelligence that the latter became extremely worried when contact with him was lost. The Soviets dispatched a cut-out — who was an agent of the Soviet residency in Stockholm — to assess the situation. He turned out to be a double agent for the Germans. Two illegals (probably ethnic Germans) were dispatched in the fall of 1942 to make contact. Apparently Soviet intelligence did not know that Schulze-Boysen had already been arrested. The Gestapo arrested "Bart" and "Kessler," shot Kessler because he would not cooperate, and used "Bart" in a radio playback. Bart was later captured by U.S. forces, turned over to the Soviets at the end of the war, and interrogated; after admitting that he had cooperated with the Gestapo, he was duly shot.[202]

By mid-July 1942 German counterintelligence had identified several major players in the Berlin Red Orchestra, including Schulze-Boysen and Avrid Harnack, and patiently placed numerous members under surveillance. In addition to Schulze-Boysen and Harnack, the Gestapo also caught Corporal Horst Heilmann, a radio intercept specialist and cryptographer assigned to the Abwehr office responsible for intercepting and decoding Soviet agent transmissions in the East (Signals Security). Heilmann and Schulze-Boysen had become acquainted when they were studying in a Berlin university. Heilmann fell under Schulze-Boysen's spell and was converted to Marxism. He was fluent in French, English, and Russian, and with Schulze-Boysen's help, he eventually obtained a position with the Eastern section of the Abwehr's radio intercept service.[203] Heilmann told the Soviets that the Gestapo had broken the cipher used by Soviet agents operating in Germany.[204] He also passed on information obtained from coworker Alfred Traxl.[205] Traxl showed Heilmann decoded messages from Moscow that clearly indicated that Schulze-Boysen was a Soviet agent. The Gestapo arrested Heilmann while he was trying to warn Schulze-Boysen; however, he managed to warn Schulze-Boysen's wife of his discovery before his arrest.[206] The Gestapo arrested Schulze-Boysen on 30 August 1942, and he was executed at the Berlin-Ploetzensee Prison on 22 December 1942. Heilmann also was sentenced to death and most certainly was executed.[207]

Soviet counterintelligence appears to have been well informed regarding German commando operations behind Soviet lines. Schulze-Boysen's network had access to the plans and intentions of Leitstelle II Ost (Walli II), which directed sabotage missions against the USSR. The Soviets were forewarned about German intentions to occupy the Baku oil fields using airborne forces and had knowledge of specific German plans to infiltrate agents into Britain.[208]

Lieutenant Herbert Gollonow, a desk officer in Abwehr II, unwittingly passed information to the Soviets on German sabotage operations behind Soviet lines; Canaris claimed that this resulted in the deaths of thirty-six German agents. Gollonow was taking English lessons from Mildred Harnack and ended up sleeping with her. Mildred was the wife of Avrid Harnack (Soviet code name "the Corsican"), leader of a group of Soviet agents in Germany — part of the Rote Kapelle — commonly referred to as the Harnack Group. Mildred Harnack would make subtle negative references to how the war was going, and Gollonow would counter her pessimistic remarks with details of how well German agent operations in the East were carried out. Harnack then passed on that information to the Soviets.[209] Wolfgang Havemann, also a member of Avrid Harnack's group and a lieutenant in German naval intelligence, was arrested by the Gestapo, let go because of lack of evidence, and sent to an infantry division on the Eastern Front.[210]

The Soviets did not limit their penetrations of the German services solely to the Abwehr. Willi Lehman, a long-term career counterintelligence officer recruited in the 1930s and code-named "Breitenbach" or "Breitman" by the Russians, provided the Soviets with a wide variety of information on the techniques the Gestapo used to track down Soviet agents.[211] Lehman passed the Soviets an extensive Gestapo report, submitted to Himmler and dated 10 June 1941, on Soviet subversion in Germany that apparently indicated the Gestapo's substantial lack of knowledge of Soviet agent activity on German territory.[212] As Lehman, at one point in his long career, was responsible for industrial security, he gave the Soviets several reports on new Nazi weapons systems, including details on liquid-fuel rockets.[213] Armed with information on how the Gestapo conducted its counterintelligence operations, the Soviets ensured for several years that the Berlin networks of the Rote Kapelle could avoid capture.[214] Lehman last met with Soviet intelligence on 19 June 1941 and told his handler that the invasion was scheduled for 22 June at 0300 hours.[215]

After the war the Russians discovered that Breitenbach's career as an agent for the Soviet intelligence service came to an end in 1942. In his memoirs Sudoplatov relates that on 5 August 1942 the Soviets parachuted two agents into Nazi Germany, one of whom was Albert Barth.[216] The Gestapo captured Barth and initiated a *Funkspiel.* During his interrogation Barth revealed that Lehman was a Soviet agent.[217] The Gestapo then secretly arrested Lehman and executed him without fanfare.[218] The British took Barth prisoner after the war; however, Barth returned to the Soviet Union in 1946 and was subsequently tried and shot for treason by the Soviets.[219] According to volume 4 of the *History of Russian Foreign Intelligence,* Barth might also have been dispatched to contact the Schulze-Boysen Group.[220] Volume 3 briefly describes an operation to recontact Breitenbach by a Soviet intelligence-trained German Communist code-named "Beck," who was also infiltrated deep into the German rear in mid- to late 1942. He, too, came under Gestapo control and was shot in November 1945.[221]

Although by no means a main source of information on German operations in the USSR, Soviet intelligence also penetrated the Washington, D.C., headquarters staff of the Office of Strategic Services (OSS), the wartime forerunner of the Central Intelligence Agency. Although there is no specific evidence that OSS officers working for the Soviets had access to information on German agent activity on the Eastern Front, large intelligence organizations receive information from a variety of sources. Therefore the possibility cannot be excluded that OSS may have been in possession of some material on German activity in the East and that one or more of the Soviet sources in the OSS passed this kind of information to Soviet intelligence. What follows are brief highlights of the major Soviet intelligence penetrations of the OSS.

Elizabeth Bentley, a former Soviet agent, testified before Congress in 1948 that at least seven members of the OSS were working for the Soviets.[222] Recent scholarship indicates that the figure could be more than twenty.[223] Four of the most important agents were Maurice Halperin, Major Duncan Lee, J. Julius Joseph, and Helen Tenney.[224] Halperin was chief of research and analysis in the Latin American Division; Lee was a counterespionage officer and legal adviser to the head of the OSS, General William Donovan; Joseph was employed by the Japanese Division of OSS; and Tenney was employed by the Spanish Division.[225]

Halperin had access to the secret OSS cable room, to information on OSS agents abroad, and to State Department traffic. According to Bentley, Halperin's information was of great interest to the NKVD.[226] Lee provided Bentley, in the spring of 1944, with a list of "Reds within OSS," as well as information on OSS agents and OSS anti-Soviet activities.[227] Lee probably had access to such data because of his position as counterespionage adviser to Donovan. Such a list would have provided the Soviets with leads to several potential agent candidates or served as a warning that several communist sympathizers within OSS (or Soviet agents) were under investigation.[228] In addition to providing the Soviets with information on his work in the Japanese Division, Joseph also passed information given to him by colleagues in the Russian Division.[229] Tenney gave Bentley stacks of OSS reports, some of which concerned OSS operations as far away as Kurdistan and Iran.[230]

Some evidence suggests that the Russians succeeded in infiltrating a staff officer of Soviet intelligence, posing as a German citizen, into the Abwehr in Germany. John Erickson, in his *Road to Berlin,* described an operation in which one Major Ilya Svetlov — a Soviet intelligence officer — was dispatched to Germany in the 1930s under a false German identity and gradually took on the identity of another German citizen. He married the daughter of a German Foreign Ministry official, joined the Nazi Party, and finally became a full-fledged staff officer of the Abwehr in 1941. In 1943 this man, Svetlov-Schultz, was apparently loaned to SD/Ausland and given an assignment to pave the way for a commando team — code-named "Operation Long Jump" — to kill Churchill, Stalin, and Roosevelt while they were in Tehran. The plot ultimately failed and resulted in Svetlov-Schultz's wife turning him in to the SD as a Soviet agent. Svetlov-Schultz was apparently able to escape to the USSR. Erickson states that he found no substantive Soviet documentation for this operation other than these two memoirs, which he called "documentary fiction." Even volume 4 of the most recent *History of State Security* mentions Long Jump only in passing.[231] Otto Skorzeny, Hitler's chief of Nazi special operations, basically called Long Jump an invention of the Soviet intelligence designed to separate Churchill and Roosevelt at the conference in order to better install bugs in their quarters.[232] Nevertheless, given the number of ethnic Germans in the USSR, it is by no means inconceivable that the Abwehr harbored a few such agents.[233]

State Security's penetrations of both the German and Allied services contributed substantially to Soviet knowledge of the capabilities and intentions of the Nazi leadership and the German armed forces. Unrelenting massive Soviet attacks on the German security and intelligence services, combined with high German agent failure rates and significant circumstantial evidence that the higher levels of the Abwehr and the Gestapo harbored well-placed Soviet agents, strongly suggest that staff officers of the German intelligence services on the Eastern Front worked for the Russians.

Sabotage, Kidnapping, and Assassination

Violence was the muscle behind Soviet offensive counterintelligence operations. State Security units conducted sabotage operations behind German lines, and kidnapped and assassinated German officers and officials. Assassination squads killed many of those who refused to cooperate with the Chekisty.[234] According to Sudoplatov's memoirs, the Fourth Directorate of State Security annihilated 137,000 German soldiers, killed 87 high-ranking German officers, and liquidated 2,045 agents and police officers in the service of the Germans.[235] The Fourth Directorate of the NKVD/NKGB of the USSR and its territorial counterparts deployed some 2,222 operational groups during the entire war. The Special Departments inserted only 20 sabotage or "operational" groups behind German lines, many of which performed intelligence or sabotage missions.[236]

For example, FAK 304 noted in one of its daily reports on 8 May 1944 that the OKR/Smersh of the Baltic Fleet for the first time deployed a sabotage team to blow up a factory near Kivioli. These types of OO missions often supported Soviet military intelligence.[237] Although the Germans kept detailed records (for example, in January 1944, out of 419 Soviet agents caught, 62 were assigned sabotage missions), the Germans did not have a category of agents who were subordinate to a Soviet counterintelligence organization and assigned a sabotage mission.[238] Partisan units also carried out sabotage operations of all types, some of which were planned by Soviet counterintelligence.[239]

Soviet counterintelligence operations of this type yielded significant results. For example, State Security kidnapped three German intelligence and counterintelligence officers in 1942.[240] An NKVD lieutenant, using the name of Captain Firsanov, was in charge of a locally recruited German auxiliary military police unit of about 120 men.[241] On the instructions of the NKVD, he systematically murdered several members of his unit for being anti-Soviet, purposely sent the unit into partisan traps, and made life unbearable for the other troops.[242] Firsanov escaped when the unit was reorganized. In January 1942 a female Abwehr agent, who was actually under the control of the counterintelligence element of a partisan unit, was arrested for having poisoned two Abwehr counterintelligence officers.[243]

Not all Soviet sabotage operations involved kidnapping or assassinating German intelligence officers using partisan or Soviet-controlled agents behind German lines. During the course of conducting a *Funkspiel* in July 1944, FAT 326 in Army Group North induced the Soviets to air-drop more supplies.[244] The Soviets dropped the material according to plan, and when members of

FAT 326 opened the load it exploded, killing and injuring several members of FAT 326.[245]

Soviet sabotage, kidnapping, and assassination operations against the Germans served as an integral part of the overall Soviet counterintelligence offensive. Soviet sabotage operations strained the already overburdened resources of German military counterintelligence. FAK/FAT III units devoted to hunting saboteurs to preserve German rear-area security had less time to uncover and turn around Soviet espionage agents. The killing and kidnapping of Nazi intelligence officers by the Soviets (often by partisans) resulted in a shortage of officers available to train and deploy agents behind Soviet lines. Schmalschlaeger, for example, attributed the 30 percent casualty rate of Abwehr III officers and men largely to partisan operations.[246] By any measure Soviet sabotage of German intelligence facilities, installations, and equipment, as well as assassinations and kidnappings of German intelligence officers, clearly hurt the German clandestine collection capability against the USSR.

Russian mud *(Rasputitsa)* (*Der Weltkrieg 1939-1945 in seiner rauhen Wirklichkeit "Das Frontkaempfer-Bildwerk"* [Verlag Justin Moser, Munich, n.d.], p. 404).

German munitions transport in Russian winter (*Der Weltkrieg 1939-1945 in seiner rauhen Wirklichkeit "Das Frontkaempfer-Bildwerk"* [Verlag Justin Moser, Munich, n.d.], p. 399).

German troops in combat, Donetsk region, April 1942 (*Der Weltkrieg 1939–1945 in seiner rauhen Wirklichkeit "Das Frontkaempfer-Bildwerk"* [Verlag Justin Moser, Munich, n.d.], p. 410).

German defensive positions in winter (*Der Weltkrieg 1939–1945 in seiner rauhen Wirklichkeit "Das Frontkaempfer-Bildwerk"* [Verlag Justin Moser, Munich, n.d.], p. 474).

NKVD emblem (FSB, *Liubianka II*, p. 230).

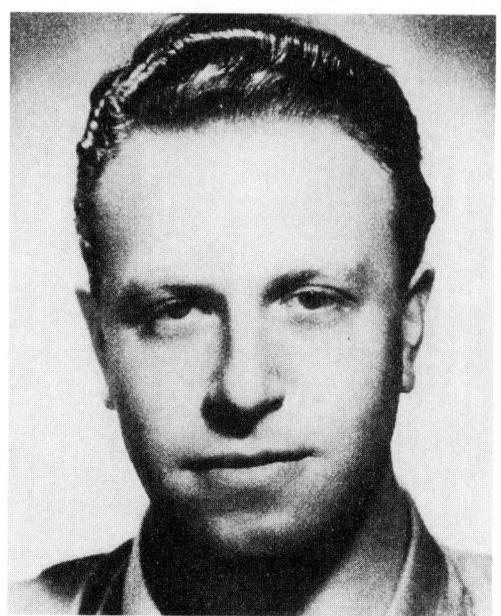

Ivar Lissner (Meyer, *Unternehmen Sieben*, p. 153).

Gestapo officer and Soviet agent Willi Lehman (Russian Intelligence Archive).

Chief of the Gestapo Heinrich Mueller (Berlin Document Center [U.S. National Archives]).

2. Die Auftraggeber der im Januar festgenommenen Feindagenten.

Auftraggeber		Hegru A	Hegru Süd	Hegru Mitte	Hegru Nord	Ges.Oper. Gebiet
Truppen-Agentendienste						
Generalstab der RA	RU	-	-	1	1	2
	UOKR	-	-	-	-	-
Fronten	RO	7	3	2	12	24
	OKR	1	-	-	-	1
Armeen	RO	2	1	1	1	5
	OKR	-	1	-	-	1
Divisionen u. unterstellte Einheiten	RO	-	8	2	2	12
	OKR	-	1	2	2	5
Tru-Agt-Dienst gesamt		10	14	8	18	50
Banden-Agentendienste						
Zentralstab		-	-	-	2	2
Bandenstäbe u.Op.Grupp.		-	-	1	2	3
Banden diess.d.Front		27	34	85	131	277
Bd.Agt.Dienst gesamt		27	34	86	135	282
NKWD-(NKGB-)Agt.-Dienste						
Zentrale Moskau		65	-	-	-	65
Gebietsverwaltung		-	-	1	14	15
Nachgeordn.Dienstst.		-	2	1	-	3
NKWD-Agt-Dienst gesamt		65	2	2	14	83
Partei-Agenten-Dienste						
Zentralkomitee		-	-	-	-	-
Nachgeordn. Stellen		-	2	-	-	2
Partei-Agt-Dienst gesamt		-	2	-	-	2
Sonstige und ungeklärte Feind-Agt.-Dienste gesamt		-	2	-	-	2
Feind-Agenten-Dienste ges.		102	54	96	167	419

Sample of Abwehr III Statistics for captured Soviet agents, January 1944 (broken down by Soviet organization) (U.S. National Archives, Record Group 242. Captured German Records).

Im allgemeinen blieb der Anteil der verschiedenen Agentendienststellen des Gegners an den erkannten Einsätzen gegenüber den Vormonaten gleich. Bemerkenswert ist das weitere Ansteigen derjenigen unschädlich gemachten Agenten, die vom NKWD(NKGB)gesteuert wurden.

3. Die Aufträge der Agenten

Auftragsart	Hegru A	Hegru Süd	Hegru Mitte	Hegru Nord	Ges.Oper. Gebiet
Militärische Erkundung	18	19	33	8o	15o
Politische Erkundung	-	-	-	-	-
Allgemeine Erkundung	1	3	12	5	21
Spionage-Organisation	-	1	-	1	2
Gegenspionage	65	-	2	3	7o
Sabotage	-	14	11	27	62
Propaganda u.Zersetzg.	18	17	38	4o	113
Sonderaufträge	-	-	-	1	1
Insgesamt	1o2	54	96	167	419

(48 gemischte Aufträge wurden nach dem Hauptauftrag eingeordnet)
Gegenüber dem Vormonat starke Zunahme der zur milit.Spionage angesetzten Agenten und der Zersetzungsagenten. – Auf der Krim Aushebung einer grossen Gegenspionageorganisation.

4. Die verschiedenen Kategorien der ausgemerzten Agenten.

Kategorie	Hegru A	Hegru Süd	Hegru Mitte	Hegru Nord	Ges.Oper. Gebiet
Voll-Agent (bewährt)	8	-	5	3	16
Voll-Agent (Anfänger)	5	8	11	9	33
Agent i.Nebenauftrag	2	5	2	2	11
Agentenmäßig angesetzte Truppenangehörige	3	1o	5	7	25
Gelegenheitsagenten	1o	8	11	44	73
Agentenhelfer (Kuriere, Versorger usw.)	7o	23	57	98	248
Agentenfunker	4	-	-	4	8
Ungeklärt	-	-	5	-	4
Insgesamt	1o2	54	96	167	419

Sample of Abwehr III Statistics for captured Soviet agents, January 1944 (broken down by mission and type of agent) (U.S. National Archives, Record Group 242. Captured German Records).

Chief of the Abwehr, Admiral Wilhelm Canaris (Otto Renfeld-Haus, Koenge/N, as cited in Meyer, *Unternehmen Sieben*, pp. 24, 623).

Chief of Staff of the Abwehr, Colonel Hans Oster (Bundesarchiv/Militaerarchiv, Freiburg, as cited in Meyer, *Unternehmen Sieben*, pp. 24, 623).

Chief of Abwehr I, 1935-1943, Colonel (later General) Hans Piekenbrock (Kahn, *Hilter's Spies* [author's personal collection; used with permission]).

Chief, Sicherheitsdienst/Ausland, Walter Schellenberg (Center for American History, University of Texas at Austin, Whellis Papers).

Chief, Leitstelle I Ost (Stab Walli I), Colonel Hermann Baun (Hoehne, *The General Was a Spy* [Hoehne, citing *Der Spiegel,* n.d.]).

American postwar interrogation center at Oberursel (U.S. Army).

Chief, Fremde Heere Ost (FHO), Colonel (later General) Reinhard Gehlen (Hoehne, *The General Was a Spy* [citing Jochen Wilke; no further identifying data]).

Wartime headquarters for FHO shown here in Angerburg, East Prussia (Gehlen, *The Service)*.

Reinhard Gehlen, 1944 (Gehlen, *The Service*).

FHO staff (Gehlen marked with X, his deputy Gerhard Wessel with XX; front row) (Gehlen, *The Service*).

Chief of Smersh, Viktor S. Abakumov (FSB, *Liubianka II*, p. 243).

Chief of Soviet military counterintelligence radio playbacks in World War II, Vladimir Y. Baryshnikov (FSB, *Liubianka II*, p. 250).

Chief, Fourth Directorate NKGB, Lieutenant General Pavel Sudoplatov (Schecter, *Special Tasks* [author's personal collection; used with permission]).

Aleksandr Dem'ianov (Heine), principal Soviet agent in Operation Monastery (Schecter, *Special Tasks* [author's personal collection; used with permission]).

Case officer Mikail M. Makliarskii (left) and Aleksandr Dem'ianov (right) (FSB, *Liubianka II*, p. 245).

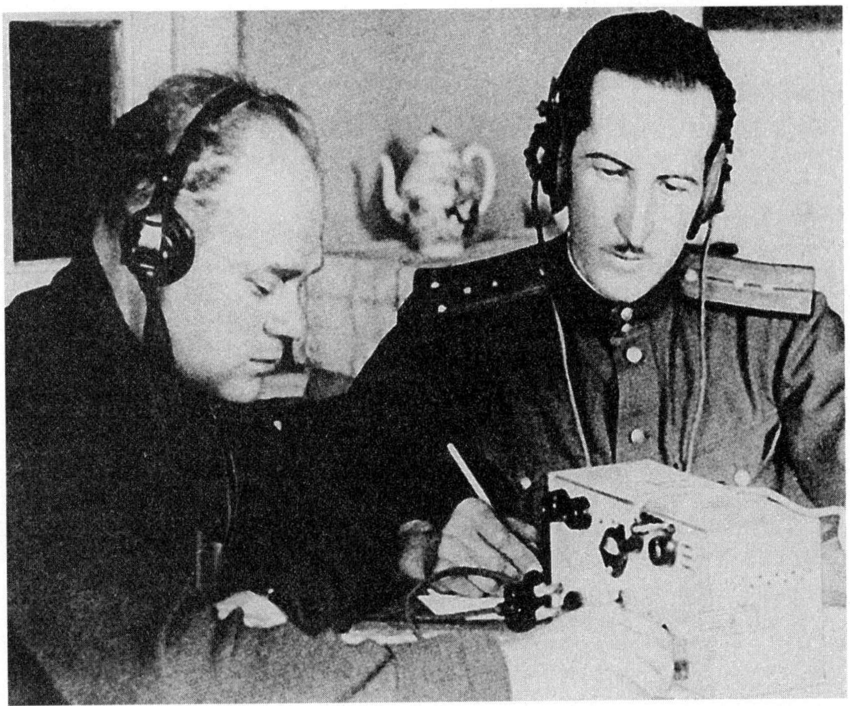

Aleksandr Dem'ianov (right) during a radio-playback transmission session (FSB, *Liubianka II*, p. 247).

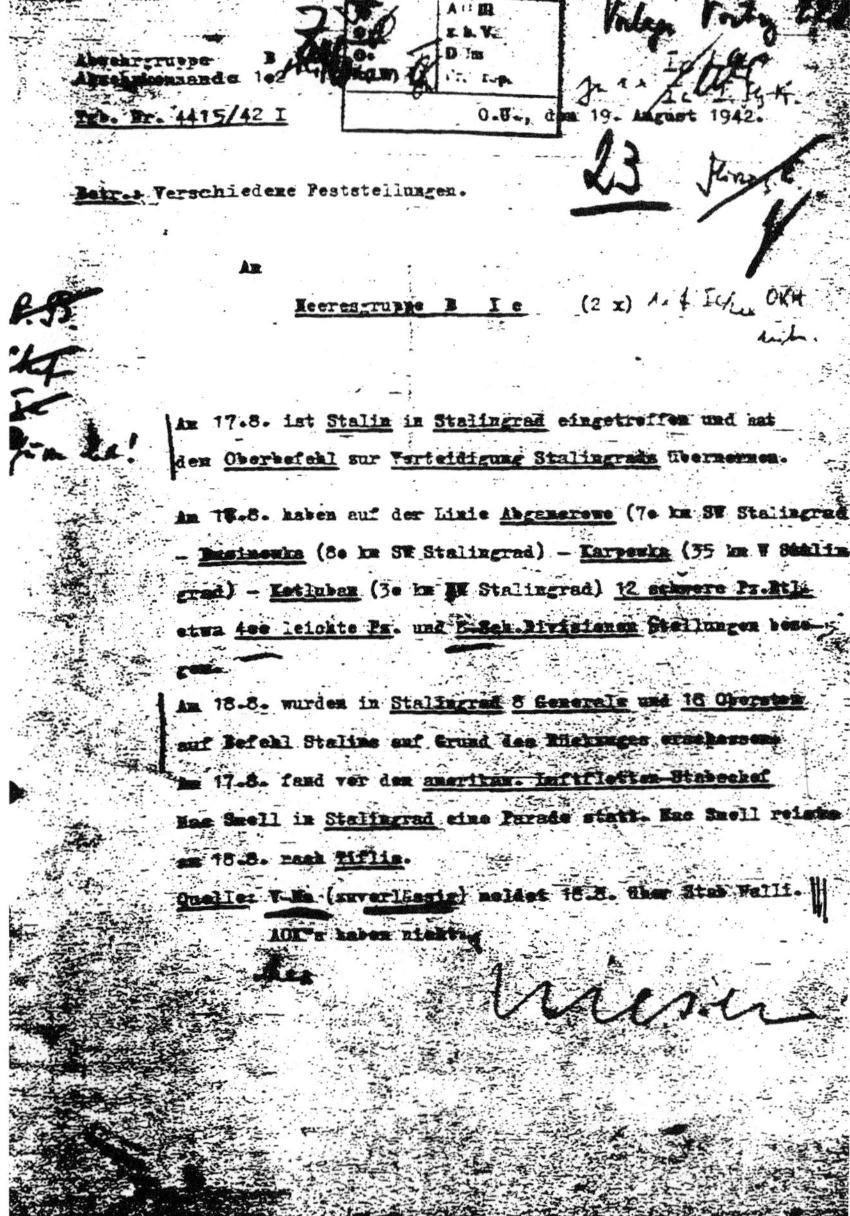

Abwehrgruppe B
Abwehrkommando 1o2

Tgb. Nr. 4415/42 I

O.U., den 19. August 1942.

Betr.: Verschiedene Feststellungen.

An

Heeresgruppe B I c (2 x)

Am 17.8. ist Stalin in Stalingrad eingetroffen und hat den Oberbefehl zur Verteidigung Stalingrads übernommen.

Am 18.8. haben auf der Linie Abganerowo (7o km SW Stalingrad – Basinowka (8o km SW Stalingrad) – Karpowka (35 km W Stalingrad) – Kotluban (3o km NW Stalingrad) 12 schwere Pz.Btl. etwa 4oo leichte Pz. und [illegible] Divisionen Stellungen bezogen.

Am 18.8. wurden in Stalingrad 8 Generale und 16 Obersten auf Befehl Stalins auf Grund des Rückzuges erschossen.

Am 17.8. fand vor dem amerikan. Luftflotten-Stabschef [illegible] Snell in Stalingrad eine Parade statt. [illegible] Snell reiste am 18.8. nach Tiflis.

Quelle: V-Ma (zuverlässig) meldet 18.8. über Stab Walli.

AOK's haben nichts.

German intelligence report from agent "Max" (probably from Dem'ianov) (U.S. National Archives, Record Group 242. Captured German Records).

Anlage zur Feind-
beurteilung v.3.1o.42.

Wichtigere Abwehrmeldungen allgemeiner Art.

1.) 2.1o. V – Mann (Max) :

Am 1.1o. wurde die Militärkonferenz in Moskau beendet. Es wurde beschlossen, die Verteidigung des Kaukasus durch neue Truppen zu verstärken u. neue Verteidigungslinien nördl. Stalingrad zwischen Wolga u. Don anzulegen. Hierzu sollen aus Reservebeständen aus dem Osten noch 25 Div. gebildet u. herangezogen werden.

2.) 2.1o. V – Mann (Max) :

Jn Krasnaja – Sloboda (gegenüber Stalingrad am linken Wolgaufer) sind Pioniere, 2 Rgt. GPU u. 1 Btl. Minenwerfer eingetroffen, die nachts nach Stalingrad Nord übergesetzt werden.

3.) 2.1o. V – Mann (Max) :

Jn Murmansk werden 2 Divisionen (Ski-Truppen), Art., MG -Truppen u. Minenwerfer-Truppen (mit Hunden u. Renntieren) zusammengestellt.
Zur Hafenverteidigung von Murmansk trafen amerik. u. engl. Flak, 60 engl. Ballone u. Fernkampfartillerie ein.

More reports from agent Max (U.S. National Archives, Record Group 242. Captured German Records).

Lieutenant Colonel Roland von Wahl-Welskirch, chief, Abwehr I Luft, Ast Vienna, one of Richard Kauder's (aka Klatt) handling officers (Vienna State Archives [cited in Meyer, *Unternehmen Sieben*, pp. 153, 623]).

One of Richard Kauder's benefactors, Chief, Ast Vienna, Count Rudolph von Marogna-Redwitz (Meyer, *Unternehmen Sieben*, pp. 187, 623).

Lieutenant Colonel Heinrich Scherhorn (FSB, *Liubianka II*, 248).

Deputy Chief of "Zeppelin-North" H. Greif (left) and P. I. Polotov (aka Tavrin) (FSB, *Liubianka II*, 254).

P. I. Polotov-Tavrin in a Soviet army uniform (FSB, *Liubianka II,* 253).

L. Ia. Shilova in a Red Army uniform (FSB, *Liubianka II,* 253).

German Intelligence and Counterintelligence Operations

All we got from Canaris was rubbish.

Major Horst Hiemenz, Chief, Fremde Heere Ost, Gruppe II

It was better to have a controlled agent than none at all.

Anonymous Abwehr officer

No study of Soviet counterintelligence effectiveness against the Nazis would be complete without analyzing the strengths and weaknesses of both the organization and operations of the German intelligence and security services.[1] What can be loosely described as "Germany's intelligence problem" can be broken down into two broad categories, organizational and cultural. The organizational problem had two basic components: the lack of a centralized, well-developed system for collecting, processing, and disseminating intelligence — the responsibility for which lay largely with Hitler, Himmler, and Heydrich — and the lack of institutional support by the Army's High Command for the professionalization of intelligence within the armed forces; this affected personnel assignments and training.[2] The cultural component to "Germany's intelligence problem" encompasses interrelated attitudes: the effect of Nazi ideology — which basically viewed Germany as superior — on the thought processes of senior intelligence officers both within the armed forces and in the RSHA; and the natural tendency in any intelligence organization — especially under the stress of combat — for intelligence officers to ignore bad news, to disbelieve the unthinkable, and generally to deceive themselves.[3]

The Abwehr and the German Intelligence Problem in Russia

Much of the "German intelligence problem" during the Nazi era can be attributed to a fragmented organizational structure (even after the Abwehr was amalgamated into the RSHA in 1944), poor leadership, cronyism, arrogance, and the fact that throughout the war the armed forces were contemptuous of intelligence work. In fact, the rivalry between SD-Ausland and the Abwehr became so contentious that the SD often betrayed the work of the Abwehr and vice versa.[4] These problems severely affected the performance of the German intelligence in the East, as did the assumption that obliterating Bolshevism could be done in a few short months. By the spring of 1942, when the Germans realized the need for better intelligence on the USSR, Soviet counterintelligence had mirrored the recovery of the Red Army from the initial disasters in 1941 and had effectively positioned itself to blunt any German intelligence offensive. Schmalschlaeger believed that by the spring of 1942 "the defensive activities of the Soviet intelligence services had reached their peak" and that the objective of "combating all efforts to protect the Soviet Union from secret attack" (a phrase frequently found in Soviet orders) had been achieved. Canaris was forced to stop large-scale airdrops of agents by September 1942. Although at the beginning of the war almost half the Soviet military counterintelligence officers had little experience, by the end of 1941 many had begun to acquire it.[5] The Soviet intelligence and security services neither suffered from organizational fragmentation on the scale of the Germans nor were they subjected to an inherent contempt for intelligence or counterintelligence work by the country's leadership or senior officers of the armed forces.[6]

The well-known British historian Hugh Trevor-Roper, who served in British intelligence during the war, wrote an analysis — which has now been declassified — on the successes and failures of the German intelligence services. He assessed Admiral Wilhelm Canaris, chief of the Abwehr, as a poor organizer and an even worse judge of men, as he gave worthless officers considerable independence.[7] Canaris appointed so many personal friends that German General Staff officers often referred to the Abwehr as "Canaris Familie GmbH" (loosely translated, it meant "Canaris and Sons, Inc.").[8]

The corruption and inefficiency of the Abwehr as a whole was so well known that British intelligence took it into account in its operational planning. British intelligence knew so much about the Abwehr that SIS (MI6) feared a collapse of "Canaris Familie GmbH" as much as Canaris. Richard Curdes, a former Abwehr officer who served on the Eastern Front, told U.S. army interrogators that, during a short visit to Stab Walli I in May 1942, he noted that Abwehr officers and their agents, including many high-ranking officers, spent their time drinking and looting, and work came to a standstill. According to Curdes, the loot was shipped back to Germany in Abwehr cars.[9] As a result, Nazi arrogance and a reluctance of many German intelligence officers to share with their superiors suspicions that sources may have been controlled by an enemy intelligence service provided added impetus for Abwehr officers to continue running suspect agents.[10] Hitler, of course, often ignored, or refused to believe, the intelligence estimates he received.[11]

Gehlen did not believe that the Soviets engaged in strategic "radio deception," but his interrogation report provides unique insights into Soviet military camouflage and concealment efforts, as well as Soviet use of the open press and political lectures for transmitting misleading information.[12] He was well aware that frontline propaganda delivered to Soviet troops was designed to skew German perceptions of the actual situation should captured Soviet soldiers talk. This awareness of Soviet tactical-level deception, however, did not extend to strategic deception. To quote Gehlen's interrogation report, "no major radio-deception scheme has ever been attempted by the Russian who realized that such a scheme is easily detected if it is not accompanied by thoroughly planned deceptive measures in all other fields. Tactical radio deception has been employed, but was only of limited importance."[13] It is not clear from this quotation if Gehlen was referring to the use of radio games by Soviet counterintelligence or to the Soviets purposely transmitting over military and governmental communications nets strategic information that they wanted the Germans to receive. In either case, the report shows that Gehlen was predisposed to believe that the Soviets were incapable of conducting a well-coordinated deception effort on a strategic scale.

During the initial stages of World War II the repeated successes of the German armies implied good intelligence. The shock of the Blitzkrieg, which had been extraordinarily effective until it halted at the gates of Leningrad in the late summer and early fall of 1941, no doubt masked the Germans' intelligence problems. Even then, the Abwehr's reputation was not seriously questioned until December 1941, when the Soviets stopped the German army in its tracks just before Moscow.[14] Therefore, when the direction of the war began to shift in the Allies' favor in 1942, intelligence assumed greater importance. Its performance was subjected to greater criticism, and its failures became regular and conspicuous.[15] In 1944 Hitler and Himmler "rewarded" the Abwehr's poor performance by subordinating the bulk of it to the RSHA under Schellenberg's control; some of its counterintelligence functions were subordinated to Amt IV (Gestapo).[16]

Trevor-Roper's analysis shows that Abwehr I (intelligence collection) consistently performed poorly, Abwehr II (sabotage and subversion) performed marginally better than Abwehr I, and Abwehr III (counterintelligence) actually achieved some degree of success.[17] Despite the massive Soviet counterintelligence attack on the German intelligence services, overall FHO performed better than its counterpart in the West, Fremde Heere West (Foreign Armies West, or FHW).[18] SD/Ausland (Amt VI of the RSHA) — the foreign intelligence service of the SS — had a few isolated successes (mostly in the West), and the Gestapo, in its counterintelligence role, achieved a satisfactory performance in catching spies.[19] The German services on the Eastern Front exhibited roughly the same performance pattern. Although Soviet counterintelligence soundly defeated German clandestine collection operations, the German services as a whole — and FHO and Abwehr III in particular — functioned better in the East than in the West.[20]

The German intelligence failure against the USSR did not begin with Operation Barbarossa. The refusal of the German Army High Command to professionalize intelligence and the Nazi view that Germany and Germans were superior significantly detracted from the ability of the armed forces to learn anything from German military intelligence experiences in Russia during World War I.[21] In 1927 Major General Gempp, former commander of German military intelligence in the East during World War I, initiated a secret study of German intelligence operations during that war.[22] By 1938 six volumes had been published; volume 6, which concerned German intelligence operations in Russia from May 1915 to the end of 1916, concluded the following:

> – As soon as the war broke out, we tried to plant agents in the ranks of the Russian army with the task of gathering information and then deserting to our side. To the best of our knowledge, only one of these attempts succeeded during the period covered by this report.
> – By far the most successful in dealing with agents were the few regular officers who had complete command of the enemy languages and were familiar with the country and the people from prewar times, as well as many reserve officers who had done business in Russia, merchants, etc.
> – In contrast to the mass-production methods used by the Russian espionage schools, we insisted on the individual training and employment of agents in order to eliminate the danger that one might reveal the other's identity to the enemy.[23]

Colonel Walter Nicolai, chief of German military intelligence during World War I, reinforced Gempp's conclusions. Nicolai stated that German military intelligence found the difficulties in the East "practically insurmountable."[24] The huge expanse of Russia, the scarcity of roads and railways, and the hostility of the population significantly hampered German agent operations in Russia during the Great War. The German army heavily relied on interrogations of POWs as a substitute for clandestine collection. The great distances an agent needed to cover, the inability of agents to establish rapid communications from the interior of Russia, and the efficiency of the Russian counterintelligence service convinced Colonel Nicolai that agent operations could only be useful at the tactical level.[25]

The German army as an institution did not view the lack of adequate planning and poor organization as serious problems; the repeated successes of the German armies from the late 1930s to the Battle for Moscow in December 1941 reinforced a preexisting notion that clandestinely acquired intelligence was not necessary for military success.[26]

Consequently, before and during World War II, the Germans did not succeed in penetrating the Red Army to any significant extent. There was a constant shortage of Abwehr officers who spoke fluent Russian. While the Germans used thousands of Soviet POWs as agents, they often did so without regard for the quality of those agents.[27] Last-minute planning by ill-equipped bureaucracies to insert large numbers of agents into the USSR — in the hope that they would produce at least some information of value — could not overcome the difficult operating environment in the Soviet Union. For example, Heinrich von Westarp, who was chief of Abwehr I T/Lw (air technical intelligence) for Abwehrstelle Wien (Vienna), unequivocally stated in his postwar debriefing that the entire effort of Abwehr I T/Lw against the USSR began too late. He went on to elaborate that if the effort had begun before the commencement of hostilities, the results would have been of "inestimably greater worth." Given the Soviet counterintelligence effort, Westarp's statement is arguable; however, Westarp did not recall a single instance in which a report submitted by an agent indicated that the agent had gained access to an aircraft research center.[28]

In the 1920s and early 1930s German military intelligence was reasonably well informed about the capabilities of Soviet weapons, aircraft, and the composition of the Soviet armed forces largely because of the cooperation between the Soviet and German armed forces during that time.[29] In 1932 the Germans estimated the size of the Red Army to be 600,000. It was actually 562,000. However, Lieutenant Colonel Hartman, an artillery officer by training who in 1932 was attached to the Intelligence Department of Reichswehr, assessed the Red Army as being unable to wage a successful defensive war against any enemy. Hartman went on to state that the strength of the USSR lies in its "little-known military power, invulnerable ample spaces, and the impossibility to study its inner state."[30] The German-Russian military cooperation ended in 1933 when Hitler came to power; however, the Germans had no major penetrations of the Soviet military when the cooperation ended.[31] After the invasion of Poland in 1939, Polish intelligence documents captured by the Germans revealed that the

Poles had been as unsuccessful as the Germans in penetrating the interior of the Soviet Union — at least after 1933.[32] As a result, when the Soviets invaded Poland in 1939, the Germans even failed to correctly identify the army headquarters of the invading force.[33]

From the late 1930s until the invasion in June 1941 the Germans often lacked basic information needed to conduct military operations in the USSR more efficiently — despite having collected a significant amount of information from all sources, particularly on Soviet forces in the border areas.[34] For example, topographical intelligence was poor, and the Germans had no experience on how climate and topography in the USSR would affect their aircraft, motor vehicles, and tanks.[35] Maps of the USSR were difficult to acquire and obviously could not be obtained by signals intercept or photo reconnaissance. The existing maps reproduced by the German army were of such poor quality that the Germans often had to rely on more limited photo intelligence.[36]

The Germans attempted to conduct agent operations against the USSR prior to the Soviet occupation of the Baltic states in 1940. This effort, in which the Abwehr tried to infiltrate agents through the 300 miles of swampland on the border between Lithuania and the USSR, ended in failure.[37] In fact, the Soviets anticipated that the Germans would use the Baltics as a staging base for intelligence operations and, from the late 1930s on, conducted numerous operations to thwart German clandestine collection.[38] One operation involved the expulsion of a German representative to Estonia — code-named "Bremen" — who dealt with issues concerning the repatriation of Germans. Bremen was suspected of engaging in intelligence activity. Soviet agents got Bremen thoroughly drunk, and not until later did he realize his suitcases were missing. He demanded an investigation. Two Soviet counterintelligence officers showed up posing as criminal investigators, searched the area, and found the suitcases. When they searched the bags, they found 180 photographs of important industrial facilities, 10,000 rubles, and sketches of a military vessel done on tracing paper. Bremen was expelled from the USSR.[39]

Selecting and outfitting agents to operate in the Soviet Union presented significant difficulties. Ensuring that agents had proper documentation and that the documents were error-free was especially difficult, largely because strict Soviet security measures could easily result in uncovering a minor mistake. Minor errors in such documents as identification papers, Party cards, travel passes, and military orders often led to the arrest or death of an agent. Using Russian émigrés residing in Germany to operate in the USSR proved equally fruitless. Most of the information obtained by the émigrés was either false or of little value.[40]

Soon after Colonel Piekenbrock's appointment in 1936 as chief of Abwehr I, he attempted to enlist the aid of the Austrian and Hungarian secret services to infiltrate agents into the USSR. He also tried to deploy agents into the USSR from Romania, China, Japan, and Bulgaria; however, all to no avail.[41] The Germans even attempted to insert agents into the Soviet Union from merchant ships that called at Soviet ports. These agents either produced little or were quickly caught by Soviet counterintelligence.[42] The Abwehr tried to solicit the cooperation of German businessmen and students who had traveled to Russia to report on their observations and to report the locations of factories where agents could be inserted. This, too, proved unsuccessful, as many businessmen refused to cooperate and risk jeopardizing their profits. Students also proved to be uncooperative.[43] Surprisingly the Abwehr failed to exploit the reservoir of large-scale dissatisfaction with the Soviet regime among the Volga Germans.[44]

The Nazi-Soviet Pact in August 1939 resulted in an immediate decrease in the number of clandestine agent deployments to the USSR. Even after Hitler issued the directive for Operation Barbarossa on 18 December 1940 Abwehr I activities remained severely circumscribed.[45] In January 1941 the chief of the Operations Department of the High Command of the German armed forces (OKW), General Alfred Jodl, told Piekenbrock and Canaris that OKW did not need information on the Soviet armed forces as a whole and ordered the Abwehr to limit its agent activities to the border area.[46]

As a result of Jodl's order, the Abwehr sent hundreds of agents across the border; although some succeeded, even more were caught.[47] Soviet histories of the war between the German and Soviet secret services claim that, from January 1940 to March 1941, Soviet counterintelligence caught 1,300 to 1,500 German agents in the western parts of the USSR.[48] One Soviet history in particular — which described numerous Soviet military counterintelligence successes in destroying various anti-Soviet groups in the western part of the USSR prior to the Nazi invasion — asserts that "all Abwehr attempts in the prewar years to create a stable intelligence network within the USSR failed." It goes on to say that the "discovery of thousands of enemy agents in 1940 and during the first half of 1941 by Soviet State Security hindered German access to Soviet military secrets.[49] Though these Soviet figures may well be inflated — especially with regard to the number of real German agents actually caught — the Abwehr's poor record certainly lends considerable credence to Soviet claims.

Initially Admiral Canaris contributed significantly to the German military intelligence service's inability to effectively conduct agent operations against the Soviet Union prior to the start of Barbarossa. Canaris, who was vehemently opposed to an invasion of the USSR, followed Hitler's prohibition against spying on the USSR to the letter.[50] On several occasions Abwehr officers refused assistance from the Romanian and Japanese secret services either to provide the

Abwehr with information about the Soviet Union or to assist in the infiltration of agents.[51] Lieutenant Colonel Heldach, former chief of FHO's Soviet Group, remarked that it was almost impossible to obtain secret information on the USSR.[52] Canaris finally sanctioned a gradual relaxation of the ban, after FHO officers brought to his attention the dearth of information in FHO holdings on the Red Army.[53] Although he urged Piekenbrock to expand agent operations against the Soviet Union, the expansion did not substantially alter preinvasion German intelligence assessments of the USSR.[54] The FAKs/FATs acted as the primary clandestine collectors on the Eastern Front. On 15 June 1941 approximately 200 men from the Eastern sections of Abwehr I took up their positions with the various German armies and army groups for the attack on the Soviet Union.[55]

The "Baun Agency" (Agent Operations)

Canaris appointed then-Major Hermann Baun, formerly head of the USSR desk at Abwehr I headquarters, as chief of the German clandestine collection effort against the Soviet Union.[56] Baun, who was born in Odessa in 1897 and spoke — in addition to German — Russian, Ukrainian, English, and French, had joined the Abwehr in 1939 after having served as an infantry officer. He knew Russia well and was considered the "cleverest Russian expert on Canaris's staff."[57] Although the FAKs/FATs functioned better in the East than in the West, the limited quality of agent reporting deteriorated even further after the RSHA took over the Abwehr in 1944.[58]

The "Baun Agency," as Walli I was often called, inserted its agents behind Soviet lines to a depth of 200 kilometers.[59] FAKs/FATs subordinate to Baun reconnoitered the area just ahead of the advancing German armies and infiltrated agents behind Soviet lines, dressed in Soviet uniforms and equipped with radios and vehicles. Baun had some initial success in penetrating Soviet army field headquarters and in inserting agents in the Soviet rear.[60] However, the success was only temporary. As the German advance ground to a halt and Soviet counterintelligence recovered from the initial defeats, the extensive Soviet rear-area security system began to take shape, thereby making German clandestine collection against the USSR exceedingly difficult.[61] According to one Soviet source, by the end of 1941 most of the prewar German agents were killed or captured, largely through good (presumably ruthless) rear-area security measures. This forced the Germans to rely on Soviet POWs for potential agent candidates. For example, three Russian émigrés, who were dispatched by the Germans in September 1941 on a mission near Luga, were arrested and shot by Soviet counterintelligence when they forgot to take off their gold crosses when they entered a public bath.[62]

The German agent training infrastructure in the East expanded rapidly in 1941.[63] The Abwehr converted its emphasis on individual training to group training, and by 1943 it had set up nine schools on conquered Soviet territory capable of training approximately 10,000 agents annually, with training lasting from three to six weeks.[64] Although standing orders to prevent agents from knowing one another remained, the sheer bulk of the German effort made such regulations difficult to follow. The Soviets, in turn, made training schools for German agents a high priority target. As a result of the breakdown in compartmentalization, many German agents were identified before they were even deployed.[65]

Vetting procedures could be brutal. One method the Germans used to accelerate the cooperation of a potential agent candidate was to order a Soviet POW, who was a prospective agent, to shoot another Soviet prisoner while the Germans photographed the process.[66] During the course of the war Walli I expanded to 500 men, excluding agents.[67] Agent training generally took from three to six weeks, radio training took somewhat longer, and missions generally lasted only a few days, as Soviet counterintelligence made long-range penetration of the USSR problematic at best.[68] The "Baun Agency" relied primarily on the "cooperation" of Soviet POWs, thousands of whom agreed to work for the Germans in the hope that they could save themselves from starvation, torture, and almost certain death.[69] On deployment behind Soviet lines, many immediately turned themselves in to Soviet counterintelligence.[70]

Operating conditions in the Soviet Union for the FATs, as for the German army as a whole, were abysmal. For example, one Abwehr officer recorded the following in his diary:

> 28 November 1942. We seemed to have picked up some slippery customers today. Among them are a section chief of the 3rd Section of the NKVD (counterespionage) and the office chief of the local Komsomol (Communist Youth). We set out at 2200 to get them. Horribly dark and the roads knee-deep in mud. The batteries of our pocket lamps gave out, I could not get through to the *Trupp* [*sic*] with my car because the roads were too muddy. We struck matches to see the house numbers, since our agent who had traced the two men for us could not accompany us, otherwise he would be a dead man. All the stenches of the East reigned in the tumbledown hovel. And a man like this is the section chief of a Russian government office. Or is this dirt just camouflage? Anyway these people think methodically and in a dispassionate and logical way which is alien to most of us.[71]

German officers and men assigned to the FAKs/FATs found themselves isolated from German ground units, under constant threat of ambush, and surrounded by Soviets (who were German agents) whose language and mentality they could only partially grasp. German frontline intelligence officers became bogged down in the interpersonal intrigues of their Soviet collaborators largely because the FAKs/FATs had no staff organizations that either could equip the FAKs/FATs with the latest technology or that could handle the day-to-day personnel affairs of FAK/FAT agents.[72] Lack of staff organizations and time did not allow the German officers and men assigned to mobile frontline intelligence units the luxury of gradually adapting to the operating conditions in the USSR. This further reduced the effectiveness of German clandestine collection.[73]

A typical Abwehr I mission involved a two-week deployment behind Soviet lines and a subsequent detailed debriefing of the agent's observations. The bulk of the information was tactical in nature. For example, FAT 113, attached to the Third Panzer Army of Army Group Center, dispatched agent numbers 2391 and 2384 from 28 February to 11 March 1944 in the area around Vitebsk.[74] Over the course of their two weeks behind Soviet lines, 2391 and 2384 observed, for example, that one Soviet rifle battalion, consisting of 300 to 400 men, had 10 armed women within its ranks. Both agents also noted that there was an artillery ammunition dump located in the area of Liosno; the 1st Rifle Regiment of the 33rd Army was located 10 kilometers south southwest of Liosno; and truck traffic on the road to Vitebsk only moved at night.[75]

Shortly after the agents' deployment, Soviet security guards manning a checkpoint on a bridge examined their papers and asked them about their mission. Agents 2391 and 2384 showed the guards their identity papers and replied that their task was to pick up a cable from army headquarters.[76] Without further questioning, the Soviet guards took the agents' documentation, removed the bolts from their rifles, and locked the agents up for a few days. On 1 March 1944 the Soviet guards brought both agents, along with a deserter, to another village where an NKVD lieutenant interrogated them. The lieutenant did not believe the agents' story either and explained that nothing would happen to them if they told the truth. Both 2391 and 2384 decided to fall back on another prearranged cover story. They told the NKVD lieutenant that they actually had deserted from the 629th Rifle Regiment.[77]

After a single interrogation, the NKVD lieutenant believed their story and neglected to thoroughly examine the agents' identity papers. However, agents 2391 and 2384 were then assigned to the 145th Penal Company in the area of the 164th Rifle Division. There both agents volunteered to be messengers. Agent 2391 was later assigned to a reconnaissance company. While on a mission, 2391 managed to break away and return to German lines on 11 March. Agent 2384 became a messenger for the commander of the 145th Penal Company and managed to return to German lines on 14 March. Both sources were assessed as "believable" by their German debriefers.[78]

German intelligence officers knew that Soviet counterintelligence conducted double-agent operations, at least on a tactical level. Many Abwehr documents analyzed by the Allies after the war cautioned that every German agent returning from Soviet-held territory "had to be suspected" of being turned by the Soviets.[79] For example, FAT 113 in Army Group North inserted agent 2385 on 5 March 1944 about ten kilometers south southwest of Vitebsk.[80] Agent 2385 returned to German lines on 9 June 1944, having spent almost three months in the rear area of the Soviet army. During his debriefing, agent 2385 stated that two Soviet security guards had detained him at a crossroad, taken him to a village, and locked him up for a few days, and that an NKVD lieutenant interrogated him while he had been locked up.[81]

Agent 2385 reported that he had told his Soviet interrogator that he had been captured by the Germans and had offered to work for them so he could return to Soviet lines. The Soviet lieutenant had questioned agent 2385 on the details of his treatment in the POW camp and about his military career, and ordered the agent to write out his autobiography.[82] On 16 March the Soviets apparently had released 2385 because he was sick; after his interrogation he subsequently had spent almost two months in a Soviet field hospital. On 30 May 1944 agent 2385 had been assigned to a replacement unit and, on 9 June 1944, had taken advantage of an opportunity while in the forward area to escape back to German lines.[83]

Agent 2385 provided his German debriefer with information on the makeup of a Soviet field hospital, on the locations of various Soviet units, and some minor tidbits of information gleaned from conversations with Soviet officers on awards and assignments given to Marshals Zhukov and Vassilevskiy, as well as some vague information on upcoming Soviet plans for an offensive. The German debriefer evaluated 2385's information as basically worthless, commenting that the agent's story resembled those of agents known to be controlled by the Soviets. He expressed considerable skepticism about the ability of a replacement officer to view so much of the forward area by himself and in the daytime. The German debriefer further commented that agent 2385 had provided better information when he was interrogated as a POW. The FAT commander sent agent 2385 back to a prison camp on the strong suspicion that he was actually a Soviet double agent.[84]

In addition to the German institutional lack of willingness to plan for secret war prior to the invasion, Baun himself may have contributed to his organization's lack of success. In his memoirs Reinhard Gehlen assessed Baun as having a complex personality.[85] Since Baun had spent the formative years of his childhood in the USSR, Gehlen believed that Baun had "absorbed the Russian mentality," that is, "there was something of the Russian soul in him, that emotional sentimental something that distinguishes Russians from other peoples." Gehlen went on to elaborate that Baun had an uncontrollable imagination, which made it hard for Baun to pass sober judgment on hard facts and inclined him to chase "will-o'-the-wisps."[86] Like other FHO officers, Gehlen was also suspicious of Baun, no doubt because of his "Russianness," as well as the gulf between Baun's alleged reputation as the "cleverest Russian expert on Canaris' staff" and his record during the initial phases of the German invasion of the USSR.[87] Just prior to Gehlen's takeover of FHO in April 1942, Baun's credibility had significantly eroded largely because of failed agent deployments deep inside the Soviet Union.[88] His reports were the object of ridicule within FHO.[89] Although Baun's record improved somewhat when Gehlen breathed new life into FHO, many of Baun's sources continued to be caught or controlled by the Soviets.[90]

For example, one German intelligence document, dated 14 November 1944, evaluated the reliability of almost 159 Abwehr I agents — many were targeted against the Soviet Union, but very few were actually operating on Soviet territory — and assessed agent R-4927's information as very valuable to usable. R-4927 was described as "operating in Russia for many years" and engaged in the "supervision of internal Russian radio traffic." However, the information of two other German agents on the list who were operating on Soviet territory — "a radio counteragent" who was a former Soviet lieutenant and POW, and an agent whose designator was 102 and who was identified as a former German officer working at the Siberia Institute in Vladivostok — was assessed as usable. Of the 159 sources evaluated, only 41 were rated as having provided very valuable to usable information.[91] Given the abysmal Abwehr I record in the East, it is doubtful that these operations were genuine.

By the end of the war the FAKs/FATs on the Eastern Front could only use compromised agents whose sole choice was to serve their conquerors. As a result, clandestinely acquired intelligence production was reduced to a trickle.[92] Although the Abwehr I effort in the East functioned somewhat better and appears to have been less corrupt than the effort in the West, ruthless Soviet counterintelligence operations made the German clandestine effort just as ineffective as in the West. Relentless Soviet pressure exacerbated the Abwehr's and SD's problems caused by lack of preparation, poor leadership, insufficient training, a shortage of Russian-speaking German intelligence officers, and brutal

Nazi occupation policies. After the war, former members of the Abwehr and the RSHA conceded that their organizations did not supply Germany with vital intelligence.[93]

"Set the East Ablaze" (Sabotage and Sedition)

Abwehr II conducted a wide variety of operations ranging from destroying vital civilian and military targets such as bridges, communications centers, and rail lines to spreading propaganda in the rear of the Soviet army and preventing the Soviets from carrying out their scorched earth policy.[94] The operations were loosely divided into three main categories: guerrilla warfare, sabotage, and operations conducted to further the disintegration of enemy morale.[95] One Abwehr II report summarizing the effectiveness of sabotage operations for 1942 indicated, at least up to that time, that Abwehr II operations were somewhat more successful than those of Abwehr I. The Abwehr II report stated that, as of the end of 1942, a total of 525 officers and men had trained 7,027 agents, dispatched 3,262 of those trained behind Soviet lines, and recovered 2,510 of them.[96] Those agents, according to the same report, carried out 504 missions, of which 302 had been successful.[97] Abwehr II FAKs/FATs lost 5 killed, 9 wounded, and 18 missing during 1942. Of the agents deployed, 532 had been killed and several hundred never returned to German lines.[98]

However, the Germans may well have inflated the success rates. For example, FAK 202, which was attached to Army Group South in 1942, reported that, in a six-month period it had mounted fifty-nine sabotage operations, of which eleven had been ostensibly successful. Further evaluation revealed that, in nine of these successful cases, the determination was based solely on the statements of the returning agents.[99] According to a London Counterintelligence War Room report of the debriefings of several Abwehr II officers who had served in FAK 202, many agents did not have the courage to remain in the area to verify the results of their work.[100] These officers assessed FAK 202 over the course of the war as having had "some success."[101]

The inaccessibility of much of the Soviet defense industry and strict Soviet security controls at defense plants and factories further reduced the ability of Abwehr II to sabotage the Soviet war effort.[102] The Germans realized that precise planning was needed to effectively sabotage factories. However, because of the demands placed on the German agent training system and the fluidity of combat operations, many Abwehr II agents could not receive the required intensive training — that is, where exactly to plant the explosives to achieve the most damage and what to do if alternate sites were as inaccessible as the original one — and therefore would need to rely largely on their wits. If an agent were not able to gain entry to the factory himself, planning called for him to be given the name of a suitable anti-Soviet contact in the particular factory who would be able to carry out the act of sabotage (an inherently risky process).[103] Given that the physical security in Soviet factories was extensive and that the factories were riddled with informants, Abwehr II success rates against this type of target were probably not high.[104]

The difficulty in measuring Soviet counterintelligence success against Abwehr II operations designed to covertly subvert the morale of Soviet troops largely stems from the fact that neither the German documents nor the Soviet counterintelligence histories of World War II tend to focus on these activities. Another difficulty in measuring Soviet counterintelligence effectiveness against these kinds of operations is the lack of feedback on their successes or failures. For example, in 1944 the Germans captured a Soviet lieutenant who was strongly suspected of being a Soviet agent.[105] The Germans trained him as an agent and arranged for him — without his knowledge — to overhear a conversation indicating that the Abwehr was in touch with a group of Soviet officers planning to overthrow Stalin.[106] The lieutenant was given an encoded letter and 50,000 rubles, and, under the guise of a Red Army officer who was on his way to a hospital, was infiltrated behind Soviet lines with instructions to contact a certain Soviet officer and give him the letter and the money.[107] The German handler explained to the agent in somewhat vague terms that there was a conspiracy of sorts. The officers the agent was told to contact were actually active-duty Soviet officers known to the Germans but who were not in their employ.[108]

The Abwehr assumed that their agent would be arrested and interrogated and that the letter and money would be easily discovered by the Soviets. The Germans planned to create such suspicion about these Soviet officers, some of whom were high ranking, that they would be arrested as traitors or, at a minimum, that Smersh would launch a witchhunt for nonexistent conspirators.[109] The Germans further planned to send other agents into Soviet territory who would also have information ostensibly confirming that there was a conspiracy of Soviet officers plotting against Stalin. On 28 July 1944 the Soviet lieutenant was infiltrated behind Soviet lines; however, original German documentation did not provide any information on the success or failure of the mission.[110]

Soviet sources admit that in the first part of the war German sabotage operations achieved substantial successes. German saboteurs blew up bridges, destroyed railway lines, power stations, and communications lines, acted as forward air controllers for German bombers, poisoned water supplies, distributed anti-Soviet literature, and killed hundreds of political commissars, Party workers, commanders, and police officers.[111] As the Abwehr II report for 1942 demonstrates, sabotage operations became less successful during the war. For example, FAK 207 dispatched four agents to blow up the rail line from Yelets to Yefremov in May 1942. All four were captured before they could carry out their mission.[112] In 1943 FAK 204 launched Operation Jungle to blow up sections of the Vorutka-Ktolas railroad and several bridges. The group was composed of twelve Russians, including two radio operators, all dressed in NKVD uniforms. The Germans issued them rations for twenty days and a total of 60,000 rubles. After blowing up the rail line, the group was to release political prisoners from an NKVD prison and use them as a nucleus to start a resistance movement. The Germans later concluded that this operation had been turned by the Soviets.[113]

The Soviets also defeated German efforts to conduct guerrilla warfare behind Soviet lines. For example, one Soviet history described the failure of Operation Dromedar — the German code name for efforts to create guerrilla movements and foment dissent among the people of the Caucasus.[114] From 1942 to 1943 German intelligence dispatched some twenty sabotage groups to that region, equipped with explosives, radios, anti-Soviet propaganda, and millions of rubles. Soviet military counterintelligence captured many of the agents, and a large percentage of them volunteered their services on arrival in the Soviet rear area. The German figurehead for these series of operations was an anti-Soviet Armenian émigré, General Dro Kananyan. At the direction of Soviet counterintelligence, Kananyan's former adjutant — who was still in Soviet-held territory — infiltrated German lines posing as a deserter. He mentioned to his German interrogators that he knew Kananyan well and asked to work for him. The Germans obliged, and the adjutant subsequently played a key role in destroying Operation Dromedar by passing to the Soviets a considerable amount of detailed information on German agent deployments originating from the training schools at Pyatigorsk, Georgievesk, and Nal'chik.[115]

However, Nazi ambivalence toward fully exploiting the anti-Soviet sentiments of a large number of Soviet citizens — including those located in the non-Slavic regions of the USSR — severely handicapped the Germans from establishing a broad base of resistance in the rear of the Red Army.[116] Nevertheless, German support for Ukrainian nationalist organizations both before and during the war was real; Canaris's Abwehr used many members of these groups to subvert the Soviet rear.[117] Soviet histories reflect this German emphasis on the Ukraine.

State Security devoted considerable resources to countering the "threat" posed by Ukrainian nationalist organizations and suffered substantial losses in the process.[118] To date, historians are unable to check either the accuracy of the Soviet figures (see below) or determine how many of those arrested actually had been in the employ of the Germans; no corroborating official documentation has been released, if it exists. Nevertheless, the Soviet versions of their operations against Ukrainian nationalist groups no doubt reflect the counterintelligence pressure put on these groups by the Soviet State Security organs, which in turn made it difficult for real German agents to operate. For example:

One Soviet history claimed that, from April to October 1940, Soviet counterintelligence destroyed thirty-eight armed groups consisting of several hundred Ukrainian nationalists.[119]

Almost one-third of the German agents captured by Soviet military counterintelligence from 1940 to 1941 were identified as Ukrainian nationalists.[120]

From April to May 1944, in the area of the First Ukrainian Front, Soviet military counterintelligence officers conducted 166 operations against 47 Ukrainian "bandit groups," killed or captured 930 of the members, and destroyed 61 arms caches. In the spring of 1944 another 1,400 Ukrainian nationalists were killed or captured.[121] The Soviets claimed that in the first 40 days of 1945, in the area of the First Belorussian Front, Smersh officers arrested 129 German agents who had been assigned sabotage missions.[122]

Soviet histories also praise "counterintelligence successes" against other nationalist groups ostensibly supported by the Germans. In 1939 the Soviets claimed to have liquidated 2,500 members of the "Union of Armed Struggle," a German-supported anti-Soviet organization in Belorussia.[123] Just prior to the war the Lithuanian NKVD arrested another 100 members of an anti-Soviet organization. In the spring of 1941 the Latvian NKVD arrested an additional 100 members of a German-supported anti-Soviet organization.[124]

Exaggerations aside, the Soviet claim that destruction of these groups was so extensive that, beginning in late 1940, the Germans could no longer rely on any organized underground support directed against "Soviet power" appears generally credible.[125] Although Nazi policy undermined organized efforts to substantially exploit the population's anti-Soviet sentiments, the effectiveness of even minor or misguided efforts to subvert the Soviet rear was severely reduced by ruthless Soviet operations to detect and destroy real or imagined enemies of the regime.

Soviet counterintelligence, for all practical purposes, destroyed the potential threat posed by Abwehr II, despite some Abwehr II successes throughout the war.[126] German documents strongly suggest, and Soviet sources appear to confirm, that the Germans never succeeded in establishing a broad-based agent network inside the Soviet Union capable of carrying out a sustained campaign of sabotage, sedition, and guerrilla warfare over the long term.[127] Documentary evidence shows that Abwehr II also could not conduct effective sabotage operations against the Soviet defense industry. Although some Abwehr II missions, such as those targeting the immediate rear of the Red Army, may have been successful at times, Soviet counterintelligence was effective where it counted most, against direct threats to the stability of the regime.

Schmalschlaeger's Spy Catchers (Counterintelligence)

German counterintelligence as a whole, particularly Abwehr III, achieved considerable success against Soviet agent deployments in the rear of the German army. However, despite identifying and rendering ineffective a little over 50 percent of the known Soviet agents operating in the rear of the German army, Abwehr III did not prevent a German intelligence service defeat.[128] Abwehr III also did not penetrate the Soviet intelligence service's agent training system to the extent that the Soviets penetrated the German system, nor did Abwehr III succeed in penetrating the higher levels of the Soviet intelligence services. One difficulty the Germans had in penetrating Soviet intelligence was the lack of a qualified agent pool. Although the Germans captured NKVD and Smersh officers, many destroyed their personal documents and disguised their identities by wearing the uniforms of ordinary soldiers. Many escaped at the first opportunity, committed suicide, or were murdered by other POWs because of their affiliation with State Security.[129] Finally, Abwehr III was unable to conduct offensive counterintelligence operations behind Soviet lines largely because of the effectiveness of Soviet counterintelligence.[130]

During the first few months of the invasion, German mobile counterintelligence teams primarily focused on collecting documents by searching important government, Party, and Soviet intelligence service offices, as well as military command posts and buildings. The FAKs/FATs captured few Soviet agents during this period; however, they seized enormous quantities of documents.[131] Abwehr III's FAKs/FATs, with the aid of former Latvian and Estonian intelligence officers, captured large amounts of material on the Soviet intelligence services in the Baltics.[132] This success decreased as the German advanced slowed. By November 1941 casualties began to mount, the troops of the FATs/FAKs were exhausted, and supplies such as winter clothing and motor vehicles were inadequate. In addition, Soviet agent activity began to increase, and mobile counterintelligence teams began to divert resources to combat Soviet agent deployments behind German lines.[133]

Although the Germans never again achieved the same success in seizing documents as in 1941, the documents initially seized yielded a reasonably accurate picture of the Soviet intelligence services and played an important role in how Abwehr III operated on the Eastern Front.[134] These documents revealed that the NKVD planned — even before the war — to have its informants report on the activities of the Germans as well as to attempt to penetrate all German organizations in those areas likely to be occupied. The NKVD's prewar planning included using the intelligence officers in partisan units as agent controllers and using the partisan structure as a whole to communicate with Soviet intelligence elements in the rear of the Red Army.[135] The increased Soviet agent commitments caught the Germans unprepared and forced them to redirect the efforts of the FAKs/FATs III toward combating Soviet agent deployments. The FATs/FAKs III had originally been designed to exploit enemy intelligence documents and run agents, not to hunt down Soviet agents.[136] Because there were no mobile units specifically dedicated to combating Soviet agents in the German rear, starting in autumn 1942 the FAKs/FATs III began to attack Soviet agents behind German lines. In addition, no component existed to systematically exploit and evaluate information gleaned from captured Soviet agents (the Asts and Nests were too far removed from combat operations to be useful).[137]

Nevertheless, in the spring of 1942 Walli III recognized the potential threat posed by Soviet partisans residing in the rear of the German army and issued one of the first comprehensive reports on the subject. Despite the warning, the German military establishment and the occupation authorities underestimated the importance of the partisans and considered them merely "bandits." By the time they realized that the partisans indeed posed a substantial threat to the German rear area, few troops could be spared to combat them.[138] The German governor of the Ukraine initially boasted that he could eliminate the partisans on a moment's notice; one and a half years later he was forced to travel in an armored car.[139] Schmalschlaeger was convinced that German counterintelligence could have defeated the massive Soviet intelligence offensive, which, by his calculations, started in autumn 1942, had not the partisans provided staging areas and communications links for Soviet agents in German-occupied areas.[140]

To meet the Soviet increase in intelligence activity, OKH ordered the FAKs/FATs III to take on full-fledged counterintelligence duties. FAKs/FATs could now conduct radio playbacks, systematically analyze the methods of operation used by the Soviet intelligence services, apprehend Soviet agents, and attempt to gauge Soviet military intentions by analyzing agent deployments.[141] To implement those orders, Schmalschlaeger reconstructed his FATs to cover larger areas. He also increased the quality of personnel assigned to the FAKs/FATs III, improved training, established a network of almost 1,000 agents to cover the huge operational area, improved the communications links of the FAKs/FATs III, and increased the awareness of German troops so that they were better able to spot Soviet agents.[142]

Schmalschlaeger instituted some rigorous training standards. FAT commanders served as specialists in counterintelligence as well as advisers to German military intelligence officers (1c) assigned directly to German military formations. NCOs were required to be able to command small outposts and maintain strict discipline (no sleeping with local women, no excessive drunkenness, no looting, etc.), and both new and experienced personnel were required to take examinations and pass them in order to continue serving as counterintelligence officers. FAT leaders also needed to be intimately familiar with the complicated process of how to conduct a radio playback. None of this was done during the planning for Operation Barbarossa.[143] As a result, regular German army combat units apprehended 35 to 40 percent of all Soviet agents operating behind German lines.[144]

During the war German military counterintelligence conducted numerous double-agent operations and approximately thirty-five *Funkspiele* with some degree of success.[145] However, even the success of these kinds of operations was limited. In the beginning of the war many German double-agent operations failed because of lax security.[146] Later in the war both the *Funkspiele* and double-agent operations became somewhat more successful; however, as one German officer put it, "the reliability of turned agents constantly varied directly with the fortunes and, especially, the misfortunes of war."[147]

In one successful case the Germans detected through a double agent a large Soviet agent network, whose leader — a Russian mayor — had been directed by Soviet counterintelligence to gain favor with the Germans and offer to set up an agent network for them.[148] The mayor carried out his assignment well and eventually became highly esteemed by the local German civil administration because of his efficiency and ostensibly pro-German attitude. To enhance his bona fides with the Germans, the mayor even regularly denounced hidden Soviet Jews as well as anyone who threatened his personal security. The Germans conducted a lengthy radio playback and subsequently exposed forty-two agents in the mayor's net as actually working for Soviet counterintelligence.[149]

Abwehr III purposely circulated rumors that cooperation with German counterintelligence would reap substantial benefits. As a result, a Latvian doctor, who was a specialist in venereal diseases, told German naval counterintelligence officers in August 1941 that he had been required to treat a Soviet counterintelligence officer for gonorrhea during the Soviet occupation of Riga.[150] The Soviet officer threatened the doctor with arrest unless he became an informant.

The doctor agreed and then, under duress, turned over a list of his patients to Soviet counterintelligence. The patients were subsequently recruited as informants. The doctor's information led to the German discovery of an extensive network of Soviet stay-behind agents.[151]

Of the thirty-five wartime *Funkspiele* conducted by German military counterintelligence in the East — many of which were run simultaneously — some lasted well over a year.[152] In contrast to the Soviets, Abwehr III officers in the East did not need special headquarters authority to conduct a *Funkspiel,* as obtaining such authority would have impaired the security of the operation. However, many German radio playbacks were detected by the Soviets, because the Soviets required that agents adhere to strict time limits for an initial call after arrival behind German lines. This operational security measure was adopted on the theory that any delay would likely indicate that the agent had been captured and was under German control.[153]

Nevertheless, the Germans ran some successful radio playbacks. According to one Abwehr III officer, Ast Krakow conducted the most successful radio playback of the war in the East. The operation began in Warsaw in the summer of 1943, lasted approximately one year, and resulted in the capture of fifty two-man Soviet agent teams.[154] The success of this operation enabled the Germans to determine the timing and scope of some Soviet military offensives in Poland, Czechoslovakia, and Upper Silesia for an entire year.[155] In other radio playbacks, the Germans deceived Soviet commanders so effectively that captured agents were decorated in absentia by the Soviet government, and Soviet supply planes were either shot down or captured intact.[156] In another case FAT 326 initiated a radio playback in the autumn of 1943 against the Central Partisan Staff. The playback lasted almost eight months and resulted in the Soviets losing thirty-four out of thirty-five agents and a considerable amount of supplies.[157]

Although additional precautions that the Germans took later in the war to enhance the security of the FAKs/FATs III deterred Soviet agent penetrations to some extent, security was still extremely difficult to maintain. For example, one Soviet-controlled partisan agent of a FAT III unit led a band of partisans to the FAT commander's home, where the partisans killed him. In the ensuing battle, several other FAT members were also killed.[158] One Soviet woman offered her services to a FAT III unit, claiming that she did not want to carry out the mission that Soviet intelligence had given her; she had only accepted it so she could visit her relatives in the occupied area. The Germans vetted her and hired her to work directly for one of the FAT III interpreters. The Soviet woman and the FAT III interpreter developed a close personal relationship, and shortly thereafter she began to copy official documents in the interpreter's possession. At the first opportunity she fled, but she was captured when the truck she was riding in crashed. She survived the crash and, on interrogation, confessed that she had been under the control of Soviet counterintelligence.[159]

To detect Soviet agents, the Germans used such methods as planting informants in German civil administrations, establishing curfews in coordination with house-to-house searches, searching the desks, personal belongings, and work spaces of non-German employees, and instituting "security days" in which the GFP (Geheime Feldpolizei; Secret Field Police) and the military police simultaneously set up checkpoints to inspect documents.[160] In Kiev the Germans caught fifty Soviet agents in one day by searching the work spaces and personal belongings of non-German employees working for the army or the occupation authorities. The Germans even limited the validity of identity papers to one month, but this still gave the Soviets ample time to equip their agents with the necessary papers.[161] Monitoring the traffic of Soviet radio agents gave the Germans an indication of agent locations; however, the Germans were never able to break Soviet agent ciphers.[162] Leitstelle III Ost identified approximately 11,000 Soviet agents annually by using a combination of all the counterintelligence methods in its arsenal. In 1944 Colonel Georg Buntrock, who after the amalgamation of the Abwehr into the RSHA became chief of all the FAKs/FATs in the East, stated that the Germans captured an average of 600 Soviet agents a month. This would mean that the Germans captured an average of 7,200 Soviet agents a year for a total of 28,800 for the entire war.[163]

During the course of the war Leitstelle III Ost developed an impressive analytical capability. German counterintelligence officers plotted Soviet agent commitments in minute detail, kept index card records on thousands of Soviet intelligence and counterintelligence officers and agents, and issued numerous situation reports on Soviet agent deployments based on intercepts of Soviet agent communications, captured agent interrogations, POW debriefings, and information provided by German double agents run against the partisans.[164] German military counterintelligence officers analyzed Soviet operational methods in such detail that Soviet agents' subordination could often be identified by the type of agent-radio used or the specific documents an agent possessed. For example, Leitstelle III Ost could invariably identify Soviet agents subordinate to Baltic Fleet naval intelligence units because that fleet's intelligence units equipped their agents with Kambala radios. One regional NKVD unit always issued its agents with the forged stamps and documents only associated with a particular German civil administrator.[165]

Leitstelle III Ost produced daily, weekly, and monthly statistics and reports on significant events and every aspect of Soviet agent commitments.[166] Reports on Soviet agent commitments included such details as targets, subordination, age, sex, occupation, organization, cover stories, Party membership, location and method of apprehension, method of recruitment, and method of infiltration. Leitstelle III Ost also produced reports and statistics on intercepted agent transmissions. The statistics were used to measure the success and failure of various FATs as well as to refine FAK/FAT III targets and deployments.[167]

Schmalschlaeger claimed in his postwar debriefing that occasionally analysis of enemy agent concentrations resulted in the ability to predict Soviet offensives several months in advance.[168] For example, he stated that, on 6 July 1944, Soviet partisan headquarters in Kiev issued an order to all subordinate units to intensify their intelligence and sabotage activities in Slovakia; Leitstelle III Ost noticed the increase. Schmalschlaeger believed that the order was a precursor to the Soviet offensive launched on 28 September 1944, via the Carpathian Mountains.[169] Schmalschlaeger was convinced that Soviet agent concentrations enabled German counterintelligence to predict the Soviet offensive toward Minsk in July 1944 and, as early as January 1945, the Soviet offensive in the direction of Stettin in March of the same year.[170] Colonel Buntrock went even further and stated that, during the last two years of the war, "no Russian offensive came off which FA III had not known about weeks in advance." Buntrock also made the observation that efforts to predict enemy offensives in the West by analyzing Allied agent deployments were not successful, largely because the capture of huge numbers of enemy agents was not possible.[171]

However, the "success" of Schmalschlaeger's innovative approach to the operational analysis of Soviet agent deployments must be qualified. According to the premier Western analyst of Soviet military deception during World War II, former U.S. Army colonel David Glantz, the Soviets deceived the Germans more often about the scope, magnitude, and exact locations of Soviet attacks; however, the Soviets could not totally deceive the Germans on whether an offensive was likely.[172] The Soviets also took some precautions with their agents by deploying them to locations far from their intended target areas and assigning them tasks and intelligence collection requirements which, if revealed to the Germans, would not necessarily compromise the details of a planned offensive.[173]

In his final evaluation of German military counterintelligence performance in the East, Schmalschlaeger concluded that the effectiveness of the FAK/FAT III units was limited and that by the time the effectiveness of Soviet tactics became apparent it was too late for the Germans to take "corrective action."[174] He acknowledged that even during the first few years of the war the Soviets had "concealed their own strength from all foreign observers." They had spread rumors about the deficiencies of their army and, by using foreign intelligence services, created the impression that the Soviet armed forces were much weaker than they actually were. Although projecting "weakness" was out of character for

Soviet Cold War "perception management," it was not uncommon to make the Germans believe, at certain times and on certain sectors of the Eastern Front, that Soviet forces were not as strong as they actually were. As Stalin did not want war in 1941, he had a vested interest in making sure that his adversaries believed that the Soviet armed forces were deployed defensively. Schmalschlaeger concluded that the German services "had fallen prey to misinformation." However, Leitstelle III Ost had succeeded in establishing the utility of counterintelligence analysis to support military operations.[175]

The "Gehlen Organization" (Fremde Heere Ost)

Reinhard Gehlen inherited an almost impossible task when he took over FHO in April 1942. After ten months of constant combat and few resources, Gehlen set out to build a military intelligence organization capable of effectively serving OKH.[176] He succeeded only in part. Under combat conditions, he established an excellent system for the reporting on and the analysis of every aspect of the Soviet war effort.[177] He attempted to furnish OKH with long-range forecasts of Soviet operational intentions, which was an innovation for German military intelligence, and he established a training program for new intelligence officers.[178] However, his inability to correctly predict Soviet operational intentions on a number of occasions, his inflexible belief in German superiority, his arrogance, and a fundamental unwillingness to believe that the Soviets were capable of strategic deception seriously impaired the effectiveness of FHO. Gehlen's attitude — exploited by Soviet counterintelligence and the Soviet General Staff — made what little strategic intelligence FHO collected positively dangerous, because OKH based some of its operational planning on Gehlen's analyses.[179]

An officer without previous intelligence or foreign-language training ran Germany's most successful intelligence organization. In fact, during his military career, Gehlen purposely avoided modern languages so he would not have to serve in intelligence.[180] Gehlen received his commission in 1921, became a General Staff officer in 1935, and was posted to the Operations Department of the General Staff in 1936. At the outbreak of World War II he was assigned as the senior General Staff officer of an infantry division. During the Polish campaign he won the Iron Cross Second Class. In October 1940 General Franz Halder appointed then-Major Gehlen to the Eastern Group of the Operations Section of OKH, which dealt, in part, with overall German military strategy in the East. For Barbarossa, Gehlen drafted the details for the dividing lines between the three German army groups and resolved the initial transport problems of the invasion. Because of the abysmal intelligence failures of FHO, starting from the initial planning for Barbarossa through March 1942, Halder reassigned Gehlen to head FHO in April 1942, largely because of Gehlen's reputation for organization.[181]

To a significant degree, the Abwehr's lack of mid- to high-level agent penetrations of the Soviet government, the armed forces, the intelligence and security services, the CPSU, and the Soviet defense industry contributed to FHO's underestimation of the overall number of Soviet divisions, tanks, and aircraft prior to the onset of Barbarossa, as well as to FHO's underestimation of the Soviet ability to mobilize reserves in December 1941. Halder believed that in February 1941 the Soviets possessed 10,000 tanks when, in reality, they possessed somewhere between 20,000 and 24,000. The Germans estimated that the Red Air Force had 6,000 to 10,500 aircraft when the actual figure was closer to 18,000. The day before the invasion the Germans estimated the total Soviet strength at 226 large formations in European Russia. By the fifty-first day of the campaign Halder noted that German intelligence had increased its estimates of the number of Soviet divisions to 360. OKW's War Diary asserts that, as of 1 December 1941, the Soviets had no substantial reserve units left. German intelligence, on 4 December 1941, believed that for the time being the Soviet armed forces were incapable of launching a major offensive.[182]

With little or no meaningful intelligence gleaned from agents deep inside the Soviet Union, FHO became highly dependent on the incomplete intelligence obtained from other sources such as aerial photography, signals interceptions, troop reconnaissance on the border, and analysis of the Soviet press and radio broadcasts.[183] In short, the Germans had no agents capable of producing information that would have seriously challenged either FHO's or OKH's preconceived notions that the Red Army and the Soviet Union would quickly collapse under the might of the Wehrmacht.[184]

OKH firmly believed that it had a satisfactory grasp of the most important elements of the Soviet army and therefore never seriously tried to collect strategic intelligence on the USSR. The "widespread sense of superiority toward Russia infected the personnel in intelligence as it did their superiors" and "over optimism made them lazy." The Germans let the challenges of collecting intelligence inside Russia blunt their efforts. In addition, the lack of telephones in the USSR, excellent Soviet radio telephone security, and the inability of the Germans to break higher-level Soviet crypto-systems resulted in German signals intelligence units largely relying on direction finding to update the order of battle information on Soviet forces. The 250 German receivers faced 10,000 Soviet transmitters. German signals intelligence never obtained solid information on how large the Red Army actually was. Aerial reconnaissance, of course, provided excellent, albeit incomplete, intelligence, owing to the limitations inherent in this type of reconnaissance such as weather, range of the aircraft, and Soviet camouflage and concealment measures.[185]

The attitude of General Guenther von Blummentritt, Chief of Staff of the German Fourth Army, was not uncommon. Overstimulated by his prejudices, he believed that conquering the largest country in the world (the USSR) would take a mere fourteen days. Given such attitudes among senior German officers, as well as Hitler, it is doubtful that any contradictory information would have been believed, even if it had come from an excellent source. Because of the lack of mid- to high-level agents in the USSR, German intelligence never even had a real opportunity to authoritatively question the preconceived notions about the certainty of a quick and successful campaign in the USSR so that operational planning could have been adjusted accordingly. David Kahn, in his book *Hitler's Spies,* takes this line of argument even further by stating that, in his opinion, German intelligence — by having avoided a detailed and critical examination of all possibilities, both pessimistic as well as optimistic — preserved the illusion of certain victory. Victory seemed so certain that an all-out effort to collect intelligence against the USSR seemed pointless. Schellenberg claimed in his memoirs that he suggested to Heydrich that German planning be based on Stalin's ability to reinforce the Party-government structure and that a war might be a source of strength for him. Schellenberg said that Heydrich rebuffed him twice.[186]

One Western historian recently challenged the conventional wisdom that the Germans grossly underestimated the rigors of a campaign in the USSR.[187] R. H. Stolfi, a professor of modern European history at the Naval Postgraduate School in Monterey, California, argues that the Germans were well aware of the problems of conducting a campaign in the Soviet Union — as well as of the strengths and weaknesses of the Red Army — and, had Hitler adhered to Halder's original plan to continue the German attack on Moscow in the summer of 1941, the Soviet armed forces would have been quickly and soundly defeated.[188] The decision not to take Moscow at that time enabled Soviet forces to regroup and eventually launch a devastating counterattack in December 1941 against Army Group Center. Stolfi maintains that the Soviets survived Barbarossa not because of weather, the tenacity of the Soviet soldier, or the fanatical ruthlessness of a communist bureaucracy. He believes that Hitler's decision to delay the drive on Moscow for two months cost the Germans the war, because it gave the Soviets time to reinforce their forces around Moscow.[189]

Recent scholarship by David Glantz calls Stolfi's argument into question. Army Group Center's best opportunity to capture Moscow was in October 1941, as Soviet forces were far weaker at that time than in September.[190] The Germans also needed to ensure that the flanks of Army Group Center were secure before taking Moscow. In short, Glantz's scholarship supports the contention of the former commander of the German Fourth Army's 43rd Army Corps at Moscow, General Gotthard von Heinrici, that taking Moscow early would have been a close call.[191]

According to Stolfi, that it took the Soviets almost three and a half more years to defeat the German army demonstrated the magnitude of the initial German victories.[192] Stolfi further argues that if the Soviets took so long to defeat the Germans, the Germans could not have underestimated the Soviets, particularly if the only reason the Germans lost the war in the East was Hitler's decision, in the summer of 1941, to divert elements of Army Group Center southward toward the Ukraine instead of Moscow.[193] Seen in this light, German assessments of the Red Army were neither unreasonable nor illogical.[194]

If one accepts Stolfi's argument, subsequent German intelligence failures are irrelevant and, by implication, not worth analyzing largely because German prewar assessments of the USSR were essentially accurate. In Stolfi's view, historians have been able to characterize preinvasion German intelligence judgments on the USSR as the product of an unbridled contempt for everything Russian only because Hitler's decision not to attack Moscow led to the German defeat.[195] Stolfi's argument supports Kahn's observation that, to the Germans, serious strategic intelligence collection against the USSR seemed pointless prior to the invasion because victory was assumed.[196]

However, Stolfi's provocative hypothesis does not take into account the likely decrease in the rapidity of the initial German advance — or the almost certain increase in German casualties — had Stalin decided to put Soviet forces on full alert and order complete mobilization. As Stalin possessed an overwhelming amount of information on the imminence of a German invasion, he could have easily raised the alert status of Soviet forces.[197] The stubborn resistance of the Red Army as early as July 1941 in some sectors of the front — even under chaotic conditions — shows that if Soviet forces had been on full alert in late June 1941, the German advance would have been slowed and German casualties would have increased.[198] If the German defeat in the East is not seen primarily as the result of Hitler's decision to delay the drive on Moscow, then FHO preinvasion underestimations of Soviet military capabilities assume greater importance.[199] In fact, as early as July 1941, the Germans knew that they could not simultaneously launch offensives on all fronts. This weakening of assault strength indicated that the Germans had theoretically lost their chance to defeat the Soviet Union. The Germans knew in early August that they could not reach Murmansk or the Caucasus, that their units had to be refurbished and resupplied, and that a drive on Moscow would risk a Soviet counterattack in the North or the South and there were no reserves to meet such a contingency.[200]

The overall poor performance of German intelligence in the East is worth analyzing, as FHO's faulty analyses deprived OKH of the opportunity to adjust German military operational planning prior to the attack.[201] If the battle for Moscow were considered to be the decisive battle on the Eastern Front, then the single biggest mistake of German intelligence was its failure to correctly gauge the degree to which the Soviet state could mobilize its resources as well as its reserve forces. That failure is a direct result of ignoring the need for strategic intelligence and having no good sources inside the Soviet Union.[202]

The Germans never recovered from their preinvasion intelligence failures. Although the FAKs/FATs seized thousands of Soviet documents during the initial advances, the data could not be processed in time to correct FHO estimates. On 11 August 1941 General Franz Halder stated that the "Russian colossus has been underrated and could still dispose of manpower reserves for new formations."[203] FHO also did not anticipate the formation of new Soviet reserves behind the Moscow front; on 4 December FHO informed OKH that Soviet forces in front of Army Group Center were incapable of a large-scale offensive.[204] The Soviets launched their counteroffensive against Army Group Center on 5 December 1941. By the end of the winter the Germans lost almost 376,000 men as a result of the Soviet counterattack.[205]

When Gehlen took over FHO, Halder elevated FHO from a statistical organization to one that was authorized to formulate its own judgments on enemy operational intentions. Gehlen made substantial improvements to the organization. He assembled the best people he could find and reorganized FHO to make it more responsive to OKH. The status FHO achieved within OKH was unprecedented. Gehlen's streamlining of the combat intelligence process was a major innovation for the German army.[206]

However, Gehlen's statements, both during and after the war, that FHO had predicted almost every Soviet offensive do not hold up under scrutiny.[207] In fact, FHO had a poor record of predicting Soviet operational intentions at critical junctures during the war. Gehlen's attitude toward the USSR, faulty analysis conducted under the stress of intense combat, and serious gaps in intelligence collection — generated by the difficulty in collecting against the USSR, Soviet deception measures, scarce resources, and poor organization — to a large extent account for FHO's less than satisfactory performance.[208]

For example, before the Soviet offensive at Khar'kov in May 1942, FHO predicted that the Red Army did not have the capability to compel the Germans to divert significant numbers of troops from their planned offensive into the Ukraine.[209] Contrary to FHO's prediction, the Red Army launched a full-scale attack that pushed back the German summer offensive in the Ukraine until late

June 1942.[210] On 6 November 1942 Gehlen produced an estimate predicting that the main Soviet offensive would be launched against Army Group Center. The Soviets launched their Stalingrad offensive on 19 November 1942, which eventually resulted in the total destruction of the German Sixth Army.[211] Gehlen had correctly assessed Soviet force dispositions and strengths in the Kursk salient; however, he was less accurate in predicting the strength of the subsequent Soviet counterattacks.[212]

Gehlen's most serious intelligence error of the war resulted from FHO's failure to predict the Soviet offensive in June 1944, code-named Operation Bagration, which culminated in the complete destruction of Army Group Center.[213] By August 1944 the Soviets had ripped a 250-mile-wide gap in the German front, obliterated more than thirty German divisions (450,000 men), and had seriously shaken up Army Group North Ukraine. When Operation Bagration ended, the Red Army had reached the eastern borders of the Reich.[214] Just before the Soviet attack Gehlen's final estimate concluded that all available intelligence "confirms FHO's previous evaluation that the main blow would be delivered against Army Group North Ukraine."[215]

Not only did the Soviets launch the attack against Army Group Center, but Gehlen also had underestimated the total number of Soviet forces opposite Army Group Center by almost 50 percent (1,230,000 men); actual Soviet strength totaled 2,411,600 men. Glantz, citing both original FHO documents and a declassified secret Soviet General Staff Academy paper on Operation Bagration, says that German tactical intelligence on Soviet forces opposite Army Group Center was generally accurate. However, Soviet *maskirovka* discipline, lack of aircraft, Soviet radio silence, and the inability of German agents to move around in the rear areas of the Soviet army resulted in the Germans not detecting three Soviet combined-arms armies, a tank army, and several mobile corps.[216] While FHO acknowledged Soviet attack preparations in front of Army Group Center, it assessed them as being of secondary importance.[217]

German intelligence possessed little or no information on Soviet strategic reserves and did not acknowledge, until late July 1944, that the attack in progress was a major offensive that would unequivocally decide the outcome of the war.[218] In commenting on Operation Bagration, General Shtemenko, deputy chief of the Soviet General Staff, stated bluntly: "This system of operational deceptive measures proved its worth. History has shown that the enemy was profoundly misled concerning our real intentions."[219] What Shtemenko did not mention was that Soviet counterintelligence, through clever use of double agents, radio games, and ruthless rear-area security measures, significantly contributed to the success of those "operational deceptive measures."

German intelligence made serious mistakes in evaluating the capabilities of the Soviet armed forces and their operational intentions, as they had no significant agent penetrations of Soviet military, security, or Party organizations. One Soviet history acknowledged that the Germans not only underestimated the total number of Soviet divisions, but they also completely missed the fact that the USSR recognized the need to establish a second military-industrial base that would be invulnerable to air strikes from the east and west.[220] By 1941 almost one-fifth of all Soviet military factories had been moved to the Urals and parts of Siberia.[221] On the Leningrad front, German military intelligence did not succeed in obtaining even a single Soviet attack plan, nor did it succeed in placing a single agent on the staff of a higher-level military unit.[222] Another Soviet history stated that the Abwehr's major error lay in anticipating an uprising shortly after the invasion.[223]

S. Ostryakov, in *Military Chekists,* acknowledged that Soviet double-agent operations contributed to Gehlen's incorrect conclusion that the main scope and direction of the Soviet attack in Operation Bagration would fall on Army Group North Ukraine.[224] According to Ostryakov, Soviet disinformation aimed at convincing the Germans that the main Soviet offensive would be launched in the south and that the Soviet forces opposite Army Group Center would be only on the defensive. By using a variety of camouflage, concealment, and security measures, and three radio playbacks involving at least three double agents, the Soviets successfully convinced the Germans that the Red Army would attack in the south.[225]

Gehlen's pronouncements that he predicted all Soviet offensives are, to quote one Western historian of the intelligence war on the Eastern Front, "proof that the greatest deception senior intelligence officers suffer is from their own opinions."[226] Nazi Germany's "intelligence problem," that is, arrogance, Hitler's unwillingness to listen to unpleasant news, an unshakable belief in ultimate victory, unrelenting internecine bureaucratic infighting, and lack of preparation for contingencies all contributed to the belief that the Soviets were incapable of strategic deception by using double agents.

German failures, however, should be placed in context. The Abwehr itself was a hotbed of resistance to Hitler throughout most of the war. Many of the Red Orchestra's sources were in the Abwehr or close to it. Canaris's role in sabotaging the effectiveness of the German military intelligence cannot be overlooked.[227] He viscerally opposed the invasion of the Soviet Union and, when ordered to stand down on intelligence operations against Russia in the late 1930s and early 1940s, dutifully abided by the order. Although Canaris gradually came around to supporting what may arguably be viewed as a preventive war by the

Germans, he was always uncomfortable with fighting a two-front war. Relations between FHO and Canaris were not good.[228]

Since the early days of the Bolshevik Revolution, Soviet counterintelligence made it exceedingly difficult for any service to run clandestine operations in the USSR. The Trust Operation, in which the Soviets used double agents and false defectors for the better part of ten years, effectively destroyed émigré opposition to the Bolshevik regime and established beyond any doubt that the security services of the USSR were a worldwide force "to be reckoned with."[229]

Soviet counterintelligence was so effective that the British Secret Intelligence Service (SIS) could not establish an SIS station in Moscow and therefore was forced to run operations against the USSR using stations in bordering countries as staging areas for agent deployments.[230] Former SIS chief Admiral Hugh Sinclair considered the Bolsheviks masters at espionage and counterintelligence.[231] By the 1930s — even when the USSR became the primary target of SIS — SIS had no agents in the USSR capable of collecting significant intelligence and had to rely on information provided by the intelligence services of Czechoslovakia, Poland, Finland, and the Baltic states.[232] When the Germans overran most of Europe in the late 1930s and early 1940s SIS had to withdraw its stations all over occupied Europe, further limiting its collection against the Soviet Union.[233] Throughout the war the British considered the NKVD an efficient security service.[234] Both the Polish and Japanese intelligence services also had substantial difficulties operating in the USSR.[235]

Therefore the Nazi intelligence service defeat in the East cannot be dismissed solely as a German self-induced failure. Since the Bolshevik Revolution, the Soviet security services established a well-earned reputation for countering the clandestine operations of foreign intelligence organizations. The Germans faced an enemy who over a quarter of a century had elevated counterintelligence to the status of a fine art, albeit a brutal and ruthless one. Even taking into account the exaggerations, the distortions, the homage paid to the CPSU, and the triumphs of "fatherland security," Soviet State Security waged an impressive worldwide offensive counterintelligence war against the Germans, the Japanese, as well as the USSR's allies while under tremendous stress.[236] The British effort was much more refined, involved fewer numbers of agents, and had the advantage of Ultra.[237] Stalin's Chekists, decimated by the purges before the war and the initial German onslaught in 1941, recovered and, through sheer terror and cunning, smashed the Abwehr's ability to generate a viable clandestine collection effort in Russia.

Operation Monastery, the Soviet counterintelligence exploitation of an alleged network of agents in Russia ostensibly run by the Abwehr's principal agent in the Balkans, Richard Kauder (alias Klatt), Operation Berezino, and those operations that defeated the SD's Zeppelin project show just how sophisticated and cunning State Security could be in exploiting German vulnerabilities. These operations will be discussed in detail in the next two chapters and were selected not only because of their contribution to the Soviet counterintelligence effort but also because both German and Russian sources were available for these particular operations, as were declassified allied intelligence documents.

Operation Monastery and "Case Klatt"

When looking at Russian affairs it is so easy to fix your attention on the patent inefficiencies that the magnitude of the achievement is liable to escape from view altogether.

Christopher Duffy, *Russia's Military Way*, 1981

In Operation Monastery, which was run by Lieutenant General Sudoplatov's Fourth Directorate of the NKVD/NKGB, the Soviets, over the course of the war, passed to the Germans disinformation that seriously affected FHO estimates of Soviet military intentions at critical junctures. One of the principal Soviet figures in this operation was Aleksandr Petrovich Dem'ianov, code-named Heine. He was a long-term source, who — under Soviet direction — functioned ostensibly as a principal agent for the Germans and "recruited" or elicited information from several alleged sub-sources in the USSR. Heine primarily operated in the area of Army Group Center. The German code name — according to Sudoplatov and some German documents for Dem'ianov and his "organization of sub-sources" — was Max.[1] Heine was also used in Operation Berezino (German code name Rennstrecke, better known as Operation Scherhorn), which entailed an elaborate scheme by the Russians to deceive the Germans into diverting valuable agents, supplies, radios, and ammunition to a nonexistent group of 1,800 German soldiers stranded by Russian lines from mid-summer 1944 to the end of the war. Berezino is discussed in detail in the next chapter.

What makes Monastery so complex is its probable connection — at least in the components at the higher levels of the NKGB, Smersh, and the General Staff where disinformation was coordinated — to an ostensible German agent network operating inside the USSR. That German network, which has been extensively analyzed by several Western counterintelligence organizations after the war, passed thousands of messages to an Abwehr-controlled station in the Balkans that transmitted the intelligence to the Abwehr station in Vienna. From Vienna, it was forwarded to Berlin. The organization, Luftmeldekopf Suedost (translated as Air Intelligence Station, Southeast), headed by a German agent named Richard Kauder alias Richard Klatt, was subordinate to Abwehr I Luft of Ast Vienna. In the beginning of the war Klatt's primary station was based in Sofia and toward the end of the war in Budapest. The German code name for this operation was also Max.[2]

Strangely no Russian or Soviet sources, including the 1977 classified history of State Security, have definitively connected "Case Klatt" to Operation Monastery. In fact, recent scholarship based on apparently reliable information acquired in Russia over the last few years by two Western scholars suggests that Klatt's organization basically passed off newspaper articles as intelligence to the Abwehr (without Russian knowledge), or that if Klatt's organization had been controlled by the Russians, it was a separate operation from Monastery, albeit with possibly the same code name.[3] Whether swindler or a conduit for Soviet disinformation, "Max South" (Kauder/Klatt) as well as "Max North" (Dem'ianov/Heine) were not Abwehr or FHO success stories, contrary to what Reinhard Gehlen and many authors writing even in the 1990s have claimed.[4]

As with all issues relating to the Soviet intelligence and security services, many of the details of both Monastery and Richard Kauder probably will remain unknown for the foreseeable future. Nevertheless, based on an extensive analysis of currently available information — some of it Russian — a strong circumstantial case can be made to show that Klatt's organization was used by Soviet counterintelligence to pass the Germans disinformation and that Monastery and "Case Klatt" were connected, at least at the top. This does not exclude the possibility that Klatt swindled the Abwehr by passing off newspaper articles or other open source information as intelligence. The salient points for Klatt's organization having been used by Soviet intelligence, and Heine's and Klatt's information having been coordinated, include:

– Many of Klatt's associates were seen visiting the Soviet Legation in Sofia.[5]

– Ira Longin, Klatt's primary source for information on the USSR who was suspected of being a Soviet agent himself, had a close girlfriend who frequented the Soviet legation in Sofia.[6]

– Virtually every Soviet radio playback was a spinoff from the other. Monastery had three phases to it, the first two of which could have been used to feed all or some of the information demands of Klatt's organization.[7]

– The Soviets set up Heine as a communications operator with sub-sources often in the same kind of jobs. Klatt's alleged sources in the USSR were also Red Army communications officers.[8]

– Volume 4 of the recent official *History of Soviet Foreign Intelligence* mentioned the Klatt affair for the first time. The brief description of the Klatt case was placed just after a history of Operation Monastery; although the history does not connect the two, the clear implication is that these operations are related.[9]

– Lev Bezymenskii, a well-known Russian journalist and former GRU officer, in an article based partially on interviews with Sudoplatov, connected Monastery to Klatt's organization by strongly implying that Klatt received "radio reports" from Dem'ianov.[10]

– Although the Soviets apparently have no record of a Joseph Schultz being a Russian agent, Arnold Silver, who was one of Klatt's and Longin's interrogators after the war, believed that Joseph Schultz was one of Klatt's close associates and a Soviet agent.[11]

– The Soviets tried to kidnap both Klatt and his wife several times after the war was over.[12]

– Members of the Cambridge Five — specifically Philby, Blunt, and Cairncross — passed much information on Klatt's organization to the Soviets.[13]

Sudoplatov — the first high-ranking Soviet official to describe the history of both Operations Monastery and Berezino — called Operation Monastery one of the most successful deception games of the war.[14] The classified history of State Security called it "exceptionally important."[15] By early 1943 Operation Monastery resulted in the capture of twenty-three German agents and the seizure of 2 million rubles, several radio sets, as well as ammunition, provisions, and documents.[16] Sudoplatov claimed that Monastery apprehended fifty Abwehr agents, and many were turned into double agents.[17] Sudoplatov's figure might not be exaggerated as the classified history of State Security, without giving exact figures, clearly indicates that, after Stalingrad and Kursk, Monastery was expanded.[18] During the war Gehlen relied heavily on the information that the Soviets provided through Monastery, as did several German generals, including Heinz Guderian.[19] Even twenty years after the war Gehlen still praised the information provided by Max (North).[20]

The classified history of State Security, and even the newly published *History of Soviet Foreign Intelligence* (volume 4), have largely corroborated Sudoplatov's basic contention that Dem'ianov (Max North) actually worked for the Soviets. The limitations of Sudoplatov's memoirs aside — and there are many — should not preclude using his narrative as a baseline for further inquiry into Soviet counterintelligence operations in World War II.[21] His descriptions of Soviet counterintelligence operations during the war, to date, generally have been good, given the limitations of a sharp and lucid eighty-seven-year-old man's memory at the time the book was published.[22] Although Sudoplatov's account of Operations Monastery and Berezino raise numerous questions about the details of how those operations were actually run, Western analyses of German and Soviet military operations as well as analyses of FHO records, support Sudoplatov's statements on the effects of Soviet military disinformation during the war.[23]

Nevertheless, Sudoplatov's memoirs with some additions from volume 4 of the *History of Russian Foreign Intelligence* represent the most detailed account of Operation Monastery to date. Therefore, before describing the "Max South" (Klatt) portion of this complex case, Operation Monastery will be discussed in detail below. In July 1941 Soviet counterintelligence, in cooperation with the GRU, originally designed Operation Monastery to penetrate the Abwehr's agent network inside the USSR by creating an ostensibly pro-German, anti-Soviet organization inside the Soviet Union, code-named Throne. The Soviets believed that German intelligence would not be able to resist supporting such an organization. Throne's mission was to seek contacts with the German High Command and to offer its support. In return, the Germans were to give Throne's leaders lucrative positions in the administrative apparatus of a provisional German government in the USSR, no doubt a credible motive in the eyes of the Germans.[24] State Security reasoned that it then would have at least some agents in key positions in any potential future puppet government established by the Germans.[25]

After the careful screening of numerous agent files, Soviet counterintelligence selected Aleksandr Dem'ianov to make the initial contact with the Germans.[26] Dem'ianov, who had been an agent of Soviet counterintelligence since 1929, possessed an almost perfect background for such an operation. His grandfather had been a leader of the Kuban Cossacks, and his father had been killed in 1915 while serving as an officer in the tsarist army. The younger brother of Dem'ianov's father had served as chief of counterintelligence for the White Army in the Northern Caucasus during the Russian civil war, had been captured by the Cheka, and had died of typhus while in captivity. Dem'ianov's mother was well known in St. Petersburg high society, as well as in Russian émigré circles in France. She had received and rejected several invitations to emigrate there.[27]

In the late 1920s Aleksandr began working as a junior electrical technician and was admitted to a polytechnical institute in Leningrad (now St. Petersburg) but was soon expelled because of his "gentrified origin."[28] Shortly after his expulsion, one of Dem'ianov's friends denounced him for anti-Soviet activities in a letter to the OGPU (the abbreviation for the Soviet secret police at that time). According to Sudoplatov, the OGPU arrested Dem'ianov and found an illegal weapon and some anti-Soviet propaganda during a search of his apartment. The OGPU determined that the weapon belonged to Dem'ianov's friend and that Aleksandr had been sincere in his statements to the OGPU. Nevertheless, the OGPU believed it had a hold over Dem'ianov and that he could be potentially useful to State Security because of his family's connections to émigré circles. Therefore, instead of sentencing him to "administrative exile," the OGPU recruited him as an agent to report on possible terrorist acts by Russian émigrés returning to the USSR.[29]

Dem'ianov's controllers, Viktor Ilyin and Mikhail Makliarskii, used him primarily to report on activities of the foreign and Muscovite cultural elite.[30] In Moscow Dem'ianov easily mixed with writers, actors, poets, film directors, foreign diplomats, and journalists. Through word of mouth he cleverly made use of his family origins to gain the trust and confidence of the Russian émigré community, as well as of numerous individuals professing anti-Soviet or promonarchist sympathies. His family origins could easily be verified through Russian émigré circles all over Europe. Because he did not conceal his family origins, he came into contact with people who took little care to hide their anti-Soviet leanings.[31] Dem'ianov's natural ability to make friends enabled the NKVD to place more people under surveillance and to subsequently recruit more informants.[32] By the outbreak of the war Dem'ianov had more than ten years of experience as an agent, working on more sophisticated operations than those normally assigned to most NKVD informants.

According to Sudoplatov, Dem'ianov's family origins and his high profile within Moscow's cultural elite brought him to the attention of the Abwehr and the Gestapo.[33] Shortly before the outbreak of the war, Aleksandr reported that, during a conversation with a member of the German Trade Mission in Moscow, the German official made casual references to Russian émigrés who had been close to Dem'ianov's family before the Bolshevik Revolution. Ilyin (one of Dem'ianov's Soviet counterintelligence handlers) believed that this was the Germans' first step toward the eventual recruitment of Dem'ianov. Ilyin instructed Dem'ianov to show little interest so as not to appear overeager; the Germans might interpret overeagerness as a sign that Dem'ianov was actually controlled by Soviet counterintelligence.[34] Because of Dem'ianov's contact with the Germans, Makliarskii placed a special stamp in Dem'ianov's file. The stamp indicated that in case of war Dem'ianov would be a prime candidate to work as a Soviet double agent against the Germans. According to Sudoplatov, at this stage the Abwehr assigned Dem'ianov the code name Max; however, one Russian history indicates that Heine might have been assigned the code name during his German espionage training in 1942.[35]

When the war broke out Dem'ianov enlisted in the cavalry, and by July 1941 he had become an agent for Sudoplatov's Directorate of Special Tasks.[36] To increase his anti-Soviet bona fides, Dem'ianov — under Soviet counterintelligence direction — established a relationship with a seventy-year-old former chairman of the Gentry Assembly in Nizhni Novgorod, whom Sudoplatov remembered only by the name of Glebov. Glebov was well known in Russian aristocratic society, and his wife had been a member of the late tsar's court.[37] Makliarskii ensured that any monarchist sympathizers Dem'ianov introduced to Glebov were actually trusted agents of the NKVD. This process continued until Soviet counterintelligence dispatched Dem'ianov behind German lines.[38]

Pretending to be a deserter, Dem'ianov crossed over to German lines in December 1941 near Gzhatsk, 120 miles southwest of Moscow.[39] Inadvertently he had skied over a newly laid Soviet minefield. When the Abwehr captured him they did not believe he was a deserter, largely because he had traversed a minefield unscathed.[40] His German interrogators professed no interest in the anti-Soviet organization Throne, which Dem'ianov claimed to represent, and were disappointed that he did not reveal, or had no knowledge of, Soviet troop deployments. The Germans staged a mock execution to compel him to admit that he was under Soviet control, but Dem'ianov adhered to his story and was subsequently transferred to an Abwehr camp in Smolensk and trained in an apartment in the city. Two German intelligence officers instructed Heine in secret writing (SW), radio operations, and tradecraft in general.[41] When the Germans checked his background more thoroughly, they discovered that he already had been given the code name Max and had been under development by the Abwehr before the war.[42] The Abwehr took no immediate interest in Throne but proceeded to train Dem'ianov as an agent and instructed him to set up an espionage ring in Moscow using his connections.[43]

The Soviets took precautions against possible Abwehr checks. To make Dem'ianov's bona fides even more credible, Soviet counterintelligence briefed Dem'ianov's wife, father-in-law, and his father-in-law's daughter on every detail of Monastery. Dem'ianov's wife was well known in Muscovite theater and cinema circles for her technical work in Mosfilm. Dem'ianov's father-in-law, Professor Berezantsov, served as a primary consultant to the Kremlin clinics, was regarded as a "medical god," and one of the few top-level doctors allowed to have a private practice. He was educated in Germany and spoke fluent English, German, and French. Soviet counterintelligence used Berezantsov's apartment as a meeting place for members of Throne and later for operational meetings related to the conduct of Monastery. The Soviets reasoned that these steps would greatly enhance Dem'ianov's credibility as a principal agent in the eyes of the Germans, because the whole family would appear to be pro-monarchist and anti-Soviet. Dem'ianov's connections would also have enabled him to plausibly report on the activities of the Soviet leadership.[44]

Files of the German "secret services" apparently captured by the Russians after the war show that before Dem'ianov was actually dropped behind Soviet lines the Germans put him up in an apartment in Minsk for three days. Although nobody bothered him, the Germans herded and beat partisans outside his window and had his neighbors not only report on his reactions but tell him of other atrocities the Germans committed against the partisans. The primary goal of this test was to determine whether Dem'ianov was actually in the employ of the Soviet counterintelligence. In March 1942 the Germans parachuted Dem'ianov and an assistant named "Krasnov"deep behind Soviet lines in the vicinity of Arefino, Yaroslavl' oblast'. Heine hurt his knee on landing, turned himself into Soviet counterintelligence, and was transported to Moscow. Dem'ianov gave his description to State Security officers and Krasnov was captured later.[45] This account differs slightly from Sudoplatov's in that, according to Sudoplatov, Heine was dropped with two assistants in a blinding snowstorm, the three men lost contact with one another, and each had to make his way to Moscow on his own. Dem'ianov then managed to contact Soviet counterintelligence, and his two assistants were arrested.[46]

The Soviets quickly established Heine as a principal agent for German intelligence in Moscow and he began to broadcast within two weeks of having landed. For the first four months Heine did not ask for any couriers, new radios, batteries, or money. Finally, in August 1942 he requested a new transmitter.[47] The Germans began to dispatch couriers to contact Max, many of whom were turned by the Soviets. Some couriers were allowed to return to German lines so they could report that Max's network was functioning properly.[48] Under Soviet direction, Dem'ianov created the impression that his group had successfully sabotaged railways near Gorkii. The Soviets also published press articles to indicate that a railway accident had taken place in that area.[49] When two Abwehr agents contacted Max in Moscow to give him a new radio, money, and one-time pads, Dem'ianov's controllers, rather than kill them, employed a team of experts that drugged the couriers, put blanks in their weapons, photographed them, and disabled their explosives to prevent the team from carrying out their sabotage mission. In the morning the two members of the team were allowed to walk around Moscow, and were duly arrested and used in a radio playback. To enhance Heine's credibility, one of the team members who had been arrested was purposely compromised by the Russians. Heine told his German controllers that Shakurov "drank too much, was lazy and afraid." The Germans told Heine to kill him in any way possible. After a suitable period Heine told the Germans that Shakurov had been killed.[50]

Subsequently Dem'ianov ostensibly became a junior communications officer on the staff of the Red Army High Command in Moscow, and the Soviets placed William Fisher in charge of transmitting Dem'ianov's controlled material to the Abwehr.[51] William Fisher — a Soviet intelligence officer since 1927 — was the true name of Colonel Rudolph Abel, the Soviet illegal who was arrested by the FBI on 21 June 1957 in New York City. Abel was exchanged in 1962 for downed U-2 pilot Francis Gary Powers who had been shot down over the USSR in 1960 while on a reconnaissance mission.[52]

Dem'ianov — at the behest of his handlers — ostensibly recruited numerous sub-sources, all of whom the Soviets used as channels for the passage of misleading information. According to Sudoplatov, Operation Monastery contributed significantly to the German army's defeat in at least two cases, largely because Max underreported Soviet strength, and many of his "predicted" offensives, provided to the Germans at critical times, were actually only diversions.[53] Sudoplatov is generally backed up by Western sources. For example:

On the eve of the Battle of Stalingrad Max correctly predicted that the Red Army would launch an offensive against Army Group Center in the area near Rzhev and in the North Caucasus.[54] Zhukov was unaware that Stalin had planned to warn the Germans via Max of the coming Soviet offensive. When Zhukov launched his offensive near Rzhev in July 1942, the result was the loss of 193,000 troops in one month.[55] While Max's credibility was enhanced because he predicted the attack, Army Group Center received reinforcements totaling twelve divisions. Many of these reinforcements had been originally destined for Army Group South. The Soviets achieved their overall objective of diverting German forces away from Stalingrad and misleading the Germans as to their intentions.[56]

Sudoplatov attributes the Soviet victory at the Battle of Kursk in May 1943 to disinformation Max supplied. Dem'ianov sent misleading reports to the Germans, which indicated that, although the Red Army had strong reserves to the east and south of the Kursk salient, they lacked maneuverability.[57] The basic Soviet plan was to let the expected German offensive against the Kursk salient run its course and then rapidly switch over to the offensive.[58] While Gehlen accurately warned OKH of the difficulties it would face in launching an offensive against well-prepared Soviet defenses, as well as the possibility of subsequent Soviet counteroffensives, he underestimated the scale and scope of those counterattacks.[59]

Although Sudoplatov's memoirs contain only two examples (both generally substantiated by Western sources) in which Max provided the Germans with disinformation at critical junctures, Western historians have unearthed some of the more important "Max North" messages, which influenced FHO estimates and OKH operational decisions (the "Max South" [Klatt] messages have not been made public). Probably because of the fluidity of combat operations, and the fact that undoubtedly the Soviets gave the Germans a credible mix of truths, half-truths, and outright lies, FHO estimates are devoid of any speculation on whether the intelligence it was receiving was actually disinformation. Examples of some of the more important Max messages include the following:

Max reported that, at a high-level conference in Moscow on 4 November 1942, Stalin and twelve marshals and generals decided on a careful advance in all operations to avoid heavy losses; loss of ground was deemed unimportant and all planned offensives were to be carried out before 15 November, weather permitting. Main offensives would be in areas near Grozny, Voronezh, Rzhev, and south of Lake Ilmen near Leningrad.[60] The Stalingrad offensive took place on 19 November 1942.[61]

On 27 April 1944 Max reported the results of another high-level military conference in Moscow in which two plans for the coming summer offensive against the Germans were being considered. One plan under consideration was to launch an offensive against the Germans with the objective of taking Brest-Litovsk and reaching the Weichsel River. The other was to launch an offensive against Army Group South Ukraine toward the Balkans. Max stated that Stalin approved the second plan. Gehlen incorporated this report into his estimate on 13 June 1944, stating that the main Soviet offensive would take place in the south and not against Army Group Center. The Soviets launched their 2.4-million-man offensive (Operation Bagration) against Army Group Center on 23 June 1944, which resulted in 450,000 German troops killed, captured, or wounded.[62]

Although much of the Russian material, including Sudoplatov's memoirs, and recent Western scholarship (much of it based on an analysis of FHO estimates) on the Max case all agree that "Max North" information negatively affected the Germans, Sudoplatov's memoirs, as well as other Russian sources' versions of Operation Monastery, contain some critical gaps. For example, the questions of how the Soviets manipulated Dem'ianov's many sub-sources as well as how he went about "recruiting" his "agents" are crucial to assessing the level of Soviet sophistication in making disinformation credible to the Germans.

Details of exactly how Soviet counterintelligence bolstered Dem'ianov's bona fides as well as those of his sub-sources would go a long way toward better assessing the sophistication of German intelligence and counterintelligence in the East.

Sudoplatov's memoirs as well as other Russian sources offer no insights on why Soviet counterintelligence apparently allowed Dem'ianov, after his initial contact in December 1941, to cross German lines twice, once in 1942 and once in 1943, to meet face-to-face with his German controllers.[63] Directing a double agent of Dem'ianov's importance to come into face-to-face contact several times with German counterintelligence officers was extraordinarily risky; those officers easily could have questioned Dem'ianov in detail on his activities, potentially resulting in Dem'ianov's exposure of Monastery. It is even more surprising when a plausible excuse for Dem'ianov's inability to contact the Germans probably could have been easily fabricated.

Such risky behavior on the part of a counterintelligence service with a strong tradition of effectively running long-term double-agent operations suggests that the Soviets were reasonably sure that Heine himself could withstand any renewed German counterintelligence scrutiny. One possible explanation is that the Soviets had an agent in an organization such as Leitstelle I Ost who had detailed knowledge of exactly how Heine was being handled. This would have enabled the Russians to coach Dem'ianov on how best to comport himself to maintain his bona fides, refine their disinformation, and manipulate the operation in such a way so that the Germans would not suspect Dem'ianov or drop contact with him. But, even then, the risk would still be substantial. If Heine would have given up a major operation on the scale of Monastery, further investigation by the Germans might have led to the uncovering of a Soviet agent at the higher levels of Leitstelle I Ost. In short, the Russians risked a great deal for reasons yet to be made public.[64] It begs the question of whether the Russians have systematically omitted specifics on Dem'ianov's activities to purposely avoid disclosing information concerning well-placed Soviet penetrations of the German intelligence services, whether human, technical, or a combination of both.

The only feedback mechanism to gauge the performance of "Max North" (and "Max South") mentioned either by Russian or Western sources originates with the Cambridge Five and the British government. Blunt, Philby, and Cairncross, and the British government, all warned the Russians that the Germans had a widespread agent organization inside the USSR.[65] The Cambridge Five passed summaries of Ultra intercepts, and Philby, Blunt, and Cairncross, in particular, passed the Russians extensive information on British intercepts of Klatt's messages from his station in Sofia.[66] It strains credulity to believe that the only "feedback mechanism" available to the Russians was the "Cambridge Three."

Attributing Sudoplatov's omissions solely to fading memory is problematic; he stated that Operation Monastery "remains the classic classified textbook in counterintelligence tradecraft for cadets at the security schools," which has turned out to be true. The classified *History of State Security* devotes a total of about six sanitized pages to both Monastery and Berezino.[67] Arguably Sudoplatov should have remembered more details of such a prominent operation, especially since he stated that Operation Monastery involved the manipulation of more than fifty Abwehr agents.[68] Given the importance of Dem'ianov to the Soviet military deception program and the war effort in general, it is curious why Sudoplatov, Bezymenskii, as well as other Russian sources omit important details of this operation.

The 1993 publication of Bezymenskii's article on Operation Monastery made a loose but unclear connection between Aleksandr Dem'ianov and Richard Kauder's organization, Luftmeldekopf Suedost in Sofia, which the Germans also code-named Max. Bezymenskii — who based his article on interviews with Sudoplatov — stated that Kauder received "radio reports" from Max, meaning Dem'ianov. However, in his memoirs, which were published in 1994, Sudoplatov did not mention Klatt at all.[69] Nigel West, in his book *The Crown Jewels,* which details the mountains of information the Cambridge Five passed to the Russians over the course of their entire espionage careers, makes a solid case that the Germans might have used the same code name for two different operations.

Even Walter Schellenberg, chief of SD/Ausland (Amt VI), might also have believed that Klatt and Dem'ianov were separate operations, although he did not mention Dem'ianov by name or code name, only by position.[70] Schellenberg said that the "secret service" had connections to two of Marshal Rokossovskii's general staff officers, both of whom expressed doubts about Marshal Rokossovskii's loyalty.[71] Sudoplatov states that Dem'ianov was originally selected as a double agent specifically because of his family's impeccable pro-monarchist credentials, that during the war Dem'ianov was a signals officer and had served on Marshal Rokossovskii's staff.[72] In Operation Berezino (see the next chapter), the Germans were in contact with an "Aleksandr" — probably Dem'ianov or one of his sub-sources — who was a communications officer.[73] These source descriptions strongly suggest that Schellenberg was referring to Dem'ianov or at least sources who might have been offshoots of "Max North." In his memoirs Schellenberg went on to state that after the SD took over the Abwehr in 1944, he inherited a "very important center," the chief of which was a "German Jew" and whose "network penetrated every stratum of society," and who was "able to report large scale strategic plans as well as details of troop movements." Schellenberg went on to say that the "evaluating section of our own Army Supreme Command" attached special significance to some of the reports that originated from senior staff of the Russian army.[74]

Citing a Russian Intelligence Service file on the Klatt organization, West states that, based on an investigation that lasted two years and resulted in a sixty-one-page report by Smersh that went to Stalin in 1947, only an insignificant amount of Klatt's material was genuine. According to West, a longer, more detailed Russian study of Klatt's messages from mid-1942 to January 1945 revealed that 8 percent were authentic. To add credence to the idea that Klatt was a "swindler extraordinaire," West adds that the NKVD concluded that, of the Klatt messages that were true, Ira Longin (aka Lang) — Klatt's primary source of information — acquired the information from Russian émigrés who had interrogated Soviet POWs on behalf of the Germans.[75] Klatt might also have acquired his information from a variety of other sources including, but not limited to, contacts in foreign embassies and possibly even an ingenious scheme in which Klatt bought information from German intelligence officers, corrected it using newspaper articles, and then fabricated believable possibilities using his own imagination and experience or the services of his contacts.[76] Though there is no evidence that Klatt actually carried out such a scheme, a White Russian émigré by the name of Vasilyev did exactly that, remarking, when questioned, that deceiving the Germans was a "safe undertaking" because the amount of dubious intelligence reports in circulation made it difficult to single him out.[77] German author Winfried Meyer, in a book detailing the histories of several Jewish Abwehr agents, states that FHO was independently receiving much of the same information as that provided by Klatt and therefore tended not to question Klatt's bona fides.[78]

Without the Russians making the full truth public and the British or the Americans declassifying Klatt's messages so they can be compared to those of Dem'ianov, the best explanation appears to be that the Germans gave the same name to both Dem'ianov's and Klatt's organizations (different German intelligence organizations ran "Max North" and "Max South") and that Soviet State Security used both as conduits to pass disinformation, albeit possibly using "Max South" somewhat less often than "Max North." Though there is considerable evidence to indicate that Klatt and his associates were substantially less than trustworthy and could easily have passed doctored information to the Abwehr on their own at least some of the time, solid circumstantial evidence — Smersh reports aside — strongly indicates that the opportunity to use Klatt's channel was too good for the Soviets to pass up, especially since the Russians were well aware that the Germans had high regard for Klatt's intelligence.[79] Disinformation is more effective if it reinforces an existing belief. If 8 percent of the thousands of messages on the USSR passed by "Max South" were true, it could still represent a respectable effort by the Soviets to use Klatt's channel for controlled information.

Western efforts to piece together Klatt's organization centered on investigating and analyzing activities of six people who were either Soviet agents or were used to varying degrees as conduits for Soviet disinformation. Richard Kauder, alias Richard Klatt, alias Richard Karmany, a Jewish sports equipment salesman, who marketed himself to the Abwehr in Vienna, played a key role in forwarding "Max South" reports to the Abwehr. Kauder passed on his reports through an Abwehr-supported station in Sofia, which allegedly received intelligence reports from the USSR via a relay in Turkey.[80] Joseph Schultz, allegedly a longtime Soviet agent and friend of Kauder, introduced Kauder to the Abwehr.[81] According to West, the NKVD had no record of Schultz having been a Soviet agent.[82] General Anton Turkul, a former White officer who fought in the Russian civil war, lent Kauder his name to add an air of authenticity to Kauder's claim to the Abwehr that there were high-level sub-sources in the USSR willing to help the Germans.[83] Ira Longin, alias Ilya Lang — another Russian émigré and possible Soviet agent — had served in the White Army and was described by his U.S. Army interrogator as an intelligent liar. He appears to have provided Kauder with at least some of the reports from the USSR, either via Turkey or directly from the Soviet Embassy in Sofia.[84] Two Abwehr officers involved in the operation were Colonel Rudolph Count von Marogna-Redwitz, chief of Ast Vienna, and Lieutenant Colonel Otto Wagner, chief of the Abwehr Kriegsorganization (KO) in Sofia.[85]

Just as the reporting from Dem'ianov and his sub-sources was code-named Max, so, too, was the reporting from Klatt's alleged organization in the USSR (reporting other than that of the USSR was code-named Moritz).[86] The documentary evidence tends to support Bezymenskii's claim that Kauder was receiving reports (not necessarily directly by radio) from the USSR and that the intelligence was high-grade.[87] The modus operandi between Dem'ianov's alleged network and Klatt's is similar.

For example, the former chief of air intelligence at Abwehr I headquarters, Major Brede, stated in his postwar debriefing that the Max organization consisted of sources who were "signalers on Russian signals staffs at high levels." Brede stated that the organization "was said" to consist of a net of radio agents among Russian soldiers who were members of families which had been anti-Soviet. Brede stated that the "reports were said to have been collated in Russia at one or more centers" and that from "these centers the reports were sent via intermediaries to Istanbul and Samsun and then on to Sofia."[88] A declassified postwar study, "The German Intelligence Services and the War," indicates that Kauder forwarded reports to the Abwehr that ostensibly originated from such wide-ranging locations as Leningrad, Kuibyshev, Novorossisk, and the western desert.[89] The army file on Turkul contains an interrogation report of one Franz Bergler who was a member of Kauder's station in Sofia. Bergler said that he overheard Longin, in February 1945, reveal the system for obtaining information from the USSR. According to Bergler, Longin received his information via radio (W/T) from ten to thirteen "well-placed informants, all radio operators with top-level Soviet ministries and units."[90]

However, while all sources agree that Kauder was actually receiving information on the USSR at his sub-station in Sofia and passing that information to the Abwehr, there is considerable confusion among numerous sources about precisely how Kauder received and forwarded his reports.[91] For example, according to Lieutenant Colonel Wagner, Kauder initially received numerous transmissions from the USSR via a radio receiver belonging to the Bulgarian police immediately after the war started.[92] Wagner also believed that Ira Longin — one of General Turkul's right-hand men — provided Kauder with information from "sources" in the USSR.[93] However, Longin — whom Arnold Silver (Longin's interrogator) assessed as a habitual liar — told his interrogators that he never personally received radio messages in Sofia but received them in bars, on street corners, and in an Orthodox Church from two individuals whom Longin ostensibly knew only as "Trotsky" and "Matchenko."[94]

According to Turkul, Longin told him in 1941 that agents were being sent into the USSR and that some were already communicating with Longin via couriers. Turkul also told his interrogators that, during one of Longin's visits in 1942, Longin said that he was receiving radio communications six times weekly from a radio school in the USSR run by one Colonel Samarov (or Samoilov) and that the radios at the school were operating constantly.[95] In November 1946 U.S. Army CIC officers interrogated George Romanoff — a Soviet émigré and journalist who joined Turkul's organization in 1943 — on a variety of issues, one of which was Romanoff's three-week stay in Longin's Sofia apartment in 1942. Romanoff was convinced that Longin was not operating a radio out of the Sofia apartment for the following reasons: during Romanoff's three-week visit, he never left the apartment and therefore was aware of all the activity in the house; there was no place to hide all the radio equipment needed to receive messages from the USSR; Longin had a radio but never listened in; and every morning Longin went to his girlfriend's apartment — who may have been a Soviet agent — to pick up messages for Klatt.[96] According to Longin's unnamed British interrogator, the only Soviet transmissions to Bulgaria that the British could intercept during the war were the traffic from the USSR to the Soviet embassy in Sofia. Romanoff's statements and the lack of British intercepts of Soviet wireless transmissions to receivers in Bulgaria cast substantial doubt on the possibility that Longin himself was receiving his information via wireless transmissions from the USSR.[97]

Based on a review of Silver's interrogations of Kauder and the Abwehr officers who had handled him, the transcripts from the bugging of Kauder's quarters in Oberursel, the extensive U.S. Army investigative file on Turkul, author David Kahn's interviews and correspondence with Wagner, and Major Brede's post-war debriefing, a detailed — albeit incomplete — picture emerges of Kauder's activities.[98] After foiling a Soviet kidnapping attempt of Kauder in January 1946, Allied counterintelligence in Austria sent Kauder, along with General Turkul and Ira Longin, to the U.S. Army interrogation center at Oberursel, near Frankfurt-am-Main.[99] Much of the information below was obtained while Kauder was at Oberursel.

Richard Kauder was born in Vienna on 6 September 1900. His mother was of Jewish origin and his father, a former colonel in the Austro-Hungarian army, converted to Judaism but later decided to be re-baptized as a Christian.[100] The younger Kauder, who was a mechanical engineer by training, became a salesman for various sporting goods firms in Berlin. In 1932 he left Berlin, and from June 1932 to July 1938 he sold real estate in Vienna. In August 1938 he fled from Austria to Hungary because of Jewish persecutions by the Nazis. While living in Budapest, he published a travel atlas for Hungary, but the Hungarian police arrested him in 1939 for lacking a residency permit. The Hungarians turned him over to the German border police, who then turned him over to the Gestapo. The Gestapo briefly questioned him and then released him.[101]

In the summer of 1939 Kauder's mother unwittingly made the acquaintance of an Abwehr officer. When she told him that her son was living in Budapest without proper papers, the Abwehr officer offered to help. He contacted Kauder in Budapest and asked him to come to Vienna to meet some people. When Kauder discovered that the Germans wanted him to work for the Abwehr, he turned down the offer and was rearrested by the Gestapo in December 1940.[102]

On 4 February 1940 Colonel Count Rudolph Marogna-Redwitz summoned Kauder from prison and again asked him to work for the Abwehr. Kauder agreed on the condition that his mother, who lived in Vienna, not be persecuted.[103] Kauder, an opportunist, may also have wanted to become "aryanized"; he had complained to the Abwehr that his application for aryanization had not been acted on. According to Major Brede, the application was finally turned down.[104] The Abwehr provided Kauder with the required documentation and assigned him to work for Abwehr I Luft in Ast Vienna. His first assignment, in May

1940, was to travel to Sofia to establish contacts and spot potential agents who could obtain order-of-battle information on the Bulgarian air force.[105]

In June 1940 Kauder met Ira Longin in Budapest. Both had been in prison together when Kauder had been arrested for lacking a residency permit. Kauder asked Longin — probably because Longin was a member of a Soviet émigré organization — about the possibilities of obtaining intelligence on the Soviet air force.[106] Longin stated that he would have to seek the approval of his chief, General Anton Turkul, to work for the Abwehr. After several conversations with Abwehr officers in Ast Vienna, and after obtaining Turkul's approval, the Abwehr issued Longin documents under the name of Ilya Lang. Longin and Kauder then set up what became known as Luftmeldekopf Suedost (air intelligence post, southeast).[107] Lieutenant Colonel Wagner, chief of the Abwehr KO in Sofia, was to have administrative control over it. The Germans codenamed the transmitters "Max and Moritz," since one was emanating from the Kremlin and one from behind the Urals. When Moritz eventually dropped out of the picture, the Germans gave the code name Max to the entire operation. Kauder claimed, in one of his interrogation reports, that the Moritz messages numbered about 1,000 over the course of the war; they concerned the Near East and Anglo-American matters, and Berlin assessed the reports as basically worthless. According to Kauder, Longin said that he obtained the reports from a Russian émigré. According to Kahn, Kauder was put in charge of the radio.[108]

Although the interrogation reports of Kauder contained in the U.S. Army file on Turkul do not mention Joseph Schultz, Arnold Silver believed that Schultz was an important figure in Kauder's organization. According to Silver's article — which was probably based on his memory and his extraordinary knowledge of the case — in the summer of 1941 Schultz, a friend of Kauder, introduced Kauder to General Anton Turkul in Vienna.[109] Turkul told Kauder that he could activate friends in the USSR who could report on Soviet military movements. Schultz then arranged to have Kauder meet with the chief of the Abwehr in Vienna, Count Marogna-Redwitz. Kauder impressed Marogna-Redwitz, and the Abwehr agreed to hire Kauder on a temporary basis. Kauder then met Ira Longin through Turkul, and, without asking probing questions, Kauder accepted Longin's claim that he had a network in the USSR already in place and could run it from Istanbul.[110]

Kauder-Klatt's operation began to produce substantial results almost immediately after the war started. Ast Vienna's explanation for the surge in reporting was that, in anticipation of the war, Klatt had managed to brief his sources on wartime requirements, so when the war broke out messages started to come into Klatt's station.[111] Lieutenant Colonel Wagner raised suspicions about Kauder's operation to Admiral Canaris, chief of the Abwehr, almost as soon as Kauder established Luftmeldekopf Suedost. Canaris, citing the objections of the Luftwaffefuehrungsstab (general staff of the German air force), instructed Wagner to abstain from interfering in Kauder's activities. Finally, in late 1942 Wagner became so disgusted that he ordered Sonderfuehrer (specialist) Kleinhampel of Abwehr IIIF in Prague to conduct an unofficial investigation into Kauder's activities.[112]

Kleinhampel could not identify any radio station in Bulgaria handling Kauder's traffic. When Kleinhampel confronted Kauder, Kauder explained that the messages were transmitted to a station in Samsun, Turkey, then transmitted by telephone to Istanbul, and from there by railroad and courier to Sofia.[113] Further investigation by Kleinhampel revealed that to establish a telephone connection from Samsun to Istanbul would have taken four weeks and that railroad transportation from Istanbul to the Bulgarian border was not feasible because an important bridge had been destroyed. Therefore the question still remained as to how Kauder was receiving his information on such a timely basis.[114] The German radio counterintelligence service noted that there were no wireless transmissions at all on the days that Klatt claimed he received radio transmissions.[115]

Kleinhampel also discovered that some of Kauder's close associates had been seen drinking with a Soviet intelligence officer — who was assigned to the Soviet Legation in Sofia — in the bar in the basement of the Royal Theater. Kleinhampel's investigation further revealed that Ira Longin had been seen leaving the Soviet Legation in 1943 and that Kauder's girlfriend had daily contact with the same Soviet intelligence officer who had been drinking with Kauder's associates.[116]

Wagner also did not view this as conclusive proof that Longin and Kauder were receiving their information directly from the Soviet Legation in Sofia. In 1944 Wagner ran a Hungarian military attaché named Otto Hatz as a double agent against the Soviets to test the origin of Kauder's material. Hatz was recalled from his post in Turkey and arrested by the Gestapo on suspicion of working for the Soviet intelligence service. Wagner convinced the Gestapo to release him, and Wagner gave Hatz the task of collecting military information. During May and June 1944 both Kauder and Hatz produced identical reports that conveyed the impression that certain Soviet units were going to retreat and that the Germans should hold their positions. This tends to indicate that the Soviets might have been somewhat careless; such a practice would have run the risk of compromising an operation by giving two double agents in different parts of the world the exact same report.[117]

Unfortunately there is no mention in Wagner's interrogation report of how Hatz obtained his information or on the details of any disinformation passed by the Soviets. Nevertheless, Kleinhampel's investigation raises more questions than it answers on the Soviet handling of the case. In a country well known to be pro-German, why were Soviet intelligence officers having what appears to be almost overt contact with their agents?[118]

According to volume 4 of *The History of Soviet Foreign Intelligence*, the NKGB appears to have been quite successful in Bulgaria. Prior to the outbreak of the war, the residency in Sofia recruited an agent network close to Bulgarian leaders that enabled the Soviets to read at least some Bulgarian communications channels.[119] The Soviets also recruited agents on Bulgarian counterintelligence surveillance teams.[120] Following Barbarossa, the Sofia residency was the only legal residency in Hitler's Europe, and, as expected, the Germans and their Bulgarian allies set about attacking the Soviet intelligence presence and acquired a highly accurate picture of it.[121]

Nevertheless, Soviet foreign intelligence managed to recruit a source, apparently code-named "Grey," and generally supported the underground to prepare the way for Soviet forces. Grey represented an ally of Germany and elicited important information from the German military attaché in Sofia on the direction of the German attack toward Stalingrad. Grey was probably Japanese, as he acquired significant information on the "influence of the Germans on the Japanese leadership."[122] Several credible sources have intimated that Klatt received at least some of his information from a well-connected Japanese journalist strongly suspected of being in the employ of Japanese intelligence. A 15 July 1946 U.S. Army memo commenting on an analysis of the interrogation of Klatt noted that when Klatt's mistress was interrogated by the Russians, the Russians displayed a deep interest in a Japanese journalist by the name of Enomoto.[123]

In short, although Luftmeldekopf Suedost was transferred to Budapest in September 1943, there was ample opportunity for the Russians to have planted controlled information in Klatt's organization in Sofia, despite claims by the NKVD or Smersh that they could not find Longin's contact in the Soviet Embassy there.[124] The Russians knew the mechanics of how the organization worked and that the Germans thought highly of at least some of Klatt's information on Russia and recruited excellent sources in Bulgaria. The Russians, through Schulze-Boysen and no doubt others, knew that Abwehr I Luft (which ran Klatt) was a hotbed of anti-Hitlerism. All this, combined with the fact that Klatt's associates and Longin were known to have had contacts with Soviet intelligence officers in Sofia, and the fact that Russian émigré circles were a high priority target for Soviet intelligence since the early days of the Bolshevik Revolution, call into serious doubt the NKVD claim that Russian intelligence or counterintelligence had little or nothing to do with Klatt's operation.

Klatt and his associates sent Ast Vienna thousands of reports, many of them accurate and timely. According to Klatt's first interrogation, he sent 3,000 reports to Ast Vienna in 1942 alone, 3,700 in 1943, and 4,500 in 1944.[125] Even if these numbers are exaggerated, there can be no doubt that Klatt's station generated thousands of reports over the course of the war, not all of them intercepted and decrypted by the British or the Russians. Interrogations of Klatt and Longin revealed that most of the questions asked by OKW were answered in two to five days.[126] Rolf Wodarg, former chief of the 1c of OKL, told his interrogators that a study of the Max reports (meaning Klatt's information) showed that, between the summer of 1943 and the summer of 1944, thirty of the thirty-four reports studied proved to be "absolutely accurate," one partially correct, and the other three inaccurate. According to Wodarg, the Max reports from Klatt were highly valued by OKL, and many Soviet air operations were predicted a month in advance.[127] Heinrich Walter Viktor von Westarp, a senior Abwehr officer assigned to Abwehr I/t Luft, said that Colonel Baron von Marogna-Redwitz, chief of Ast Vienna, once examined fifty-six of Klatt's more important reports and concluded that all but four contained accurate information on Soviet troop movements.[128] Westarp went on to state that, in his opinion, Klatt was being used as a channel for controlled information, most of which was true but deceptive at critical moments.

It would have been a relatively simple process for Sudoplatov's organization, or even the GRU, occasionally to have transmitted "feed material" to the residency in Sofia via secure communications — complete with false but plausible sourcing — with instructions to make sure that Klatt, Longin, or any of their associates receive the controlled information through a source (or sources) working for the Russians. In fact, during one of Klatt's interrogations on 28 January 1947, the interrogator told Klatt that they had information that a Soviet military attaché in Sofia by the name of Yakovlyev — who had been in the Soviet Legation in Sofia throughout the war — gave a Russian (possibly a Russian woman by the name of Alexandrova) messages marked "Fuer Ira Lang — Klatt." Although the interrogator did not tell Klatt, the source of this information came from inside the Bulgarian intelligence service.[129] Klatt, of course, denied it.

During Arnold Silver's interrogation of senior SD officer Wilhelm Hoettel in May 1946, Hoettel said that Klatt received information on "Russian Intelligence from 1942 to 1944 from Bucharest and Budapest" from an individual named Kowalewsky. According to Hoettel, Kowalewsky resided at Klatt's residence in Budapest and worked with the Japanese journalist Enomoto. The same report noted that, according to Lieutenant Colonel Freund of Amt VI of the RSHA, one of Klatt's "star reporters" in Istanbul, Schenschin, was a Soviet agent.[130]

Smersh might not have known about a "notional" offshoot of Monastery to which some of the "Max South" messages could have been sourced. There would have been no wireless transmissions, and Smersh might not have known about agents run in Sofia by the NKGB or even the GRU. Many of Dem'ianov's sources in Monastery were notional, that is, they did not exist but the Germans thought they did. Klatt's and Longin's sources inside the USSR did not actually exist, but the descriptions of the kind of sources claimed (communicators) strongly resemble the notional positions that Dem'ianov used in Operations Monastery and Berezino. That the Germans gave both Klatt and Dem'ianov the same operational code name for similar kinds of reporting is also intriguing. That Klatt was a swindler, liar, blackmarketeer, and generally unreliable might not have deterred the Soviets from using his organization at critical junctures to ensure that the Germans would receive the desired controlled information. After all, the Russians knew that critical elements of the German High Command valued the channel highly. The "Klatt Buero," and its colorful associates, at a minimum, made tempting targets.

Wagner informed Canaris of the results of Kleinhampel's investigation, but both Canaris and Piekenbrock again refused to shut down Kauder's operations.[131] The controversy dragged on for much of the war. FHO praised the Max reports as "indispensable," even though Wagner raised the possibility that Max's information might have been under Soviet control.[132] In fact, FHO was so impressed with Max's information that it required Max reports to be forwarded daily from Vienna to FHO.[133] Wagner again raised his suspicions concerning Kauder in the autumn of 1944 at a conference chaired by Walter Schellenberg — then head of all German intelligence — and attended by representatives of the German High Command.[134] Schellenberg ordered a formal investigation into Klatt's activities. The Abwehr was split as to whether the Russians were using Klatt as a double agent. To solve the dilemma, Schellenberg showed Heinz Guderian (who had become chief of OKH after the 20 July 1944 attempt on Hitler's life) a few of Klatt's reports. Guderian said that to close down the Max organization was an act of "criminal irresponsibility."[135] The High Command still could not be swayed by Wagner's arguments and instead insisted that Kauder be kept on because his material was judged to be authentic.[136] At the conference Schellenberg initially sided with the High Command, but, according to Wagner, Schellenberg eventually changed his mind late in the war.[137]

In 1947 Silver and Klop Ustinov, one of the top interrogators of MI-6 and father of the actor Peter Ustinov, questioned Kauder at length regarding whether he was a Soviet double agent.[138] After Kauder attempted suicide, his will to resist was shaken but not completely broken. Silver and Ustinov concluded that Kauder had not been a Soviet agent but had suspected early on that, through Schultz, the Soviets were using his network to pass disinformation to the

Germans. However, Kauder had to keep his suspicions to himself for fear that the Abwehr would withdraw its protection of him and the Gestapo would then arrest him.[139]

Kauder told his interrogators that Joseph Schultz, his longtime friend, had admitted to him just before the end of the war to being a Soviet agent since 1939 and to conspiring with the Soviets to fabricate Kauder's network.[140] According to Kauder, who attributed the information to Schultz, Turkul and Longin had not been knowing conspirators but were merely figureheads used to enhance the bona fides of the network inside the USSR.[141]

That numerous unresolved issues remain regarding how and under what conditions the "Max South" traffic reached the Germans in no way diminishes the impact of the information on German military operational decision making. Few high-ranking German military officers questioned the bona fides of the "Max North" or "Max South" information, including Gehlen, one of the most innovative German intelligence officers during the war.[142] Gehlen, as well as other German officers, could not conceive of the Soviets engaging in strategic deception on such a scale.[143] Nazi arrogance accounts for some of the German mistakes. The German inability to acquire high-level bona fide penetrations of any major Soviet governmental or Party organization capable of providing details on Soviet strategic deception planning cost the lives of tens of thousands of German soldiers and significantly contributed to the pace of the Soviet victory.[144]

One of the most significant questions to be answered, not only for Operation Monastery but also for the entire Soviet offensive counterintelligence effort against the Germans, concerns the nature of the Soviet feedback mechanism for monitoring the success of their offensive counterintelligence and deception efforts.[145] Sudoplatov mentions, as does Bezymenskii, that the Soviets received several indicators from the British that both "Max North" and "Max South" were working. The Soviets received feedback on Dem'ianov's information from Blunt, Philby, and Cairncross, all of whom provided the Soviets with copies of the Ultra intercepts and decrypts containing information that originated from both "Max North" and "Max South." The Soviets may have also received various versions of Max feed material from their agents who were members of the Red Orchestra. The British even warned the Soviets officially that the Germans had a highly placed source in Moscow.[146] That these were the only Soviet feedback mechanisms, other than routine collection and analysis of military intelligence (aerial reconnaissance, POW interrogations, signals intercepts, patrol debriefings, captured documents, etc.), defies logic, especially in light of the Soviets allowing Dem'ianov to meet face-to-face with the Germans twice after his initial contact.

Nevertheless, despite frustrating gaps in the accounts of both these operations, it is clear that both the Germans and the Russians highly valued the contributions of Operation Monastery (Max North) and that the Germans were also impressed — rightly or wrongly — with the information provided by Richard Kauder's organization (Max South). German intelligence was ultimately convinced it had good sources at the higher levels of the Soviet army and that information was factored into OKH operational planning much to its detriment. However, what is most important about these two cases — other than that they were assigned the same code name and that the Germans relied heavily on them — is that both operations have more than coincidental similarities in the ostensible positions of the Russian sub-sources. It is nothing short of astounding that both Kauder and Lognin could concoct similar stories for their sub-sources that are remarkably like those used by the NKVD/NKGB for Dem'ianov in Operation Monastery. This means that there is a high probability that the Soviet equivalent of the British Twenty Committee coordinated not only the feed material for both operations but also the cover stories for the various "sources."

Operations Berezino and Zeppelin

The three-phased operational game "Monastery," "Courier," and "Berezino," which was conducted by the central apparatus of the NKVD-NKGB of the USSR from the end of 1941 to 9 May 1945 was exceptionally important in the plan for disinforming enemy intelligence organs, and the exposure and halting of his subversive activity.

Top Secret History of the State Security Organs, 1977

On the other hand, there is a great probability that in the forests near Berezino, there is indeed a larger group of stranded German soldiers who under no circumstances can be let without support.

German intelligence report on Operation Scherhorn, 1944

Operation Berezino (German code names Rennstrecke and Scherhorn) began in the late summer of 1944, when Stalin ordered Operation Monastery to be expanded.[1] The Soviet General Staff wanted to persuade OKH that German units left behind after the destruction of Army Group Center in the summer of 1944 still retained the ability to sabotage Soviet supply and communications lines.[2] According to Sudoplatov, such an operation was intended to entice the Germans to divert scarce resources to support units trapped behind Soviet lines in the mistaken hope of inflicting damage in the Soviet rear, and facilitating the return of those trapped units to German lines.[3]

The basic operational concept devised by Soviet counterintelligence centered on using radio playbacks to create the impression that the remnants of an obscure German unit, commanded by Lieutenant Colonel Heinrich Scherhorn, was attempting to make its way back to German lines. Scherhorn had been captured on 9 July 1944 near Minsk, and his unit, the 36th Security Regiment of the 286th Security Division, had been totally destroyed. The Soviets based their operation on some degree of truth. A group of 1,800 German soldiers was defending a position near the Berezino River. In a two-week battle the Soviets destroyed the entire force, and the 200 remaining troops, one of whom was Scherhorn, became POWs. The Soviets chose Scherhorn largely because they believed that his unit was not well known to the Germans, and therefore this would make it harder for the Germans to verify the various Soviet-manufactured "facts" about the group.[4]

The Soviets recruited Scherhorn while he was in captivity and used him as a figurehead to facilitate the doubling of agents the Germans dispatched to aid the Scherhorn group. By using Aleksandr Dem'ianov — who was, of course, already well known to the Germans — as a cut-out between Army Group Center and the Scherhorn group, Soviet counterintelligence induced the Germans to divert substantial resources to aid the remnants of a nonexistent unit trapped behind Soviet lines. This long-term Soviet double-agent effort succeeded despite initial German suspicions that the operation might have been controlled by the Soviets.

An NKGB evaluation of the results of Operation Berezino revealed that, from September 1944 to May 1945, Soviet counterintelligence captured a total of 25 German agents and intelligence officers, 13 radio sets, 225 "cargo packs" containing uniforms, ammunition, food, and medicine, and more than 2 million rubles.[5] Thirty-two NKGB officers and 255 servicemen participated in the operation.[6] During the same period the Luftwaffe flew at least 39 sorties and, by the time the operation was over, OKH promoted Lieutenant Colonel Heinrich Scherhorn to colonel and awarded him the Knight's Cross.[7] Dem'ianov — again the primary agent in this operation — was awarded the Red Star, and his wife, who was also an NKGB agent, was given the medal "For Combat Service."[8] Sudoplatov claimed that the Soviets used Operation Berezino to feed disinformation to the Germans regarding ostensible sabotage operations conducted against the Red Army by Scherhorn's unit.[9]

Dem'ianov, who was the principal agent in Operation Monastery, also played a crucial role in deceiving the Germans regarding the "plight" of Lieutenant Colonel Scherhorn's unit. In July 1944 Dem'ianov, using the name "Aleksandr," reported to Soviet counterintelligence that the Germans believed that significant remnants of their units in the forests of Belorussia were cut off and were attempting to reunite with German forces.[10] The Soviets confirmed Aleksandr's reporting through other agents behind German lines and through radio intercepts.[11] On 19 August 1944 *Agenten-Funktrupp* (translated as agent radio-troop) Flamingo relayed a message from the Throne organization in Moscow to FAK 103.[12] The message contained information — attributed to Aleksandr's ostensible conversation with a captured German corporal — about a German unit, somewhat larger than a regiment, commanded by a Lieutenant Colonel Heinrich Scherhorn and hidden in the forests of Berezino. According to Aleksandr's message, the unit was unwilling to surrender and wanted to break through to German lines. The breakout was supposedly complicated by the ostensible presence of fifty wounded soldiers and a shortage of ammunition, medicine, and food.[13]

Credibly fabricating the plight of a regiment-size unit using primarily radios for communications, and sustaining such a deception for nine months, demonstrates the skill with which Soviet counterintelligence carried out Operation Berezino. Dem'ianov's communications system provides a glimpse of the complexity of such an undertaking. Many of the messages Dem'ianov sent to Scherhorn, which were relayed by *Agenten-Funktrupp* Flamingo, were signed "Throne" (*Prestol,* in Russian).[14] Throne was the code name the Soviets assigned to a nonexistent organization in Operation Monastery, notionally consisting of several pro-German Soviet officers who were allegedly Aleksandr's subsources.[15] The FHO report on Scherhorn clearly identifies "Aleksandr" as the radio operator for *Agenten-Funktrupp* Flamingo. It also indicates that Flamingo was based in Moscow, originally dispatched by FAK 103, and was the relay for messages concerning Scherhorn originating with the Soviet-controlled organization Throne, which was also based in Moscow.[16]

Knowledge of the details of Dem'ianov's communications system in Operation Berezino becomes even more important, especially in light of two of Gehlen's biographers — albeit unwittingly — having raised the possibility that Dem'ianov played a major role in yet another operation involving agent radiotroop Flamingo.[17] They cite Flamingo as an operation involving a Communist Party functionary named Minzhinskiy, who had been captured by the Germans, recruited by Baun's organization, and dispatched back to Moscow to work for the Germans as an agent. However, according to Hoehne and Cookridge, Minzhinskiy was in contact with Flamingo's radio operator, a man named "Aleksandr." If true, this indicates that Dem'ianov might also have been a relay for Minzhinskiy's information, especially as Dem'ianov ostensibly had several assignments as a radio operator.[18]

However, neither the Soviets nor Sudoplatov himself have explained how Aleksandr's pattern of assignments was manipulated to deflect German suspicion. For example, it is curious that a communications officer would interrogate a German POW, as Aleksandr's relayed message of 19 August 1944 indicated.[19] That a communications officer of Dem'ianov's caliber could be assigned to a construction battalion, or that a communications officer could travel back and forth from the battle zone to Moscow, sometimes with his wife, looks — at least in hindsight — inherently suspicious given the constant attention that the Soviets paid to security.[20] Dem'ianov had several ostensible assignments, and, at least in his role as Max, his assignments appear to have had a degree of consistency that would probably have been believable to the Germans.[21]

Aleksandr's relayed message of 19 August 1944 describing the plight of the Scherhorn group further explained that, although the German corporal had not yet provided exact information on the location of the unit, Aleksandr thought that the information had been important enough to make a special duty-related trip to Moscow, just to report the information on Scherhorn's unit to Army Group Center. The message also indicated that Aleksandr, through his agents in Berezino, could contact the Scherhorn group should the Germans be interested.[22]

Aleksandr's information generated considerable skepticism and confusion in Army Group Center's headquarters.[23] The Germans knew, of course, that a great number of their soldiers had been lost in the forests of Belorussia as a result of the recent Soviet offensive. Other than the obvious questions of why a German corporal would impart such detailed information to a Soviet communications officer and whether the message was a Soviet ploy, the Germans also had additional doubts about Scherhorn's identity. They wondered whether the Scherhorn mentioned in the message was the same man listed in German army records as the commander of the 675th Rifle Battalion; whether the Soviets possessed only the papers of a Lieutenant Colonel Scherhorn and were using them to lure the Germans into a radio playback; and whether Aleksandr was trustworthy despite the Germans having used him in other operations.[24]

After lengthy discussions Colonel Worgitzky, chief of military intelligence for Army Group Center, decided that the probability of a sizable group of German soldiers stranded behind Soviet lines was high, and that Army Group Center absolutely could not leave them without supplies.[25] Therefore, on 25 August 1944, FAK 103, which was operating in Army Group Center's area, transmitted a message to agent radio-troop Flamingo asking Aleksandr — probably because of his contacts, his access, and "proven reliability" — to contact Scherhorn. The message asked Flamingo for Scherhorn's exact position and informed Flamingo that Army Group Center intended to support the isolated group by dropping supplies and sending in radio operators to establish direct communications. The message also asked Flamingo to suggest the best location for an airdrop and the best way for the radio operators to avoid being apprehended; the operators were to be dressed in Soviet uniforms.[26]

On 30 August 1944 Flamingo informed Army Group Center (via FAK 103) that Aleksandr planned to contact Scherhorn, and that Aleksandr needed money and a radio to accomplish his mission.[27] Army Group Center waited for a more detailed reply and received it on 6 September. Flamingo's message indicated that Aleksandr had actually contacted the group, which was short of ammunition, food, medicine, and supplies; however, the group still had the will to fight its way back to German lines. Flamingo gave a detailed description of the group's position (thirty miles northwest of Berezino), the exact location for the airdrop as well as the signals to be used in case of danger.[28]

After the Soviets passed the Germans the coordinates for an airdrop, Soviet counterintelligence dispatched sixteen officers to the area. The group consisted of, among others, Sudoplatov's deputy, Leonid Aleksandrovich Eitingon (the architect of Trotsky's assassination), Major William Fisher (later known as Rudolph Abel), Lieutenant Isidor Makliarskii, Iakov Serebrianskii (who was one of Sudoplatov's department chiefs), and Lieutenant Colonel Scherhorn. Serebrianskii, Makliarskii, and Eitingon recruited Scherhorn and his radio operators while they were in captivity. Eitingon wrote most of Aleksandr's and Scherhorn's messages, and the Soviets used German POWs, who had been recruited to create the impression of the existence of an actual German camp, complete with dugouts and tents.[29] On 14 September 1944 FAK 103 told "Aleksandr" via Flamingo that the first airdrop would take place on the night of 15 September.[30] The Germans would attempt to verify the existence of the Scherhorn group and to establish direct communication with it.

As planned, the Germans dropped the supplies, along with two German agents, one of whom was a radio operator. However, shortly after landing, the Soviets caught one of the agents along with the radio, and the other agent escaped.[31] The Soviets sent two short messages to buy time and to placate Army Group Center's worries over whether the whole operation was a hoax; the Germans, however, still remained suspicious. On 20 September, just as the Germans planned to cease supporting Scherhorn, Army Group Center received a detailed message via Flamingo, ostensibly originating from Scherhorn himself.[32]

The message provided more details on the Scherhorn group. It said that Scherhorn had established personal contact with Aleksandr, that the group now totaled more than 2,500 men (including 16 officers, some of whom Scherhorn mentioned by name but who had been previously captured by the Soviets), and that it had 884 wounded soldiers and needed more medicine, explosives, ammunition, and clothes, as well as a doctor. In addition, Scherhorn stated that the group needed German radio operators, two radios, and maps. He mentioned that he had arranged a series of supply drops with "a Russian captain" and also wanted to know the best location to break through to German lines. Scherhorn informed Army Group Center that both agents who had been dropped on the night of 15 September had arrived, but he did not explain why the agents had not yet contacted Army Group Center via Flamingo.[33]

A quick follow-up message from Flamingo to Army Group Center further explained what reportedly happened to the two agents. Ostensibly the parachute attached to the radio did not open, and the radio was damaged beyond repair upon landing. The follow-up message also explained that the lack of communication was because Aleksandr was unable to travel to Moscow to relay his messages; Aleksandr instead had helped one of the two agents with his papers so that the agent could travel to Moscow himself to facilitate better contact with Army Group Center. Aleksandr also asked for more money and another radio.[34]

The 20 September message and the follow-up to it caused the Germans even more concern. For example, the Germans wondered that if the Soviets actually had captured one of the agents, did they use his papers to send one of their trusted agents to Aleksandr? The Germans noted that Aleksandr did not personally know the agent and that Scherhorn had mentioned names of officers in his "group" who were known to Army Group Center to have been in Soviet captivity. Shortly after receipt of the 20 September message and its follow-up, Army Group Center sent two other messages to Scherhorn promising the supplies and men, but also asking pointed questions about the fate of the second agent and the location of Aleksandr, and requesting that Aleksandr describe his observations while traveling to and from Moscow. The German sense of duty, and the potential political and military value of rescuing 2,500 troops trapped behind Soviet lines, proved stronger than the suspicions surrounding the operation. Therefore Army Group Center continued its quest to verify the existence of the Scherhorn group.[35]

On 7 October 1944 the Germans dropped a carefully selected radio operator and supplies without having informed Scherhorn in advance, hoping to confirm the group's existence. On landing, however, the radio operator — an individual using the name Del'nikov — had a change of heart, surrendered to the Soviets, and turned over his codebook, his transmission schedule, and his safe arrival instructions. Under the close scrutiny of Soviet counterintelligence, Del'nikov informed the Germans of his "safe arrival." In Army Group Center's view, direct daily communications had now been established with Scherhorn. However, Army Group Center was still not completely satisfied. On 9 October the Luftwaffe dropped two radio-equipped SS agent teams — both consisting of four men — for the express purpose of identifying Scherhorn's group. They, too, were captured.[36]

One of the SS radio operators, an individual using the name Vedenin, had informed Soviet counterintelligence of his group's arrival, unbeknownst to other group members. As Soviet motorcyclists were approaching the group's position, Vedenin shot his comrades and surrendered. Members of the other SS group were also captured. One group did not report back at all, and the other radioed back that they were engaged in a firefight with Soviet troops. The members of the SS agent teams who were dropped behind Soviet lines to rescue Scherhorn were disguised as members of a work battalion made up of German POWs, although a few members of the groups were documented as sergeants in the Red Army. In early October 1944 the Soviets finally captured the radio operator who disappeared after he was dropped behind Soviet lines on 15 September. However, the Soviets had previously sent a message to Army Group Center stating that he probably was still trying to return to his unit.[37]

Despite lingering doubts, the Germans continued to drop supplies, men, and equipment. Army Group Center dispatched an air force officer to supervise the building of a runway to evacuate Scherhorn's wounded. On 4 November Army Group Center received a message from a member of the missing SS group indicating that he had been in a firefight with Soviet troops. In several more messages Scherhorn repeatedly requested food and ammunition, and even reported successfully attacking a Soviet supply column destroying more than 100 vehicles and acquiring 70 tons of foodstuffs.[38]

To sustain German interest, Soviet counterintelligence began sending messages to Army Group Center indicating that Scherhorn would have to cancel some airdrops because of approaching Soviet troops. The messages also told Army Group Center that the "Scherhorn group" was planning to organize into two groups to reconnoiter the best route for breaking through to German lines, and that construction of the runway was suspended because of weather and the proximity of Soviet troops. Although supply drops continued at a trickle — largely because of a lack of resources — it nevertheless became apparent over time that a rescue mission was impossible.[39]

Despite the attention of the German High Command and Hitler's approval to allow Otto Skorzeny — the infamous commander of all German commando units during the war — to escort the Scherhorn group back to German lines, the plan was dropped and Scherhorn was not rescued. On 23 March 1944 Hitler sent a message to Scherhorn announcing the promotions of some of the group's officers, previously recommended by Scherhorn. Hitler also awarded Scherhorn the Knight's Cross and promoted him to colonel. The Soviets continued the radio playback up to the end of the war. They fabricated the group's marching route, its casualties, and its "approach" to the East Prussian frontier. The operation ended on 5 May 1945, when the Germans sent a message to Scherhorn stating that they could no longer support his efforts. Colonel Scherhorn remained in Soviet captivity until 1949, when he was returned to Germany — having been one of the few surviving German witnesses to Operation Berezino.[40]

The Soviets spared no effort to convince the Germans that a group under the command of Lieutenant Colonel Scherhorn actually existed. For example, Soviet State Security personnel who spoke German were relocated to the area around Berezino and dressed in German uniforms. At Soviet direction, Scherhorn initially talked to the captured German parachutists to reinforce the illusion that the group actually existed. After having talked to Scherhorn and while walking along through the woods to their bivouac, the German parachutists were captured by actual NKVD security troops and taken into custody. The Soviets had also set up communications with radio-intercept posts, security troops, and anti-aircraft units that had been deployed around the drop zone.[41] Every time the Germans asked detailed questions about various officers, the Soviets located them, isolated them from the rest of the prisoner population, and obtained the required information.[42] At one point in the operation, *Oberleutnant* Barfeldt, commander of FAK 103, planned a personal visit to Scherhorn. However, on landing at an airfield to meet Scherhorn, Barfeldt was in a hurry and jumped out of the aircraft as it was still taxiing. A propeller blade cut off his head. The crew recovered Barfeldt's body and the aircraft took off immediately, possibly saving Operation Berezino from being compromised to the Germans.[43]

Attributing the success of Operation Berezino solely to German credulity fails to take into account the sophistication and complexity of such an operation. The Soviets selected Scherhorn precisely because he was not well known to the Germans. They used Aleksandr because of his proven reliability as Max and possibly because of his role in transmitting information from Minzhinskiy to the Germans. The Soviets knew that the Germans praised troops who escaped encirclements or prisons, showered them with promotions and decorations, and often extended their leaves for rest and recuperation. The Russians were so thorough that they checked German food drops for poison by testing the contents on dogs.[44] Therefore the Soviets offered the Germans an attractive opportunity to significantly boost the morale of German troops if the Scherhorn group had been rescued. While the Soviet operation was not perfect in every detail, it was good enough to overrule nagging German doubts about whether to support the nonexistent Scherhorn group.

In August 1942 Heinrich Himmler (chief of the SS) and Reinhard Heydrich (chief of the RSHA) put pressure on Walter Schellenberg (head of SD/Ausland of the RSHA) to improve the intelligence collected on the USSR and to form reconnaissance and partisan groups similar to those employed by Soviet intelligence and counterintelligence against the Germans. Despite the success of the German armies, both Himmler and Heydrich expressed concern over the quality and quantity of the information obtained on the USSR, as well as over the increasing threat posed by Soviet partisans.[45]

Schellenberg told his U.S. Army interrogators that partisan attacks on German convoys became so frequent and menacing that even members of Himmler's staff had been killed during some attacks. Therefore Himmler believed that Soviet partisan operations had demonstrated their effectiveness so well that he ordered Schellenberg to establish German-supported partisan groups in the Soviet rear.[46] Both Himmler and Heydrich also demanded to know why the RSHA intelligence reports on the USSR were not as extensive or as successful as the military situation required.[47] Schellenberg admitted that intelligence reporting on the Soviet political situation and Soviet war production was deficient, and told both Himmler and Heydrich that such poor reporting was primarily owing to a lack of personnel and resources. For example, Schellenberg stated in his memoirs that German intelligence in general was astonished by the quality and quantity of Soviet armor.[48]

Himmler ordered Schellenberg to set up an organization to accomplish the dual goals of obtaining better intelligence on the USSR and establishing a partisan movement in the Soviet rear. Schellenberg subordinated the operation to Group VI of SD/Ausland and code-named the activity Operation Zeppelin. The SD/Ausland component responsible for the administration of Zeppelin was Gruppe C/Z. The officers chiefly responsible for Zeppelin at Amt VI headquarters were SS Lieutenant Colonels *(Obersturmbannfuehrer)* Graefe, Hengelhaupt, and Roeder, SS Majors *(Sturmbannfuehrer)* Willy Teich, Peter Siepen, Krauss, and Lumm, and Colonel *(Standartenfuehrer)* Albert Rapp.[49] In the end, Operation Zeppelin, like other German clandestine operations in the East, fell far short of its goals, achieved little, and ended in failure. While Nazi arrogance, lack of resources (such as aircraft), and little or no prior planning contributed to the failure of Zeppelin, effective Soviet counterintelligence destroyed the major SD clandestine collection and subversion effort in the East.[50]

Operation Zeppelin began as an ambitious enterprise in which Schellenberg envisioned masses of SD-trained agents — recruited from POW camps — being deployed behind Soviet lines to collect intelligence and to conduct guerrilla warfare in the Soviet rear. Intelligence collection objectives included, but were not limited to, obtaining information on the food supply in the USSR, the Soviet coal and petroleum industries, anti-Soviet movements, and how best to employ anti-Soviet propaganda within the USSR.[51] These agents were to be given the status of German soldiers and allowed to wear Wehrmacht uniforms. They were also to be given clean clothes, clean quarters, and the best food, along with strong doses of Nazi propaganda and trips through Germany to reinforce their motivation. The SD also recruited informants among the agent trainees to root out those who were pro-Soviet and those who were more interested in material benefits than in serving the German cause.[52]

Initially 10,000 to 15,000 Soviet citizens volunteered their services to the Germans, but this figure was reduced to 2,000 to 3,000 by screening out those who were unsuitable for employment as agents.[53] The SD could not deploy all the remaining agents largely because of the lack of air and logistical support. In 1943 the SD managed to dispatch behind Soviet lines a total of 115 men divided into 19 agent groups. Only half produced any information, and many of those who returned and were no longer of use to the Germans were shot.[54]

In addition to the lack of logistical support, Schellenberg could not convince Heydrich or Himmler that Soviet POWs, especially those from Central Asia and the Caucasus, could not be motivated solely by demonstrations of and appeals to higher living standards, anti-Sovietism, and the virtues of National Socialism. Schellenberg realized that the only effective way to enlist more agents was to recruit them based on the promise of future national autonomy for their regions. Heinrich Fenner, who was commander of Hauptkommando Sued (the SD version of a FAK) from 1943 to 1944 and who, in his late twenties, fled the Bolsheviks, was also of roughly the same opinion as Schellenberg. Fenner told his interrogators that many of the Central Asians could not understand Nazi propaganda since they did not speak German. Fenner said that "German attempts to make National Socialists out of the Turkmen [*sic*] were ridiculous" and that he tried to motivate his agents by pointing out that the Soviet government would never allow the Central Asian Republics of the USSR to become independent. Heydrich did not want to listen to this recommendation and sarcastically told Schellenberg: "Be careful you don't get a medal from Stalin one day."[55] Volunteers began to decline after 1942 as a result of German mismanagement and the fact that the war began to turn in the Soviets' favor.[56]

Some Soviet versions of Operation Zeppelin exaggerate its scale. For example, one Soviet history of the intelligence war against Germany stated that, in 1942, the Abwehr had deployed 20,000 agents in Operation Zeppelin alone.[57] In fact, the Abwehr does not even appear to have been a major player in Operation Zeppelin. Fenner attributed part of the failure of Zeppelin to a lack of cooperation with the Abwehr and said that the Zeppelin field units exchanged information with Stab Walli I (the "Baun Agency") on Soviet documentation but otherwise did not cooperate.[58] Given German logistical constraints, it would have been virtually impossible for the SD to have deployed 20,000 agents. Schellenberg repeatedly complained about the shortages of aircraft and said that "nothing is more destructive of an agent's nerve than to keep him waiting too long before sending him out." Fenner said that postponed flights and lack of aircraft even jeopardized mission security. During a several-week period, in which a group of Georgian agents had to wait for an available aircraft, the agents became drunk and unruly. Soviet agents managed to approach members of the group and elicit details of its mission. In one case, a Georgian agent proposed to a comrade that they both give themselves up to Soviet counterintelligence on arrival in Soviet territory. Willy Teich, a *Hauptsturmfuehrer* in the group in Schellenberg's SD/Ausland that was responsible for Zeppelin, described an elaborate plan, code-named Operation Ulm, in which the SD would drop saboteurs deep inside Soviet territory to blow up a few key transformers supplying electrical power to the Soviet defense industry. According to Teich, this operation had to be postponed because of a lack of aircraft.[59]

However, Soviet descriptions of counterintelligence successes against German agents in Operation Zeppelin mirror those against the Abwehr. In one operation, the SD parachuted a group of twenty-five agents behind Soviet lines in the area around Grozny, located in the northern Caucasus. The SD had assigned the group the mission of blowing up an oil refinery. Soviet state security apparently had received advance warning of the mission and machine-gunned the agents while they were still in their parachutes.[60] Another Soviet history stated that, in 1943, the SD dropped nineteen agent groups behind Soviet lines, of which fifteen were eliminated by the Soviets; members of the remaining groups surrendered immediately after landing.[61]

German assessments generally substantiate Soviet accounts of the failure of Zeppelin. Schellenberg said that the NKVD had inflicted sizable losses on Zeppelin and had thus undermined it from within.[62] One SD officer explained that several groups of agents had been deployed deep inside Soviet territory with various missions; one group was assigned the task of destroying an oil pipeline running northward from the Caspian Sea. Although the agent groups were able to move around and use radios for communication, the SD officer stated that the pipeline had not been blown up and that the information the other agent groups provided was of no great value.[63]

The SD assigned some Zeppelin agent groups, which could not be deployed because of the lack of aircraft, to anti-partisan missions in the rear of the German army. The Soviets even reduced the effectiveness of these groups. Schellenberg recounted an incident involving one Colonel Rodionov, who had been assigned to command an SD-organized anti-partisan combat unit code-named Druzhina by the Germans.[64] The unit consisted of Zeppelin-trained agents who, subsequent to their training, could not be deployed because of a lack of aircraft. On one occasion, the unit ruthlessly "screened" a village suspected of sympathizing with the partisans. While marching prisoners back to a concentration camp, Rodionov ordered his men to kill the SS guards accompanying the prisoners. According to Schellenberg, Rodionov had made contact with Soviet counterintelligence while he was working for the Germans and had been instructed to suborn his colleague to work for the Soviets. After Rodionov had returned to Moscow, he was decorated by Stalin personally.[65]

State Security also used agents deployed in Operation Zeppelin in radio playbacks. One Soviet history, without citing specific cases, asserted that, in

June 1944, Zeppelin-trained agents had been turned by Soviet counterintelligence and were used in radio playbacks that transmitted disinformation to the Germans concerning the upcoming Soviet offensive against Army Group Center. The same history also stated that disinformation transmitted through radio playbacks had resulted in the Luftwaffe diverting raids from Soviet defense plants.[66]

Another Soviet history described in detail an operation code-named Shturm in which a former Soviet artillery officer named G. Lezhava had been trained by the SD and dropped into the mountains around Tbilisi, Georgia, on 19 June 1943, along with several other agents. The Germans had instructed Lezhava and the other agents to collect military information on Soviet forces, conduct sabotage operations, and establish an anti-Soviet underground.[67] However, the agents surrendered to Soviet counterintelligence and were used in a radio playback that neutralized several German agent groups sent to reinforce Lezhava's group. The radio playback also convinced the Germans that other groups were successfully carrying out their missions.[68] Operation Shturm lasted two years, resulted in the apprehension of thirty German agents, the seizure of several million rubles, and the capture of several tons of arms and other military supplies. The Soviet deception had been so successful that the SD believed it no longer needed to send any more agent groups to Georgia to establish an underground.[69]

One of the most significant Soviet counterintelligence successes against Zeppelin-trained agents occurred in September 1944, when Soviet security officers arrested one Major Tavrin (real name Politov) and his accomplice, Liya Shilova, who were operating behind Soviet lines with documents identifying them as Smersh officers. The SD had trained both agents for almost one year and given them the task of assassinating Stalin and other high-level Soviet military leaders scheduled to attend a conference in Moscow commemorating the twenty-seventh anniversary of the Bolshevik Revolution.[70] The extended training period probably allowed the Soviets time to obtain advance warning of their deployment from an agent in Politov-Tavrin's school.[71] However, both agents landed a considerable distance away from the intended site, despite a well-planned Soviet radio playback. They were arrested shortly after their arrival behind Soviet lines because of good counterintelligence and security work by Smersh.[72] In a subsequent search of both agents, the Soviets found seven pistols with poison-filled bullets, a radio set, an antitank weapon, hand grenades, a remote control bomb built into a briefcase, 428,000 rubles, 116 genuine and fabricated Soviet seals and stamps, along with several blank Soviet documents, codes, and secret writing materials.[73]

According to Soviet sources, Politov-Tavrin had an unusual background. From 1933 to 1940 he lived in the Ukraine, Tashkent, and Uzbekistan and in the Bashkir Autonomous Republic. He was a manager of a petroleum storage plant in Ayaguz, Kazakhstan, embezzled a large sum of money and evaded prosecution by using aliases and fake documents. He finally found a job as an investigator in the public prosecutor's office in Voronezh.[74] In November 1941 Politov-Tavrin was drafted into the Red Army and subsequently became a platoon commander and then a company commander. On 30 May 1942 he surrendered to the Germans near Rzhev.[75]

The SD recruited Politov-Tavrin in 1943 and sent him to Austria to be trained as an agent. The Gestapo used him as an agent provocateur against Soviet partisans.[76] Politov-Tavrin performed his duties well, and the SD selected him for an assassination mission behind Soviet lines. In Berlin, Pskov, and later in Riga, Politov-Tavrin received individual instruction in such disciplines as marksmanship, motorcycle driving, explosives, and how to handle a special kind of advanced antitank weapon.[77] He also was required to memorize his cover story as a Smersh officer.[78] Shilova was trained as a radio operator.[79] The plan was to infiltrate Politov-Tavrin and Shilova behind Soviet lines in a specially modified transport aircraft that could carry a Soviet M-72 motorcycle. Politov-Tavrin and Shilova were then to use it to transport themselves to Moscow to carry out their mission.[80]

The Germans spared no effort to ensure that every detail of Politov's cover story could stand up to scrutiny by the Soviet security service. The SD had issued Politov documents in the name of Major Tavrin, assistant director of the OOs of the 39th Army of the 3rd Belorussian Front, who was going to Moscow on business after having been wounded and treated in a field hospital.[81] At SD direction, he underwent plastic surgery to simulate wounds on his hands and stomach. In addition to the standard array of documentation that a Soviet military counterintelligence officer was required to carry (leave orders, pay book, soldier's book, military orders, Smersh credentials, etc.), Politov-Tavrin was furnished with numerous medals and false papers entitling him to wear those medals. The Germans even forged copies of *Pravda* and *Izvestiia* with fabricated articles showing Politov-Tavrin's picture to substantiate his right to wear various decorations.[82]

Circumstantial evidence suggests that Soviet counterintelligence pieced together Politov-Tavrin's SD affiliation and his mission from a variety of sources. As with all German agent training schools, the SD training school at Pskov had long been kept under observation by Soviet agents. A Smersh staff officer had even penetrated the school and became commander of the school's guard platoon. With the aid of the Smersh staff officer inside the school and three partisans, Soviet counterintelligence officers kidnapped the deputy commander of the Pskov school on New Year's Eve, 1944, and stole several suitcases full of documents.[83] After the kidnapping, Politov-Tavrin was transferred to Riga. The Soviet account strongly implies that some information on Politov-Tavrin's affiliation with the SD had been obtained as a result of an evaluation of the stolen documents and the kidnapping of the deputy commander of the school.[84]

While in Riga Politov-Tavrin needed to have a Soviet-style long leather coat custom-made, with the right sleeve lengthened and two pockets sewn on the left-hand side of the coat. The tailor, who was a Soviet agent, viewed this as strange and alerted Soviet counterintelligence.[85] The Soviets then placed Politov-Tavrin under surveillance, quickly confirming his affiliation with the SD. Soviet state security then discovered from other sources that the Germans were planning to deploy a group of agents behind Soviet lines to select a suitable landing site for a special aircraft.[86]

In June 1944 the Germans parachuted a three-man radio-equipped agent team behind Soviet lines near Smolensk. According to Soviet accounts, the agents immediately surrendered on landing, gave up their codebooks, radio call signs, and code words, and told Soviet counterintelligence officers all they knew about the identities of German agents and future agent deployments, including Politov-Tavrin's.[87] The Soviets immediately engaged in a radio playback and assisted the Germans in selecting a landing site for Politov-Tavrin's aircraft.[88]

Soviet counterintelligence supervised the preparation of the airfield to facilitate the capture of the aircraft, the crew, and any agents. To preclude the aircraft from taking off after unloading its cargo, the Soviets placed a searchlight in the bushes to blind the pilot, built camouflaged firing pits around the runway, and camouflaged a trench about halfway down the runway to thwart the plane's taxiing.[89] A security unit waited out of sight just in case the Germans discharged a large group of saboteurs. Through the radio playback, the Soviets informed the Germans that the landing site was ready, and the Germans scheduled a date for Politov-Tavrin's arrival.[90]

The Soviets waited, but the German aircraft did not arrive. At the direction of Soviet counterintelligence the radio operator of the agent group, which had been dropped in June 1944, sent an angry radio message to Riga threatening not to carry out the mission if such an act were to be repeated. Riga sent back a message apologizing and citing bad weather as the reason for aborting the mission. However, the Soviets radioed back that the weather had been perfect over the landing site.[91] Therefore Soviet state security concluded that the

Germans suspected that the agent group given the task of finding a landing site might have come under Soviet control.[92] The Germans confirmed Soviet suspicions when a few days later they asked in a radio message where the head of the group had spent the night before flying out of Riga. The Soviets gave the Germans the correct answer and added that if "you do not trust us, we can fare easier without you than you can without us."[93]

The Germans, satisfied that the Soviets had not turned the group, planned to have the aircraft carrying Politov-Tavrin and Shilova land on the preselected runway in the early morning hours of 6 September 1944. Flying over Smolensk the plane was hit by Soviet anti-aircraft fire and veered off course. The pilot finally landed the aircraft on an airstrip he had used in 1941, which was located 150 kilometers northeast of the intended site.[94] The aircraft hit a tree, tearing off a wing. Politov-Tavrin and Shilova survived the crash, exited the aircraft on their motorcycle as fast as possible, and disappeared. Soviet security troops — acting on a tip from the air defense forces — arrived quickly, captured five of the plane's crew members, and killed one who resisted.[95]

On the same day Politov-Tavrin and Shilova were traveling on a country road leading to the Rzhev-Riga road. They presented their documents to the security guards, who initially observed nothing suspicious. However, on closer inspection, the guards noticed that two of Politov-Tavrin's medals, the Order of the Red Star and the Order of Aleksandr Nevskii, were pinned on the left side of his uniform instead of on the right. When asked which city they were coming from, Politov-Tavrin named a city about 200 kilometers to the west. The Soviet security guards thought this answer was suspicious, because Politov-Tavrin and Shilova did not look tired and had no mud on their uniforms even though it had rained heavily the night before. Politov-Tavrin's incorrect arrangement of the medals, the absence of mud on their uniforms, and the fact that the guards knew that a German plane had crashed in the area all convinced the guards to arrest both German agents. Soviet counterintelligence then engaged the Germans in a radio playback lasting several months in an attempt to deceive the Germans about Politov-Tavrin's and Shilova's progress in fulfilling their missions.[96]

Operations Monastery, Berezino, and Zeppelin clearly demonstrate that Soviet combat counterintelligence conducted sophisticated operations under difficult conditions that affected, minimally, German intelligence estimates and ultimately some German military operational decisions. The scale, scope, and complexity of many of these Soviet operations rivaled or arguably exceeded those of the British Twenty Committee. In every case the Germans were aware that these operations might have been under Soviet control, and every time they elected to take the chance and treat the information from these sources as genuine.[97] While an intensive examination of the Soviet execution of all three of these operations would no doubt reveal a multitude of flaws, operations of any type are seldom perfect under combat conditions and almost none proceed according to plan. To quote Prussian General Helmuth von Moltke, "no plan survives the first shot."[98] These Soviet operations succeeded well enough to compel German intelligence to overrule whatever doubts it might have had about some of its major sources of clandestinely acquired information.

The Sword and Shield

Much of the data on the Soviet Union before and during World War II suggest that it should not have won the war, that it could have been defeated. It was not. A host of western rationalizations exist for its victory. Too often they are based on the deficiencies and errors of Russia's enemies, the exceptional contributions of its allies and any number of other avenues but that of answering the historian's question, "What did the Soviet Union do right and do well?"

Proceedings of the Twelfth Military History Symposium, United States Air Force Academy, 1986

In a secret war, waged with unprecedented ferocity over a four-year period on a 2,400-mile front and involving more than 175,000 agents, Soviet counterintelligence soundly defeated the Nazi security and intelligence services. The most significant contribution made by Soviet counterintelligence to victory in World War II was its active participation in, and support for, Soviet military deception operations. Disinformation passed through both Max Operations (Monastery, and Richard Kauder's Luftmeldekopf Suedost), the 183 radio playbacks of Soviet military counterintelligence, and hundreds, if not thousands, of non–radio-equipped double agents made a substantial contribution toward leading German intelligence to incorrectly assess Soviet military operational intentions.

Combined with a GULAG-like security regime in the rear areas, an unceasing quest to ferret out and destroy "enemies of the state," real or imagined, and relentless massive attacks on the Abwehr, SD, and Gestapo infrastructure in the East, "fatherland counterintelligence" (to use the Russian phrase du jour) provided little or no opportunity for the Nazis to clandestinely acquire agents with access to Soviet military intentions after the war began. Even years before the outbreak of the war, the Nazis never felt it necessary to systematically target the mid- to higher levels of the CPSU, the intelligence and security services, and the armed forces, as well as the recuperative capacity of the Soviet state.

This critical mistake ensured that the senior leadership of the German armed forces would have considerably less ability to adjust military operational planning before the invasion or even in the early days of Barbarossa when access to such sources might have been a bit less difficult. The Soviet intelligence services had the advantage of being able to exploit a good many communist sympathizers, who were already operating clandestinely or semi-clandestinely long before the outbreak of the war, and used them extensively to collect high-grade intelligence and counterintelligence information. The Soviets always had an appreciation of the necessity for strategic intelligence. The Nazis did not.

In short, the Germans "blew" the secret war in the East, and the Russians have not "come clean" as to exactly why and how. Therefore, while the case for the existence of a Soviet version of a British "Twenty Committee" is compelling, the details of its contribution remain elusive, largely because the Russians have not made public exactly how they monitored the effectiveness of their deception measures.[1] Nevertheless, though FHO estimates were clearly based on a myriad of sources, the fact that the Germans lacked sources deep in the Soviet rear made them more susceptible to believing the controlled information they did receive, especially since they were disinclined to believe that the Soviets could deceive on a grand scale.

The single biggest failure of German intelligence — other than its poor understanding of the Red Army's mobilization system before the onset of Barbarossa—was its systematic underestimation of the scale and scope of Soviet attacks and counterattacks at critical junctures during the war, despite having several excellent Russian-speaking intelligence officers in FHO (albeit not enough).[2]

As late as 4 December 1941 FHO believed that Russian forces facing Army Group Center were not in a position to mount a large-scale attack "without significant reinforcements."[3] The Soviets counterattacked on 5 December with a vengeance. The Russians had hastily put into effect a *maskirovka* plan within six days. Nevertheless, the Germans not only wrongly assessed Soviet intentions but underestimated Soviet forces by at least 200,000 troops, even though they had known as early as mid-November that Siberian divisions "keen for battle and well trained" were in Army Group Center's area of responsibility, that divisions were being transferred from the Far East, and that the Soviet leadership had an unknown number of "army troops" at its disposal. Though no Soviet sources claim that radio playbacks or double agents played a role, Soviet OO-enforced operational security measures undoubtedly did.[4]

In the spring and summer of 1942 German intelligence failed to detect the formation of fifteen new Soviet tank corps and five new tank armies.[5] In May 1942 FHO assessed Soviet intentions as defensive, stating that "forces sufficient for a large-scale offensive are lacking" and underestimated Soviet strength. This delayed the German summer offensive until late June.[6]

Although as early as August 1942 FHO foresaw the possibility of a Soviet counteroffensive against Army Group B in Stalingrad, it never envisioned major simultaneous attacks on the flanks of Paulus's Sixth Army. In fact, the Soviets deluded Gehlen into believing that the main attack would take place against Army Group Center and that Soviet forces were too weak to mount large-scale operations. Gehlen had received a report from Max (probably Dem'ianov) citing a "Council of War on 4 December presided over by Stalin" which essentially indicated that the Russians would not launch a large-scale offensive.[7] On 19 November 1942 the Soviets launched a 1.1-million-man offensive that resulted in the destruction of the German Sixth Army.[8] Stalingrad terminated Germany's bid for world power.[9]

The gross underestimation of Soviet intentions and reserves at Kursk, the Belorussian offensive (Bagration) in the summer of 1944 against Army Group Center, as well as the Vistula-Oder offensive in early 1945 inflicted tremendous damage on German forces.[10] Kursk precluded the Germans from launching any other major offensives in the East for the rest of the war.[11] Operation Bagration wiped Army Group Center off the map, and the Vistula-Oder put Soviet forces within sixty miles of Berlin in record time. Soviet double agents, radio games, penetrations of the British services, and NKVD security forces, combined with military deception operations, worked in concert to totally confound FHO and OKH operational planning.

Military victory results from a variety of factors such as good generalship, logistics, intelligence, superior training and morale, and often just plain luck. The Soviet ability to exploit the weaknesses and biases in the decision-making process of senior German officers also played an important part in the Soviet victory over the Nazis.[12] The Soviets used combat counterintelligence as an integral part of the process of manipulating German military decision making and turned what is often viewed as a defensive weapon into a substantial force multiplier and ultimately a strategic asset.[13]

If commanders have confidence in their intelligence and counterintelligence officers, and the information being produced is accurate, well sourced, and authoritative, the stress of making decisions in the "fog of war" can be reduced. High-quality intelligence and counterintelligence information might lessen the negative impact of stress by increasing a commander's confidence that he has made the right decision and giving him at least some battlefield predictability. During the Soviet-German war of 1941–1945, the stress became particularly acute when commanders tried to impose order on the chaos of combat by executing plans involving millions of troops, equipped with thousands of tanks, artillery, and aircraft, in an environment where adversaries were determined to exterminate each other in an area at least half the size of the United States, and in a climate barely suitable for human habitation.[14]

Although accurate intelligence and counterintelligence information can reduce the stress of combat decision making, acquiring it often eludes the best efforts of intelligence services. The data tend to be fragmentary, distorted, and incomplete.[15] Therefore combat intelligence and counterintelligence cannot free commanders from ultimately relying on their own intuitive grasp of the situation to make a decision. The necessity for commanders to make decisions based on insufficient and oftentimes manipulated data — especially under the chaotic and stressful conditions of the Eastern Front — created an environment highly conducive to the success of Soviet military deception operations. One of the major missions of Soviet combat counterintelligence operations — both offensive and defensive — was to support the manipulation of that environment by Soviet deception planners for the express purpose of exacerbating the stress on the invader of making decisions in the "fog of war."

Nazi arrogance, the German army's negative attitude toward intelligence (compared to the more positive one in the Soviet military), internecine bureaucratic warfare, Hitler's decision to prohibit clandestine collection beyond sixty miles of the border prior to the invasion, and the poor overall record of German intelligence would suggest that Soviet counterintelligence won because German intelligence was dysfunctional and ineffective. Despite the Abwehr's well-deserved reputation for anti-Nazism, mismanagement, and even outright fabrication of agents, FHO amassed a substantial amount of data on the USSR, especially after Gehlen took over in April 1942.[16] Gehlen injected new life into Foreign Armies East.

Gehlen systematically produced a myriad of analyses and reports on such subjects as the military situation, Soviet order-of-battle, the Soviet defense industry, the partisan movement, internal conditions within the USSR, and the Soviet intelligence and security services.[17] He based these reports and estimates on the evaluation of thousands of pieces of data gleaned from POW and captured agent interrogations, newspapers, radio intercepts, aerial photography, and clandestine collection.[18] His organization produced the best results of any German intelligence organization during the war.[19] Nevertheless, to quote one historian of the intelligence war on the Eastern Front, "more knowledge about capabilities does not vouchsafe better understanding of intentions."[20] Gehlen, like many other German officers, suffered from an inflexible conviction of German superiority and therefore discounted any possibility that the Soviets were capable of strategic deception on a wide scale.[21]

The effectiveness of Soviet military deception operations strongly suggests that the Russians had a German source (or sources) capable of monitoring the effects of Soviet deception operations throughout the entire war, as well as a source that knew details of German agent deployments.[22] Philby, Blunt, and Cairncross — all well-known penetrations of British intelligence — provided the Soviets with some feedback on German military operations and on Luftmeldekopf Suedost. Gehlen's assertion that after the war he received proof from behind the Iron Curtain that Martin Bormann worked for the Soviet intelligence service requires substantially more evidence than Gehlen provided in his memoirs.[23] It is not clear whether Colonel Rudolph von Gersdorff, chief of Army Group Center's Ic (Abwehr liaison officer) knowingly worked for the Soviets when he passed high-grade intelligence to Rudolph Roessler in Switzerland and, if so, whether Gersdorff acted as a Soviet agent while in Army Group Center.[24] The issue of whether Heinrich Mueller, chief of the Gestapo, was an agent for the Soviet intelligence service during the war remains highly controversial. The investigation of Hermann Baun immediately after the war for espionage on behalf of the USSR by the U.S. Army Counterintelligence Corps found no conclusive evidence that Baun worked for Soviet intelligence. Sudoplatov might have purposely omitted details of Soviet penetrations of the German services, and the Russian government, to date, has not shed any light on whether the Soviets broke any high-grade German ciphers after having captured numerous Enigma machines, German codes, and radio operators.[25]

Other than Baun and possibly Gersdorff, neither Bormann nor Mueller would have had sustained access to details of agent deployments in the East nor the details of how well Soviet military deception plans were working. The number of German agents who volunteered to the Soviets accounts for some degree of Soviet success, as does the number of German agents caught through Soviet rear-area security measures. Soviet penetrations of German agent training schools could explain more Soviet successes. But to achieve an 80 to 90 percent success rate in the destruction of German agent deployments suggests a level of Soviet foreknowledge that the current available record does not explain.

The notable lack of Soviet and Russian books, articles, or documents addressing these two crucial issues suggests several possibilities: that there were no sources; that disclosure of such sources would embarrass the Russians (and possibly the Germans) or their intelligence service in some way; that the Russian intelligence service does not want to make what it knows public because no credible revelations have yet appeared in the Western press; and that the Russians do not want to be seen officially initiating the disclosure of one of their agents in a public forum. Until these issues are credibly resolved, to include the declassification of all the relevant documents and making all of them available to researchers, histories of the "invisible war" on the Eastern Front will be missing a key element of an important story.

One of the major contributions of State Security to the war effort centered on its ability to deny the Germans the opportunity to attain a better understanding of Soviet intentions.[26] The German failure to place good agents in key positions within the USSR significantly contributed to the decisiveness of the German defeat. A strong argument could be made that the German acceptance of the "Max South" reports (the Kauder/Klatt organization) — despite substantial counterintelligence problems that were clearly visible at the time and brought to the attention of OKW, OKH, and the German intelligence leadership — goes a long way toward substantiating the Soviet claims that no serious German intelligence effort during the war was successful. The assumption here, of course, is that a sustained bona fide, high-level German penetration of the CPSU, the armed forces, or the Soviet intelligence services would have been able to cast serious doubt on the credibility of the Max information and that the Germans would have taken any ensuing doubts about that information seriously.

Prior to Barbarossa and during the early months of the war when hundreds of thousands of Soviet soldiers deserted or voluntarily surrendered, the Germans had the means and arguably some opportunity to obtain the necessary accurate intelligence, but they lacked the will.[27] By early 1942 the Soviet counterintelligence system virtually guaranteed that even if the opportunity arose for the Germans to penetrate the higher levels of the USSR, German success would be short-lived or nonexistent. The hostile operating environment in the USSR caused the Germans to view information provided by low-level tactical agent deployments as being of limited reliability though somewhat useful.[28] Under these conditions the Germans often ignored strong indications that their sources that actually managed to report intelligence information were controlled by the Soviets.

The Germans, no doubt, felt forced to continue running such agents as Richard Kauder, and deployed thousands of other agents behind Soviet lines despite abysmal success rates, largely in the hope that some valuable information might be obtained. The Soviet willingness to provide accurate military and political information to enhance the credibility of their double agents made it extremely difficult for the Germans to terminate operations, even though many of those operations were suspected of having been under Soviet control. By 1944 the lack of reconnaissance aircraft, poor results in tactical agent deployments, and no bona fide, high-level penetrations of organizations that mattered forced the Germans to rely heavily on signals intercepts. That increased FHO's vulnerability to Soviet deception.[29]

The Russians had a quarter of a century prior to the Nazi invasion to perfect counterintelligence operations and to embed redundancy into their security services much as they did in their military. After the initial shock of the German invasion, State Security recovered and proved to be a resilient and tenacious opponent. As soon as the front became stationary, the Soviets began using masses of agents against the Germans.[30] The ability of State Security to deploy thousands of agents even after heavy blows to its agent and informant networks confirms the claims of Abwehr officers that the Soviets had a well-prepared counterintelligence system.[31] The Russians positioned themselves to systematically exploit German weaknesses, despite initial setbacks in the latter half of 1941. The Soviet effort was highly focused: eliminate all real or perceived threats to the armed forces and the regime, support military deception, and destroy the German capability to run clandestine operations in the USSR.

There is no question that the constant emphasis on repression bred resentment among loyal Soviet citizens and that more work was created because many of them became vehement opponents of the Soviet regime. However, one of the salient features of a totalitarian state is its ability to militarize the efforts of every organization and stratum of society to achieve Herculean feats. The Soviet secret police was the primary instrument in sustaining the complete and total mobilization of the Soviet state for war, with German atrocities (as well as atrocities committed by the Soviets and blamed on the Germans), Soviet propaganda, and Russian patriotism also making substantial contributions to defeating the Germans.

However, without the coercive power of the NKVD (and gross mismanagement of occupation policies by the Nazi leadership), the Bolshevik regime might have taken significantly longer to recover, and possibly might not have recovered at all. It is ironic that the primary weapon preferred by Stalin's secret police, that is, terror or the threat of terror, which initially drove thousands of Soviet soldiers to desert or surrender en masse to German troops, was also the weapon that contributed significantly to preventing the Soviet state from total collapse.[32] State Security's long-standing brutal war against the Soviet population to eradicate every vestige of disloyalty to Comrade Stalin and the Communist Party might have been wasteful, inefficient, and a "crime against humanity," but it did not prohibit "fatherland counterintelligence" from conducting highly sophisticated operations or apprehending the majority of German agents. German intelligence officers repeatedly asserted that it was exceedingly difficult to operate behind Soviet lines and that almost all German operations ended in failure.[33]

This does not mean that no German agents operated behind Soviet lines. A 1946 U.S. Army study, which was largely based on German documents, stated that "despite the great scope and unusual rigor of Soviet counterintelligence measures, its actual effectiveness during World War II was surprisingly spotty."[34] The study asserted that constant emphasis on repression bred resentment and disaffection even among normally loyal persons and that emphasis on extensive security measures diluted efforts to detect "skilled foreign agents with authentic credentials" who were able to operate with "considerable impunity."[35] Although this may have been true in some cases, even when German agents could operate in the Soviet rear undetected, German officers suspected that the information was deliberately passed to them by the Soviets or was of marginal quality. Schellenberg conceded that because of the enormous size of the USSR, agents could move about without hindrance for "months on end." However, he acknowledged that the NKVD caught most of them.[36]

Chekisty "spottiness" aside, the historical ruthlessness and effectiveness of the Soviet secret police had made it exceedingly difficult for any agent to operate there, and even more so in wartime.[37] World War II was no exception. Smuggling secret documents in and out of the country or across enemy lines, inconspicuously moving about, and securely communicating with or meeting an agent at all would have presented almost insurmountable challenges to any foreign intelligence service operating in the prison-like atmosphere that was the USSR.[38] Therefore to attribute the German loss of the intelligence war in the East solely to Nazi arrogance, lack of planning, and disdain for clandestinely acquired intelligence implies that the Germans could have won the intelligence war had these problems within the German services not been present. Yet the agent operations of Western intelligence services inside the USSR prior to the German invasion in 1941 also met with generally poor results.[39] Polish intelligence experienced considerable difficulties operating in the prewar USSR, and Japanese intelligence fell victim to Soviet military deception when it was completely surprised by the Soviet Manchurian offensive in mid-1945.[40] These examples demonstrate that, although German blunders played a major role in the magnitude of the German defeat in the East, they were by no means the only reasons for it.

The effectiveness of Soviet counterintelligence should be measured by its two main objectives: preservation of the regime in power and eradication of enemy spies. It achieved both goals. At the end of the war Stalin not only remained in power, but the USSR was well on its way to achieving superpower status. The Abwehr and the SD achieved almost none of their objectives. Although much blame has been placed on the Germans for failing to successfully exploit the anti-Soviet sympathies of the numerous ethnic minorities in the USSR, as well as the population at large, such foresight would have been a major departure from Nazi ideology.[41] The Russians preempted any potential German plans to foment significant unrest by terrorizing and deporting hundreds of thousands of ethnic minorities living within the territories of the USSR and ruthlessly punishing real or perceived collaborators and their families.[42]

Had Soviet counterintelligence been less effective, German intelligence would have undoubtedly uncovered true Soviet military intentions, laid bare the full extent of *maskirovka,* as well as uncovered the detailed plans, intentions, and operations of the Soviet intelligence services. If "forewarned is forearmed," in the best case the combined efforts of OKH, the Abwehr, and the RSHA — at least from December 1941 on — might have resulted in fighting the Bolsheviks to a stalemate. Minimally OKH could have slowed the pace of the Soviet victory, increased Soviet casualties, and limited the havoc that Russian forces wreaked on the German population during the race to Berlin. Those potential but nevertheless realistic outcomes illuminate the critical importance of counterintelligence to the Soviet war effort. Good counterintelligence becomes a force multiplier when used as a strategic weapon, but by itself it does not win wars. The absence of it, however, can lose them.

APPENDIXES

Appendix A. Soviet Organization for Secret War

Western estimates of the number of personnel assigned to the Soviet intelligence and security services during the war range from 500,000 to 2 million.[1] The majority of them were assigned to NKVD (People's Commissariat of Internal Affairs) troop units, Border Guard units, Signal Troops, and various other rear-area support formations. With the exception of Soviet military counterintelligence, virtually no detailed information is available on numbers of personnel assigned to other NKGB (People's Commissariat for State Security) and NKVD entities. One Soviet document placed the total number of personnel (or authorized personnel) in the NKVD headquarters area at 32,642 men as of 1 January 1940.[2] The range of numbers reflects the fact that the Germans mainly came into contact with military counterintelligence units and NKVD formations, and therefore had more information on the organization, personnel, and functions of these types of units.

Throughout Soviet history, the functions of the Soviet intelligence and security services have been divided into two general categories: those functions associated with State Security (Gosudarstvennaia Bezopasnost', or GB) and those associated with Internal Affairs (Vnutrennye Dela or VD).[3] Missions assigned to State Security included, but were not limited to, conducting counterintelligence and counterespionage operations, collecting foreign intelligence, running informant networks, carrying out sabotage and assassinations, protecting the leadership, ensuring the security of the armed forces, conducting covert action operations, guarding the borders, and maintaining the security of the economy by devoting an entire directorate to economic counterintelligence.[4]

Missions assigned to Internal Affairs were generally those associated in Western countries with various police functions, for example, investigating criminal activities (militia), directing traffic, firefighting, administering labor camps and prisons, administering the internal passport system, suppressing riots, policing the highways and railways, and serving as convoy guards.[5] At various times in Soviet history Internal Affairs has also been assigned such functions as securing rear areas, guarding borders, running POW camps, and constructing and guarding sensitive installations.[6]

During World War II State Security functions were performed by Glavnoe Upravlenie Gosudarstvennoi Bezopasnosti (GUGB, or Main Directorate for State Security) and Narodnyi Komissariat Gosudarstvennoi Bezopasnosti (NKGB, or People's Commissariat for State Security). The GRU, the military intelligence organization of the Soviet General Staff, did not have a counterintelligence mission. The state security function for the armed forces was performed by two successive organizations: Osobye Otdeli

(OOs, or Special Departments) of the NKVD (commonly referred to as OO/NKVD) and Glavnoe Upravlenie Kontrrazvedki–Narodnyi Komissariat Oboroni–Smersh (GUKR–NKO–Smersh — Smert' Shpionam, or Main Directorate for Counterintelligence of the People's Commissariat for Defense — Death to Spies). The internal security functions were performed by Narodnyi Komissariat Vnutrennykh Del' (NKVD, or People's Commissariat for Internal Affairs).[7]

Before describing in detail the missions and organizations of the Soviet intelligence and security services, a brief description of two major wartime reorganizations of State Security is essential to understanding the arcane nomenclature of Stalin's secret police. The GUGB was a main directorate of the NKVD from 10 July 1934 until February 1941, when it became the NKGB, an independent commissariat. On 20 July 1941 it reverted to its previous status as a main directorate of the NKVD until 14 April 1943, when it again became an independent People's Commissariat. It remained the NKGB until the end of the war. In both February 1941 and April 1943 OO/NKVD was transferred to the People's Commissariat of Defense (NKO). In July 1941 it reverted back to the NKVD, but in April 1943 it became the Third Main Directorate for Counterintelligence of the People's Commissariat for Defense — Death to Spies (GUKR–NKO–Smersh — Smert' Shpionam), where it remained until the end of the war. These organizational changes appeared to have affected only the senior leadership of the NKVD and the GUGB; the functions, personnel, and operations of the Soviet counterintelligence and security services changed little (see also Appendixes B–D).[8]

STATE SECURITY (GUGB/NKGB)

The GUGB/NKGB was essentially responsible for all espionage and counterintelligence operations against nonmilitary targets. It worked closely with the NKVD and military counterintelligence and was the primary organization responsible for running the informant networks inside the USSR, for prosecuting crimes against the state such as treason and anti-Soviet activity, and for ferreting out German agents deep inside the USSR. It was also responsible for collecting foreign intelligence. The organization of the NKGB (and probably the GUGB as well) consisted of eight directorates (*upravleniia*, often referred to by the Germans as Verwaltungen, and sometimes as Abteilungen), several departments and special departments (see chart A.1). The organization of republic NKGBs resembled that of the all-Union NKGB, but on a much smaller scale.[9] Many of the details of how the entities discussed below were organized are based on an analysis of Soviet documents in 1942–1943 as well as on the information provided by German counterintelligence officers. While the organizations of State Security directorates are based on documents dated 1943, the detailed breakout of the sections and departments of those directorates are based on a 1942 Soviet document.[10]

The First Directorate (Inostrannoe Upravlenie [INU], or Foreign Directorate; also referred to as Razvedyvatel'noe, or Intelligence Directorate) was responsible for conducting clandestine operations abroad and targeting foreigners inside the USSR for recruitment, especially diplomats and attachés.[11] It worked closely with the People's Commissariat for Foreign Affairs to place its officers abroad under official cover in Soviet

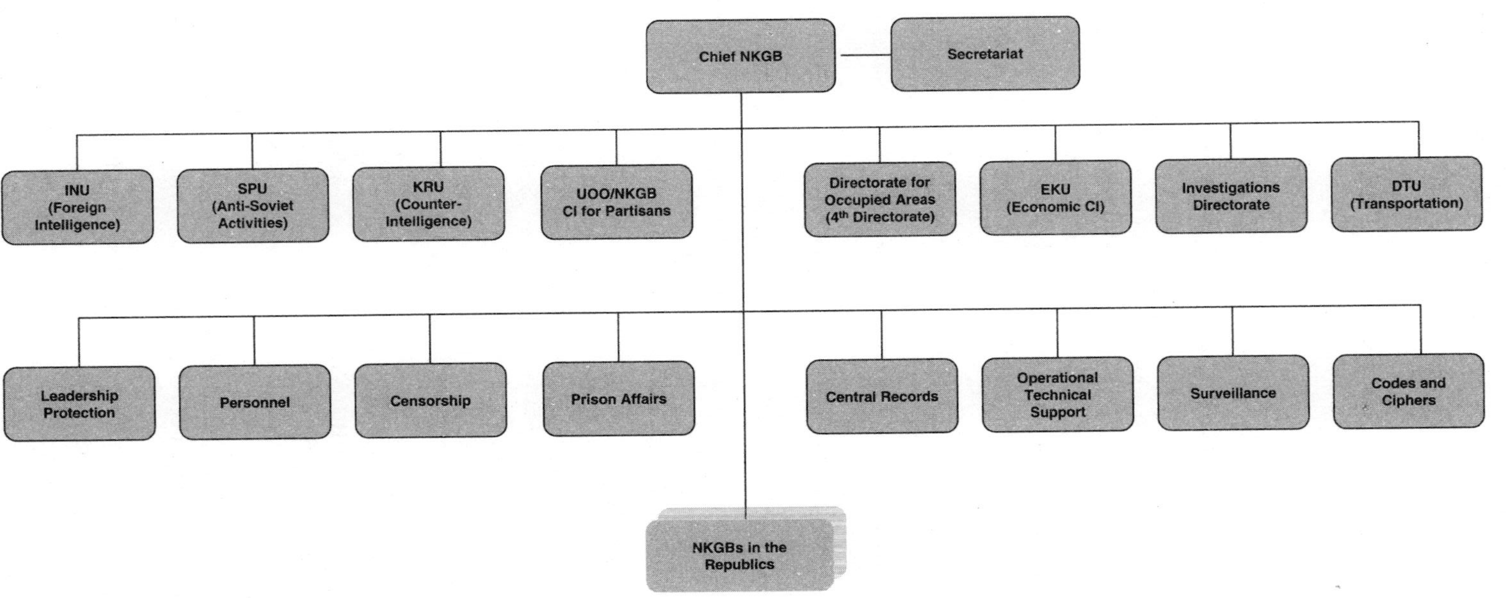

Chart A.1. Basic Organization of the NKGB

embassies and trade missions and also placed Soviet intelligence officers abroad with fabricated non-Soviet identities. It infiltrated émigré organizations outside the USSR and may even have had a section dedicated solely to the neutralization of the émigré intelligentsia overseas, although a Soviet document dated 1942 outlining the departments and sections of the INU does not appear to have such a dedicated component. The headquarters staff of the directorate numbered 135 officers and was divided into six departments. It had five separate geographic departments covering Western Europe, Eastern Europe, the Western Hemisphere (this department had a technical section), the Far East, and the Middle East, which included South Asia. The South Asian department included a section (third) entitled "Caucasian Emigration."[12] The sixth department comprised roughly six sections or components that covered the security of Soviets stationed abroad (Soviet Colony), an operational registry, a section for "entry and departure" (probably responsible for alias documents), a communications section, a "Group A" whose function was not identified, and a section to handle the operations of the INU's training school.[13] The Soviets apparently, at this stage, had no coverage in Africa.

A U.S. Army CIC report, dated 1946, stated that German counterintelligence units on the Eastern Front detected few INU officers or agents. Therefore the INU's direct contribution to defeating the German army was difficult to measure.[14] However, another U.S. Army document, basing its figures on German sources, estimated that the INU deployed a total of approximately 4,000 agents during the war.[15] An FHO document, dated 1 December 1944, stated that a Commissar of State Security named Titius was chief of the directorate. However, former KGB colonel Oleg Gordievsky, who defected to the West in 1985 and was well versed in the history of Soviet intelligence, and Lieutenant General Sudoplatov stated that Pavel Mikhailovich Fitin was chief of the INU during the war.[16] A recently published Soviet document placed Fitin as head of the INU at least as of July 1941.[17]

Counterintelligence and counterespionage operations (excluding those of Soviet military counterintelligence) within the territory of the USSR were the primary responsibility of the Second Directorate (Kontrrazvedevatel'noe Upravlenie [KRU], or Counterintelligence Directorate) of the NKGB (and, in 1942, the NKVD). In January 1943 the chief of the KRU was Petr Vasil'evich Fedotov, and the KRU had 227 personnel on its headquarters staff.[18] This directorate ran the majority of the informants within the USSR and cooperated extensively with military counterintelligence and other components of both the NKVD and the NKGB. It was, along with its republic counterparts, the backbone of the Soviet police system among the civilian population.[19] In April 1943 the Secret Political Directorate and the Economic Directorate of the NKVD were merged into the KRU.[20]

The duties of the KRU included, but were not necessarily limited to, the apprehension of enemy spies and saboteurs, the penetration of foreign intelligence services both inside the USSR and abroad, the surveillance of foreign officials and establishments in the USSR, the surveillance of agents of other Soviet intelligence services such as the GRU and the INU, the checking of the effectiveness and reliability of operational security and surveillance performed by other Soviet intelligence and security organizations, the screening of Soviet officials returning from abroad for signs of disaffection with the regime or recruitment by a foreign intelligence service, and the ferreting out of sedition and "anti-Sovietism" among the population at large.[21] German documents essentially divide the functions of this directorate into counterintelligence abroad and counterintelligence within the USSR.[22]

According to Soviet sources, the First Department of the KRU comprised six sections, all of which focused on counterintelligence operations. The First Section conducted counterintelligence operations to ensure that liberated areas were free of German spies; the Second Section probably engaged in double-agent operations; the Third Section hunted for German agents in the area of Moscow; the Fourth Section conducted agent operations in POW and internment camps working closely with the local NKVD; and the Fifth Section conducted counterintelligence operations to root out traitors, German agents, and their supporters. The Sixth Section was an investigative element.[23]

The Second, Third, and Fourth Departments essentially covered the foreign embassies and personnel inside the USSR, primarily in Moscow. Each of these departments had an investigative section or group with the Fifth Section of the Second Department dedicated to countering Polish intelligence in the USSR, including prison camps.[24] The Fifth Department — "Special Measures" — comprised two sections and two groups, most of which were probably dedicated to surveillance operations. The Sixth Department protected the diplomatic corps and appears to have been dedicated to recruiting Russian service personnel working in foreign embassies and consulates.[25] German documents reflect no detailed knowledge of the KRU but correctly identify its basic functions. An FHO document stated that Commissar of State Security Blinov was chief of the KRU.[26] Blinov was actually chief of the Secret Political Directorate as of January 1943, and N. D. Gorlinskii headed it before Blinov.[27]

The Third Directorate (Sekretnoe Politicheskoe Upravlenie [SPU], or Secret Political Directorate) was charged with the responsibility to combat all anti-Soviet activities in political, religious, or cultural organizations, to neutralize the anti-Soviet intelligentsia, and to infiltrate and neutralize vocal national minority groups. Although German documents reflect the existence of this organization, it appears not to have had an offensive counterintelligence mission behind German lines. Nevertheless, the SPU ran an extensive nationwide informant network the existence of which no doubt contributed to denying German agents access to these organizations.[28] To the extent that the Germans used minority, cultural, or religious groups in the USSR as a basis for subversion, the SPU probably would have been their principal adversary.

Until it was merged into the KRU in April 1943, the SPU headquarters staff in May 1942 numbered 197 people and was divided into five departments, an investigative unit, and an operational group. A Soviet document dated 1942 provides too much detail on the directorate's organization to examine here. However, a quick overview of the functions of each department provides a glimpse of the resources devoted to this mission. The First Department combated anti-Soviet political parties and organizations. It had three sections, one of which was devoted to looking for former "provocateurs and members of anti-Soviet groups." The Second Department targeted anti-Soviet elements in academia, literary and artistic circles, scientific and medical communities and institutions, and the Soviet government apparatus, and conducted agent operations among youth groups.[29] The Third Department combated "national counterrevolutionary" movements all over the USSR and even included operations against "Tatar-Mongol" counterrevolutionary elements. The Fourth Department ferreted out counterrevolutionaries among such groups as former White Guards, "kulaks," and the "collective farm intelligentsia," and in the villages within the territory of Russia proper. The Fifth Department targeted such "elements" as anti-Soviet authors and anonymous articles with anti-Soviet content. The sections of the investigative unit paralleled those of the SPU departments.[30] Again, the Germans do not appear to have had detailed knowledge of the SPU.

Prior to the publication of the memoirs of Lieutenant General P. A. Sudoplatov, information on the organization, missions, and functions of the NKGB's Fourth Directorate was sparse. The directorate was often erroneously referred to as the partisan directorate and cited in German documents as the Directorate for the Occupied Areas. German documents shed little light on this organization and German counterintelligence analyses of Soviet agent deployments do not specifically refer to agents deployed by the Fourth Directorate.[31]

However, one FHO document on the organization and operations of the Soviet security services, dated October 1944, stated that most of the agents deployed in the German-occupied areas by the NKGB were agents subordinate to the Fourth Directorate.[32] Nevertheless, according to other German documents and Sudoplatov's memoirs, the main task of the Fourth Directorate was to organize guerrilla movements and infiltrate agents behind German lines, recruit agents, and conduct deception operations. Sudoplatov stated that the Fourth Directorate deployed behind German lines a total of 212 detachments comprising 7,316 men during the course of the war, usually divided into groups of 160 men that were further divided into platoons of 30 men each. These groups were commanded by experienced officers of State Security and consisted of former agents or detailees from other NKVD and NKGB units. Strict compartmentalization of missions was maintained between the sabotage and reconnaissance groups deployed by the Fourth Directorate. The directorate trained a further 1,000 officers and technicians in sabotage operations for the Red Army and either infiltrated or dropped behind German lines an additional 6,500 civilian saboteurs and guerrillas.[33]

According to Sudoplatov, the Fourth Directorate comprised sixteen geographic sections and two departments; one department trained and supported partisans and the other trained and deployed agents.[34] The basic course for the Fourth Directorate was 100 hours long and included such subjects as annihilation of enemy paratroopers, espionage, sabotage, and instruction on how to train partisans. Fourth Directorate officers specialized in such subjects as radio operations, reconnaissance, sabotage, terrorism, parachuting, propaganda, and foreign languages.[35]

In May 1942, according to a recently published collection of Soviet documents, the Fourth Directorate of the NKVD — later, in April 1943, the Fourth Directorate of the NKGB — possessed a headquarters staff of 113 officers and was officially entitled

"Terror and Sabotage in Occupied Enemy Territory." It had four departments and a separate staff (fifteen people) dedicated to overseeing the operations of the interference *(istrebitel'nye)* battalions and partisan detachments. The First and Second Departments had eleven geographic sections covering the world as well as the former territories of the USSR occupied by the Germans, two sections for operations in POW and internment camps, and a registry. The functions of the Third and Fourth Departments are vague, and range from technical supply and "operations" to sections "D" and "TN."[36] The operations, functions, and exploits of this directorate are still highly secret. The Germans assessed the basic functions of this directorate correctly but probably did not realize the scope of its operations.

Although little is known of the two NKGB counterintelligence directorates charged with rooting out sabotage and espionage in the Soviet economy and in the Soviet transportation system, these entities contributed to the Germans' difficulties operating in the interior of the USSR. Neither NKGB directorate had the mission of deploying agents in the rear of the German army, thereby depriving the Germans of the ability to glean counterintelligence information from captured agents.

The Ekonomicheskoe Kontrrazvedyvatel'noe Upravlenie (EKU, or Economic Counterintelligence Directorate) (no number), which merged with the KRU in 1943, was, according to German sources, divided into four departments, one each for heavy industry, commerce, agriculture, and all other industries. Although data on its functions are scarce, the directorate's mission was to ferret out saboteurs and enemy agents within Soviet industry and agriculture. The Dorozhno-Transportnoe Upravlenie (DTU, or Road and Transportation Department) — later the Third Directorate of the NKGB — was charged with detecting espionage and sabotage on the highways, railroads, and internal waterways.[37] The DTU deployed its agents in all major transportation and railroad facilities. This informant network functioned both as a mechanism to spot foreign agents as well as to keep Soviet citizens in check. The DTU and its subordinate elements in the republics acted as additional eyes and ears of both the KRU (counterintelligence) and the SPU (Secret Political Directorate) by augmenting the surveillance capabilities of these NKGB components.[38]

Again, although the Germans were able to piece together the basic functions of the EKU and DTU, details were lacking. The EKU had a headquarters staff of 165 people and the DTU 166.[39] When compared to the recently published May 1942 organization of the NKVD, which lays out every department and section of both directorates, the Germans never realized the full extent of the Soviet counterintelligence services' penetration of society or the redundancy built into the security organs. For example, the ETU's First Department was dedicated solely to the aviation industry and even had a section devoted to plants that made aircraft engines. The Third Department was responsible for the defense industry. There was no specific element devoted to agriculture. Moreover, Germans apparently had no idea that the First Section of the Third Department of the DTU covered civil aviation.[40]

By April 1943 the NKGB also had its own administration and communications directorates (including communications security and intercept), an investigations directorate, a directorate for guarding the Kremlin, and a directorate for leadership protection.[41] The Sixth Directorate (protection of Party and government leadership) was created out of the old NKVD's First Department.[42] Departments "A," "B," and "V" were respectively responsible for "exploitation of statistics and archives," operational-technical support possibly including surveillance and radio counterintelligence, and military correspondent censorship.[43] The NKGB, like all other directorates and Commissariats, had its own secretariat and staff as well as a "Cadres Department."

In May 1942 the First Department of the NKVD (leadership protection) had a headquarters staff of 354 persons. It consisted of twenty-four sections plus units for the protection of the leadership of the Ministry of Foreign Affairs, the Ministry of Defense, the Central Committee, employees of special laboratories (not specified) and installations.[44] It also had an investigative unit, duty officers, and responsibility for a training school. By April 1943 another directorate specifically dedicated to protecting the Kremlin may have been created out of the resources of the Sixth Directorate of the NKGB.[45] Sections of the First Special Department of the NKVD (archives and registry) and of the Special Operational-Technical Department probably went to the NKGB.[46]

Since partisan units were in constant contact with the population in German-occupied areas and were more likely to have prolonged contact with the Germans, the Soviet security services considered them more susceptible to being infected with "fascist ideas." Therefore the CPSU charged both the NKVD and probably later the NKGB with ensuring the political security and reliability of the partisan movement. The Directorate for Special Departments of the NKGB (Upravleniye Osobykh Otdeli [OO]) was responsible for security and counterintelligence within the partisan movement. Before 1943 this function was performed by the Special Departments of the NKVD.[47]

The organization and structure were patterned after the Special Departments in the Red Army (see below). Although the main function of this organization was to maintain the political reliability and security of partisan units, it was not uncommon for OO/NKGB officers also to act as chief of intelligence for some partisan units as well as a deputy brigade or battalion commander.[48] In addition to conducting interrogations of suspected German agents, providing operational security for partisan-directed agents, and ferreting out Soviet citizens who collaborated with the Germans, OO/NKGB officers in partisan units also recruited, coerced, or suborned Soviets working in German-occupied areas who were in leading positions to work against the Germans.[49] Neither the top secret *History of State Security* nor the collection of documents detailing the history of the headquarters staff of the security organs reflects a military counterintelligence component dedicated to the partisan movement, unless it was buried in the organization of the Fourth Directorate of the NKVD/NKGB.[50] However, this function appears to have been transferred to Smersh in 1943.[51]

The NKVD in May 1942 possessed a number of departments and special departments (*spetsial'nye otedeli*, or SO) for a variety of functions. Many of these were subsumed in April 1943 into one of the lettered departments (A, B, or V — see above) of the NKGB.[52] German documents, which by and large conform to available Soviet documents, show that there were special departments for the following functions: SO 1 maintained the NKGB's central records system on enemy agents, domestic informants, and persons under arrest; SO 2 provided agents with all the technical equipment necessary to communicate with their handlers securely (forged documents, radios, etc.), issued NKGB passes, established security regulations for government communications, conducted communications intercept, located and seized unauthorized radio stations, and in border zones conducted mail intercepts; SO 3 was charged with the surveillance of suspected persons (including NKGB personnel), carrying out searches, seizures, and arrests in conjunction with the Investigations Bureau, the KRU, the SPU, the Fourth Directorate, and Soviet military counterintelligence; SO 4 was responsible for censorship and carried out its mission by monitoring telephone calls, manning secret broadcasting stations, and intercepting mail (it was also responsible for developing invisible inks [secret writing systems] for Soviet agents); and SO 5 was charged with making codes and ciphers for the Soviet government and with attempting to intercept and break non-Soviet government codes and ciphers for communications security purposes. According to the Germans, the Department of Prison Affairs (Gefaengniswesen) was specifically charged with running the informant networks within the political prisons, and the NKVD was responsible for the physical security and administration of them.[53] The NKVD also had a department (unnumbered) that was responsible for combating "bandits." It had a headquarters staff of 37 and was divided into three geographical departments covering all the republics of the USSR.[54] Virtually all this is accurate, including the SO numbering system. The only major discrepancy between German and Soviet documents is that a "Department of Prison Affairs" was not an NKGB function but a function of the NKVD, and the Germans did not identify a special department to combat "bandits." The NKVD had a Directorate for POW and Internee Affairs with a headquarters staff of 30, and a Main Directorate for Concentration Camps (GULAG) with a headquarters staff of 456. The Fourth Section of the First Department of the KRU of the NKVD/NKGB ran agent operations in POW and internment camps. However, by April 1943, Smersh had dedicated an entire directorate (the second) to nothing but work in POW and internment camps.[55]

MILITARY COUNTERINTELLIGENCE (GUKR-SMERSH)

Soviet military counterintelligence — often referred to as Smersh, or simply OOs — was the primary organization charged with the neutralization and apprehension of German agents directly behind Russian lines. Its main purpose, however, was to maintain the security and political reliability of the Soviet armed forces. Its tasks included, but were not limited to, preventing desertion, neutralizing (including arresting) enemy spies, running double agents and conducting radio playbacks, combating counterrevolutionary activities, investigating crimes by military personnel, and protecting the operational security of the armed forces. Personnel assigned to Smersh probably ranged anywhere from 15,000 to 30,000, with a headquarters staff of 225, in May 1942.[56]

During World War II Soviet military counterintelligence consisted of two successive organizations: OO/NKVD and GUKR/NKO–Smersh. Smersh, short for Smert' Shpionam (Death to Spies), was established on 15 April 1943 in conjunction with the elevation of the NKGB to a separate Commissariat (see appendix B).[57] Colonel General Viktor S. Abakumov, who was formerly chief of OO/NKVD, was named chief of Smersh and elevated to the position of deputy minister of defense. For the first time since the early stages of the Bolshevik Revolution (with the exception of a brief period from February 1941 to July 1941), Soviet military counterintelligence was subordinated to the armed forces.[58] In 1946 it was resubordinated to State Security. Although there were two separate organizations, virtually no significant changes were made in the functions of military counterintelligence throughout the war. These organizations have been referred to as GUKR-NKO Smersh, OO/NKVD, military counterintelligence, and Osobye Otdeli (Special Departments, or OOs).[59]

According to largely German-originated documents, the headquarters components of Smersh consisted of six directorates and six departments. Although Smersh was responsible for the security of all the armed forces, a separate organization was set up in the navy and designated GUKR–NKVMF–Smersh. German counterintelligence documents and Soviet sources do not generally refer to a separate military counterintelligence component for the Soviet air force; however, a 1944 FHO document shows that a directorate of Smersh was responsible for overseeing surveillance activities for each branch of the Soviet armed forces, including the air force. Given this information, it is possible to conclude that the Directorate for Troop Surveillance at Smersh headquarters may have been further divided by branch of service.[60]

Smersh headquarters was organized into directorates for staff surveillance, troop surveillance, counterespionage, cooperation with partisans, investigations, and personnel, as well as several housekeeping and functional departments. The staff and troop surveillance directorates were responsible for surveillance of staff officers assigned to the Soviet General Staff headquarters in Moscow and with surveillance of troop units stationed in and around Moscow. Both directorates also controlled and coordinated the surveillance activities of lower-echelon Smersh elements.[61]

The counterespionage directorate controlled and coordinated all counterespionage operations down to army level (including double agents) and had responsibility for collecting some military intelligence and sabotage operations.[62] The partisan directorate carried out Smersh functions in partisan units and the investigations directorate carried out investigations of individuals deemed suspicious by the troop and staff surveillance directorates or by the communications security organization. The Personnel Directorate handled all employee records and selected personnel for promotions, training, and assignments.[63]

Smersh headquarters also consisted of approximately seven functional departments, a Kommendatura, a secretariat, and the military courts *(troikas)*. The Technical and Signal Surveillance Department was responsible for communications security and for intercepting and jamming enemy agent communications. The Military Censorship Department censored all military mail, which would make it difficult for the Germans to communicate with an agent by mail; the Security Control Department ensured that security regulations were properly carried out; the Cipher Department encoded and decoded messages, and maintained crypto-equipment; and the Special Inspection Department investigated all offenses committed by Smersh personnel and important agents. Another department was responsible for keeping agent files and case histories. The Kommendatura guarded Smersh installations and administered the day-to-day operations of Smersh prisons. The *troikas* were essentially military courts and could punish lesser offenses without a hearing of the accused. The Administrative Bureau served as the staff for Abakumov (the head of Smersh) and the Secretariat was the focal point for CPSU activities within Smersh. The Main Administration for Military Tribunals was subordinate to the Ministry of Defense. However, military regulations and discipline that did not stem from civil law and applied only to members of the Red Army were not within the sphere of the Military Tribunals. Therefore, the *troikas,* which were infamous during the war for their brutality and ruthlessness, possessed considerable latitude in administering punishments for various offenses (see chart A.2).[64]

The Smersh organization at front (or military district) and army-level headquarters resembled scaled-down versions of Smersh headquarters in Moscow (see Chart A.3). Both front and army Smersh units were the primary entities responsible for running double agents, conducting counterespionage operations, and passing on any military intelligence information collected as a result of those operations. Front and army Smersh units ranged in size from 70 to 110 men, not counting the guard companies, which numbered 100 to 150 men. Generals commanded front-level units, and colonels or brigadier generals commanded army-level units.[65]

To combat German agents and maintain both political and military discipline within the Red Army, front-level and army-level Smersh units had at their disposal "security troops" formed from elements of the Border Guards and NKVD Internal Troops.[66] Military counterintelligence officers commanded these units, even though these "security troops" were probably technically and administratively subordinate to the NKVD's Main Administration for the Rear Area.[67] These units, often referred to as blocking or annihilation detachments, were infamous at the beginning of the war for shooting retreating Soviet soldiers.[68] As the war progressed, the blocking detachments were instrumental in sweeping rear areas for German agents and for setting up ambushes for newly deployed agents. Five or six such regiments were attached to fronts. Each regiment numbered approximately 1,650 men and consisted of three rifle battalions, a reconnaissance company, a submachine-gun and machine-gun company, a signal company, an antitank company, an engineer platoon, and maintenance, chemical warfare, and transportation units.[69]

The primary mission for Smersh organizations assigned to Soviet military units from corps to battalion level was to run the informant networks. Units below the army level had no capability to conduct offensive counterintelligence operations against German forces and therefore could concentrate on troop surveillance. A division-level Smersh unit consisted of approximately 15 to 20 men, and a guard platoon of 20 to 30 troops.

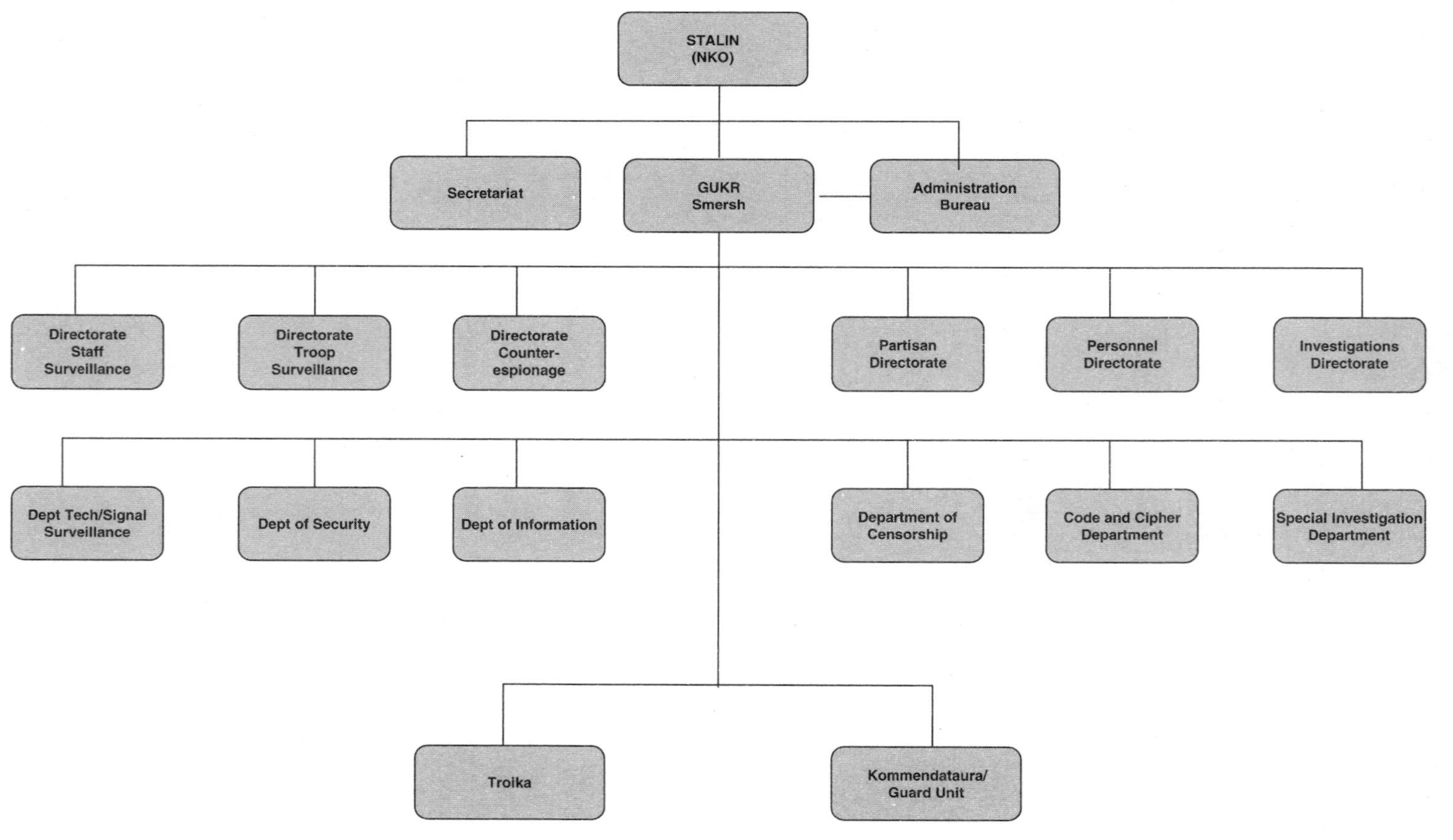

Chart A.2. German View of the Organization of GUKR-NKO Smersh

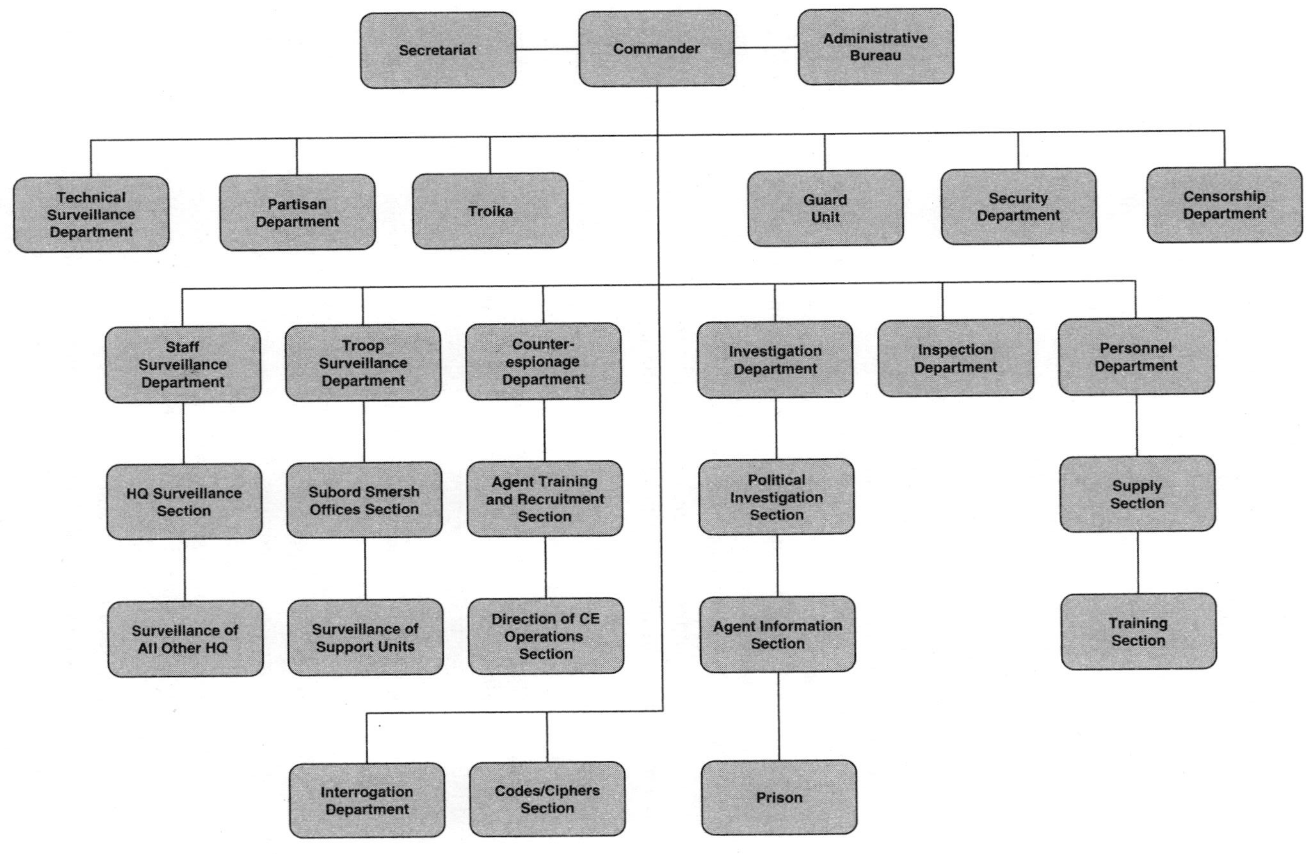

Chart A.3. German View of the Organization of Smersh at Front

One officer was assigned to each regiment, and one to a battalion. Each battalion officer recruited resident agents, and, in turn, resident agents recruited informants.[70]

Available Soviet documentation on military counterintelligence consists of a broad organization outline of Smersh (eight departments) in April 1943 and a breakdown of OO/NKVD in May 1942 by department and section[71] (see chart A.4). German counterintelligence amassed a reasonably detailed and accurate picture of Smersh at the front level and below and had a good grasp on Soviet military counterintelligence operations. However, there were considerable discrepancies in how the headquarters staff was organized. It appears that Smersh underwent considerable reorganization from OO/NKVD (see chart A.5). For example, recent Soviet documentation shows that Smersh was organized into departments for counterintelligence for the "central organs" of the Red Army (First Department), "work among POWs and internees" (Second), the "rooting out of agents and radio games" (Third), counterintelligence operations behind the front (Fourth), surveillance of the leadership of the military districts (Fifth), investigations (Sixth), dossiers, archives, and statistics (Seventh), and communications (Eighth).[72]

The headquarters staff of OO/NKVD (Fifth Directorate) in May 1942 totaled 225 persons, all divided into ten numbered departments and one unnumbered one.[73] The responsibilities broke down as follows. It had a secretariat and an unidentified operation section. Department 1 covered the General Staff of the Red Army, as well as staffs of the fronts and armies, including the GRU and the intelligence staffs of the fronts and armies. Department 2 was responsible for the air force, the air defense forces, and the airborne forces. Department 3 covered armored, rocket, and artillery units and their staffs, including those at the Ministry of Defense level, as well as the archives of the Red Army. Department 4 conducted "agent-operational work" in the infantry, artillery, sappers (engineers), and cavalry, was responsible for combating desertion, treason, and self-inflicted wounds, and even had a section that covered military academies and the military procuracy. Department 5 had counterintelligence responsibility for a variety of disparate entities that included the main supply directorate of the Red Army, the Ministry of Defense, various military administrative functions, medical service, veterans affairs, and military construction.[74]

Department 6 covered the NKVD troops to include the Border Guards, Internal Troops, and convoy and supply troops. Department 7 (operations) conducted a wide range of counterintelligence activities. Areas of responsibility included the Special Departments themselves; communications security; keeping track and possibly rooting out traitors of the motherland — spies, deserters, saboteurs, terrorists, cowards, "panic-mongers," those who inflicted wounds on themselves, and anti-Soviet elements; and maintaining card indexes on enemy agents and personnel, traitors to the motherland, and those compromised by the testimony of enemy agents. Department 8 was responsible for communications security (codes and ciphers), and department 9 had counterintelligence responsibility for the navy. Another entity functioning as a department had responsibility for the NKVD staff itself and the Dzerzhinksii Division.[75] The top secret *History of State Security* shows a tenth department responsible for rooting out enemy agents and conducing counterintelligence in POW and internment camps.[76]

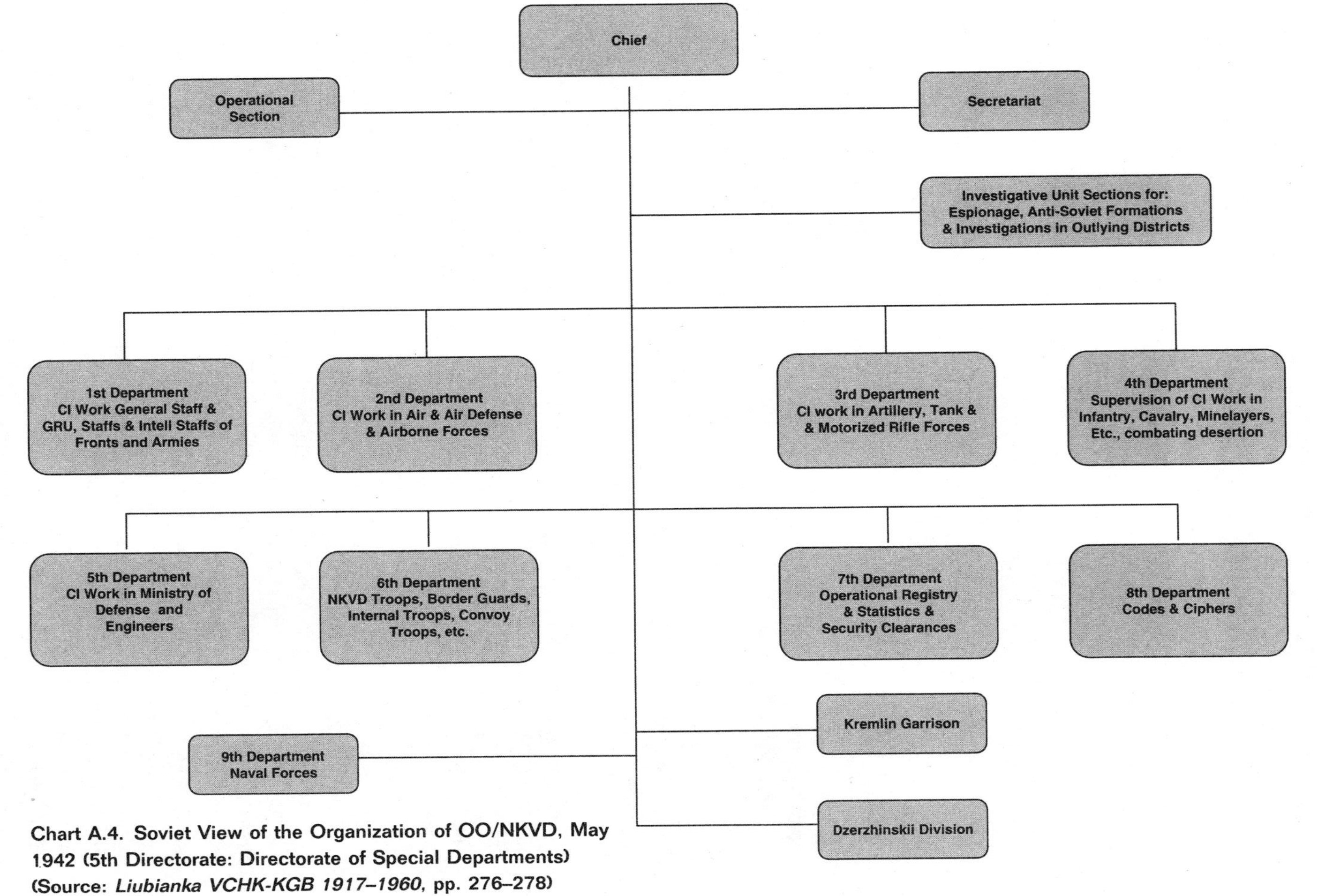

Chart A.4. Soviet View of the Organization of OO/NKVD, May 1942 (5th Directorate: Directorate of Special Departments) (Source: *Liubianka VCHK-KGB 1917–1960*, pp. 276–278)

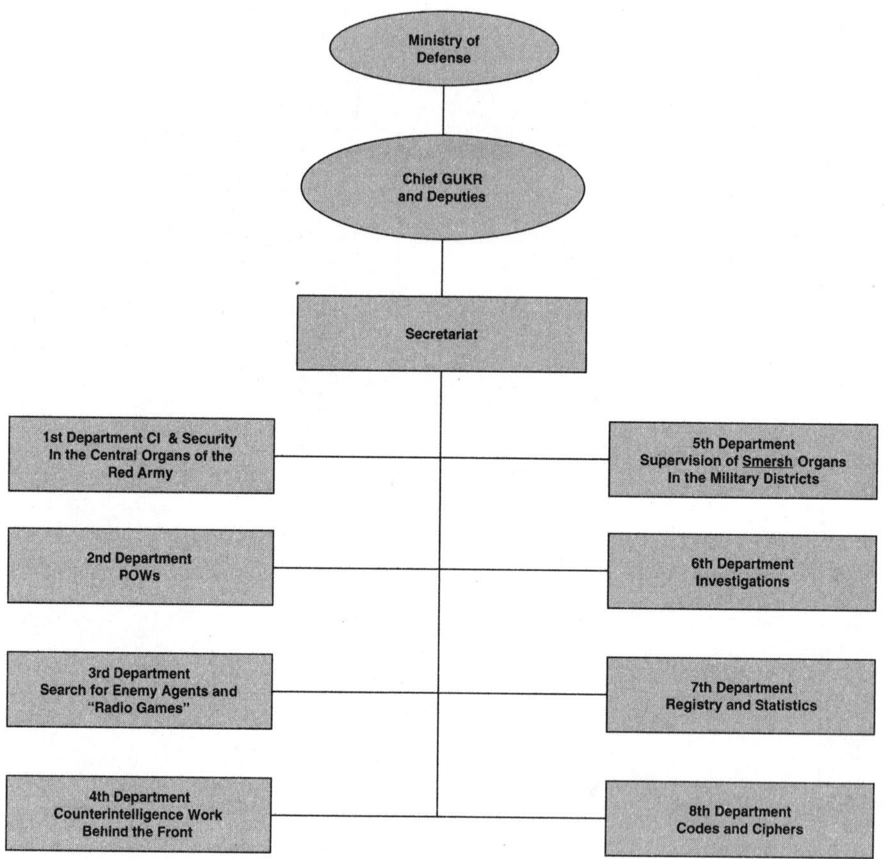

Chart A.5. Soviet View of the Organization of Smersh, May 1943 (Source: FSB, *Liubianka II*, p. 233)

PEOPLE'S COMMISSARIAT FOR INTERNAL AFFAIRS (NKVD)

After the reorganization of the Soviet intelligence and security services in 1943, the NKVD no longer had a foreign intelligence mission and ceased to be responsible for counterespionage and counterintelligence operations. However, Beria's NKVD was still a formidable security organization. It remained responsible for law and order, the maintenance and operation of government communications and the physical security of sensitive installations (including those related to the atomic bomb project) and the infrastructure of the country's interior. It still retained control over Soviet borders, as well as the administration and operation of POW and concentration camps (GULAG); it was also responsible for the physical security of the Red Army's rear area, to include providing security for such special weapons as the Katyusha multiple rocket launchers (see chart A.6).[77] The NKVD of 1943 strongly resembled Himmler's SS without the counterintelligence and political security functions of the Gestapo and the SD.

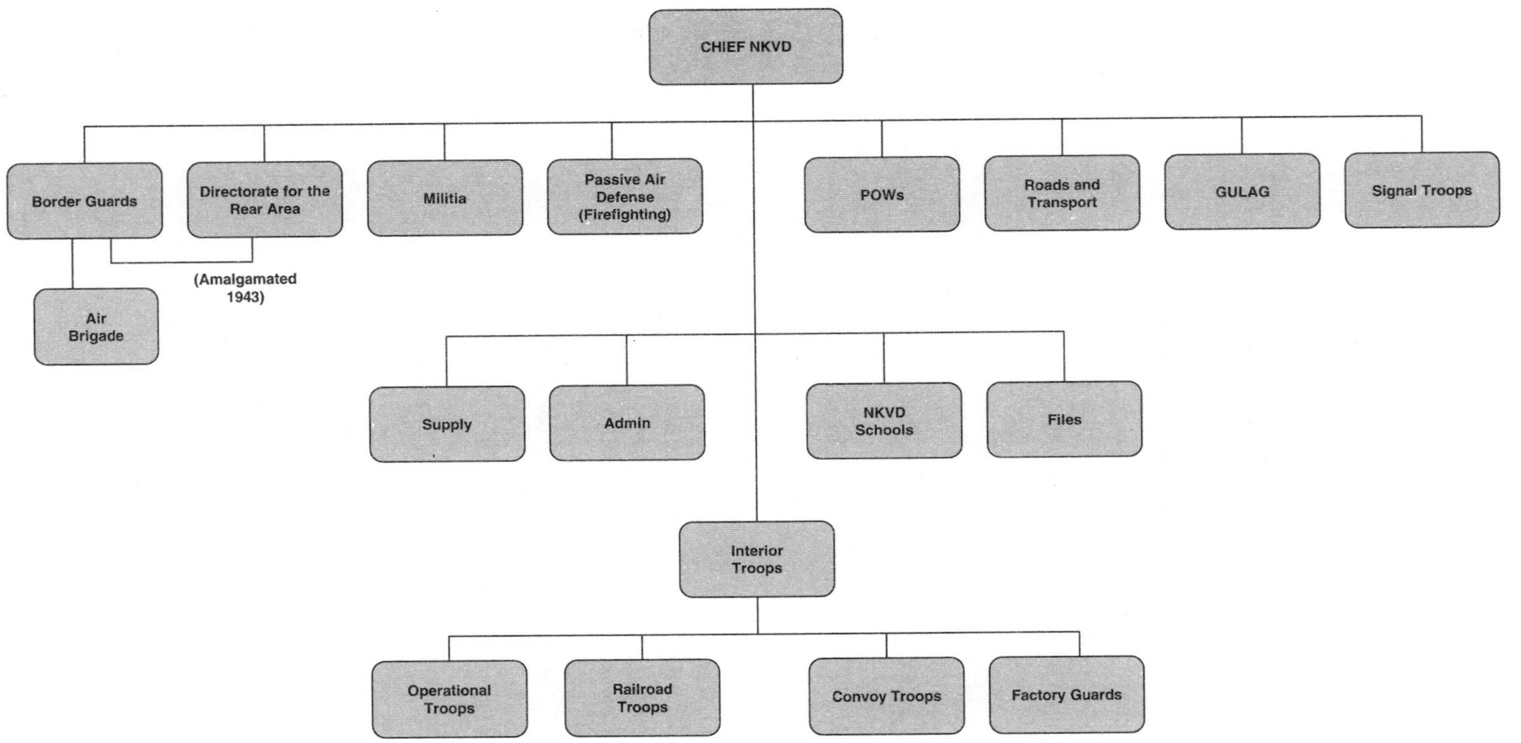

Chart A.6. Basic Organization of the NKVD, 1944

Estimates for the size of the NKVD troops during World War II — which include the Border Guards, interior troops, communications and transport troops of all types, the militia, prison guards, and firefighters — range from a low of 850,000 to a high of 2 million. Given the size of the USSR and the wide-ranging functions of the NKVD, an estimate of 2 million may not be an exaggerated figure.[78] On the eve of the war the Border Guards themselves numbered from about 157,000 to 158,000 men.[79] One U.S. intelligence document, based on 1944 FHO data, estimated the Border Guard strength at sixty-eight regiments and interior troop strength at thirty-one divisions and twenty-one brigades.[80]

The primary NKVD components responsible for physically thwarting the activities of German agents operating behind Soviet lines were the Main Directorate for Interior Troops (headquarters staff of 174 in May 1942) and the Main Directorate of Border Guards (headquarters staff of 246). Much of the German-originated material, and even some Soviet primary sources, indicate that both directorates might have been amalgamated into a Main Directorate for the Security of the Rear Area (often referred to as the Main Directorate for Security Troops).[81] A Soviet document, dated 1 January 1944, shows that there was a Main Directorate for Internal troops, a Main Directorate for Rear-Area Security (headquarters staff of 43 in May 1942), and a Main Directorate for Border Guards. In May 1942 rear-area security was a directorate subordinated to the Main Directorate for Interior Troops.[82]

Both interior troops and Border Guard units were highly mobile, and it was not uncommon for both Border Guard and NKVD interior troop units to fight on the front line alongside regular units of the Red Army. The Border Guard Directorate had an air brigade subordinate to it. The Border Guards' main mission prior to the war was to maintain the security of the Soviet frontiers and to conduct intelligence and some counterintelligence operations in the immediate border area. After the German attack, their main mission became rear-area security.[83]

The Main Directorate for Interior Troops was divided into four directorates: one each for railroad troops, convoy troops, and factory guards, and one directorate for operations troops. Railroad troops guarded railway lines and were organized into divisions, regiments, and battalions. Convoy troops protected the movement of troops, supplies, and POWs on the roads, waterways, and railroads. Factory guards provided protection for major defense industry facilities. Operations troops guarded the rear area of the Red Army.[84] However, recently published Soviet documents, dated 20 May 1942 and 1 January 1943, indicate that railroad, convoy, and numerous security troop formations, such as the Main Directorate for Troops Guarding Especially Important Enterprises (headquarters staff of eighty-one), might not have been subordinated to the Main Directorate for Interior Troops.[85]

The primary missions for Border Guard units (or rear-area security units) during the war, in addition to maintaining the security of the frontier, were to apprehend enemy agents and Red Army stragglers, to prevent Soviet troops from retreating (blocking detachments), and to guard key installations in the immediate rear of the Red Army. Prior to the German invasion, Border Guard units also had a well-developed intelligence and counterintelligence system. The main missions of the interior troops (especially operations troops) were to apprehend enemy agents and guard key installations in the interior of the USSR, to suppress insurrection, civil disorder, and uprisings, to defend against enemy airborne troops, and, if necessary, to put down mutiny within the armed forces. Both Border Guard units and NKVD interior troops also participated in mopping up remnants of enemy units behind Soviet lines, as well as in the deportation and outright murder of hundreds of thousands, if not millions, of ethnic minorities to other areas of the USSR.[86] Border Guards and interior troops were also employed as snipers and sharpshooters, and destroyed key installations in the face of the German advance.[87]

The NKVD permeated every aspect of the war effort. For example, the Main Directorate for Firefighting, which was renamed the Main Directorate for Passive Air Defense, was responsible for organizing passive air defense measures within the civilian population. One air defense group consisted of 31 people for every 200 to 500 residents. These groups ensured, among other things, that preparatory measures, such as camouflage, were carried out; they were also responsible for damage control. Further, these groups were prepared to organize into partisan bands in the event they were overrun by the enemy. Other highlights of the NKVD organization included main directorates for police (militia), concentration camps (GULAG), firefighting (also known as the Main Directorate for Passive Air Defense), supply, signal troops, POWs, and the main directorates for transport and the construction of roads. As in any large organization, the NKVD also had components for its own organizational administration, files, and for the administration of NKVD schools.[88] Vladimir Petrov, a Soviet intelligence officer who served in the NKVD during World War II and defected with his wife to the West after the war, stated that the Moscow headquarters staff of the Main Directorate for Concentration Camps numbered 2,000. However, according to a May 1942 Soviet document, the actual number might have been as low as 456, with an authorized strength of 1,810.[89] The signal troops, in addition to being responsible for the operations, maintenance, and security of all NKVD communications, were also charged with intercepting some types of enemy communications as well as with monitoring friendly communications for operational security reasons and may have numbered about 15,000 men.[90]

Liquidation units and territorial groups augmented NKVD troop security efforts and probably NKGB counterintelligence efforts as well. Liquidation units were organized by local and regional NKVD offices and were composed of politically reliable individuals ineligible for military service. These units further aided NKVD/NKGB operations to combat enemy agents and ferret out dissident groups and citizens exhibiting anti-Soviet behavior. The liquidation units consisted of approximately 75 to 200 men, divided into platoons of 25 men each, and further divided into 8-man squads. They patrolled city and village streets looking for suspect activity. Territorial groups consisted of 8 to 10 men whose occupations included, among others, that of a shepherd, a watchman, a forester, and a railroad employee. They were charged with assisting the Border Guards in monitoring frontier areas for suspicious activity and for apprehending enemy agents.[91]

Appendix B. Chronology of the Soviet Intelligence and Security Services[92]

VCheka	20 December 1917–6 February 1922
GPU	6 February 1922–15 November 1923
OGPU	15 November 1923–10 July 1934
GUGB/NKVD	10 July 1934–3 February 1941
NKGB and NKVD	3 February 1941–20 July 1941
GUGB/NKVD	20 July 1941–14 April 1943
NKGB and NKVD	14 April 1943–19 March 1946
MGB and MVD	19 March 1946–7 March 1953

(The KI was established in 1947 and absorbed the foreign intelligence missions of the MGB and the GRU. It was abolished in 1951, and the MGB and the GRU were given back their foreign intelligence missions. The MVD also existed at this time but with slightly different responsibilities.).

MGB merged with MVD	7 March 1953–13 March 1954
KGB and MVD	13 March 1954–August 1991

(From 1962 to 1968 the MVD was renamed *Ministerstvo Okhrany Obshchestvennovo Poriadki* [Ministry for the Maintenance of Public Order, or MOOP].)

Appendix C. Chiefs of the Soviet Intelligence and Security Services[93]

Felix Dzerzhinskii	VCheka	20 December 1917–6 February 1922
Felix Dzerzhinskii	GPU	6 February 1922–15 November 1923
Felix Dzerzhinskii	OGPU	15 November 1923–20 July 1926
Vyacheslav Menzhinskiy	OGPU	20 July 1926–10 May 1934
Genrikh Yagoda	GUGB/NKVD	10 May 1934–25 September 1936
Nikolai Yezhov	GUGB/NKVD	25 September 1936–8 December 1938
Lavrenty Beria Merkulov	GUGB/NKVD	8 December 1938–3 February 1941
V. N. Merkulov	NKGB	3 February 1941–20 July 1941
Lavrenty Beria	NKVD	3 February 1941–20 July 1941
Lavrenty Beria (Merkulov, Chief of GUGB)	GUGB/NKVD	20 July 1941–14 April 1943
V. N. Merkulov	NKGB	14 April 1943–19 March 1946
Lavrenty Beria	NKVD	14 April 1943–19 March 1946

V. S. Abakumov	MGB	October 1946–August 1951
S. N. Kruglov	MVD	19 March 1946–7 March 1953

(The KI was established in 1947 and absorbed the foreign intelligence missions of the MGB and the GRU. Both the MVD and the MGB existed but with slightly different responsibilities. Abakumov was replaced as head of the MGB in 1952 by S. D. Ignat'ev. Kruglov continued on as chief of the MVD.)

S. N. Kruglov (MGB merged with MVD)	MVD	7 March 1953–13 March 1953
Ivan Serov (Chief of KGB) (The KGB and MVD became separate organizations.)	KGB and MVD	13 March 1954–25 December 1958
Alexander Shelepin	KGB	25 December1958–31 October 1961
Vladimir Semichastny	KGB	13 November 1961–18 May 1967
Yuri Andropov	KGB	18 May 1967–26 May 1982
Vitalii Fedorchuk	KGB	26 May 1982–15 December 1982
Viktor Chebrikov	KGB	16 December 1982–1988
Vladimir Kryuchkov	KGB	1988–1991

Appendix D. Evolution of Soviet Military Counterintelligence (1918–1949)[94]

May 1918	Voenkontrol' (Military Control) placed under Commissar for War to conduct counterespionage and counterintelligence operations in the army.
July 1918	Chekas established to fight counterrevolution on both the Eastern and Western Fronts. VCheka establishes a military sub-department to coordinate work of Front Chekas.
September 1918	Various organizations dealing with counterintelligence in the military placed under the Military Supervision Sub-department of the Registration Office of the Revvoensovet.
November 1918	Military Sub-department of the VCheka given full department status.
19 December 1918	Special Departments of the VCheka established. Considered official birthday of Soviet military counterintelligence.
6 February 1922	OOs (Special Departments of VCheka) become OOs of the GPU.
15 November 1923	OO GPU becomes OO OGPU.

10 July 1934	OO OGPU becomes OO/GUGB of the newly formed NKVD.
3 February 1941	OO/GUGB of the NKVD (often referred to as OO/NKVD) is transferred to the armed forces as Third Directorate of the NKO, a Third Directorate of the NKVMF (Narodnyi Kommissariat Voennoi Morskoi Flot) is established, and a Third Directorate was left behind in the GUGB of the NKVD to watch the internal troops, frontier troops, and so on.
20 July 1941	Third Directorate (OOs) of the NKO and the NKVMF transferred to GUGB/NKVD and again referred to as OO/NKVD.
14 April 1943	OO/NKVD is transferred to the NKO as the Third Main Directorate of the People's Commissariat of Defense —Death to Spies (GUKR–NKO–Smersh — Smert' Shipionam). A Third Main Directorate was set up in the Navy (GUKR–NKVMF–Smersh). An OO contingent was left behind in the NKVD to ensure the security of the interior and frontier troops. An OO contingent also remained in the NKGB to ensure the security of partisan units.
19 May 1946	Smersh was dissolved and its functions were absorbed by the newly created MGB. When the NKVMF was subordinated to the Ministry of Defense, OO/MGB assumed responsibility for the security of the navy. OO/MGB became GUKR/MGB.
7 March 1953	GUKR/MGB becomes OO/MVD.
13 March 1954	OO/MVD becomes OO/KGB and remained so until the KGB was abolished in 1991.

Appendix E. German Organization for Secret War

An initial assessment of Nazi Germany could conclude that it, as well as the USSR, belonged to the ranks of counterintelligence states. Nazi Germany established a party-subordinated intelligence and security service, the Reichssicherheitshauptamt (Reich Security Main Office, or RSHA) that obsessively pursued real or imagined enemies of the state. Himmler's RSHA of the SS, and the Gestapo in particular, inspired fear, used terror on a mass scale, and blanketed Germany and the occupied territories with informants and extermination camps.[95] However, the similarities with the USSR as a counterintelligence state end there. The Nazi Party and the SS lasted only twelve years; because of the diffusion of intelligence and security resources, the Party and the SS security service never achieved the almost coterminous relationship — a key ingredient of a counterintelligence state — that existed between the CPSU and the Soviet State Security organs.[96]

The lack of centralization of the German services played a significant role in their defeat. It hampered the Germans' ability to fully grasp the depth and scope of the Soviet counterintelligence assault on the Nazi intelligence and security services. Internecine bureaucratic warfare between Himmler's SS and the Abwehr and the overextension of scarce intelligence and counterintelligence resources further hindered German clandestine collection efforts in the USSR. By the end of 1941 German armies occupied most of Europe and parts of North Africa. With the exception of Fremde Heere Ost (Foreign Armies East, or FHO) — the all-source intelligence analysis organization for the German army in the East — almost every other German intelligence organization had elements deployed from Scandinavia to North Africa.[97] Therefore the Germans could not commit all their resources to the Eastern Front. In stark contrast, the Soviets focused the overwhelming majority of their intelligence and counterintelligence resources on defeating Germany.[98]

The major German organizations charged with initiating clandestine operations behind Russian lines were the Abwehr (military intelligence) and Sicherheitsdienst/Ausland (SD/Ausland — the foreign intelligence organization of the SS).[99] The Abwehr was subordinate to the High Command of the German Army (Oberkommando der Wehrmacht, or OKW), and SD/Ausland was subordinate to the RSHA, also known as Amt (office) VI of the RSHA.[100] The Nazis dispersed counterintelligence and counterespionage functions among components of the Abwehr (Abwehr III, in particular), the German army's Geheime Feldpolizei (GFP, or Secret Field Police), and the Gestapo (also known as Amt IV of the RSHA).[101] FHO and the intelligence staffs of the German army groups in the Soviet Union (also known as the 1c or Abwehr Liaison Officer, roughly equivalent to the G-2 in a U.S. army-level formation) analyzed the bulk of the intelligence and counterintelligence information obtained from clandestine sources, including captured Soviet agents.[102]

AMT/AUSLAND ABWEHR

Admiral Wilhelm Canaris headed Amt/Ausland/Abwehr until late 1944, when it was officially taken over by the RSHA. The Abwehr was divided into three main components, one each for clandestine collection (Abwehr I), sabotage (Abwehr II), and counterintelligence (Abwehr III).[103] Abteilung Z (central department) was responsible for archives and administration, and Amtsgruppe Ausland (Foreign Department) briefed OKW on military policy, conducted liaison with foreign military attachés, and supervised the German military attaché system.[104] To conduct operations, the Abwehr broke down further into regional controllers, stations, outstations, and outposts (roughly translated as Abwehrleitstellen, Abwehrstellen (Asts), Nebenstellen (Nests), and Aussenstellen respectively; see chart A.7).[105] The Abwehrleitstellen, the Asts, and some Nests mirrored the organization of Abwehr headquarters on a smaller scale. By 1942 Abwehr field elements consisted of thirty-three Asts, twenty-six Nests, and twenty-three Aussen-

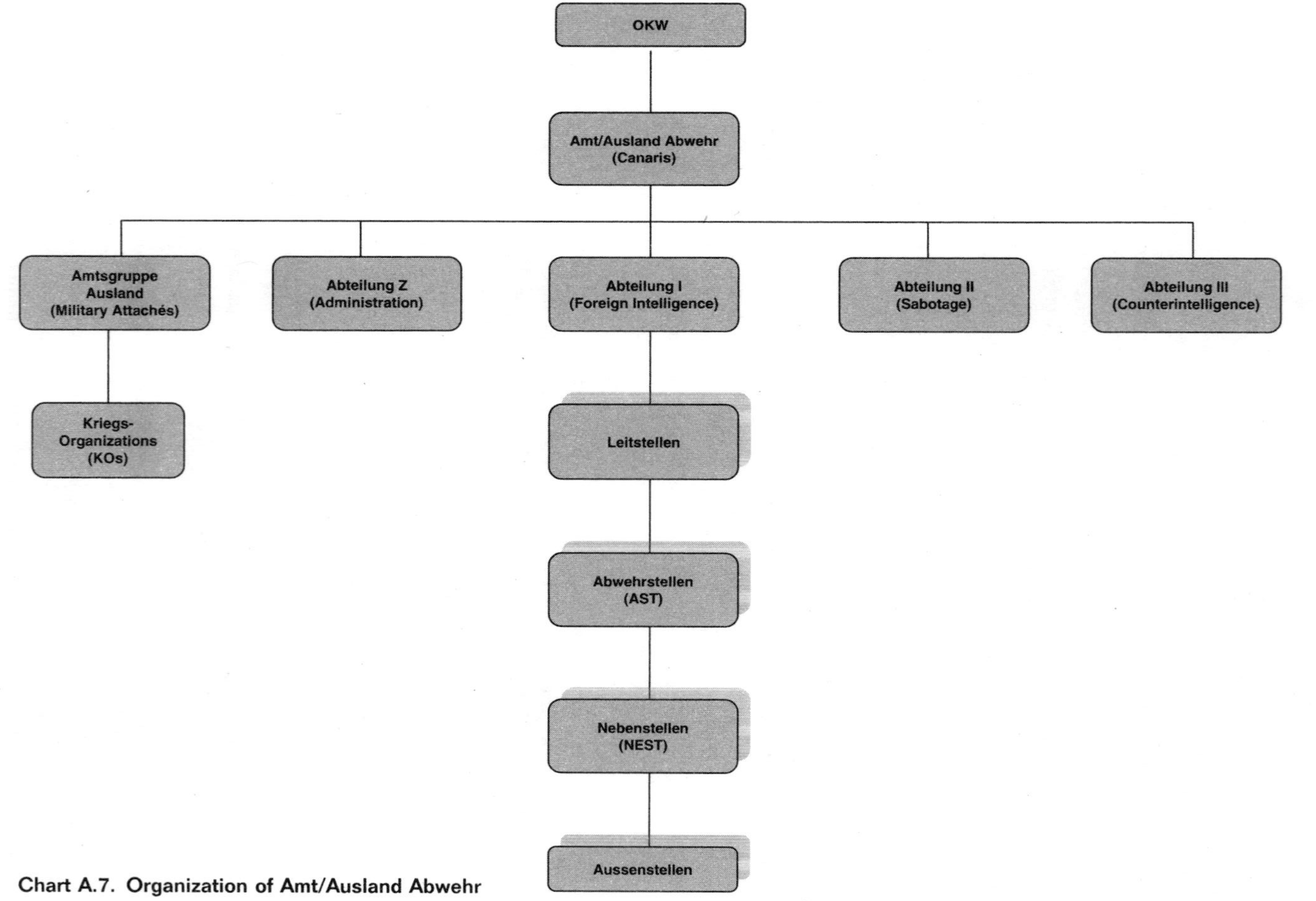

Chart A.7. Organization of Amt/Ausland Abwehr

stellen. Although there were wide variations in size, each Ast and its subordinate elements consisted of approximately 150 people.[106]

On the Eastern Front, among the main adversaries of Soviet military counterintelligence were Abwehr mobile units — designated Frontaufklaerungskommandos (front reconnaissance commands, or FAKs) and Frontaufklaerungstruppen (front reconnaissance troops, or FATs) — which were attached to the German Army Groups (see chart A.8).[107] FAKs controlled several FATs and their duties corresponded with Abwehr functions. For example, the FAKs/FATs charged with seizing enemy documents and collecting intelligence on the size, strength, and disposition of Soviet forces were given three-digit numbers starting with 1. Those FAKs/FATs charged with conducting sabotage operations were given three-digit numbers starting with 2, and the FAKs/FATs conducting counterintelligence operations and combating partisans were given three-digit numbers starting with 3. Abwehr II also had at its disposal the Brandenburg Division, upgraded from a regiment in 1942, which largely conducted guerrilla warfare and sabotage behind enemy lines and seized military objectives in advance of regular forces.[108] FAKs consisted of thirty to forty men and FATs numbered approximately fifteen to thirty men.[109] Training camps run by FAKs could have forty to fifty agents in various stages of training.[110] FAT training camps could accommodate from twenty to thirty agents at any given time.[111] As the situation in the East was extremely fluid, the strengths and capabilities of FAKs/FATs varied considerably throughout the war.[112]

The total number of Abwehr officers on the Eastern Front engaged in collecting intelligence and counterintelligence information from clandestine human sources, supporting those operations, and evaluating information gleaned from them cannot be unequivocally determined from available evidence. David Kahn, in *Hitler's Spies,* estimated that, by 1944, a total of 9,200 officers and men were assigned to FAKs/FATs on all fronts. An additional 5,000 were assigned to Asts, and approximately 1,000 Abwehr employees were assigned to intelligence duties in German embassies in neutral countries.[113] When adding these figures to the roughly 650 officers assigned to Abwehr headquarters and the troops assigned to the Brandenburg Division, Amt/Ausland Abwehr totaled at least 16,000 men.[114] Although a large part of these resources were devoted to the Eastern Front, it was still a small effort compared to the size of the area to be covered and the magnitude of the Soviet counterintelligence effort.

FREMDE HEERE OST (FHO)

FHO was subordinate to Oberkommando des Heeres (High Command of the German Army, or OKH) and provided OKH with critical all-source analysis of the operations, plans, and intentions of the Soviet armed forces, as well as with counterintelligence information and analyses on the Soviet intelligence and security services.[115] In addition to obtaining intelligence from the FAKs/FATs, FHO also did so from a variety of organizations, including Amt/Ausland Abwehr, Fremde Luftwaffe Ost (Foreign Air Forces, East), and the Wehrmacht signals intelligence organization Leitstelle fuer Nachrichtenaufklaerung Ost.[116] FHO was officially established on 10 November 1938

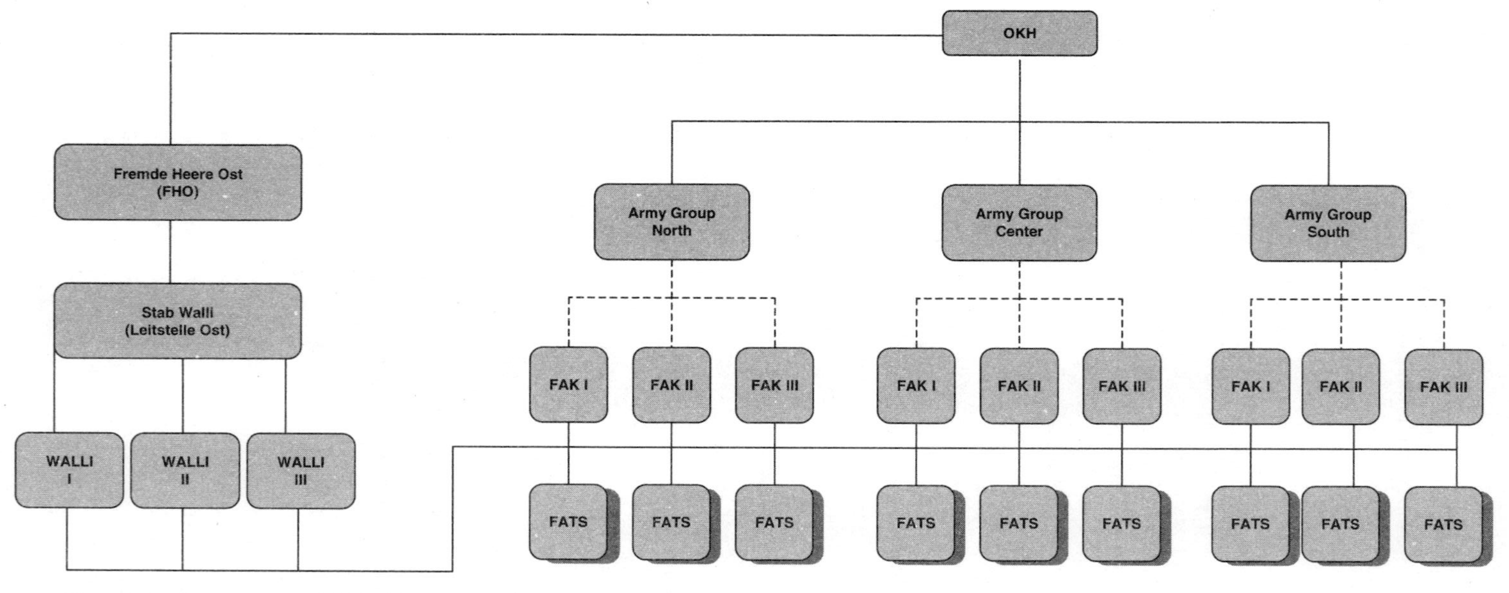

Chart A.8. Organization of FAKs/FATs

and was headed by Lieutenant Colonel Eberhard Kinzel until March 1942, when the chief of the General Staff, General Franz Halder, replaced him with Lieutenant Colonel Reinhard Gehlen. Gehlen was later promoted to *Generalmajor* (Brigadier General). On 10 April 1945 Lieutenant Colonel Gerhard Wessel became head of FHO until its dissolution on 21 April 1945.[117]

When Gehlen became head of FHO in March 1942, the Abwehr field organizations (regional controllers) responsible for intelligence and counterintelligence (Stab Walli I and Stab Walli III — all of which later became Leitstellen) and the FAKs/FATs subordinate to Walli I and Walli III came under the operational control of FHO. The Abwehr, however, retained control over sabotage operations.[118] Gehlen reorganized FHO in May 1942 (see chart A.9) and, with only minor modifications until the end of the war, he divided FHO into six groups (Gruppen) consisting of several subgroups (Referate).[119] Group I prepared daily situation reports, and Group II was responsible for detailed research and analysis on all aspects of the Soviet military effort, including the Soviet war-making potential. Gehlen required Group II to be able to give a competent written answer within two hours to any question concerning intelligence it had gathered or evaluated.[120] Subgroup IIc maintained a 30,000-card index on the order of battle for the Soviet armed forces, including biographical information on Soviet division commanders.[121] Group III translated captured documents, radio broadcasts, and Soviet propaganda and periodicals. Groups IV, V, and VI were responsible, respectively, for Scandinavia, for preparing situation maps, and for administration.[122] According to Gehlen's debriefing at the end of the war, FHO consisted of fifty officers, seventy NCOs, and sixty clerks.[123] Again, given the magnitude of the Soviet war effort, this was a small allocation of resources.

REICHSSICHERHEITSHAUPTAMT: SICHERHEITSDIENST/AUSLAND (RSHA)

The RSHA functioned largely as the security and intelligence service of the SS.[124] Reinhard Heydrich headed the RSHA until his assassination in 1942.[125] After a hiatus of some months, he was succeeded by Ernst Kaltenbrunner.[126] The RSHA was directly subordinate to the *Reichsfuehrer* SS, Heinrich Himmler, and was organized into seven departments (see chart A.10), of which Schellenberg's SD/Ausland and Heinrich Mueller's Gestapo were the most important. According to the testimony provided by Ernst Kaltenbrunner and Otto Ohlendorf (chief of SD/Inland) at the Nuremberg war crimes trials, the SS totaled 5 million members, the Gestapo 40,000 members, and the Sicherheitsdienst 3,000 members.[127] SD/Ausland was organized geographically into groups and consisted of approximately 1,000 officers, including the personnel stationed in occupied territories.[128] Group VI Referat (section) C collected and analyzed political and economic intelligence on the Soviet Union, Poland, the Eastern Balkans, the Far East (including Japan), and the Near East.[129] According to a Supreme Headquarters Allied Expeditionary Force (SHAFE) Counterintelligence War Room report dated 23 April 1945, Group VI C also had a large special section "CZ" (Z was for Operation Zeppelin), which was responsible for directing SS sabotage and guerrilla warfare on the Eastern Front.[130]

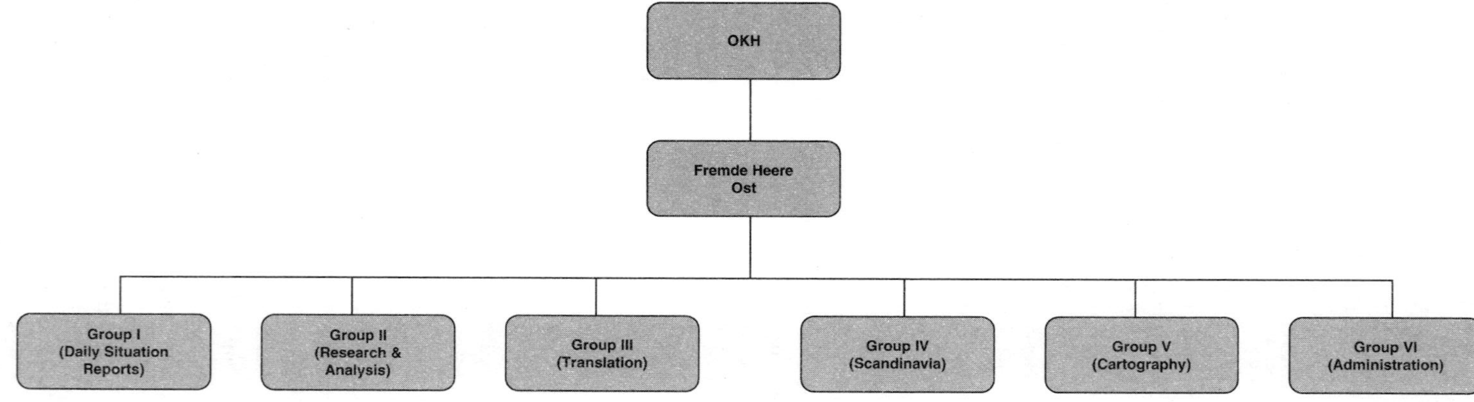

Chart A.9. Organization of Fremde Heere Ost

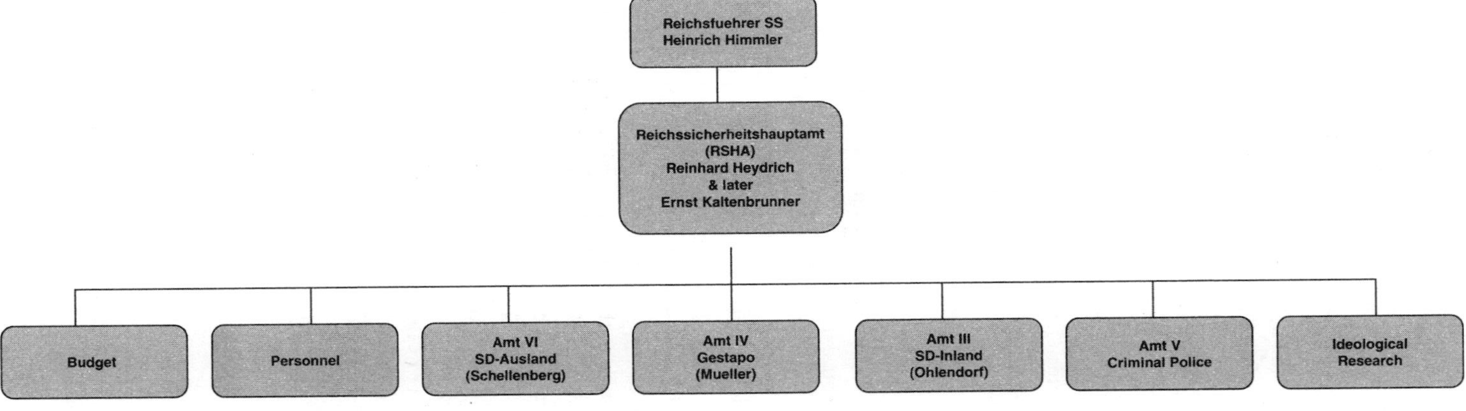

Chart A.10. Organization of the Reichssicherheitshauptamt (RSHA)

Schellenberg expanded SD foreign intelligence operations. Operation Zeppelin — which ultimately ended in failure — was an enormous undertaking in which SD/Ausland expected to deploy thousands of agents behind Russian lines.[131] Section C Zeppelin controlled the SD/Ausland field elements that were attached to various SS police units operating in the areas of the German army groups, and Zeppelin field elements functioned much like FAKs/FATs except that reports were forwarded directly to Berlin.[132] By the end of 1942 Schellenberg ordered the deployment of two more mobile units (Hauptkommandos) to the Eastern Front. One Hauptkommando was assigned to cover the area of Army Group North and another was assigned to the area of Army Group South. Aussenkommandos were subordinate to Hauptkommandos and were expanded in size. Aussenkommandos by then consisted of fifteen to twenty Soviet interrogators or agents, one German officer, and several German NCOs.[133] Their missions were largely the same as those of the Abwehr I FAKs, that is, to train and deploy agents behind Soviet lines.[134] Like Schellenberg, many of the men assigned to SD/Ausland, and Group C in particular, were in their early to mid-thirties and held military ranks equivalent to majors, lieutenant colonels, and colonels.[135] To fulfill the requirement for service at the front and to accelerate their promotions, many served in the notorious Einsatzkommandos (death squads).[136]

As a result of numerous Abwehr intelligence failures and problems with the political reliability of several senior Abwehr officers, Hitler signed a decree on 12 February 1944 abolishing the Abwehr.[137] Canaris was removed from his post six days later, and Hitler ordered Himmler to take command of a new unified German intelligence service, the details of which were to be worked out with the chief of OKW, Field Marshal Wilhelm Keitel.[138] At a conference of RSHA and Abwehr officers in mid-May 1944, Himmler announced the details of the agreement between the RSHA and OKW. The agreement basically placed Abwehr I and II into a Militaerisches Amt (Military Office, referred to as the Milamt) under the RSHA, pending a gradual merger of the Milamt into Schellenberg's SD/Ausland. The Gestapo took over many of Abwehr III's functions. The FAKs/FATs (I and II) were to remain administratively subordinate to OKW (or OKH). The Abwehr budget was transferred to the SD.[139] By 1 December 1944, the RSHA completed its takeover of the seventy-eight-year-old German military intelligence organization.[140] To quote one historian of the German intelligence services, "the organizational chaos of the German spy service was complete."[141]

NOTES

Introduction

1. For example, see David Glantz, *Soviet Military Deception in the Second World War* (London: Frank Cass, 1989), for the best comprehensive work to date on Soviet military deception in World War II.

2. See, for example, Security and Intelligence Foundation, *The Trust* (Arlington, Va., 1989; originally prepared by the Central Intelligence Agency, reprinted by SIF, and obtained under the FOIA). This concise, well-organized, and well-written monograph describes Soviet State Security's ten-year counterintelligence war to defeat the external émigré opposition to the Bolshevik regime.

3. For the first scholarly treatment solely dedicated to how badly German military intelligence underestimated Soviet military strength during the entire war, see David Thomas, "Foreign Armies East and German Military Intelligence in Russia, 1941–1945," *Journal of Contemporary History* 22 (1987): 261–301. For details of Soviet deception during the Belorussian offensive (Soviet code name Bagration), see Glantz, *Deception*, 360–379; and David M. Glantz and Jonathan House, *When Titans Clashed: How the Red Army Stopped Hitler* (Lawrence: University Press of Kansas, 1995), 195–215, 358.

4. F. H. Hinsley and C. A. G. Simkins, *British Intelligence in the Second World War*, Volume 4: *Security and Counterintelligence* (London: Her Majesty's Stationery Office, 1990).

5. For in-depth analyses of the problems in using Russian intelligence service and military archives, see Amy Knight, "Russian Archives and Opportunities and Obstacles," *International Journal of Intelligence and Counterintelligence* 12, no. 3 (1999): 325–337; and Glantz and House, *When Titans Clashed*, 309–321.

6. See, for example, John Costello and Oleg Tsarev, *Deadly Illusions* (New York: Crown, 1993); Nigel West and Oleg Tsarev, *The Crown Jewels: The British Secrets at the Heart of the KGB Archives* (New Haven, Conn.: Yale University Press, 1999); and Allen Weinstein and Alexander Vassiliev, *The Haunted Wood: Soviet Espionage in America. The Stalin Era* (New York: Random House, 1999).

7. See Amy Knight, "The Alger Hiss Story: The Selling of the KGB," *Wilson Quarterly* (winter 2000): 1–10 (available on the journal's website), for a highly skeptical look at the new literature on Soviet foreign espionage.

8. David E. Murphy, Sergei A. Kondrashev, and George Bailey, *Battleground Berlin: CIA vs. KGB in the Cold War* (New Haven, Conn.: Yale University Press, 1997).

9. Ibid., xi.

10. See V. I. Trubnikov, ed., *Ocherki Istorii Rossiiskoi Vneshnei Razvedki, Tom 4, 1941–1945* (Moscow: Mezhdunarodnye Otonosheniia, 1999); U.S. Congress, Senate, Subcommittee to Investigate the Administration of the Internal Security Act and Other Internal Security Laws, Committee on the Judiciary, *Soviet Intelligence and Security Services, 1964–1970: A Selected Bibliography of Soviet Publications with Additional Titles from Other Sources,* vol. 1, 92nd Congress, 1st Session (Washington, D.C., 1975) and the following volume by the same committee covering the years 1971 to 1972.

11. See volume 4, in particular, covering World War II, of Trubnikov, *Ocherki Istorii;* and A. N. Iakovlev, ed., *Rossiia XX Vek: Dokumenty; Liubianka, VCHK-OGPU-NKVD-MGB-MVD-KGB, 1917–1960, Spravochnik* (Moscow: Mezhdunarodnyi Fond, Demokratiia, 1997).

12. Federal'naia Sluzhba Kontrrazvedki Rossiiski Federatsii, Akademiia Federal'noi Sluzhby Kontrrazvedki, Rossisski Federatsii, *Organy Gosudarstvennoi Bezopasnosti SSSR v Velikoi Otechestvennoi Voine: Sbornik Dokumentoi, Tom I, Kniga Perovaia, Noiabr' 1938 g.–Dekabr' 1940 g.: Kniga Vtoria 1 Ianvaria–21 Iiunia 1941 g.* (Moscow, 1995); and Federal'naia Sluzhba Kontrrazvedki Rossiiski Federatsii, Akademiia Federal'noi Sluzhby Kontrrazvedki, Rossisski Federatsii, *Organy Gosudarstvennoi Bezopasnosti SSSR v Velikoi Otechestvennoi Voine: Sbornik Dokumentoi, Tom 2, Kniga Perovaia, Nachalo, 22 Iiunia–31 Avgusta 1941 goda I Kniga Dva, 1 Sentiabria–31 Dekabria 1941 goda* (Moscow: Izdatel'stvo Rus', 2000).

13. Federal'naia Sluzhba Bezopasnosti Rossiiskoi Federatsii i Moskovskoe Gorodskoe Obiedinennie Arkhivov, *Lubianka II: Iz Istorii Otechestvennoi Kontrrazvedki* (Moscow: Izdatel'stvo Obiedinennia Mosgorrkhiv, 1999).

14. Vyshaia Krasnoznamennaia Shkola Komiteta Gosudarstvennoi Bezopasnosti pri Sovete Ministrov SSSR imeni F. Z. Dzerzhinskovo, Spetsial'naia Kafedra No. 9, *Istoriia Sovetskikh Organov Gosudarstvennoi Bezopasnosti,* Uchebnik, No. 12179, Sovershenno Sekretno, 2192 (Moscow, 1977). Document is available, as of 31 August 2002, at http://www.fas.harvard.edu. See also Michael Waller, "The Secret History of the KGB," *Insight Magazine* 15, no 37 (4–11 October 1999): 1–7 (copy obtained from magazine's website).

15. Dmitrii Petrovich Tarasov, *Bol'shaia Igra (Dokumental'nii Obzor i Khudozhestvenno-dokumental'nii Ocherk "Pamiatnaia duel'")* (Moscow: Zhizn', 1997).

16. For example, see Thomas, "Foreign Armies East"; David Kahn, *Hitler's Spies: German Military Intelligence in World War II* (New York: Macmillan, 1978); and Timothy Mulligan, "Spies, Ciphers, and 'Zitadelle': Intelligence in the Battle of Kursk, 1943," *Journal of Contemporary History* 22, no. 2 (1987): 235–260.

17. J. C. Masterman, *The Double-Cross System in the War of 1939–1945* (New Haven, Conn.: Yale University Press, 1972).

18. Michael Parrish, *Soviet Security and Intelligence Organizations, 1917–1990: A Biographical Dictionary and Review of Literature in English* (New York: Greenwood, 1992); Michel Parrish, *The Lesser Terror: Soviet State Security, 1939–1953* (Westport, Conn.: Praeger, 1996); Amy W. Knight, *Beria: Stalin's First Lieutenant* (Princeton, N.J.:

Princeton University Press, 1993); Robert Conquest, *Inside Stalin's Secret Police: NKVD Politics, 1936–1939* (Stanford, Calif.: Hoover Institution Press, 1985).

19. Kahn, *Hitler's Spies,* 361.

20. West, The *Crown Jewels,* 187–204.

21. See also Timothy Naftali, "Im Zerrspiegel: US-Gegenspionage in Deutschland 1945–1948," in Wolfgang Krieger and Juergen Weber, *Spione fuer den Frieden: Nachrichtendienste in Deutschland waehrend des Kalten Krieges,* 98–102 (Munich Guenter Olzog Verland GmbH, 1997).

22. David Glantz, "The Red Mask: The Nature and Legacy of Soviet Military Deception in the Second World War," *Intelligence and National Security* 2, no. 3 (July 1987): 175–259.

23. Militaergeschichtliches Forschungsamt, ed., *Germany and the Second World War,* Volume 4: *The Attack on the Soviet Union* (New York: Oxford University Press, 1996).

24. U.S. Army, Office of the Chief of Military History, Special Studies Division, *The German Campaign in Russia, Planning and Operations (1940–1942),* Department of Army Pamphlet No. 20-26a (Washington, D.C.: U.S. Government Printing Office, March 1955).

25. *Sovetskaia Voennaia Entsiklopediia,* vol. 4, 1977, s.v. *Kontrrazvedka,* 326; Wilhelm Moll, Eric Waldman, and Earl Ziemke, *Project Cleopatra: Soviet Agent Operations in the German Occupied Territories during World War II,* Bureau of Applied Social Research, Columbia University, on contract to the U.S. Government, May 1955, 1–3.

26. See Glantz, "The Red Mask," 175–259; and John J. Dziak, "Soviet Deception: The Organizational and Operational Tradition," in Brain D. Dailey and Patrick J. Parker, eds., *Soviet Strategic Deception* (Lexington, Mass.: Lexington Books, 1987), 3–21. See also Department of the Army, *U.S. Army Field Manual 34-60: Counterintelligence* (Washington, D.C., October 1995), for an unclassified comprehensive description of the current U.S. Army concept of counterintelligence. In that manual "counter-reconnaissance" basically refers to counterintelligence support to the concept of destroying enemy intelligence collection capability through degrading enemy intelligence facilities and personnel, and especially the wide array of technical intelligence collection capabilities deployed by today's more sophisticated armies. This level of conceptual sophistication did not exist in the U.S. Army of World War II. The modern battlefield has, of course, necessitated an updating of U.S. Army counterintelligence doctrine.

27. *Sovetskaia Voyennaia Entsiklopediia,* vol. 4, s.v. "Kontrrazvedka."

28. See Vysshaia Krasnoznamennaia Shkola, Komiteta Gosudarstvennoi Bezopasnosti, pri Sovete Ministrov SSR imeni F. Z. Dzherinskovo, Sovershno Sekretno, *Kontrrazedyvatel'ni Slovar',* no. 10064 (1972): 142–143.

29. See U.S. Army, *The German Intelligence Service and the War,* NARS Record Group 319, XE 003641, Box 5, Folders 1–3; and Michel Geyer, "National Socialist Germany: The Politics of Information," in Ernest R. May, ed., *Knowing One's Enemies: Intelligence Assessment before the Two World Wars,* 310–347 (Princeton, N.J.: Princeton University Press, 1984).

30. Idea based on U.S. Army FM 34-60, chapter 1. The U.S. Army's current definition of counterintelligence has not essentially changed over the years, and the concept is used by most other government organizations including the CIA and the FBI. The Army's concept has been substantially refined since World War II to take into account operational analysis to defeat technical sensors.

31. *Kontrrazvedyvatel'nyi Slovar'*, 9.

CHAPTER 1. "The World Will Hold Its Breath"

1. Richard Overy, *Russia's War: A History of the Soviet War Effort* (New York: Penguin, 1998), 72; Earl F. Ziemke, *Stalingrad to Berlin: The German Defeat in the East* (Washington, D.C.: Center for Military History, 1966), 500–501; Earl F. Ziemke and Magna E. Bauer, *Moscow to Stalingrad: Decision in the East* (New York: Military Heritage, 1988), 7; Glantz and House, *Titans;* 31, 42; Omar Bartov, *Hitler's Army: Soldiers, Nazis, and War in the Third Reich* (New York: Oxford University Press, 1991), 14, 17; John Erickson, *The Road to Stalingrad: Stalin's War with Germany* (Boulder, Col.: Westview, 1984), 98.

2. David Glantz, *Stumbling Colossus: The Red Army on the Eve of War* (Lawrence: University Press of Kansas, 1998), 10–24; Ziemke and Bauer, *Moscow to Stalingrad,* 10–13; Militaergeschlichtliches Forschungsamt, *Germany and the Second World War,* 4:93.

3. John Erickson, *The Soviet High Command: A Military-Political History* (New York: St. Martin's, 1962), 586; Glantz, *Stumbling Colossus,* passim; Ziemke and Bauer, *Moscow to Stalingrad,* 23.

4. Gerhard L. Weinberg, *A World at Arms: A Global History of World War II* (Cambridge: Cambridge University Press, 1994), 265; Glantz and House, *Titans,* 49–53.

5. Glantz and House, *Titans,* 49.

6. Erickson, *High Command,* 587, 593.

7. Albert Seaton, *The Russo-German War, 1941–1945* (Novato, Calif.: Presidio, 1993; reprint, New York: Praeger, 1971), 98.

8. Bartov, *Hitler's Army,* 17; Ziemke and Bauer, *Moscow to Stalingrad,* 28.

9. Weinberg, *World at Arms,* 266.

10. Mikhail Heller and Aleksandr N. Nekrich, *Utopia in Power: The History of the Soviet Union from 1917 to the Present,* trans. Phyllis B. Carlos (New York: Summit, 1986), 377.

11. Charles Burdick and Hans-Adolf Jacobsen, *The Halder War Dairy, 1939–1942* (Novato, Calif.: Presidio, 1988) 446–447.

12. Matthew Cooper, *The German Army, 1933–1945: Its Political and Military Failure* (New York: Stein and Day, 1978), 311.

13. Glantz and House, *Titans,* 292; Seaton, *Russo-German War,* 208, n. 53; Overy, *Russia's War,* 117; David Glantz, *Barbarossa: Hitler's Invasion of Russia, 1941* (Charleston, S.C.: Tempus, 2001), 210.

14. Glantz, *Barbarossa,* 210.

15. Overy, *Russia's War,* 113.
16. Ibid., 117.
17. Cooper, *German Army,* 311.
18. Ziemke, *Stalingrad to Berlin,* 13; U.S. Army, *Historical Study: The German Campaign in Russia—Planning and Operations (1940–1942),* Department of the Army Pamphlet No. 20-261a, March 1955, 88; Glantz, *Barbarossa,* 210.
19. Militaergeschichtliches Forschungsamt, *Germany and the Second World War,* 4:317.
20. Ibid.; U.S. Army, *Planning and Operations,* 88.
21. Ziemke, *Stalingrad to Berlin,* 13.
22. Ziemke and Bauer, *Moscow to Stalingrad,* 45.
23. Ibid.; Cooper, *German Army,* 331.
24. Bartov, *Hitler's Army,* 20.
25. Ibid., 22.
26. U.S. Army, Center for Military History, *Effects of Climate on Combat in European Russia,* CMH-PUB 104-6 (Washington, D.C.: U.S. Government Printing Office, 1952), 4.
27. Cooper, *German Army,* 311.
28. Ibid., 334.
29. Ibid., 312.
30. Ibid., 332; Militaergeschichtliches Forschungsamt, *Germany and the Second World War,* 4:207.
31. Overy, *Russia's War,* 119; Glantz and House, *Titans,* 89.
32. Glantz and House, *Titans,* 87.
33. Bartov, *Hitler's Army,* 22.
34. Ibid., 24.
35. Seaton, *Russo-German War,* 228.
36. Cooper, *German Army,* 336–337.
37. Seaton, *Russo-German War,* 228.
38. G. F. Krivosheev, ed., *Soviet Casualties and Combat Losses in the Twentieth Century* (London: Greenhill, 1997), 107–108.
39. U.S. Army, *Planning and Operations,* 12.
40. Militaergeschichtliches Forschungsamt, *Germany and the Second World War,* 4:569.
41. Ibid., 4:594–595.
42. Heinz Hoehne and Hermann Zolling, *The General Was a Spy: The Truth about General Gehlen and His Spy Ring,* trans. Richard Barry (New York: Coward, McCann, and Geoghegan, 1972), 303–304.
43. Militaergeschichtliches Forschungsamt, *Germany and the Second World War,* 4:586.
44. Ibid., 4:323–324.
45. Ibid., 4:586, n. 201; Kahn, *Hitler's Spies,* 460.
46. Kahn, *Hitler's Spies,* 460.

47. Militaergeschichtliches Forschungsamt, *Germany and the Second World War,* 4:586.

48. Ibid., 4:587.

49. Kahn, *Hitler's Spies,* 461–462; U.S. Army, *Planning and Operations,* 88–89.

50. Militaergeschichtliches Forschungsamt, *Germany and the Second World War,* 4:239.

51. Ibid., 4:593.

52. Ibid., 4:570.

53. Ibid., 4:586.

54. Ibid., 4:691.

55. Ibid., 4:695.

56. Ibid., 4:702.

57. Ibid., 4:525; James Lucas, *War on the Eastern Front: The German Soldier in Russia, 1941–1945* (New York: Bonanza, 1982 [1979]), 78.

58. Lucas, *German Soldier,* 78–119; Cooper, *German Army,* 333; U.S. Army, *Effects of Climate,* 4, 31, 34, 79.

59. U.S. Army, *Effects of Climate,* 4.

60. Bartov, *Hitler's Army,* 18–24.

61. Lucas, *German Soldier,* 80–85.

62. Ibid., 88.

63. Ibid., 118.

64. Bartov, *Hitler's Army,* 23.

65. John Keegan, *The Second World War* (New York: Penguin, 1989), 220.

66. Lucas, *German Soldier,* 105, 107, 114–115.

67. Ibid., 108–109; Bartov, *Hitler's Army,* 181; Ziemke and Bauer, *Moscow to Stalingrad,* 198.

68. U.S. Army, *Effects of Climate,* 31, 79.

69. Glantz and House, *Titans,* 106, 104–108.

70. Ibid., 104–108; Bartov, *Hitler's Army,* 15–25; U.S. Army, *Planning and Operations,* iv; Weinberg, *World at Arms,* 426–427.

71. Glantz and House, *Titans,* 114–120, 342–343; Keegan, *Second World War,* 223.

72. Heller and Nekrich, *Utopia in Power,* 387–392; Keegan, *Second World War,* 223–224, 226, 228.

73. Glantz and House, *Titans,* 110–111, 120–125; Weinberg, *World at Arms,* 426–427.

74. David M. Glantz, *Zhukov's Greatest Defeat: The Red Army's Epic Disaster in Operation Mars, 1942* (Lawrence: University Press of Kansas, 1999), 2, 317; Glantz and House, *Titans,* 123, 133.

75. Glantz, *Zhukov,* 20, 292, 317–319.

76. Pavel Sudoplatov, *Spetsoperatsii: Liubianka i Kreml', 1930–1950 gody* (Moscow: Izdatel'stskaia Firma, "Olma-Press, 1998), 248.

77. Ibid., 77–82.

78. Ibid., 318–319.

79. Ibid., 304, 308, 318–319.

80. Ibid., 286–287.

81. Overy, *Russia's War,* 177; Rolf-Dieter Mueller and Gerd R. Ueberschaer, *Hitler's War in the East, 1941–1945: A Critical Assessment,* trans. Bruce D. Little (Providence, Oxford: Berghahn, 1997), 112; Cooper, *German Army,* 422–423.

82. Glantz and House, *Titans,* 122–123.

83. Keegan, *Second World War,* 230.

84. Glantz and House, *Titans,* 122; Keegan, *Second World War,* 231.

85. Overy, *Russia's War,* 182.

86. Anthony Beevor, *Stalingrad: The Fateful Siege* (New York: Viking, 1998), 353–354.

87. Ziemke, *Stalingrad to Berlin,* 80.

88. Ibid., 76.

89. Ibid., 69.

90. Overy, *Russia's War,* 183; Erickson, *Road to Berlin,* 37.

91. Ziemke, *Stalingrad to Berlin,* 78, Beevor, *Stalingrad,* 376–378, 408–409.

92. Mueller and Ueberschaer, *War in the East,* 112; Krivosheev, *Casualties,* 127–128; Bruce Lee, *Marching Orders: The Untold Story of World War II* (New York: Da Capo, 2001), 69–70.

93. Erickson, *Road to Berlin,* 43; Mueller and Ueberschaer, *War in the East,* 112.

94. Krivosheev, *Casualties,* 127.

95. Beevor, *Stalingrad,* 356, 361–365.

96. Glantz and House, *Titans,* 123.

97. Ibid., 143–147.

98. Ibid., 147; Ziemke and Bauer, *Moscow to Stalingrad,* 509.

99. Seaton, *Russo-German War,* 346–350.

100. Ibid., 351–352; Glantz and House, *Titans,* 151.

101. Erickson, *Road to Berlin,* 64–65; Glantz and House, *Titans,* 147, 158–160.

102. Erickson, *Road to Berlin,* 64–69.

103. Seaton, *Russo-German War,* 360; David M. Glantz and Jonathan M. House, *The Battle of Kursk* (Lawrence: University Press of Kansas, 1999), 67.

104. Glantz and House, *Kursk,* 67.

105. Erickson, *Road to Berlin,* 72.

106. Overy, *Russia's War,* 201.

107. Erickson, *Road to Berlin,* 71; Glantz and House, *Kursk,* 274, 336–337; Glantz and House, *Titans,* 163.

108. Seaton, *Russo-German War,* 361.

109. Overy, *Russia's War,* 201; Glantz and House, *Titans,* 163.

110. Glantz and House, *Titans,* 166.

111. Erickson, *Road to Berlin,* 101; Glantz and House, *Titans,* 166.

112. Glantz and House, *Titans,* 166.

113. Erickson, *Road to Berlin,* 106–109, 112.

114. Glantz and House, *Kursk,* 278, 338.
115. Erickson, *Road to Berlin,* 112.
116. Glantz and House, *Kursk,* 276, 337.
117. Glantz and House, *Titans,* 167; Overy, *Russia's War,* 210.
118. Glantz and House, *Titans,* 167–169; Krivosheev, *Casualties,* 312–134; Overy, *Russia's War,* 210–211.
119. Figures here based on Glantz and House, *Kursk,* 276–277.
120. Overy, *Russia's War,* 212, 217; Erickson, *Road to Berlin,* 122.
121. Glantz and House, *Titans,* 176.
122. Ziemke, *Stalingrad to Berlin,* 146.
123. Overy, *Russia's War,* 234.
124. Ziemke, *Stalingrad to Berlin,* 147.
125. David Glantz, *The Battle for Leningrad, 1941–1944* (Lawrence: University Press of Kansas, 2002), 459–500.
126. Entire paragraph based on Overy, *Russia's War,* 102, 107–108, except note above on the failed Blitzkrieg.
127. Ibid., 112.
128. Ziemke, *Stalingrad to Berlin,* 197–199; Glantz, *Leningrad,* 468.
129. Glantz, *Leningrad,* 459–460.
130. Ibid., 462.
131. Ibid., 469–470.
132. Weinberg, *World at Arms,* 607–608; Glantz and House, *Titans,* 174, 184 (map).
133. Ziemke, *Stalingrad to Berlin,* 173.
134. Paragraph based on Glantz and House, *Titans,* 180, 191–194; and Seaton, *Russo-German War,* 432.
135. Paragraph based on Seaton, *Russo-German War,* 394–400.
136. Erickson, *Road to Berlin,* 326.
137. Seaton, *Russo-German War,* 436.
138. Overy, *Russia's War,* 243.
139. Glantz and House, *Titans,* 198, 201–202, 204, 209, 214–215; Krivosheev, *Casualties,* 144–145.
140. Glantz and House, *Titans,* 215.
141. Erickson, *Road to Berlin,* 326, Glantz and House, *Titans,* 214–215.
142. Paragraph based on Glantz and House, *Titans,* 216, 218, 220, 221, 227, 232; Erickson, *Road to Berlin,* 360; Seaton, *Russo-German War,* 487.
143. Glantz and House, *Titans,* 237.
144. Weinberg, *World at Arms,* 819–828.
145. Erickson, *Road to Berlin,* 444–447.
146. Anthony Beevor, *The Fall of Berlin, 1945* (New York: Viking, 2002), 165–166 (GULAG figure); Glantz and House, *Titans,* 254–255; Ziemke, *Stalingrad to Berlin,* 412, 445–466.
147. Seaton, *Russo-German War,* 566, Erickson, *Road to Berlin,* 538–539.
148. Glantz and House, *Titans,* 261.

149. See also Cornelius Ryan, *The Last Battle* (New York: Pocket Books, 1967).

150. Paragraph based on Erickson, *Road to Berlin,* 586–589, 480–481; Ziemke, *Stalingrad to Berlin,* 480–481.

151. Ziemke, *Stalingrad to Berlin,* 492 (and 469, map no. 42); Beevor, *Fall,* 322, 341, 357.

152. Krivosheev, *Casualties,* 157–158.

153. Heller and Nekrich, *Utopia in Power,* 9–11.

154. Nicholas V. Riasanovsky, *A History of Russia,* 4th ed. (New York: Oxford University Press, 1984), 73.

155. Riasanovksy, *History of Russia,* 148–151; Thomas Riha, *Readings in Russian Civilization,* Volume 1: *Russia before Peter the Great, 900–1700,* 2nd ed. (Chicago: University of Chicago Press, 1969), xviii.

156. Weinberg, *A World at Arms,* 609–615; and John H. Waller, *The Unseen War in Europe: Espionage and Conspiracy in the Second World War* (New York: Random House, 1996), 290–295. See also Radio Free Europe/Radio Liberty (RFE/RL), ed. Viktor Yasman, *Security and Terrorism Watch* 3, no. 37 (22 October 2002), subtitle: "Declassified Documents Indicate Stalin Proposed Alliance with Hitler against U.S. and Britain." RFE/RL, citing an article in the 17 October 2002 issue of *Komsomol'skaia Pravda,* which was based on two recently declassified documents, reveals that Stalin actually proposed to the Nazis in early 1942 that the USSR ally itself with Nazi Germany and restructure the world. One of the sensational revelations, among others, is that Stalin wanted to undertake an offensive with the Germans against Britain and the United States, which included exterminating Soviet Jewry on behalf of the Nazis. Karpov published the two declassified intelligence documents in his book. For a less sensational view of the issue, see Waller, *The Unseen War,* 290–295.

157. Parrish, *Lesser Terror,* 79.

158. Heller and Nekrich, *Utopia in Power,* 443.

159. Ibid., 462–453.

160. Glantz and House, *Titans,* 57, 292; Mueller, *War in the East,* 142–143, 215. For a detailed breakdown of Soviet losses of men and equipment, and insight into the complexities of analyzing combat losses, see Krivosheev, *Casualties,* 84–92. Virtually the entire book is devoted to a detailed analysis of Soviet military losses in World War II. Krivosheev's book also includes a detailed analysis of German losses. Glantz, Mueller, and Krivosheev have all based their research on either original documents or works that have used original documents. Figures above have been rounded off. See also Parrish, *Lesser Terror,* 79; and Nekrich and Heller, *Utopia in Power,* 389–90.

161. Ziemke, *Stalingrad to Berlin,* 500. Ziemke puts the overall number of military deaths in World War II at 26.8 million.

162. Krivosheev, *Casualties,* 90–92.

163. Overy, *Russia's War,* 287–289.

164. Christopher Duffy, *Red Storm on the Reich: The Soviet March on Germany, 1945* (New York: Macmillan, 1991), 3.

165. Heller and Nekrich, *Utopia in Power,* 393–394.

166. Weinberg, *World at Arms,* 894.

167. Heller and Nekirch, *Utopia in Power,* 462.

168. *World Almanac and Book of Facts, 2001* (Mahwah, N.J.: World Almanac Books, 2001), 371.

169. Heller and Nekrich, *Utopia in Power,* 463.

170. See Krivosheev, *Casualties,* 275–278, for a more in-depth exposition of these figures.

171. Krivosheev, *Casualties,* 276–277; and Ziemke, *Stalingrad to Berlin,* 500. Ziemke places the number of German dead between 3 million and 3.5 million; Krivosheev places the number at 2,230,300, with another 2,870,500 reported as missing in action or captured.

172. Krivosheev, *Casualties,* 278.

173. Duffy, *Red Storm,* 3.

174. Ian Sayer and Douglas Botting, *America's Secret Army: The Untold Story of the Counterintelligence Corps* (New York: Franklin Watts, 1989), 268–269. Sayer and Botting give an excellent and colorful introduction to the operating environment faced by the U.S. Army Counterintelligence Corps (CIC) when Allied troops overran Germany. The authors based their figures on U.S. Army documents as well as on some good secondary works.

175. Beevor, *Fall of Berlin,* 410, 419–420.

176. Seaton, *The Russo-German War,* xix; Bartov, *Hitler's Army,* 14–15; Ziemke, *Stalingrad to Berlin,* 500–501; Heller and Nekrich, *Utopia in Power,* 393.

177. Keegan, *Second World War,* 208–210.

178. Erickson, *Road to Stalingrad,* 341.

179. Cooper, *German Army,* 407.

180. Christopher Duffy, *Russia's Military West: Origins and Nature of Russian Military Power, 1700–1800* (London: Routledge, 1981), 90.

181. Arnold M. Silver, "Questions, Questions, Questions: Memories of Oberursel," *Intelligence and National Security* 8, no. 2 (April 1993):208.

CHAPTER 2. The "Invisible Front"

1. See Waller, *Unseen War;* and U.S. National Archives, Record Group 319 XE003641, Box 5, Folders 1–3, *The German Intelligence Service and the War,* which is an in-depth postwar analysis of the performance of both the German military intelligence and SD Ausland done circa 1945–1946.

2. See, for example, Central Intelligence Agency, *The Rote Kapelle: The CIA's History of the Soviet Intelligence and Espionage Networks in Western Europe, 1935–1945* (Washington, D.C.: University Publications of America, 1979), and V. E. Tarrant, *The Red Orchestra: The Soviet Spy Network inside Nazi Europe* (London: Cassell Military Classics, 1998).

3. *Istoriia Sovietskikh Organov,* 350–355; hereafter cited as *Top Secret History.*

4. Dziak, *Chekisty,* xiii–xvi.

5. See, for example, Dziak, "Organizational and Operational Tradition"; and Security and Intelligence Foundation, *The Trust: Felix Dzerzhinskiy, 1877–1926,* published in memory of James Jesus Angleton, 1989.

6. John Ferris, "Fortitude in Context: The Evolution of British Deception in the Second World War," forthcoming. Ferris traces in detail the evolution of British deception in World War II to include its skillful and precise use of double agents.

7. Glantz, "Red Mask," 223–228, 241; *Top Secret History,* 364–368; Pavel and Anatoliy Sudoplatov, with Jerrold L. and Leona P. Schecter, *Special Tasks: The Memoirs of an Unwanted Witness—A Soviet Spymaster* (Boston: Little, Brown, 1994), 152–163; Tarasov, *Igra,* 14–15; and Thomas, "Foreign Armies East," passim.

8. Ibid.

9. Ferris, "Fortitude," passim.

10. Ibid.; Masterman, *Double Cross,* 190; Hinsley and Simkins, *Security and Counterintelligence,* 309–313.

11. Stephen Ambrose, *Ike's Spies: Eisenhower and the Espionage Establishment* (Jackson: University Press of Mississippi, 1999 [1981]), 62–67.

12. FSB, *Liubianka II,* 24–241; FSB, *Nachalo (kniga 1),* 171–172; *Liubianka VCheka-KGB,* 272; *Top Secret History,* 628.

13. For details of some of Raikhman's involvement in "nonpunitive" operations, see Sudoplatov, *Special Tasks,* 131–132; FSB, *Liubianka II,* 240–241; and for a good overall description of Raikhman's career, see Parrish, *Lesser Terror,* 99, 116.

14. Parrish, *Soviet Security Organizations,* 349; Parrish, *Lesser Terror,* 99, 116; Conquest, *Inside Stalin's Secret Police,* 97.

15. Conquest, *Inside Stalin's Secret Police,* 105; Parrish, *Soviet Security Organizations,* 349.

16. S. Ostryakov, *Military Chekists (Voennie Chekisty),* trans. Defense Intelligence Agency, LN-290-80 (Moscow: Voennizdat', 1979), 165.

17. FSB, *Nachalo (kniga 2),* 455.

18. FSB, *Liubianka, VCheka-KGB,* 272.

19. Tarasov, *Igra,* 3, 16–18, 30–33.

20. Ibid., 17.

21. FSB, *Nachalo (kniga 2),* 455; *Liubianka, VCheka-KGB,* 272–273.

22. FSB, *Liubianka, VCheka-KGB,* 272–273; see Appendix A.

23. Parrish, *Soviet Security Organizations,* 431. Tarasov and Baryshnikov authored a classified study of Soviet wartime radio games entitled *Radioigry* (Moscow: Izdatel'stvo Vsh KGB, 1964). See *Top Secret History,* 364 n 1.

24. FSB, *Liubianka,* 276–278.

25. FSB, *Liubianka II,* 233.

26. Ibid.; *Top Secret History,* 630.

27. Robert W. Stephan, "The Role and Effectiveness of Soviet Combat Counterintelligence during World War II" (Ph.d. dissertation, George Washington University, 1997), 69–71.

28. Tarasov, *Igra,* 26–27. This corroborates Sudoplatov's statement on page 160 of his book, *Special Tasks,* that most of the radio games were eventually transferred to Smersh.

29. Parrish, *Soviet Security Organizations,* 431.

30. Tarasov, *Igra,* 26–27.

31. Ibid.

32. Ibid., 31.

33. *Top Secret History,* 364–367; Tarasov, *Igra,* 31–32; FSB, *Liubianka II,* 241; U.S. Army, 7707th Military Intelligence Service Center, *The Counterintelligence Organization "Smersh" of the Red Army,* Counterintelligence Special Report Number 42 (CI-SR/42) 24 March 1947, 29. U.S. National Archives (NARS), Record Group 338.

34. Sudoplatov, *Special Tasks,* 160, 167; Parrish, *Soviet Security Organizations,* 229; FSB, *Liubianka, Vcheka-KGB,* 275.

35. John Dziak, *Chekisty: A History of the KGB* (Lexington, Mass.: Lexington Books, 1987), 112; Sudoplatov, *Special Tasks,* 152–167; Erickson, *High Command,* 598–599; Seaton, *Russo-German War,* 258–260; John Dziak, "Soviet Deception: The Organizational and Operational Tradition," in Brian D. Dailey and Patrick J. Parker, eds., *Soviet Strategic Deception,* 3–21 (Lexington, Mass.: Lexington Books, 1987); B. H. Liddell Hart, ed., *The Red Army* (New York: Harcourt Brace, 1956), 258–260; FSB, *Liubianka II,* 242; Seaton, *Russo-German War,* 83.

36. Tarasov, *Igra,* 15. He states that the Soviets ran 183 radio playbacks during the war but does not identify the specific component responsible for coordinating all Soviet military deception or even the entity responsible in Soviet State Security or Smersh.

37. U.S. Army, *Report on the Case of Walter Friedrich Schellenberg,* Appendix II, page 3, NARS Record Group 319, XE001752, undated.

38. U.S. Army, 7707th Military Intelligence Service Center, *Operations and Experiences of Frontaufklaerung (FA) III OST during the Eastern Campaign,* Counterintelligence Special Report No. 32 (CI-SR/32), 27 January 1947, page 38, NARS Record Group 319, XE013988.

39. For a detailed discussion of the ability of British intelligence in World War II to precisely use double agents, see Ferris, "Fortitude."

40. For examples of how Western counterintelligence services worked in World War II, see Sayer and Botting, *Secret Army;* Hinsley and Simkins, *Security and Counterintelligence;* and Timothy Naftali's forthcoming book on OSS X-2. For a comparison of Soviet and Western security services, see John Dziak, "The Study of the Soviet Intelligence and Security Services," in Roy Godson, ed., *Comparing Foreign Intelligence Services* (London: Pergamon and Brassey's, 1988), 65–88.

41. See Parrish, *Lesser Terror;* and Robert Conquest, *The Great Terror,* rev. ed. (New York: Macmillan, 1973).

42. U.S. Army, CI-SR/42, *Counterintelligence Organization "Smersh,"* 30.

43. On Stalin ignoring Soviet warnings of the impending German attack, see Gabriel Gorodetsky, *Grand Delusion: Stalin and the German Invasion of Russia* (New Haven,

Conn.: Yale University Press, 1999); and James Barros and Richard Gregor, *Double Deception: Stalin, Hitler, and the Invasion of Russia* (De Kalb: Northern Illinois University Press, 1995).

44. For Soviet foreign espionage, see, for example, CIA, *Rote Kapelle;* West, *The Crown Jewels;* Yuri Modin, *My Five Cambridge Friends: Burgess, Maclean, Philby, Blunt, and Cairncross,* trans. Anthony Roberts (New York: Farrar, Straus and Giroux, 1994); and Weinstein and Vassiliev, *Haunted Wood,* 238–265.

45. See Knight, *Beria;* Parrish, *Lesser Terror;* Mark Kramer, ed., *The Black Book of Communism: Crimes, Terror, and Repression* (Cambridge, Mass.: Harvard University Press, 1999), 184–269.

46. Wladimir Posdnjakoff and George C. Vanderstadt, ed., *German Counterintelligence in Occupied Soviet Union, 1941–1945* (U.S. Army, Military History Institute, Historical Division, Headquarters U.S. Army Europe, Foreign Military Studies Branch, No. MS-p-122, 1952).

47. See Thomas, "FHO"; Mulligan, "Spies and Ciphers"; Kahn, *Hitler's Spies,* 445–461, 360–361; and Glantz, "Red Mask."

48. Moll et al., *Cleopatra,* iv.

49. U.S. Army, CI-SR/32, *FA III, OST,* 51–52; U.S. Army, Headquarters, U.S. Forces European Theater, Military Intelligence Service Center, *German Methods of Combating the Soviet Intelligence Service,* Counterintelligence Consolidated Interrogation Report, No. 16 (CI-CIR/16), 9 September 1945, NARS Record Group 238, 6.

50. Moll et al., *Cleopatra,* 254–255.

51. U.S. Army, CI-SR/32, *FA III, OST,* 51–52; U.S. Army, CI-CIR/16, *German Methods,* 6.

52. Moll et al., *Cleopatra,* 245, 250.

53. Rudolph Langehaueser, "Studie ueber die Beschaffung von Feindnachrichten im deutschen Heer waehrend des 2.Weltkrieges an der Ostfront" (U.S. Army Foreign Military Studies Program, No. D-407, 10 September 1954), 78.

54. Kahn, *Hitler's Spies,* 200, 360, 592, 645, 629.

55. F. Sergeev, *Tainye Operatsii Natsistskoi Razvedki, 1933–1945* (Moscow: Isdatel'stvo Politicheskoi Literatury, 1991), 254.

56. U.S. Army, CI-SR/32, *FA III, OST,* 34, 51–52; Kahn, *Hitler's Spies,* 248–250, 360–361; Moll et al., *Cleopatra,* 245, 250, 254–255.

57. Posdnjakoff, *German Counterintelligence,* 1–7, Paul Leverkuehn, *German Military Intelligence,* trans. R. H. Stevens and Constantine Fitzgibbon (New York: Praeger, 1954), 156–158; U.S. Army, CI-SR/32, *FA III, OST;* see schemata of how the Soviets sealed off the rear areas.

58. Ibid.; Kahn, *Hitler's Spies,* 445–461; Seaton, *Russo-German War,* 43–50.

59. Langehaueser, "Beschaffung," 80; Kahn, *Hitler's Spies,* 360–361.

60. U.S. Army, CI-CIR/16, *German Methods,* 6.

61. Thomas, "Foreign Armies East," 264–266; Moll et al., *Cleopatra,* iv.

62. U.S. Army, CI-CIR/16, *German Methods,* 16.

63. Mulligan, "Spies and Ciphers," and Thomas, "FHO," discuss at length the reliance the Germans placed on aerial reconnaissance and signals intercept, and the limitations of German clandestine collection.

64. U.S. Army, CI-SR/32, *FA III, OST,* 51–52.

65. Ibid.

66. Silver, "Questions, Questions, Questions," 208.

67. Ostryakov, *Military Chekists,* 209; Sergeev, *Tainye Operatsii,* 280; Dmitri Volkogonov, *Stalin: Triumph and Tragedy,* trans. Harold Shukman (New York: Grove Weidenfeld, 1991), 332.

68. Moll et al., *Cleopatra,* 251.

69. Sudoplatov, *Special Tasks,* 129–130.

70. Moll et al., *Cleopatra,* iv–v.

71. U.S. Army, CI-SR/32, *FA III, OST,* 38.

72. D. P. Nosyrev, *V poedinke s abverom, dokumental'ny ocherk o cheistakh leningradskovo fronta, 1941–1945* (Moscow: Voennizdat', 1968), 32.

73. FSB, *Liubianka II,* 234.

CHAPTER 3. "Death to Spies"

1. Sir Kenneth Strong, *Men of Intelligence: A Study of the Roles and Decisions of Chiefs of Intelligence from World War I to the Present Day* (London: Cassell, 1970), 91.

2. U.S. Department of the Navy, Office of Naval Intelligence, *Espionage-Sabotage-Conspiracy: German and Russian Operations, 1941–1945: Excerpts from the Files of the German Naval Staff and Other Captured German Documents,* April 1947, Appendix II, 4, NARS Record Group 226, Entry 120, Box 46; hereafter cited as ONI, *Espionage-Sabotage-Conspiracy.* This document contains 185 legal-size pages of translations and analyses of fifty original German documents, most of which were produced by the various components of German military intelligence. Appendixes I and II contain translations of two German studies on Soviet intelligence and the Soviet security services. Appendix II is a translation of the German document entitled *Die sowjetische Gegenspionage im Operationsgebiet der Ostfront,* which was originally produced by FHO in October 1943. The quote is in the original on page 14.

3. Parrish, *Lesser Terror,* 115, citing Mikoyan in *Pravda,* 21 December 1937.

4. Ibid., citing MGB Chief, S. D. Ignat'ev.

5. Kahn, *Hitler's Spies,* 453, 454, 460.

6. *Top Secret History,* 331, 392.

7. Seaton, *Russo-German War,* 45.

8. Ibid., 44; Leverkuehn, *Military Intelligence,* 156–157; Christopher Andrew, *Her Majesty's Secret Service: The Making of the British Intelligence Community* (New York: Viking, 1986), 285, 349–350, 462–463; Glantz, "Red Mask," 237–239.

9. Kahn, *Hitler's Spies,* 453–454; Geoffrey P. Megargee, *Inside Hitler's Command* (Lawrence: University Press of Kansas, 2000), 103, 105, 108.

10. ONI, *Espionage-Sabotage-Conspiracy,* Appendix I.

11. Both Dziak in *Chekisty,* and Simon Wolin and Robert M. Slusser in *The Soviet Secret Police* (Westport, Conn.: Greenwood, 1964), continually emphasize the point that the majority of the resources of the Soviet intelligence and security services were devoted to security and counterintelligence. The top secret 1977 classified history of the Soviet State Security organs is largely a history of counterintelligence operations.

12. Parrish, *Lesser Terror,* 116.

13. V. V. Korovin, *Sovetskaia razvedka i kontrrazvedka v gody Velikoi Otechestvennoi Voiny* (Moscow: Izdatel'stvo Rus', 1998), 83.

14. Heller and Nekrich, *Utopia in Power,* 444; Parrish, *Lesser Terror,* 88–126.

15. *Top Secret History,* 367.

16. Ibid.

17. Ibid.

18. Ibid., 351.

19. U.S. Army, CI-SR/42, *Counterintelligence Organization "Smersh,"* 2.

20. Wolin and Slusser, *Soviet Secret Police,* 195.

21. Ibid., 247; U.S. Army, CI-SR/42, *Counterintelligence Organization "Smersh,"* 8.

22. U.S. Army, CI-SR/42, *Counterintelligence Organization "Smersh,"* 25; U.S. Army, 258th Interrogation Team, *Organization and Mission of the Soviet Secret Service,* January 1948, NARS Record Group 319, 50.

23. ONI, *Espionage-Sabotage-Conspiracy,* 64–65; Kahn, *Hitler's Spies,* 282, 284; Ostryakov, *Military Chekists,* 142, 198; and General Staff, United States Army (GSUSA), Intelligence Division, *Survey of Soviet Intelligence and Counterintelligence,* 15 August 1946, NARS Record Group, 319, 152.

24. *Top Secret History,* 308–309.

25. U.S. Army, CI-SR/42, *Counterintelligence Organization "Smersh,"* 25; 258th Interrogation Team, *Organization and Mission of the Soviet Secret Services,* 50.

26. U.S. Army, CI-SR/32, *FA III, OST,* 32.

27. General Staff, United States Army (GSUSA), Intelligence Division, *Survey of Soviet Intelligence and Counterintelligence,* 9 January 1948, NARS Record Group 319, Records of the Army Staff, Declassified NND 770011, 11.

28. U.S. Army, CI-SR/42, *Counterintelligence Organization "Smersh,"* 26; 258th Interrogation Team, *Organization and Mission of the Soviet Secret Services,* 6. U.S. Army, CI-SR/42, which was based, in part, on German translations of Soviet orders, states that numerous Soviet orders energetically ordered further strengthening of the informant nets in the army and that, according to those Soviet orders, only one-ninth of all Red Army personnel worked for Smersh. If this were actually the case, and the Soviet orders were not being used solely for negative motivation, the total number of informants in the Soviet armed forces would approximate 1,540,000. The 258th Interrogation Team document, which is an edited translation of the 1944 FHO study entitled *Organisation und Aufgaben des sowjetischen Geheimdienstes im Operationsgebiet der Ostfront,* asserts that one-fifth of the Soviet Armed Forces worked for Soviet military counterintelligence as informants (German original, p. 8). This would mean that approximately

3.4 million soldiers served as informants. While neither the original version nor the translated version provide details on the methodology used in arriving at this figure, it may nevertheless not be exaggerated.

29. Wolin and Slusser, *Soviet Secret Police,* 194–195.

30. U.S. Army, Headquarters U.S. Forces European Theater, Office of the Assistant Chief of Staff, G-2, Counterintelligence Division, *The Foreign Department and the Counterintelligence Department of the NKGB,* Counterintelligence Special Interrogation Report No. 4 (CI-SIR/4), 15 July 1946, 23. NARS Record Group 84, File No. 820.02, Box 117, Central File, No. 861.20200/7-2346. This document was probably based on the debriefing of Heinrich Schmalschlaeger. It states that, by the end of the war, the German intelligence service had not yet succeeded in gaining a complete picture of the structure of the KRU (counterintelligence in the civilian sector).

31. Wolin and Slusser, *Soviet Secret Police,* 194.

32. U.S. Army, CI-SR/42, *Counterintelligence Organization "Smersh,"* 24; GSUSA, *Survey,* 154–157. To quote U.S. Army, CI-SR/42: "The basic framework of the working methods of *Smersh* is rigid and differs little from that of the KRU; . . . however, within this firm framework there is ample room for an infinite multitude of variations and innovations."

33. Walter Laqueur, *The Dream That Failed: Reflections on the Soviet Union* (Oxford: Oxford University Press, 1994), 133. The population at the end of the war was 167 million.

34. By extension, if the figure of one-fifth of military members were accepted and applied to the civilian population, this would mean that almost 40 million Soviet citizens served as informants. Such a high figure would probably have strained the resources of the Soviet internal services.

35. U.S. Army, CI-SR/42, *Counterintelligence Organization "Smersh";* U.S. Army, Information Section, Counterintelligence Branch Office of the Director of Intelligence, NARS Record Group 319, 14 August 1945, Entry 85, *Russian Counterintelligence Organizations.* The latter document is an amalgamation of a Gestapo article, dated October 1942, on the Soviet intelligence and counterintelligence services that appeared in the Gestapo secret publication *Mitteilungsblatt der Gruppe IV E,* and of a counterintelligence study done by one of the intelligence organizations of General Vlassov's Russian Liberation Army. The U.S. Army assessed the Gestapo article as general in nature but accurate and the Vlassov study as poorly organized but containing a wealth of detailed data on Smersh.

36. U.S. Army, CI-SR/42, *Counterintelligence Organization "Smersh,"* 13, 24.

37. Ibid., 6, 26. The Soviet counterintelligence term for the informant system was *massovaia agentura.* It loosely translates into English as "a general surveillance net."

38. Ostryakov, *Military Chekists,* 197–198.

39. *Top Secret History,* 351–353.

40. U.S. Army, CI-SR/42, *Counterintelligence Organization "Smersh,"* 25. If one-fifth of the Soviet population — including members of the military — were working for Soviet counterintelligence (approximately 40 million informants based on a population

of 200 million), and one-half were coerced, that would mean that about 20 million Soviet citizens were forced to work for State Security.

41. *Top Secret History,* 352.

42. U.S. Army, CI-SR/42, *Counterintelligence Organization "Smersh,"* 25; U.S. Army, *Russian Counterintelligence Organizations,* 5. Given that Smersh was a large organization, resident agents in some cases probably could recruit informants.

43. U.S. Army, *Russian Counterintelligence Organizations,* 5.

44. Ibid.; U.S. Army, CI-SR/42, *Counterintelligence Organization "Smersh,"* 13, 24, 25.

45. *Top Secret History,* 352.

46. U.S. Army, *Russian Counterintelligence Organizations,* 4.

47. U.S. Army, CI-SR/42, *Counterintelligence Organization "Smersh,"* 25–26.

48. Ibid.

49. Ibid., 13, 26; Germany, OKH, FHO, Abteilung IIb, *Truppenverbaende und truppenaehnliche Organisationen des roten Volkskommissariats des Inneren (NKWD),* 8, 16 January 1943. NARS Record Group 242, T78.563/H3/398.

50. U.S. Army, CI-SR/42, *Counterintelligence Organization "Smersh,"* 13, 26; FHO, Abteilung IIB, *Truppenverbaende und truppenaehnliche Organizationen des roten Volkskommissariats der Inneren ("NKWD"),* 16 January 1943, NARS, Record Group 242, T-78, Roll 563, Frame H3/39868, 8, 10.

51. U.S. Army, *Russian Counterintelligence Organizations,* 6.

52. Ibid.

53. *Top Secret History,* 352–354.

54. GSUSA, *Survey,* 52.

55. Ibid.

56. Ibid., 52, 157.

57. U.S. Army, CI-SR/42, *Counterintelligence Organization "Smersh,"* 26; U.S. Army, *Russian Counterintelligence Organizations,* 5.

58. U.S. Army, CI-SR/42, *Counterintelligence Organization "Smersh,"* 26; U.S. Army, *Russian Counterintelligence Organizations,* 5; Vladmir and Evdokia Petrov, *Empire of Fear* (New York: Praeger, 1956), 99.

59. U.S. Army, CI-SR/42, *Counterintelligence Organization "Smersh,"* 26; US Army, *Russian Counterintelligence Organizations,* 5.

60. Kevin Ruffner, "CIC Records: A Valuable Tool for Researchers," in Central Intelligence Agency, *Center for the Study of Intelligence Bulletin,* no. 11 (summer 2000).

61. U.S. Army, CI-SR/42, *Counterintelligence Organization "Smersh,"* 26–27.

62. Ibid.

63. Ibid.

64. U. S. Army, 258th Interrogation Team, *Organization of Soviet Secret Services,* 30.

65. Ibid., 51.

66. Ibid., 56.

67. Ibid., 57.

68. Ibid., 84.

69. GSUSA, *Survey*, 96.

70. For an excellent description of the mechanics of how the Soviet State Security organs actually controlled the population, see Peter Deriabin and T. H. Bagley, *The KGB Masters of the Soviet Union* (New York: Hippocrene, 1990).

71. ONI, *Espionage-Sabotage-Conspiracy*, Appendix II, 5–8; GSUSA, *Survey*, 148.

72. ONI, *Espionage-Sabotage-Conspiracy*, 86, Appendix I, 9–10; Appendix II, 5–8; GSUSA, *Survey*, 148. See Knight, *Beria*, 112–135. These sources give a general overview of NKVD involvement in guarding sensitive installations, taking charge of the munitions industry, and ensuring the security of the atomic bomb project.

73. ONI, *Espionage-Sabotage-Conspiracy*, 86, Appendix I, 9–10; Appendix II, 5–8; GSUSA, *Survey*, 148.

74. ONI, *Espionage-Sabotage-Conspiracy*, 86, Appendix I, 9–10; Appendix II, 5–8; GSUSA, *Survey*, 148. Germany, Panzerarmeekommando 3, Abteilung 1c/A.O., *Taetigkeitsbericht Nr. 11 fuer die Zeit 1 Januar–30 Juni 1944, Betrieb Nr. 90, 9 Mai 1944, Feindbild im Raum Rudnja-Lisos; Quelle: V-Leute Smagin und Abdurhamet*, NARS Record Group 242, T-313/309/8586/519-5. In the supplement to this report, a German captain noted that agents "Smalgin" and "Abdurhamet" observed that NKVD rear-area security units even watched swamp areas at night in search of parachute agents. See also Germany, OKH, FHO, *Die Ueberwachungsorgane im sowjetischen Staat*, Merkblatt, Geheim, 11/5, 1 December 1945, Annex 15, NARS Record Group 242, OKH H3/753, page 22, for a detailed schemata of how Soviet rear-area security units were deployed.

75. *Top Secret History*, 350–351, 357–361.

76. Ibid., 350.

77. U.S. War Department, *Handbook on U.S.S.R. Military Forces*, November 1945, Technical Manual 30-430, pages IV-2–IV-6; Germany, FHO, Abteilung I, *Die sowjetische Agenten* Abwehr *und Gegenspionage im Operationsgebiet der Ostfront (1943)*, NARS, Record Group 242, T78, Roll 562, Frame H3.323, pages 11, 18, 43; FHO, *Truppenverbaende*, 11; Vyacheslav P. Artiemiev, "OKR: State Security in the Soviet Armed Forces," *Military Review* 53 (September 1963):31; ONI, *Espionage-Sabotage-Conspiracy*, Appendix I, 9–10; Appendix II, 5–6; Romanov, *Nights Are Longest There*, 74.

78. ONI, *Espionage-Sabotage-Conspiracy*, 86, Appendix I, 9–10; Appendix II, 5–8; GSUSA, *Survey*, 148. Germany, Panzerarmeekommando 3, Abteilung 1c/A.O., *V-Leute Smagin und Abdurhamet*, 4; Germany, FHO, *Ueberwachungsorgane*, 22; *Top Secret History*, 359–360.

79. ONI, *Espionage-Sabotage-Conspiracy*, 86, Appendix I, 9–10; Appendix II, 5–8; GSUSA, *Survey*, 148.

80. GSUSA, *Survey*, 151; Germany, Oberkommando des Heeres, Abteilung 1c/A.O./Auswertung, Nr. 1231/44, *NKVD-Trupppen: Das Volkskommissariat fuer Innere Angelegenheiten*, 27 June, 1944, page 5, T-78/567/891, NARS Record Group 242.

81. U.S. Army, CI-SR/32, *FA III, OST*, 18.

82. Ibid.

83. Germany, OKH, FHO, *Die sowjetische Agenten* Abwehr *und Gegenspionage im Operationsgebiet der Ostfront (1943),* 18, NARS Record Group 242, T78/562/H3.323.

84. Ibid.

85. Ibid.

86. ONI, *Espionage-Sabotage-Conspiracy,* Appendix II, 5; Germany, FHO, *Ueberwachungsorgane,* 22.

87. U.S. Army, *Peter Report Number 576, Abwehr IG,* 10 December 1945, 6, 11 (no other identifying data); Germany, Panzerarmeekommando 3, Abteilung 1c/A.O., *V-Leute Smagin und Abdurhamet,* T-313/309/8586/519-5, 4. Agents "Smalgin" and "Abdurhamet" observed that Soviet rear-area security troops manned checkpoints along main roads every five to seven kilometers and that a tiny mistake, or the slightest lack of confidence in one's behavior, was enough to raise the suspicions of the well-trained guards.

88. ONI, *Espionage-Sabotage-Conspiracy,* Appendix II, 6.

89. U.S. Army, CI-SR/32, *German Methods,* 7.

90. U.S. Army, *Peter Report Number 576, Abwehr IG,* 6, 11; *V-Leute Smagin,* 4.

91. ONI, *Espionage-Sabotage-Conspiracy,* 64–65; Kahn, *Hitler's Spies,* 282.

92. Ibid.

93. ONI, *Espionage-Sabotage-Conspiracy,* 64.

94. Ibid., 66.

95. Ibid.

96. *Top Secret History,* 354–361.

97. ONI, *Espionage-Sabotage-Conspiracy,* 64.

98. Ibid.

99. GSUSA, *Survey,* 152.

100. Kahn, *Hitler's Spies,* 284.

101. Ostryakov, *Military Chekists,* 142, 198.

102. U.S. Army, *Russian Counterintelligence Organizations,* 7.

103. Ibid.

104. Ibid.

105. ONI, *Espionage-Sabotage-Conspiracy,* 67–68, Appendix II, 6–7; Ostryakov, *Military Chekists,* 138, 140, 158.

106. Ostryakov, *Military Chekists,* 138, 140, 158.

107. U.S. Army, CI-SR/32, *FA III, OST,* 19.

108. ONI, *Espionage-Sabotage-Conspiracy,* 68, Appendix II, 6–7; Ostryakov, *Military Chekists,* 140, 158; Sergeev, *Tainye Operatsii,* 268–269.

109. Ostryakov, *Military Chekists,* 138.

110. ONI, *Espionage-Sabotage-Conspiracy,* 67. The German translation of this Soviet document did not elaborate on exactly what "five years banishment" meant.

111. Petrov, *Empire of Fear,* 98.

112. U.S. Army, *Russian Counterintelligence Organizations,* 7.

113. GSUSA, *Survey,* 146.
114. ONI, *Espionage-Sabotage-Conspiracy,* Appendix II, 6.
115. Ibid., 68.
116. Ibid., Appendix II, 8; U.S. Army, CI-SR/42, *Counterintelligence Organization "Smersh,"* 28–30.
117. ONI, *Espionage-Sabotage-Conspiracy,* Appendix II, 8.
118. Levytsky, *Uses of Terror,* 170–171.
119. U.S. Army, CI-SR/16, *German Methods,* 8.
120. Ibid.
121. M. A. Belousov, *Unreported at the Time: Memoirs of a Military Chekist,* trans. Defense Intelligence Agency, LN 681-84 (Moscow: Voennizdat', 1978), 56.
122. ONI, *Espionage-Sabotage-Conspiracy,* Appendix II, 8–9.
123. Ibid.
124. *Top Secret History,* 392.
125. U.S. Army, CI-SR/32, *FA III, OST,* 15.
126. Belousov, *Unreported at the Time,* 65–67.
127. Ibid.
128. Ibid.
129. Ibid.
130. Ibid.
131. Ibid. Other than to say that another Abwehr agent was lost, Belousov does not mention any specifics on the disposition of the case.
132. Ibid., 45–48. The OOs were aware that the wounded soldier had this information because Chayka had been dispatched to the area to ascertain the fate of some commanders, one of whom was Goldin. The Germans subsequently overran the area, Chayka fought his way out, and, during the course of the fighting, the wounded soldier told Chayka that Goldin had surrendered. Chayka volunteered to go back again behind German lines to bring the wounded soldier out so that the soldier could make a positive identification of Goldin. Chayka knew that the wounded soldier was being hidden in a storehouse unbeknownst to the Germans.
133. Ibid., 48.
134. Ibid., 49.
135. Ibid., 50.
136. Ibid., 51.
137. Ibid.
138. Ostryakov, *Military Chekists,* 142–144.
139. Ibid.; Supreme Headquarters, Allied Expeditionary Force, Counterintelligence War Room (London), Liquidation Report Number 183, *FAK 202,* 23 November 1945. This report provides an indication of the marginal success of some German sabotage operations.
140. Ostryakov, *Military Chekists,* 158; ONI, *Espionage-Sabotage-Conspiracy,* 72–73, 86.

141. Ibid.

142. Stephanie Courtois et al., *The Black Book of Communism: Crimes, Terror, and Repression* (Cambridge, Mass.: Harvard University Press, 1999), 159.

143. Dziak, *Chekisty*, 60–73.

144. Parrish, *Lesser Terror*, xviii.

145. Ibid., quoting Sir Fitzroy Maclean.

146. Conquest, *Inside Stalin's Secret Police*, 4.

147. Courtois et al., *Black Book*, 186, 203; Heller and Nekrich, *Utopia*, 308; Robert Conquest, *The Great Terror: Stalin's Purge of the Thirties* (New York: Macmillan, 1968), 525–529.

148. Dziak, *Chekisty*, 68; Conquest, *Inside Stalin's Secret Police*, 6.

149. Dziak, *Chekisty*, 65–68; Heller and Nekrich, *Utopia in Power*, 303.

150. Ronald Hingley, *The Russian Secret Police: Muscovite, Imperial Russian, and Soviet Political Security* (New York: Simon and Schuster, 1970), 174–179.

151. Dziak, *Chekisty*, 70; Volkogonov, *Stalin*, 310; Erickson, *High Command*, 505–506.

152. Volkogonov, *Stalin*, 332; Parrish, *Lesser Terror*, 11.

153. Knight, *Beria*, 90; Parrish, *Lesser Terror*, 1.

154. Conquest, *Inside Stalin's Secret Police*, 103.

155. *Top Secret History*, 286–287.

156. Parrish, *Lesser Terror*, 15; Heller and Nekrich, *Utopia*, 305.

157. *Top Secret History*, 286–291.

158. Conquest, *Inside Stalin's Secret Police*, 101.

159. Heller and Nekrich, *Utopia in Power*, 391, 379–382, 444; Hingley, *Russian Secret Police*, 192; Petrov and Petrov, *Empire of Fear*, 98–100.

160. Hingley, *Russian Secret Police*, 190; Dziak, *Chekisty*, 114; Knight, *Beria*, 113.

161. Knight, *Beria*, 113.

162. Ibid., 114.

163. Erickson, *Road to Stalingrad*, 176.

164. U.S. Army, CI-SR/42, *Counterintelligence Organization "Smersh,"* 30. Alexander Werth, in his *Russia at War, 1941–1945* (New York: Dutton, 1964), 227, however, thought that NKVD rear-area security units were "wholly unnecessary" given that the Red Army's stubborn defense of Moscow, and the fact that the military dealt with much of the "cowardice" on its own, sufficed to halt the German advance.

165. U.S. Army, CI-SR/42, *Counterintelligence Organization "Smersh,"* 30.

166. Heller and Nekrich, *Utopia in Power*, 389; U.S. Army, CI-SR/32, *FA III, OST*, 20; United Kingdom, Combined Services Detailed Interrogation Center, BAOR, FR 53, *Final Report on Hauptman Otto Karl Soujon: Prisoner's W/T Activity on the Eastern Front (FUELI Ost)*, page 2, 9 March 1946, NARS Record Group 165, Entry 179, Box 704.

167. Beevor, *Stalingrad*, xiv.

168. Beevor, *Fall of Berlin*, 423.

169. *Liubianka VCheka-KGB*, 287; Parrish, *Lesser Terror*, 133.

170. Parrish, *Lesser Terror,* 132; Knight, also citing Soviet sources, states that by October 1944 354,590 former Soviet POWs were screened, of whom Smersh arrested 36,630. See Knight, *Beria,* 128.

171. Parrish, *Lesser Terror,* 132.

172. Heller and Nekrich, *Utopia in Power,* 393; Hingley, *Russian Secret Police,* 190–191.

173. Central Intelligence Agency, *Study of Intelligence and Counterintelligence Activities on the Eastern Front and in Adjacent Areas during World War II,* 4, NARS RG 232, Records of the Central Intelligence Agency, undated.

174. Heller and Nekrich, *Utopia in Power,* 381.

175. Hingley, *Russian Secret Police,* 192.

176. Heller and Nekrich, *Utopia in Power,* 379, 381.

177. Ibid.; Knight, *Beria,* 126.

178. Heller and Nekrich, *Utopia in Power,* 379; Knight, *Beria,* 126.

179. Knight, *Beria,* 126. Knight, citing the CPSU journal *Kommunist,* no. 3 (1991): 101–112, bases some of her description on Beria's communiqués released by the Soviet government.

180. Ibid., 126–127.

181. Heller and Nekrich, *Utopia in Power,* 381; Knight, *Beria,* 128.

182. Alexander Dallin, *German Rule in Russia* (London: Macmillan, 1957), 596–612; Heller and Nekrich, *Utopia in Power,* 429–430.

183. Heller and Nekrich, *Utopia in Power,* 596–512. Nekrich and Heller cited Patrik von Muehlen, *Zwischen Hackenkreuz und Sowjetstern* (Duesseldorf, 1971), 60.

184. Heller and Nekrich, *Utopia in Power,* 396, 428–435; Dallin, *German Rule,* 535–536.

185. Heller and Nekrich, *Utopia in Power,* 396. The population figure cited was as of 1939.

186. Dallin, *German Rule,* 536; Mulligan, *Politics of Illusion,* 24, 156–158.

187. Sergeev, *Tainye Operatsii,* 219, 279.

188. GSUSA, *Survey,* 15.

189. U.S. Army, CI-SR/32, *FA III(Ost),* 47–50.

190. Ibid.

191. Military Intelligence Division, U.S. War Department, *German Military Intelligence* (Frederick, Md.: University Publications of America, 1984), 140. For more detailed discussion of this issue, see also Horst Boog, "German Air Intelligence in the Second World War," in Michael I. Handel, ed., *Intelligence and Military Operations* (London: Frank Cass, 1990); Megargee, *Inside Hitler's High Command;* and Glantz, "Red Mask."

192. Parish, *Lesser Terror,* 131.

193. Military Intelligence Division, *German Military Intelligence,* 140.

194. Kahn, *Hitler's Spies,* 453–454.

195. *Top Secret History,* 317.

196. Ibid., 297, 317.

197. Extrapolated from Kahn, *Hitler's Spies,* 601 n. 453.

198. Ibid., 453–454, 601 n. 453; Boog, "German Air Intelligence," 376–377.

199. Military Intelligence Division, *German Military Intelligence,* 140; ONI, *Espionage-Sabotage-Conspiracy,* 43–47.

200. Kahn, *Hitler's Spies,* 358, 361; Military Intelligence Division, *German Military Intelligence,* 61–66, 195–197.

201. Kahn, *Hitler's Spies,* 361, 592; Sergeev, *Tainye Operatsii,* 97 n. 3, 187.

202. U.S. Army, CI-SR/32, *FA III, OST,* 32–33; CI-CIR/16, *German Methods,* 10.

203. ONI, *Espionage-Sabotage-Conspiracy,* 43.

204. Ibid., 46–47.

205. Mulligan, "Spies, Ciphers, and Zitadelle," 246; U.S. Army, CI-SR/32, *FA III, OST,* 32–33; Military Intelligence Division, *German Military Intelligence,* 8–9.

206. *Top Secret History,* 374, citing *Voprosii Istorii,* no. 5 (1965): 35.

207. ONI, *Espionage-Sabotage-Conspiracy,* Appendix II, 23.

208. CSDIC, BAOR, FR 53, *W/T Activity,* 2.

209. U.S. Army, CI-SR/32, *FA III, OST,* 32–33; CI-SR/16, *German Methods,* 10. See Bartov, *Hitler's Army,* for a detailed analysis of how Nazi ideology affected German soldiers and their treatment of Soviet civilians.

210. Ostryakov, *Military Chekists,* 141; Sergeev, *Tainye Operatsii,* 227; Kahn, *Hitler's Spies,* 360–361. Sergeev asserted that the Germans deployed about 10,000 agents a year. Kahn states that German Army Group Center alone deployed from eight to ten agents a day.

211. United States Joint Publications Research Service, "Book on Military Counterintelligence Agents Reviewed," No. 073162, No. 1426, *Translations of USSR Military Affairs,* 133–135. This is a translation of a review by General of the Army A. Beloborodov of the book *Voennye Kontrrazvedchiki* (Moscow: Voennizdat', 1978). Beloborodov reviewed it in *Krasnaia Zvezda,* 21 February 1979, 2.

212. Sergeev, *Tainye Operatsii,* 268–269.

213. Ibid.; Military Intelligence Division, *German Military Intelligence,* 140.

214. Seaton, *Russo-German War,* 45; ONI, *Espionage-Sabotage-Conspiracy,* Appendix II, 4.

215. Ostryakov, *Military Chekists,* 152.

216. ONI, *Espionage-Sabotage-Conspiracy,* Appendix II, 23.

217. Boog, "German Air Intelligence," 376–377; ONI, *Espionage-Sabotage-Conspiracy,* 43–47; Kahn, *Hitler's Spies,* 453–454, 460; Military Intelligence Division, *German Military Intelligence,* 140.

218. Seaton, *Russo-German War,* 45; ONI, *Espionage-Sabotage-Conspiracy,* Appendix II.

CHAPTER 4. Soviet Offensive Counterintelligence Operations

1. Glantz, *Soviet Military Deception,* xxxviii; and Thomas, "Foreign Armies East," 289. Glantz used both Soviet and German sources and made extensive use of the battle maps of both sides. His book is a comprehensive view of the use of deception during

World War II by the Soviet armed forces. Thomas's article also makes extensive use of FHO records. Both authors complement each other's work. Thomas focuses primarily on German intelligence, and Glantz focuses primarily on the Soviet military deception operations.

2. Glantz, *Soviet Military Deception,* xxviii.

3. Ibid.

4. Thomas, "Foreign Armies East," 290.

5. Glantz, *Soviet Military Deception,* 565; Thomas, "Foreign Armies East," 289.

6. Glantz, *Soviet Military Deception,* xxxix; David M. Glantz, *The Role of Intelligence in Soviet Military Strategy in World War II* (Novato, Calif.: Presidio, 1990), 2.

7. ONI, *Espionage-Sabotage-Conspiracy,* Appendix II, 23.

8. Glantz, *Soviet Military Deception,* xxxviii. For the poor performance of German intelligence throughout all theaters of the war, see Kahn, *Hitler's Spies,* 523–543; U.S. Army, *The GIS and the War,* 11–14; Military Intelligence Division, *German Military Intelligence,* 295. For the poor performance in the East, see Thomas, "Foreign Armies East," passim.

9. Thomas, "Foreign Armies East," 290; ONI, *Espionage-Sabotage-Conspiracy,* Appendix II, 1.

10. Glantz, *Soviet Military Deception,* 23, 28.

11. Ibid.

12. Reinhard Gehlen, *The Service: The Memoirs of General Reinhard Gehlen,* trans. David Irving (New York: World, 1972), 62–63.

13. Thomas, "Foreign Armies East," 290; ONI, *Espionage-Sabotage-Conspiracy,* Appendix II, 1.

14. Thomas, "Foreign Armies East," passim; U.S. Army, *The GIS and the War,* passim.

15. Glantz, *Soviet Military Deception,* 24, 591 n. 7; Kahn, *Hitler's Spies,* 459, 602 n. 458. Kahn, citing Halder's diary, states that the Germans were aware of the KV-1 but not the T-34.

16. Boog, "German Air Intelligence," 381–387; Weinberg, *A World at Arms,* 273; Kahn, *Hitler's Spies,* 455–460.

17. Boog, "German Air Intelligence," 381–387.

18. Glantz, *Soviet Military Deception,* 565, 613 n. 2.

19. For example, see Sayer and Botting, *America's Secret Army,* for a good anecdotal history of the U.S. Army Counterintelligence Corps during the war.

20. See A. I. Romanov, *Nights Are Longest There: A Memoir of the Soviet Security Services,* trans. Gerald Brooke (Boston: Little, Brown, 1972), 95–99; Nikolai Khokhlov, *In the Name of Conscience,* trans. Emily Kingsbery (New York: David McKay, 1959), 34–86. See also ONI, *Espionage-Sabotage-Conspiracy,* Appendix II, 19.

21. ONI, *Espionage-Sabotage-Conspiracy,* Appendix II, 19–24; Glantz, *Soviet Military Deception,* 2.

22. U.S. Army, CI-CIR/16, *German Methods,* 6.

23. Moll et al., *Cleopatra,* 131, 142; and Germany, *Abwehrabteilung III/Walli III: Abwehrstatistik: Operationsgebiet Ost, Folge 13,* January 1944, T-311/7118109-7118110, NARS Record Group 242; U.S. Army, CI-CIR/16, *German Methods,* 17; U.S. Army, CI-SIR/32, *FA III, OST,* 45–47.

24. U.S. Army, CI-SR/32, *FA III, OST,* 33–34, 52; 258th Interrogation Team, *Organization, Mission, and Functions of the Soviet Secret Service,* 15. The 12 percent figure may be an average for the entire war. For example, according to the 258th Interrogation Team document, German counterintelligence apprehended a total of 17,521 agents from January 1943 to 15 July 1944. Of the 5,521 Soviet agents who were interrogated and documented as having provided information to the Germans (the Germans could not obtain any detailed information from the other 12,000), 419 (7.6 percent) were identified as having been dispatched by Soviet military counterintelligence.

25. U.S. Army, CI-SIR/4, *The Foreign Department of the NKGB,* 33.

26. U.S. Army, CI/SR-32, *FA III, OST,* 34.

27. Sudoplatov, *Special Tasks,* 129.

28. FHO, *Die sowjetische Agentenabwehr,* 25.

29. See John Erickson, "New Thinking about the Eastern Front in World War II," *Journal of Military History* 56 (April 1992): 289–290; Modin, *My Five Cambridge Friends,* 112; and Glantz, *Role of Intelligence,* 216. Andrew and Gordievksy, *KGB: Inside Story,* 306–307.

30. Belousov, *Unreported at the Time,* 21. Belousov claims that while Abwehr was not invisible at the beginning of the war, many of its details were unknown to Soviet counterintelligence.

31. U.S. Army, CI-SR/42, *Smersh,* 30; U.S. Army, CI-SR/32, *FA III, OST,* 52.

32. Ibid.

33. U.S. Army, *Peter Report Number 576, Abwehr IG.*

34. ONI, *Espionage-Sabotage-Conspiracy,* 57–59.

35. Ibid.

36. Ibid., Appendix II, 14–16.

37. Barros and Gregor, *Double Deception,* 52–60, 249–250 n. 20; Hoehne, *Canaris,* 453; United Kingdom, Combined Services, Detailed Interrogation Center, Special Interrogation Report (SIR) 1716, *Notes on Gruppe I Luft, Amt/Ausland Abwehr and on the Activities of Its Outlying Centers (March 1941–January 1943),* 9 August 1945, 15, NARS Record Group 165, Entry 179, Box 665; Boog, "German Air Intelligence," 381–382, 386–387. The Lissner case, like many others, is still shrouded in mystery, as the Russian government, to date, has not published an official account of it. To write their account, Barros and Gregor extensively drew on archival sources and private papers in several languages, including recently released material from Russia. They reconstructed the maneuvering of leaders, diplomats, and military and intelligence officers to show that, contrary to widespread belief, Stalin's desire to evade war enhanced the credibility of German deception efforts prior to the invasion of the USSR. The authors, for the first time, describe the Lissner operation in as much detail

as is currently available. For a bibliography of archival and some secondary source material on the case, see Barros and Gregor, *Double Deception,* 249–250 n. 20. Barros and Gregor relied heavily on U.S. Army records of the Japanese interrogations of Lissner after his arrest in 1943, and on the Captured German Records collection in the National Archives.

38. Barros and Gregor, *Double Deception,* 52.
39. Ibid., 55.
40. Ibid.
41. Ibid.
42. Ibid., 53–54.
43. Ibid.
44. Ibid., 56.
45. Ibid., 55, 250.
46. Ibid., 56.
47. Ibid, 56–57.
48. Hoehne, *Canaris,* 453.
49. Ibid.
50. CSDIR, *Notes on Gruppe I Luft,* 9.
51. Boog, "German Air Intelligence," 381–382, 386–387.
52. ONI, *Espionage-Sabotage-Conspiracy,* 59–62.
53. Ibid.
54. Ibid.
55. Ibid., 59.
56. Ibid.
57. Ibid.
58. Ibid.
59. Ibid.
60. Ibid., 60.
61. Ibid.
62. Ibid.
63. Ibid. The ONI translation of the German document on the Puchov case renders the name as "Riech" several times.
64. Ibid.
65. Ostryakov, *Military Chekists,* 147–149.
66. Ibid.
67. Ibid.
68. Ibid.
69. Ibid., 150.
70. Ibid.
71. Ibid.
72. Belousov, *Unreported at the Time,* 81–94.
73. Ibid.

74. Ibid.

75. ONI, *Espionage-Sabotage-Conspiracy,* Appendix II, 10; Nosryev, *V poyedinke s abverom,* 155; Ostryakov, *Military Chekists,* 147–148. The Soviets may have inflated this figure — even during the war — by counting every German intelligence facility even if it did not strictly involve the training of agents.

76. FSB, *Liubianka II,* 232.

77. Ostryakov, *Military Chekists,* 150.

78. Tarasov, *Igra,* 99–104; Korovin, *Razvedka,* 269.

79. Korovin, *Razvedka,* 269.

80. Ibid., 141, 147–148; U.S. Army, CI-SR/32, *Operations of FA III, OST,* 40.

81. Ostryakov, *Military Chekists,* 150.

82. Ibid.

83. Ibid.

84. All the above examples are related by Ostryakov, *Military Chekists,* 150–152.

85. Belousov, *Unreported at the Time,* 119.

86. Ibid.

87. Ibid., 97–98.

88. Ibid.

89. Ibid.

90. Ibid., 100.

91. Ibid.

92. Ibid.

93. Ibid., 100–101. The account did not specify whether Rakhov tipped off Soviet military counterintelligence to the German operation.

94. Ibid. It is not clear if this was preplanned.

95. Ibid., 101–107.

96. Ibid., 101.

97. Ibid., 101–107. Belousov provides no further detail on how the Gestapo came to the conclusion that Rakhov was a Soviet double agent.

98. Ibid., 118–119.

99. Ibid.

100. Ibid.

101. Ibid.

102. U.S. Army, CI-SR/32, *FA III, OST,* 42.

103. Ibid.

104. Ibid., 41; FHO, *Die sowjetische Agentenabwehr,* 36.

105. ONI, *Espionage-Sabotage-Conspiracy,* Appendix II, 24.

106. Mulligan, *The Politics of Illusion,* 148; Posdnjakoff, *German Counterintelligence,* 87–89.

107. Posdnjakoff, *German Counterintelligence,* 88.

108. Ibid.

109. Ibid.

110. Tarasov, *Igra,* 15.

111. Georgi Tsinev, "Na strazhe interesov vorruzhennykh sil SSSR," *Kommunist Vorruzhennykh Sil* 24 (December 1978): 26–31, trans. United States Joint Publications Research Service No. 73037, *USSR Military Affairs,* no. 1421 (20 March 1979): 1–8. Sudoplatov, in *Special Tasks* (160), states that his department alone was engaged in forty minor radio deception operations against the Germans, all of which were eventually turned over to military counterintelligence in 1942.

112. *Top Secret History,* 365.

113. Tarasov, *Igra,* 23, 26.

114. *Top Secret History,* 364.

115. Tarasov, *Igra,* 26–27.

116. U.S. Army, CI-SR/16, *German Methods,* 10–14; Sudoplatov, *Special Tasks,* 160.

117. U.S. Army, CI-CIR/16, *German Methods,* 10–14.

118. Ibid.

119. ONI, *Espionage-Sabotage-Conspiracy,* 62–64. For the coordination of such operations, see Sudoplatov, *Special Tasks,* 126–172.

120. ONI, *Espionage-Sabotage-Conspiracy,* 62–64.

121. Account based on Sergeev, *Tainye Operatsii,* 265–267.

122. This case is based on Sudoplatov, *Special Tasks,* 160–161.

123. Tarasov, *Igra,* 14; Sergeev, *Tainye Operatsii,* 273; Sudoplatov, *Special Tasks,* 152–176.

124. Tarasaov, *Igra,* 33; *Top Secret History,* 380.

125. Sudoplatov, *Special Tasks,* 160.

126. Ostryakov, *Military Chekists,* 159–164 (Bagration and Kursk), 199 (Stalingrad); Sergeyev, *Tainye Operatsii,* 275–276 (Kursk and Stalingrad).

127. Sergeyev, *Tainye Operatsii,* 276.

128. Tarasov, *Igra,* 35.

129. Ibid., 36–41.

130. Thomas, "Foreign Armies East," passim.

131. ONI, *Espionage-Sabotage-Conspiracy,* Appendix II, 20.

132. *Top Secret History,* 364.

133. Tarasov, *Igra,* 19–20.

134. *Istoriia velikoi otechestvennoi voiny Sovetskogo Soiuza, 1941–1945,* vol. 6 (Moscow: Voennizdat', 1960), 139. It is not clear from this Soviet history whether all this misleading information was passed to the Germans through Soviet double agents. Some of the misleading information could easily have been passed through military radio communications, newspapers, radio broadcasts, and Soviet agent penetrations of various German administrations.

135. Mulligan, "Spies, Ciphers, and Zitadelle," 247; *Top Secret History,* 382–383.

136. *Top Secret History,* 382–383.

137. Ibid.

138. Ostryakov, *Military Chekists,* 163; Glantz, *Soviet Military Deception,* 161–174; Mulligan, "Spies, Ciphers, and Zitadelle," 244; Thomas, "Foreign Armies East," 286.

Glantz, Mulligan, and Thomas all confirm that FHO failed to detect the magnitude of the Soviet counterattack.

139. Tarasov, *Igra,* 35–37.

140. *Top Secret History,* 365–366.

141. Ibid. The history is citing the classified version of Tarasov's and Baryshnikov's *Radioigry* (Moscow: Izdatel'stvo Vsh KGB, 1964), 48–53.

142. Tarasov, *Igra,* 37–42.

143. Ibid., 120–126.

144. Ostryakov, *Military Chekists,* 199; Glantz and House, *Titans,* 132–133, 295; Thomas, "Foreign Armies East," 282–284.

145. *Top Secret History,* 365–366; Glantz and House, *Titans,* 174, 186–188, 298.

146. Thomas, "Foreign Armies East," 286–288; Glantz and House, *Titans,* 358 n. 8.

147. Thomas, "Foreign Armies East," 286–288; Glantz and House, *Titans,* 358 n. 8; Ostryakov, *Military Chekists,* 159–165.

148. Tarasov, *Igra,* 175–178.

149. *Top Secret History,* 366.

150. Tarasov, *Igra,* 33–34.

151. See Modin, *My Five Cambridge Friends,* 108–127; David J. Dallin, *Soviet Espionage* (New Haven, Conn.: Yale University Press, 1955), 191–257; Hoehne, *Canaris,* 258, 479; Andrew and Gordievsky, *KGB: Inside Story,* 235–331; Erickson, *Road to Berlin;* Central Intelligence Agency, *The Rote Kapelle: The CIA's History of Soviet Intelligence and Espionage Networks in Western Europe, 1936–1945* (Frederick, Md.: University Publications of America); Anthony Glees, *The Secrets of Service: A Story of Soviet Subversion of Western Intelligence* (New York: Carroll and Graf, 1987); Heinz Hoehne, *Codeword Direktor: The Story of the Red Orchestra,* trans. Richard Barry (New York: Ballantine, 1982); Costello and Tsarev, *Deadly Illusions;* West, *The Crown Jewels.* These books collectively provide the reader with an excellent description of Soviet espionage in Europe during the war and contain specific information on Soviet penetrations of the Allied and German intelligence services.

152. For details concerning the accusations and speculation on this issue, see U.S. Army, *File on Hermann Baun,* XE003134, Box 13, NARS RG 319, which contains considerable correspondence on Baun's case. See Schellenberg, *Hitler's Secret Service,* 318; Vitaliy Chernyavsky, "We Could Have Used Mueller," *New Times,* no. 36 (1991): 38; William Hood, *Mole: The True Story of the First Russian Intelligence Officer Recruited by CIA* (New York: Norton, 1982), 315–318; Gehlen, *The Service,* 70–71; West, *The Crown Jewels;* Herbert Romerstein and Eric Breindel, *The Venona Secrets: Exposing Soviet Espionage and America's Traitor* (Washington, D.C.: Regnery, 2000). See also Central Intelligence Agency, *Counterintelligence Briefs: The Hunt for "Gestapo Mueller"* (Directorate of Plans, Counterintelligence Staff, December 1971), NARS Record Group, 263 (released under the Nazi War Crimes Disclosure Act, 2000); and Timothy Naftali, "Analysis of the Name File of Heinrich Mueller," NARS Record Group 263.

153. ONI, *Espionage-Sabotage-Conspiracy,* Appendix II, 23. For example, Germany, Auswaertiges Amt, *Photocopies of Correspondence and Reports in Russian with Some*

Translations in German, Pertaining to the Autobiography of Captured NKVD Lieutenant Tschigunow and His Exploitation by German Authorities, April 1941–April 1943, NARS, RG 242, T78 Roll 287, Frame 879, EAP-3-a-11/2; Thomas, "Foreign Armies East," 272–273.

154. Baun File, XE003134. The amount of memos and CIC investigative reports dealing with these accusations are too numerous to list here.

155. U.S. Army, Headquarters, Third U.S. Army, Intelligence Center, *Preliminary Interrogation Report on Hermann Baun,* 30 August, 1945, NARS Record Group 165, ACS G-2, Captured Personnel and Material Branch, Enemy POW Interrogation File, 1943–1945, Entry 179, Box 708, Folder HTUSAIC PIR.

156. Baun File, XE003134.

157. Hoehne and Zolling, *The General Was a Spy,* 64–72.

158. Schellenberg, *Hitler's Secret Service,* 318.

159. Chernyavsky, "We Could Have Used Mueller," 38.

160. Ibid.

161. Hood, *Mole,* 315–318.

162. Ibid. To date, no evidence has been made available to suggest that Mueller might have worked for the Soviets with the idea of passing disinformation along to the Soviet intelligence service.

163. CIA, *Hunt,* 25–25a; and Naftali, "Name File," 4, 7 n. 22. See also Peter Deriabin and Frank Gibney, *The Secret World* (New York: Ballantine, 1982), for a detailed description of Deriabin's career.

164. See also Waller, *The Unseen War,* 296–303, for a good description of the machinations of Mueller, Bormann, and Heinz Pannwitz (one of Mueller's senior counterespionage experts, whose real name is Heinz Paulson) vis-à-vis establishing contact with the Soviets.

165. Gehlen, *The Service,* 70–71; Charles Whiting, *The Hunt for Martin Bormann: The Truth,* rev. ed. (London: Leo Cooper, 1996), 161–219. Whiting provides a detailed account of the hunt for Martin Bormann.

166. Gehlen, *The Service,* 70–71.

167. Ibid.; Whiting, *The Hunt,* 161–219.

168. Ibid.; Waller, *The Unseen War,* 296–303.

169. Whiting, *The Hunt,* 164–167.

170. Ibid., 126–127.

171. Ibid., 172–173.

172. Ibid., 178–179.

173. Gehlen, *The Service,* 70–71.

174. Whiting, *The Hunt,* 172.

175. Costello and Tsarev, *Deadly Illusions,* 405; Whiting, *The Hunt,* 185–187.

176. Sudoplatov, *Special Tasks,* 126.

177. Ibid., 139; CIA, *Rote Kapelle,* 132, 140–146, 353–354; Dallin, *Soviet Espionage,* 196–197, 239, 247; Hoehne, *Codeword Direktor,* 175–177, 200–251, 324 nn. 368–369; Costello and Tsarev, *Deadly Illusions,* 81–90, 399–405.

178. Sudoplatov, *Special Tasks,* 139; CIA, *Rote Kapelle,* 132, 140–146, 353–354; Dallin, *Soviet Espionage,* 196–197, 239, 247; Hoehne, *Codeword Direktor,* 175–177, 200–251, 324 nn. 368–369; Costello and Tsarev, *Deadly Illusions,* 81–90, 399–405.

179. Modin was also the handling officer in London after the war for some of these sources. The literature on these five Soviet penetrations of the British government is extensive and too voluminous to list here. However, the three most important penetrations during the war from a counterintelligence standpoint were Kim Philby (who worked for MI6, or the British external service, also known as the SIS-Secret Intelligence Service), John Cairncross (who was employed by Government Code and Cipher School at Bletchley Park and SIS), and Anthony Blunt (who worked for MI5, the British internal service, also known as the Security Service). Although one must be somewhat skeptical of books published by former Soviet intelligence officers (and Western intelligence officers as well), Modin's book conveys the impression that it is a straightforward memoir by a patriotic professional intelligence officer who had a great deal of respect, rightly or wrongly, for the agents he handled. Oleg Gordievksy, former acting KGB *rezident* [station chief] in London, who defected to the British in 1985 and wrote a history of KGB operations in Britain prior to his defection, assessed Modin as one of the ablest handling officers in KGB history (Andrew and Gordievsky, *KGB: Inside Story,* 391). Despite Modin's long association with operations against the British, Gordievsky, in *KGB: Inside Story,* has not one negative word to say about him. Contrary to many former Soviet intelligence officers, Modin does not malign the Soviet intelligence service and does not bemoan the nepotism, corruption, and incompetence of his former service that characterize other memoirs. One possible agenda is that the Russian government may have given Modin permission to divulge the details of these operations to enhance the image of the former Soviet services as highly competent. However, Modin's account of these cases does not substantially differ from those of responsible Western authors.

180. Modin, *My Five Cambridge Friends,* 113–115; West, *The Crown Jewels,* 220.

181. Modin, *My Five Cambridge Friends,* 113.

182. Ibid.

183. Ibid., 114; Andrew and Gordievsky, *KGB: Inside Story,* 304–305.

184. West, *The Crown Jewels,* 219.

185. Modin, *My Five Cambridge Friends,* 61–62; see also West, *The Crown Jewels,* Appendix 2, 294–346.

186. Modin, *My Five Cambridge Friends,* 89–94.

187. Ibid., 61–62; West, *The Crown Jewels,* Appendix 1, 279–294.

188. Modin, *My Five Cambridge Friends,* 75, 94; Glees, *Secrets of Service,* 228–229; Andrew and Gordievsky, *KGB: Inside Story,* 300.

189. Modin, *My Five Cambridge Friends,* 75, 94; Glees, *Secrets of Service,* 228–229; Andrew and Gordievsky, *KGB: Inside Story,* 300.

190. Andrew and Gordievsky, *KGB: Inside Story,* 299–300. Blunt also gave the Soviets some of the details of the "double-cross system."

191. CIA, *Rote Kapelle,* xi–xii. *Rote Kapelle* continues to serve as the most authoritative analysis of the Red Orchestra, complete with diagrams of the numerous agent net-

works in various European countries. The analysis is based on extensive evaluation of statements made by Soviet intelligence officers who were members of the Rote Kapelle and were captured by the Germans, and on the analysis of observations made by various German counterintelligence organizations. *Kapelle* (orchestra) was an accepted Abwehr term for secret wireless transmitters and the operations against them. The "orchestra" consisted of the "music" (the transmission itself), "pianists" (radio operators), a "maestro" (chief of a network), and a "conductor in Moscow" (the director). When the Gestapo/SD took over the case in July 1942 they coined the term *Rote Kapelle* (Red Orchestra) to designate all the Soviet networks in Western Europe.

192. Sudoplatov, *Special Tasks,* 138–139; Costello and Tsarev, *Deadly Illusions,* 73–90, 394–411. Soviet military intelligence ran many of these networks. Despite the fact that the German intelligence services were not the main target for Soviet military intelligence, it nevertheless became involved in supporting GUGB/NKGB recruitment of some German intelligence officers. Sudoplatov stated that some Rote Kapelle networks, one of which was the Schulze-Boysen Group in Germany, were run by the GUGB/NKGB with the help of radio operators and equipment from Soviet military intelligence. Costello, in conjunction with Oleg Tsarev, a former KGB officer and consultant to the Public Relations Department of the Russian Intelligence Service, confirms Sudoplatov's statement. Costello, with the assistance of Tsarev and the hierarchy of the Russian Intelligence Service, gained access to KGB files on Alexander Orlov, an NKVD general who defected to the United States in the late 1930s. During the course of his research he also had access to some files on the Rote Kapelle.

193. CIA, *Rote Kapelle,* 322–323.

194. Ibid., 160, 253; Hoehne, *Canaris,* 479, 649 n. 349; Waller, *Unseen War,* 300. Hoehne interviewed Dr. Manfred Roeder on 5 March 1968. According to Roeder, Canaris was so emotionally involved in the Rote Kapelle cases that his claims of the Wehrmacht losing 100,000 lives may have been exaggerated. The total number of lives lost because of Rote Kapelle will never be resolved and are, by definition, estimates. Nevertheless, given the sheer bulk of the information provided to Moscow by the agent networks of the Rote Kapelle, it would be safe to assume that a considerable number of German soldiers were killed because of it.

195. CIA, *Rote Kapelle,* 252. The CIA assessment tempers the performance of the Rote Kapelle by stating that it had too many agents, most of whom volunteered their services or accepted recruitment after Germany attacked the USSR. It elaborates that before the attack the Soviets apparently lacked high-level penetrations in Germany and that the clandestine structures to support the tremendous increase in data were built too late and in haste. Stalin's "paranoia" of the Western Allies permeated the Soviet services, and, as a result, Soviet intelligence mistrusted much of the information supplied by the Rote Kapelle. This operational assessment of the flaws in the mechanics of how the Rote Kapelle was run should not detract from the fact that Soviet intelligence managed to handle a large quantity of agents all over occupied Europe for at least two to three years. The most important of these agents were in Germany, and they obtained vital military, political, economic and some counterintelligence information. Some of

the Rote Kapelle sources had been recruited in the 1930s. For an excessively critical analysis of the weaknesses of, and damage caused by, the Rote Kapelle, see Hoehne, *Codeword Direktor,* 273–288. For a Soviet perspective on the success of the Rote Kapelle, see Costello and Tsarev, *Deadly Illusions,* 394–405.

196. Hoehne, *Codeword Direktor,* 287–288; CIA, *Rote Kapelle,* 173, 185–193, 344–345; see also Diagram 19 (the Sissy Group); Hoehne, *Canaris,* 259–269; Mulligan, "Spies, Ciphers, and Zitadelle," 237–239, 254 n. 5, 255 n. 8. The CIA's analysis of the Rote Kapelle makes a strong argument that Oster and an agent code-named "Werther" were the same person. According to the CIA analysis, Rudolph Roessler (the Soviet agent through which Oster probably passed information) before he died provided identifying data on four of his sources. One of those, he claimed, was a German major — whom he did not name — who was "chief of the Abwehr before Canaris." According to Hoehne, as he mentioned in *Canaris,* Oster was a major in the Abwehr and was head of Referat IIIC (counterespionage outside the Wehrmacht and industry) before Canaris took over. However, Hoehne, in *Codeword Direktor,* states that it was not in Oster's character to be a witting agent of the Soviet intelligence service, as his primary goal was to destroy Hitler's regime. Mulligan analyzes the contents of several of the approximately 140 messages sent to Moscow that were sourced to Rudolph Roessler's ring (code-named Lucy), some of which concerned German plans for Operation Zitadelle (Kursk). According to the CIA, "Werther" was the source of sixty-nine of them. Mulligan reaches the conclusion that, based on the contents of the intercepts analyzed, no case can be made as to the specific identity of "Werther."

197. V. E. Tarrant, *The Red Orchestra: The Soviet Spy Network inside Nazi Europe* (London: Cassell, 1995), 159, 172; CIA, *Rote Kapelle,* 189–193.

198. Sudoplatov, *Special Tasks,* 139; CIA, *Rote Kapelle,* 132, 140–146, 353–354; Dallin, *Soviet Espionage,* 196–197, 239, 247; Hoehne, *Codeword Direktor,* 137–144, 175–177, 200–251, 324 nn. 368–369; Costello and Tsarev, *Deadly Illusions,* 81–90, 399–405; Federal'naia Sluzhba Kontrrazvedki, *Organy Gosudarstvennoi Bezopasnosti SSSR v Velikoi Otechestvennoi Voine,* vol. 1, book 2 (1 January–21 June 1941), 286–296. Costello describes Schulze-Boysen's extensive contribution to warning Soviet intelligence of Operation Barbarossa. In 1995 the Russian Federal Counterintelligence Service published numerous reports from "Starshina" (Schulze-Boysen's Soviet code name) to Moscow during the period from September 1940 to June 1941. The detail in the reports confirms Western sources.

199. Dallin, *Soviet Espionage,* 196–197, 239, 247. Dallin is citing Alexander Foote, a former radio operator in the Rote Drei network (part of the Rote Kapelle) and author of the book *Handbook for Spies* (Garden City, N.Y.: Doubleday, 1949).

200. Sudoplatov, *Special Tasks,* 139; CIA, *Rote Kapelle,* 353; Hoehne, *Codeword Direktor,* 168–169; Costello and Tsarev, *Deadly Illusions,* 399–400.

201. Sudoplatov, *Special Tasks,* 139; CIA, *Rote Kapelle,* 132, 140–146, 353–354; Dallin, *Soviet Espionage,* 196–197, 239, 247; Hoehne, *Codeword Direktor,* 175–177, 200–251, 324 nn. 368–369; Costello and Tsarev, *Deadly Illusions,* 81–90, 399–405; Federal'naia Sluzhba Kontrrazvedki, *Organy Gosudarstvennoi Bezopastnosti v Velikoi Otechestvennoi*

Voine, vol. 1, book 2 (1 January–21 June 1941), 286–296. Costello describes Schulze-Boysen's extensive contribution to warning Soviet intelligence of Operation Barbarossa. In 1995 the Russian Federal Counterintelligence Service published numerous reports from "Starshina" (Schulze-Boysen) to Moscow during the period from September 1940 to June 1941. The details in the reports confirm Western sources. See also *Istorii Vneshnei Razvedki,* 4:132–133.

202. *Istorii Vneshnei Razvedki,* 4:134–137.

203. Hoehne, *Codeword Direktor,* 116, 172–173; Tarrant, *Red Orchestra,* 60–62.

204. Costello and Tsarev, *Deadly Illusions,* 403–404.

205. Hoehne, *Codeword Direktor,* 116, 172–173.

206. Ibid., 184–187; CIA, *Rote Kapelle,* 144; Costello and Tsarev, *Deadly Illusions,* 403–405; Dallin, *Soviet Espionage,* 253; Tarrant, *Red Orchestra,* 60–62. Costello, citing Russian intelligence service files on the case, gives a more detailed account of Heilmann's attempts to warn Schulze-Boysen.

207. Dallin, *Soviet Espionage,* 259–260.

208. Hoehne, *Codeword Direktor,* 177–178.

209. Ibid., 173–175; Hoehne, *Canaris,* 479–480; Tarrant, *Red Orchestra,* 83–86; CIA, *Rote Kapelle,* 146–150.

210. Tarrant, *Red Orchestra,* 95; CIA, *Rote Kapelle,* 289.

211. Sudoplatov, *Special Tasks,* 139–140; *Istorii Vneshnei Razvedki,* 3:339–348, 377–378. Sudoplatov remembers the code name Breitmann; volume 3 uses Breitenbach.

212. *Istorii Vneshnei Ravedki,* 3:339–340.

213. Ibid., 343–344.

214. Costello and Tsarev, *Deadly Illusions,* 78–79.

215. *Istorii Vneshnei Razvedki,* 3:348.

216. Ibid., 403–405. Costello confirms much of Sudoplatov's story. Costello gives the name as Robert Barth.

217. Ibid.

218. Sudoplatov, *Special Tasks,* 139–140. Sudoplatov states that no mention of Lehmann was made on the Gestapo chart of the Red Orchestra, probably to avoid the embarrassment of having harbored a Soviet agent.

219. Ibid. The account described in *Istorii Vneshnei Razvedki,* 3:347–349, of this last stage of the operation is extremely sketchy. Sudoplatov's account generally appears to be more credible.

220. *Istorii Vneshnei Razvedki,* 4:135–137.

221. Ibid., 3:348–349.

222. Herbert Romerstein and Stanislav Levchenko, *The KGB against the Main Enemy: How the Soviet Intelligence Service Operates in the United States* (Lexington, Mass.: Lexington Books, 1989), 108–109; Andrew and Gordievsky, *KGB: Inside Story,* 284–285.

223. John E. Haynes and Harvey Klehr, *Venona: Decoding Soviet Espionage in America* (New Haven, Conn.: Yale University Press, 1999), 194–196.

224. Andrew and Gordievksy, *KGB: Inside Story,* 284–285; Elizabeth Bentley, *Out of Bondage* (New York: Ivy, 1990), 125–127, 179–183, 255–257.

225. Romerstein and Levchenko, *KGB against the Main Enemy,* 108; Bentley, *Out of Bondage,* 125–127, 182–183, 255–257; Robert J. Lamphere and Tom Shachtman, *The FBI-KGB War: A Special Agent's Story* (New York: Random House, 1986), 38.

226. Bentley, *Out of Bondage,* 182–183.

227. Ibid., 256.

228. Ibid., 256, 297–298. It is not clear from Bentley's statements on page 256, or from footnote 230 on pages 297 to 298, whether "A List of Reds within OSS" meant that all were knowingly working for Soviet intelligence.

229. Ibid., 110. There is no further evidence on the exact kind of information that was given to the Soviets.

230. Ibid., 179–180; Harvey and Klehr, *Decoding,* 102–112.

231. *Istorii Vneshnei Razvedki,* 4:332.

232. Otto Skorzeny, *My Commando Operations: The Memoirs of Hitler's Most Daring Commando,* trans. David Johnston (Atglen, Pa.: Schiffer, 1995), 206–207.

233. Erickson, *Road to Berlin,* 149–154. The two sources Erickson cited were Viktor Egorov, *Zagovor pripriv Evriki* (Moscow: Sovietskaia Rossiia, 1968); and A. Lukin, "Zagovor ne sostoialsa," in *Front bez linii fronta* (Moscow: Moskovskiie Rabochii, 1970), 328–49.

234. Romanov, *Nights Are Longest There,* 90–103; ONI, *Espionage-Sabotage-Conspiracy,* Appendix II, 19; GSUSA, *Survey,* 17; FHO, *Die sowjetische Agentenabwehr,* 34.

235. Sudoplatov, *Special Tasks,* 129–130.

236. *Top Secret History,* 417.

237. Romanov, *Nights Are Longest There,* 90–103; ONI, *Espionage-Sabotage-Conspiracy,* Appendix II, 19; GSUSA, *Survey,* 17; Germany, FHO, *Die sowjetische Agentenabwehr,* 34; Ostryakov, *Military Chekists,* 146; Germany, *Abwehrkommando 304, Tagesbericht 1057, 8 Mai 1944,* Roll T-78, NARS RG 242; 258th Interrogation Team, *Organization, Mission, and Functions of the Soviet Intelligence Services,* 15.

238. *Abwehrabteilung III/Walli III, Abwehrstatistik: Operationsgebiet Ost Folge 13, Januar 1944,* T-78/311/7118109-7118110, NARS RG 242.

239. Romanov, *Nights Are Longest There,* 90–103; ONI, *Espionage-Sabotage-Conspiracy,* Appendix II, 19; GSUSA, *Survey,* 17; Germany, FHO, *Die sowjetische Agentenabwehr und Gegenspionage,* 34; Ostryakov, *Military Chekists,* 146; *Abwehrkommando 304, Tagesbericht 1057, 8 Mai 1944;* 258th Interrogation Team, *Organization, Mission, and Functions of the Soviet Intelligence Services,* 15.

240. Levytsky, *Uses of Terror,* 173. Levytsky cited a series of 1965 reports in issues of *Sovietskaia Belorussia* in which the chief of the Belorussian KGB, Lieutenant General V. Petrov, claims that the Soviets kidnapped a high-ranking German intelligence officer named von Veith and transported him to Moscow by plane. Levytsky stated that two other German security officers, Karl Kruck and Kurt Schlegel, were also kidnapped.

241. Posdnjakoff, *German Counterintelligence,* 175–177.

242. Ibid.
243. Ibid., 133.
244. U.S. Army, CI-CIR/16, *German Methods,* 13.
245. Ibid.
246. U.S. Army, CI-SR/32, *Operations of FA III, OST,* 51–52.

CHAPTER 5. German Intelligence and Counterintelligence Operations

1. This chapter is based primarily on sections in the following sources, which, in the aggregate, serve as the primary body of literature on German successes and failures overall, and the East in particular: Kahn, *Hitler's Spies;* Military Intelligence Division, *German Military Intelligence;* Thomas, "Foreign Armies East"; Mulligan, "Spies, Ciphers, and Zitadelle"; U.S. Army, *The GIS and the War;* ONI, *Espionage-Sabotage-Conspiracy;* Hoehne, *Canaris;* Hoehne and Zolling, *The General Was a Spy;* CI-SR/32, *Operations of FA III (Ost);* Glantz, *Soviet Military Deception;* Glantz, "Red Mask"; Glantz, *Titans;* U.S. Army, CI-SR/16, *German Methods;* Schellenberg, *Hitler's Secret Service;* Gehlen, *The Service;* Michael Geyer, "National Socialist Germany: The Politics of Information," in Ernest R. May, ed., *Knowing One's Enemies: Intelligence Assessments before the Two World Wars* (Princeton, N.J.: Princeton University Press, 1984), 310–347; R.H.S. Stolfi, *Hitler's Panzers East* (Norman: University of Oklahoma Press, 1993); Albert Seaton, *Russo-German War,* 43–50; Gert Buchheit, *Der deutsche Geheimdienst.*

2. See U.S. Military Intelligence Division, *German Military Intelligence,* 262–274; Geyer, "National Socialist Germany," 310–347.

3. See also Megargee, *Inside Hitler's High Command,* 102–117.

4. Military Intelligence Division, *German Military Intelligence,* 273–276, 308; U.S. Army, *The GIS and the War,* 12, 15; Kahn, *Hitler's Spies,* 523–530; Thomas, "Foreign Armies East," 290–291.

5. Military Intelligence Division, *German Military Intelligence,* 273–276, 308; U.S. Army, *The GIS and the War,* 12, 15; Kahn, *Hitler's Spies,* 523–530; Thomas, "Foreign Armies East," 290–291; CI-SR/32, *FA III, OST,* 32; Belousov, *Unreported at the Time,* 13, 58, 119; Ostryakov, *Military Chekists,* 131; D. P. Nosryev, *V poyedinke s abverom: Dokumentalny ocherk o chekistakh leningradsogo fronta, 1941–1945* (Moscow: Voenizdat', 1968), 28, 32; Sergeev, *Tainye Operatsii,* 219, 279–280.

6. Glantz, *Role of Intelligence,* 1–2, 19. Glantz makes a strong case that the best measure of Soviet military intelligence effectiveness was the flow of combat operations. He goes on to say that while FHO records understate the accomplishments of Soviet military intelligence, they reflect an imposing assessment of its capabilities.

7. U.S. Army, *The GIS and the War,* 2, 8.

8. Ibid.; Hoehne, *Canaris,* 493–496; U.S. Army, Bremen Interrogation Center, Final Interrogation Report No. 68, *Curdes, Richard,* 27 August 1945, 6, NARS RG 319 (hereafter FIR/68).

9. U.S. Army, *The GIS and the War,* 2, 8; Hoehne, *Canaris,* 493–496; FIR/68, *Curdes, Richard,* 6.

10. U.S. Army, *The GIS and the War,* 2, 8; Hoehne, *Canaris,* 493–496; FIR/68, *Curdes, Richard,* 6; Kahn, *Hitler's Spies,* 523.

11. Seaton, *Russo-German War,* 49.

12. Military Intelligence Division, *German Military Intelligence,* 293; U.S. Army, Seventh Army Interrogation Center, *Notes on the Red Army — Intelligence and Security: Preliminary Interrogation and Assessment on P/W Brigadier General Reinhard Gehlen and Major Albert Scholler, Foreign Armies East,* SAIC/2/2, 24 June 1945, 5, NARS RG 238, Records of World War II War Crimes, Entry 160, Folder 87, Box 18.

13. Military Intelligence Division, *German Military Intelligence,* 293; U.S. Army, *Notes on the Red Army,* Entry 160.

14. U.S. Army, *The GIS and the War,* 2–3.

15. Ibid.

16. Ibid.; Military Intelligence Division, *German Military Intelligence,* 308.

17. U.S. Army, *The GIS and the War,* 2.

18. Kahn, *Hitler's Spies,* 428; Military Intelligence Division, *German Military Intelligence,* 292.

19. U.S. Army, *The GIS and the War,* 15; Schellenberg, *Hitler's Secret Service,* 263; United States, Central Intelligence Agency, *Studies In Intelligence,* fall 1957, "The Labyrinth — The Memoirs of Hitler's Secret Service Chief," 124, NARS RG 263, Box 1, Folder 2, Entry 8; U.S Army, *The Case of Walter Friedrich, Walter Schellenberg, Appendix III, Amt VI, and Russia,* 1–4.

20. Kahn, *Hitler's Spies,* 428; Military Intelligence Division, *German Military Intelligence,* 198.

21. Military Intelligence Division, *German Military Intelligence,* 262.

22. ONI, *Espionage-Sabotage-Conspiracy,* 26–27. Volume 6 of Gempp's study was entitled *Betrachtungen ueber den Abwehrdienst im Osten, ins besondere im Gebiet des Oberbefehlshaber im Osten, von Mai 1915 bis zum Ende des Jahres 1916.*

23. Ibid. Gempp had several other conclusions. For example, the variety of nationalities and dialects in Russia caused tremendous language problems, thus making it more difficult to run agents in Russia. He insisted that it was better to have a few well-qualified and reliable agents than to employ masses of ill-trained and poorly motivated ones. He also observed that it was the responsibility of every intelligence officer to take every precaution in selecting and establishing the bona fides of agents.

24. Walter Nicolai, *The German Secret Service* (London: Stanley Paul, 1924), 120–121.

25. Ibid., 122–123.

26. Military Intelligence Division, *German Military Intelligence,* 274–275.

27. ONI, *Espionage-Sabotage-Conspiracy,* 25–27; Posdnjakoff, *German Counterintelligence,* 91.

28. U.S. Army, U.S. Forces European Theater, Military Intelligence Service Center, CI Preliminary Interrogation Report (CI-PIR) 98. *Heinrich von Westarp,* 31 January 1946, 5, NARS RG 319.

29. Paul Leverkuehn, *German Military Intelligence* (New York: Praeger, 1954), 155–156. For a concise history of German military intelligence after World War I, see Military Intelligence Division, *German Military Intelligence,* Appendix 5, 305–309. According to Leverkuehn, during the 1920s German military intelligence saw Poland as more of a threat than the Soviet Union.

30. Yuri Y. Dyakov and Tat'iana Bushuyeva, *The Red Army and the Wehrmacht: How the Soviets Militarized Germany, 1923–1933, and Paved the Way for Fascism* (New York: Prometheus, 1995), 286–287, 290–291, 314.

31. Seaton, *Russo-German War,* 44; Leverkuehn, *German Military Intelligence,* 156; Sergeev, *Secret Nazi Operations,* 134.

32. Leverkuehn, *German Military Intelligence,* 156; Sergeev, *Tainye Operatasii,* 183–184.

33. Seaton, *Russo-German War,* 44.

34. Ibid., 45; ONI, *Espionage-Sabotage-Conspiracy,* 43; Ostryakov, *Military Chekists,* 135. Ostryakov also admits that the Germans collected accurate information on force deployments in the border regions.

35. Seaton, *Russo-German War,* 45.

36. Ibid.

37. Kahn, *Hitler's Spies,* 452.

38. *Top Secret History,* 267–268; *Istorii Vneshnei Razvedki,* 264–282.

39. *Top Secret History,* 315–316.

40. Leverkuehn, *German Military Intelligence,* 158; Kahn, *Hitler's Spies,* 452–453.

41. Kahn, *Hitler's Spies,* 452.

42. Ibid.

43. Ibid.; CI-PIR/98, *Heinrich von Westarp,* Annex I, 12.

44. Kahn, *Hitler's Spies,* 452.

45. Ibid.

46. Ibid., 454.

47. Ibid.

48. Sergeev, *Tainye Operatsii,* 178–179; Nosryev, *V poyedinke s abverom,* 17.

49. Ostryakov, *Military Chekists,* 126.

50. Hoehne, *Canaris,* 450–453.

51. Ibid.

52. Ibid.

53. Ibid.

54. Ibid.

55. Hoehne and Zolling, *The General Was a Spy,* 16.

56. Ibid.

57. Ibid.; Kahn, *Hitler's Spies,* 249.

58. Military Intelligence Division, *German Military Intelligence,* 8, 288–289; CI-FIR/83, *Oberst Georg Buntrock.* Buntrock became Chief of the Frontaufklaerung (known as Mil F of the Milamt RSHA) in 1944 after the Abwehr was disbanded and subsumed into Amt VI of the RSHA. Buntrock believed, with considerable justification, that the

FAK/FAT system functioned better in the East than in the West. In the West the FAKs/FATs remained idle for the better part of four years (1940–1944), while in the East the FAKs/FATs worked constantly. In the West agents had to be recruited largely on a monetary basis, whereas in the East dissatisfaction with the Soviet system ensured the FAKs/FATs a steady supply of agents.

59. Hoehne and Zolling, *The General Was a Spy,* 17–19; Thomas, "Foreign Armies East," 265–266.

60. Thomas, "Foreign Armies East," 265–266; Hoehne and Zolling, *The General Was a Spy,* 16–17.

61. Thomas, "Foreign Armies East," 265–266; Hoehne and Zolling, *The General Was a Spy,* 16–17.

62. Ostryakov, *Military Chekists,* 136; Posdnjakoff, *German Counterintelligence,* 12–13.

63. Kahn, *Hitler's Spies,* 276.

64. Ibid.; Military Intelligence Division, *German Military Intelligence,* 61; Ostryakov, *Military Chekists,* 134. Ostryakov claims that the Germans were operating almost sixty schools on the Eastern Front, not counting those run by the Gestapo and SD/Ausland.

65. U.S. Army, CI-CIR 16, *German Methods,* 3; CI-SR/32, *FA III, OST,* 40–41.

66. Belousov, *Unreported at the Time,* 56.

67. Kahn, *Hitler's Spies,* 249.

68. Military Intelligence Division, *German Military Intelligence,* 196; Hoehne and Zolling, *The General Was a Spy,* 17–18; Sergeev, *Tainye Operatsii,* 97–98.

69. Kahn, *Hitler's Spies,* 144; Hoehne and Zolling, *The General Was a Spy,* 18.

70. U.S. Army, *Peter Report Number 576 (Abwehr IG),* 6.

71. ONI, *Espionage-Sabotage-Conspiracy,* 28.

72. Ibid., 26–28.

73. Ibid.

74. Germany, Panzerarmeeoberkommando 3 (Panzer A.O.K. 3) *Abteilung* 1c/AO, *Anlagenband A5, Taetigkeitsbericht-Nr. 11, 1 Januar–30 Juni 1944:* Abwehr*trupp, Pz 113: 14 Maerz 1944, Feindbild im Raum Janowitschi-Lisono,* NARS RG 242, T-313/3098586-519-5. In the jargon of German intelligence terminology an agent was referred to as a *V-Mann,* short for *Vertrauungsmann,* which loosely translates into English as a trusted individual. Agents were referred to as *V-Leute* or *V-Maenner* — trusted people or trusted men.

75. Ibid.

76. Panzer A.O.K 3, *Anlagenband A5, Taetigkeitsbericht-Nr. 11, 14 Maerz 1944,* 3.

77. Ibid.

78. Ibid.; Panzer A.O.K. 3, *Abteilung* 1c/AO, *Anlagenband A5, Taetigkeitsbericht-Nr. 11, 1 Januar–30 Juni 1944:* Abwehr*trupp, Pz 113: 20 Maerz 1944, Feindbild im Raum suedl. und nordwestl. Witebsk,* NARS RG 242, T-313/3098586-519-5.

79. ONI, *Espionage-Sabotage-Conspiracy,* 45.

80. Panzer A.O.K. 3, *Abteilung* 1c/AO, *Anlagenband A5, Taetigkeitsbericht-Nr. 11, 1 Januar–30 Juni 1944: Abwehrtrupp, Pz 113: 12 Juni 1944, Vernehmungsbericht des V-Mann 2385,* NARS RG 242, T-313/3098586-519-5.

81. Panzer A.O.K. 3, *Anlagenband A5, Taetigkeitsbericht-Nr. 11, 1 Januar–30 Juni 1944.* The term used in the German debriefing was *Oberleutnant der Sperrabteilung* (loosely translated as first lieutenant of the security department). The lieutenant could have been a Smersh officer.

82. Ibid.

83. Panzer A.O.K. 3, *Taetigkeitsbericht-Nr. 11, 1 Januar–30 Juni 1944: Abwehrtrupp, Pz 113: 12 Juni 1944, Vernehmungsbericht des V-Mann 2385,* NARS RG 242, T-313/3098586-519-5.

84. Panzer A.O.K. 3, *Anlagenband A5, Taetigkeitsbericht- Nr. 11, 1 Januar–30 Juni 1944.*

85. Gehlen, *The Service,* 127–128.

86. Ibid.

87. Hoehne and Zolling, *The General Was a Spy,* 16.

88. ONI, *Espionage-Sabotage-Conspiracy,* 46–47; Germany, *Abteilung Fremde Heere Ost (IIa), Decknamenverzeichnis der Agenten Abwehr I,* 14 November 1944, NARS RG 242, Captured German Records, T-78/673/825/H3/1510.

89. Hoehne and Zolling, *The General Was a Spy,* 17–20.

90. Ibid.; Thomas, "Foreign Armies East," passim; Silver, "Questions, Questions, Questions," 208; U.S. Army, *The Case of Walter Friedrich Schellenberg,* Appendix III, 1. Arnold Silver, Baun's interrogator after the war, attributed several false reports of a planned massive Soviet invasion of the three Western zones of Germany in 1947 to Baun's presence on Gehlen's staff. Gehlen himself had evaluated all the reports as genuine. According to Silver, Baun was a self-assured officer who was alcohol-dependent. Schellenberg, however, admitted in his interrogation that Baun's operations were better organized than those of Amt VI, Gruppe C (SD/Ausland, Group C), which were targeted against the Soviet Union.

91. ONI, *Espionage-Sabotage-Conspiracy,* 46–47; Germany, *Abteilung Fremde Heere Ost* (IIa), *Decknamenverzeichnis der Agenten* Abwehr *I,* 14 November 1944, NARS RG 242, Captured German Records, T-78/673/825/H3/1510.

92. U.S. Army, CI-CIR 16, *German Methods,* 3.

93. Kahn, *Hitler's Spies,* 370.

94. ONI, *Espionage-Sabotage-Conspiracy,* 71–119. Of the sources evaluated, this section of the ONI document represents the best information available on Abwehr II operations in the East. It is based on numerous German documents, and, though not comprehensive, it offers an excellent introduction to the subject.

95. Ibid., 72.

96. Ibid.

97. Ibid., 72, 96. Of the total number of missions, 110 were carried out by parachute, of which 23 were reported as successful. The missions were further divided into categories: 269 *Kleinkrieg* (guerrilla warfare) missions were carried out, of which 218 were successful; 132 *Sabotage* (sabotage) operations were conducted, of which 38 were successful; and 103 *Zersetzung* (sedition and subversion) operations were launched, of which

46 were successful. Operations designated *Zersetzung* were a subset of a category labeled *Insurgierung* (roughly interpreted to mean insurrection).

98. Ibid.

99. Ibid.; Supreme Headquarters, Allied Expeditionary Force, Counterintelligence War Room, London, Liquidation Report No. 187, *FAK 203*, 29 January 1946, 3. NARS RG 165, Entry 179, Box 705. The report is a debriefing of Lieutenant Colonel Gotthard Gambke, former head Referat Ost Mil. Amt D. In the sources evaluated, little information was uncovered to indicate how the Germans verified Abwehr II mission successes independent of agent statements. However, this Counterintelligence War Room Report indicated that, in 1944, FAK 203 dispatched a series of sabotage groups to blow up several sections of the rail lines connecting Riga and Daugavpils. At least some of the damage was confirmed by aerial reconnaissance, and the results were considered satisfactory.

100. Supreme Headquarters, Allied Expeditionary Force, Counterintelligence War Room, London, Liquidation Report No. 183, *FAK 202*, 3, NARS RG 165, Entry 179, Box 705.

101. Ibid., 4.

102. ONI, *Espionage-Sabotage-Conspiracy*, 81–87.

103. Ibid., 84.

104. Ibid., 86–87.

105. Ibid., 112–113.

106. Ibid.

107. Ibid.

108. Ibid.

109. ONI, *Espionage-Sabotage-Conspiracy*, 112–113.

110. Ibid., 113.

111. Ostryakov, *Military Chekists*, 135–136.

112. Ibid., 143.

113. ONI, *Espionage-Sabotage-Conspiracy*, 62–64, 108.

114. Ostryakov, *Military Chekists*, 151.

115. Ibid.

116. Mulligan, *The Politics of Illusion*, 147–183; Dallin, *German Rule*, 107–123, 506–510, 607–612; Schellenberg, *Hitler's Secret Service*, 267–276; Hoehne, *Canaris*, 316–323.

117. Hoehne, *Canaris*, 459; Dallin, *German Rule*, 107–166; U.S. Army, CI-SR/32, *FA III, OST*, 13.

118. Ostryakov, *Military Chekists*, 176–177.

119. Ibid., 125.

120. Ibid., 124–125.

121. Ibid., 176–177.

122. Ibid.

123. Ibid., 124–125.

124. Ibid.

125. Ibid.

126. Sergeev, *Tainye Operatsii,* 269–271.

127. Ostryakov, *Military Chekists,* 211; Kahn, *Hitler's Spies,* 361, 453.

128. The primary documentary sources on German counterintelligence in the East are U.S. Army, CI-SR/32, *FA III, OST;* U.S. Army, CI-SR/16, *German Methods;* Posdnjakoff, *German Counterintelligence;* U.S. Army, *The GIS and the War;* ONI, *Espionage-Sabotage-Conspiracy;* Supreme Allied Expeditionary Force, Counterintelligence War Room Situation Report No. 195, *Leitstelle III Ost (Walli III),* NARS RG, 319, XE013988. Schmalschlaeger stated that Leitstelle III Ost identified 50,000 Soviet agents and put an additional 20,000 out of action out of a total Soviet agent deployment of 130,000. Schmalschlaeger's debriefing (CI-SR/32) will be used as the primary source in this section. It is the most comprehensive analysis of German military counterintelligence in the East currently available and has not been extensively used in published books and articles.

129. Posdnjakoff, *German Counterintelligence,* 96.

130. U.S. Army, CI-SR/32, *FA III, OST,* 32–33. Measuring Gestapo effectiveness specifically against Soviet agent deployments on the Eastern Front becomes problematic largely because of the lack of source material. Nevertheless, the Gestapo had substantial success inside Germany against the Red Orchestra and other Soviet networks. See CIA, *Rote Kapelle,* xi–xiii; Gilles Perrault, *The Red Orchestra,* trans. Peter Wiles (New York: Schocken, 1969); Counterintelligence War Room, SIR/4, *Amt IV of the RSHA;* and ONI, *Espionage-Sabotage-Conspiracy,* 52–55, 128–130, for an excellent documentary introduction to the operations, missions, organization, and functions of the Gestapo. Unfortunately the Counterintelligence War Room document contains no specific operational information on the Gestapo component dealing with the East, Gruppe IV E Referat 5 (titled Abwehr Ost) headed by *Hauptsturmfuehrer* (Captain) Hausler. Schellenberg offers some details on Gruppe IV E cases in Germany against the Soviet Union, as he was chief of this group from July 1939 to July 1941. See also Schellenberg's postwar interrogation report, 2–14 and Appendix II, pages 1–3; and Schellenberg, *Hitler's Secret Service,* 149–165. Operational information on the successes of the German army's Geheime Feldpolizei (Secret Field Police) in specifically combating Soviet agents is lacking — although a few Abwehr III documents show only the number of Soviet agents apprehended by the GFP in a particular time period. The major documentary source on the GFP is U.S. Army, Foreign Military Studies, MS-C-029, *The Secret Field Police* by Wilhelm Kirchbaum, 18 May 1947. It contains little on the effectiveness of the GFP in combating Soviet agents, although it serves as a thorough introduction to the organization, missions, and functions of the GFP.

131. U.S. Army, CI-SR/32, *FA III, OST,* 11–13, 21.

132. Ibid., 13.

133. Ibid., 13–14.

134. Ibid., 13–15; Nosryev, *V poyedinke s abverom,* 193. For example, according to Nosryev, when a German officer of FAT 304 was captured and interrogated by Soviet

counterintelligence, the Soviets assessed the German officer as having possessed a good deal of knowledge of OO/NKVD activities.

135. U.S. Army, CI-SR/32, *FA III, OST,* 21–22.

136. Ibid., 22. The seizure of thousands of NKVD documents in the initial phases of Barbarossa may have hampered the ability of the German counterintelligence to accurately predict if and when a Soviet counterintelligence offensive was going to take place. Shortages of Russian-speaking officers and the demands of combat operations no doubt slowed the processing of seized documents.

137. Ibid.

138. Ibid., 23.

139. Ibid., 24

140. Ibid., 34.

141. Ibid., 30–31.

142. Ibid., 35–36; Posdnjakoff, *German Counterintelligence,* 69–142.

143. U.S. Army, CI-SR/32, *FA III, OST,* 35–36; Posdnjakoff, *German Counterintelligence,* 69–142.

144. U.S. Army, CI-SR/32, *FA III, OST,* 37.

145. Ibid., 38. See also Earl F. Ziemke, "Operation Kreml: Deception, Strategy, and the Fortunes of War," *Parameters: U.S. Army War College Quarterly* 9, no. 1 (9 March 1979): 72–82; and Ziemke and Bauer, *Moscow to Stalingrad,* 328–330, for details of this successful German deception operation against the Soviets.

146. U.S. Army, CI-CIR/16, *German Methods,* 10–11.

147. Ibid., 10–11, 14.

148. U.S. Army, CI-SR/32, *FA III, OST,* 37.

149. Ibid., 37. Schmalschlaeger did not give any details of the German radio playback operation that exposed the Soviet agent net.

150. Posdnjakoff, *German Counterintelligence,* 14.

151. Ibid.

152. U.S. Army, CI/SR-32, *FA III, OST,* 38.

153. U.S. Army, CI-CIR/16, *German Methods,* 12–14. The three Abwehr III officers who were debriefed for this report estimated that German military counterintelligence conducted an average of ten to twelve radio playbacks per month over the entire Eastern Front, with each operation extending over a period of three to six months. However, they pointed out that this figure may be somewhat suspect in that the Soviets detected many of them.

154. Ibid., 14.

155. Ibid.

156. U.S. Army, CI-SR/32, *FA III, OST,* 38.

157. U.S. Army, CI-CIR/16, *German Methods,* 14.

158. U.S. Army, CI-SR/32, *FA III, OST,* 43.

159. Ibid., 42.

160. U.S. Army, CI-CIR/16, *German Methods,* 7; U.S. Army, CI-CIR/32, *FA III, OST,* 38.

161. U.S. Army, CI-CIR/16, *German Methods,* 7; U.S. Army, CI-CIR/32, *FA III, OST,* 38.

162. U.S. Army, CI-CIR/32, *FA III, OST,* 38; U.S. Army, CI-CIR/16, *German Methods,* 7. The Germans were, however, able to read at least some of the traffic between partisan and NKGB units. After the autumn of 1943 little of this traffic remained a secret to the Germans (U.S. Army, CI-CIR/16, *German Methods,* 7).

163. U.S. Army, CI-SR/32, *FA III, OST,* 37; U.S. Army, CI-FIR/83, *Oberst Georg Buntrock,* 10.

164. U.S. Army, CI-SR/32, *FA III, OST,* 43–52; U.S. Army, CI-CIR/ 16, *German Methods,* 15–17.

165. U.S. Army, CI-CIR/16, *German Methods,* 9.

166. Ibid., 15–17.

167. Ibid.

168. U.S. Army, CI-SR/32, *FA III, OST,* 46.

169. Ibid.

170. Ibid.

171. Ibid.; U.S. Army, CI-FIR/83, *Oberst Georg Buntrock,* 10.

172. Glantz, "Red Mask," 243.

173. Posdnjakoff, *German Counterintelligence,* 160.

174. U.S. Army, CI-SR/32, *FA III, OST,* 52.

175. Ibid.

176. The major sources that discuss German military intelligence analysis in the East are Thomas, "Foreign Armies East"; Kahn, *Hitler's Spies;* Military Intelligence Division, *German Military Intelligence;* Gehlen, *The Service;* Bucheit, *Der Deutsche Geheimdienst;* Hoehne and Zolling, *The General Was a Spy;* Boog, "German Air Intelligence"; Mulligan, "Spies, Ciphers, and Zitadelle"; Hoehne, *Canaris;* and Geyer, "The Politics of Information." There are almost no books or articles published in English solely dedicated to the intelligence analysis on the USSR performed by Amt VI (SD/Ausland) of the RSHA.

177. Thomas, "Foreign Armies East," 280; Hoehne and Zolling, *The General Was a Spy,* 24–26; Kahn, *Hitler's Spies,* 429–432.

178. Thomas, "Foreign Armies East," 288–289.

179. Ibid.; Kahn, *Hitler's Spies,* 441.

180. Hoehne and Zolling, *The General Was a Spy,* 6–9, 26.

181. Ibid.; U.S. Army, *Report of Interrogation No. 5724: (Generalmajor Reinhard Gehlen).*

182. Thomas, "Foreign Armies East," 275–281, 297 nn. 33, 34; Kahn, *Hitler's Spies,* 458–460; Weinberg, *World at Arms,* 273, 1008 n. 33. Weinberg also cites the new German official history of World War II (4:600) and the first volume of OKW's *Kriegstagesbuch* (1075–1076).

183. Thomas, "Foreign Armies East," 277–278; Kahn *Hitler's Spies,* 447–451.

184. Kahn, *Hitler's Spies,* 446–447, 461; Schellenberg, *Hitler's Secret Service,* 197–200.

185. Thomas, "Foreign Armies East," 277–278; Kahn, *Hitler's Spies,* 447–451.

186. Kahn, *Hitler's Spies,* 446–447, 461; Schellenberg, *Hitler's Secret Service,* 197–200.

187. Stolfi, *Hitler's Panzers East;* Schellenberg, *Hitler's Secret Service,* 273–274. Schellenberg praises the work of the Wansee Institute, which essentially functioned as the long-range analytical arm of Amt VI primarily concentrating on the Soviet Union, but gives no details of its conclusions.

188. Stolfi, *Hitler's Panzers East,* 18–25, 140.

189. Ibid., 137–138, 143, 180–183, 229–230.

190. Glantz, *Barbarossa,* 211, 213.

191. Ibid.

192. Stolfi, *Hitler's Panzers East,* 21–23.

193. Ibid., 21.

194. Thomas, "Foreign Armies East," 278.

195. Stolfi, *Hitler's Panzers East,* 21, 180–183, 229–230.

196. Kahn, *Hitler's Spies,* 461.

197. For a detailed analysis of the information Stalin possessed regarding the German attack, see Barros and Gregor, *Double Deception,* esp. 220–227. See also Sudoplatov, *Special Tasks,* 116–125, for his perspective.

198. Weinberg, *A World at Arms,* 269–270. The Soviets started to show stubborn resistance early in the war. For example, on 20 July 1941 German troops captured Yelnya, a town twenty-five miles southeast of Smolensk, and were driven out by Soviet forces on 5 September 1941. This was one of the first local Soviet victories of the war.

199. Ibid.

200. Ibid.

201. Stolfi, *Hitler's Panzers East,* 137–138, 143.

202. Glantz, *Barbarossa,* 213–214.

203. Thomas, "Foreign Armies East," 278–279.

204. Ibid., 280.

205. Seaton, *Russo-German War,* 228; Glantz, *Titans,* 91.

206. Thomas, "Foreign Armies East," 263–265; Military Intelligence Division, *German Military Intelligence,* 13–34.

207. Thomas, "Foreign Armies East," 281.

208. Ibid.

209. Ibid., 281–282.

210. Ibid.

211. Ibid., 283–284; Kahn, *Hitler's Spies,* 437–440.

212. Thomas, "Foreign Armies East," 286; Mulligan, "Spies, Ciphers, and Zitadelle," 244; Kahn, *Hitler's Spies,* 440.

213. Thomas, "Foreign Armies East," 287–289.

214. Erickson, *Road to Berlin,* 225–228; Glantz, *Titans,* 214–215.

215. Thomas, "Foreign Armies East," 286–287; Glantz, *Titans,* 195–197; Seaton, *Russo-German War,* 591. Glantz succinctly describes the various Soviet attack options in May–June 1944 and provides an excellent map of the disposition of Soviet forces at the time. Seaton's chronology of the reorganizations of the various German Army Groups throughout the war is highly useful. Army Group South underwent consider-

able reorganization since June 1941. By January–February 1944 it had been split into Army Groups North and South Ukraine.

216. Thomas, "Foreign Armies East," 287–288; Glantz, *Titans,* 203, 358 n. 8.

217. Thomas, "Foreign Armies East," 288–289.

218. Ibid.

219. Ibid., 286.

220. Sergeev, *Tainye Operatsii,* 390–395; Ostryakov, *Military Chekists,* 126–128.

221. Sergeev, *Tainye Operatsii,* 391.

222. Nosryev, *V poyedinke s abverom,* 296.

223. Belousov, *Unreported at the Time,* 27.

224. Ostryakov, *Military Chekists,* 161–163.

225. Ibid.

226. Thomas, "Foreign Armies East," 291.

227. John H. Waller, "The Double Life of Admiral Canaris," *Journal of Intelligence and Counterintelligence* 9, no. 3 (fall 1996): 271–289.

228. Hoehne, *Canaris,* 448–491.

229. Dziak, *Chekisty,* 39–50; Waller, *The Unseen War,* 8–10.

230. Andrew, *Her Majesty's Secret Service,* 285.

231. Ibid., 422.

232. Ibid., 349–350, 462–463.

233. Ibid., 462–463.

234. Bradley F. Smith, *Sharing Secrets with Stalin: How the Allies Traded Intelligence, 1941–1945* (Lawrence: University Press of Kansas, 1996), 15.

235. Glantz, "Red Mask," 237–239; Leverkuehn, *German Military Intelligence,* 156.

236. See *Top Secret History,* 398–405, for operations against the Japanese; and Glantz, "Red Mask," 231–239, for Soviet military deception employed against the Japanese.

237. See Ferris, "Fortitude in Context," forthcoming, for a detailed discussion of this issue.

CHAPTER 6. Operation Monastery and "Case Klatt"

1. The major sources on Operation Monastery are Sudoplatov, *Special Tasks,* 152–160, 167–170; Lev Bezymenskii, "Geine po imeni Maks, ili istoriya odnoi tainoi operatsii," *Novoe Vremia,* no. 41 (1993): 40–42; V. I. Trubnikov, *Istorii Vneshnei Razvedki,* 4:108–120; Liubianka II, 244–250; *Top Secret History,* 383–386; Sudoplatov, *Spetsoperatsii,* 238–251.

2. The major sources on Kauder/Klatt are West, *The Crown Jewels,* 187–204, Thomas, "Foreign Armies East"; Silver, "Questions, Questions, Questions," 202–207; Kahn, *Hitler's Spies,* 310–318, 368–370; U.S. Army, *The GIS and the War,* 6–8; David Thomas, "The Legend of Agent Max," *Foreign Literary Intelligence Scene* 5, no. 1 (January 1986): 1–2, 5; Harris Greene, "Rescue of Max," *Foreign Literary Intelligence Scene* 5, no. 3 (May/June 1986): 1–3; CSDIC, SIR 1727, *Notes on Abwehr I Luft;* CSDIC, SIR 1716, *Notes on Gruppe I Luft;* and U.S. Army, Records of the Army Staff,

Anton Turkul, XE061758, NARS Record Group, 319; Naftali, "U.S. Gegenspionage," 97–102. The file on Turkul comprises three large folders containing hundreds of pages of correspondence, and investigative and interrogation reports on the individuals of interest to the Allies after the war (see below). See Thomas, "Foreign Armies East," 266–267, 282–290, 298 nn. 46, 51, for details of FHO estimates based on controlled information the Soviets provided the Germans through Operation Monastery.

3. West, *The Crown Jewels,* 187–204; Naftali, "U.S. Gegenspionage," 97–102.

4. See, for example, Winfried Meyer, *Unternehmen Sieben: Eine Rettungsaktion vom Holocaust Bedrohte aus dem Amt / Ausland / Abwehr* (Frankfurt-am-Main: Verlag Anton Hain GmbH, 1993), 152–162; Hoehne and Zolling, *The General Was a Spy,* 17–20; Cookridge, *Spy of the Century,* 72–90,106–107, 370, 384; Reese, *General Reinhard Gehlen,* 17; Heinz Hoehne, *Der Krieg im Dunkeln: Macht und Einfluss der deutschen und russischen Geheimdienste* (Munich: C. Bertelsmann Verlag GmbH, 1985), 433–435; Erickson, *The Road to Stalingrad,* 343–345, 546; and Gehlen, *The Service,* 57. Cookridge does not mention Max specifically but generally praises Gehlen and describes several instances of ostensibly successful German clandestine operations based on a review of FHO files. Although Kahn, in *Hitler's Spies* (310–318, 368–370), raised substantial suspicions about Max, Thomas provided, in "The Legend of Agent Max" and in his follow-up article, "Foreign Armies East," the first published scholarly correctives to Hoehne, Gehlen, and Cookridge.

5. U.S. Army, XE061758, File on Anton Turkul; see report on the "Interrogation of *Oberstleutnant* Wagner," 2.

6. Ibid.; see "Internal Memo on Source Panda," 21 January 1947.

7. Tarasov, *Igra,* 67.

8. Sudoplatov, *Special Tasks,* 158–159; *Liubianka II,* 246; CSDIC, SIR No. 1716, "Notes on Gruppe I Luft," 20–21; and numerous references throughout XE06178, which will be discussed in detail below.

9. Trubnikov, *Istorii Vneshnei Razvedki,* 116–117.

10. Bezymenskii, "Heine," 40.

11. West, *The Crown Jewels,* 202–203; Silver, "Questions, Questions, Questions," 205.

12. Thomas, "Legend of Agent Max."

13. West, *The Crown Jewels,* 187–203.

14. Sudoplatov, *Special Tasks,* 126–127, 157, 168–170. Sudoplatov also called Berezino the most successful "radio deception game" of the war (168).

15. *Top Secret History,* 383.

16. Ibid., 385.

17. Sudoplatov, *Special Tasks,* 126–127, 157. See also Reshin, "Bez Grifa Sekretno," 7. Although Reshin's article largely concerns Operation Berezino, he summarized the results of Operation Monastery because Dem'ianov played such a large role in both operations. Reshin claimed that, up to the end of 1944, fifteen German agents had been captured, four radio sets were used for radio playbacks, and seven "German collaborators" were arrested as a result of Monastery. Reshin stated that the NKGB had also captured 500,000 rubles that the Germans had earmarked for the financing of the fictitious anti-Soviet pro-German organization "Throne," the establishment of which had

been the original objective of Monastery (see below). Reshin mentioned the success of Monastery in deceiving the Germans at Kursk and Stalingrad, but he provided no further information on the seven "German collaborators" who were arrested. Dem'ianov was known to the Germans as both "Aleksandr" and "Max"; based on the documentation evaluated, however, the Germans apparently never connected "Aleksandr" and "Max" as one and the same person.

18. *Top Secret History,* 383.

19. Thomas, "The Legend of Agent Max," 1–2, 5. Guderian characterized "Max" as *erstklassig* (first class).

20. Gehlen, *The Service,* 57.

21. For limitations, see Naftali, "Pavel Sudoplatov Assassin's Tales," *Boston Book Review,* September 1994, 4, 31. Sheila Kerr, "KGB Sources on the Cambridge Network of Soviet Agents: True or False?" *Intelligence and National Security* 11, no. 3 (July 1996): 569; Sudoplatov, *Special Tasks,* vii, x. Jerrold L. Schecter has done an excellent job of putting forth Sudoplatov's views on a number of important events in Soviet history. However, in some cases — such as with Sudoplatov's descriptions of Operations Monastery and Berezino — Schecter's uncritical acceptance of Sudoplatov's narrative may indicate that Schechter did not have enough knowledge of these cases to elicit more detail from Sudoplatov. Robert Conquest, who wrote the foreword to Schecter's book, feels there is a tendency in "certain academic circles" to "reject personal reminiscences as almost by definition inferior to documents." However, he goes on to explain the necessity to use both but rightly points out how easily documents can be falsified or distorted by their originators — especially in the USSR under Stalin. Conquest also notes that "Western historical research of any value on the USSR was largely based on personal memoirs of defectors and others — and was largely validated when a mass of formerly secret Soviet documents appeared from 1989 on."

22. See Naftali, "Assassin's Tales."

23. See Thomas, "Foreign Armies East"; Silver, "Questions, Questions, Questions," 202–207; Kahn, *Hitler's Spies,* 310–318, 368–370; U.S. Army, *The GIS and the War,* 6–8; Thomas, "The Legend of Agent Max," 1–2, 5; Greene, "Rescue of Max," 1–3; CSDIC, SIR 1727, *Notes on Abwehr I Luft,* 9–10; CSDIC, SIR 1716, *Notes on Gruppe I Luft,* 20–22; U.S. Army, *Anton Turkul,* XE061758; and Dziak, *Chekisty,* 105–124.

24. Sudoplatov, *Special Tasks,* 152, 155.

25. Ibid., 155. Sudoplatov does not mention whether this meant that the Soviet intelligence services expected the war to go badly from the beginning and had started planning for such a contingency before the war broke out. In any event, since by the end of July 1941 the German army was almost in Kiev and the military situation looked bleak, that the Soviet intelligence services planned to infiltrate agents into a future German puppet government was not surprising.

26. Ibid., 152–153.

27. Ibid.

28. Ibid.

29. Ibid., 152–153. Sudoplatov made no mention in his memoirs of Dem'ianov's success in thwarting "terrorism" and gave no indication of how long Dem'ianov spent reporting on this kind of activity.

30. Ibid., 151, 154; Reshin, "Bez Grifa Sekretno," 7. Reshin identifies Makliarskii as a Lieutenant Colonel but states that his first name is Isidor. Sudoplatov identified Ilyin as a commissar of state security.

31. Sudoplatov, *Special Tasks,* 151, 154; Reshin, "Bez Grifa Sekretno," 7.

32. Sudoplatov, *Special Tasks,* 151, 154; Reshin, "Bez Grifa Sekretno," 7.

33. Ibid. Sudoplatov does not elaborate on the Gestapo interest of Dem'ianov.

34. Ibid.

35. Ibid.; *Lyiubianka II,* 246. Sudoplatov gives no explanation as to how he knew that the Germans had assigned the code name "Max" to Dem'ianov. It is not clear from Sudoplatov's memoirs if he learned that the Abwehr had assigned the code name "Max" as a result of a postwar evaluation of captured Abwehr documents or if the Soviets knew in 1940–1941 that the Abwehr had assigned the code name to Dem'ianov.

36. Sudoplatov, *Special Tasks,* 151–154.

37. Ibid., 152–153; Bezymenskii, "Geine po imeni Maks," 41; *Istorii Vneshnei Razvedki* 4:109. Sudoplatov stated that the individual was named Glebov and, in July 1941, was living in poverty under the care of the Russian Orthodox Church in the Novodevichy Monastery. Sudoplatov said that some old aristocrats survived the purges but were either placed under constant surveillance or recruited as informants. It is not clear from Sudoplatov's memoirs if Glebov had been recruited by Soviet counterintelligence. Bezymenskii identified another individual as one Prince Votbolskiy, a former leader of the nobility in the province of Nizhegorod who was under the care of the clergy of the Novodevichy Monastery. Volume 4 of the *Istorii Vneshnei Razvedki* identifies numerous others living on the grounds of the Novodevichy Monastery.

38. Sudoplatov, *Special Tasks,* 153, 155.

39. Ibid., 155; Bezymenskii, "Geine po imeni Maks," 42; *Liubianka II,* 246, states that Dem'ianov was deployed in February 1942.

40. Sudoplatov, *Special Tasks,* 155.

41. *Istorii Vneshnei Razvedki,* 4:111–112.

42. Sudoplatov, *Special Tasks,* 155.

43. Ibid., 156–157.

44. Ibid., 157–158; Bezymenskii,"Geine po imeni Maks," 42. Although Sudoplatov does not mention it in his memoirs, according to Bezymenskii (who relied on Sudoplatov for his article), Dem'ianov crossed the front lines twice in 1942–1943 to visit his German controllers, probably to enhance his bona fides. Bezymenskii merely stated that, by crossing the lines twice, Dem'ianov's prestige in the eyes of the Abwehr rose significantly, and he was awarded the Iron Cross.

45. *Istorii Vneshnei Razvedki,* 4:112–113.

46. Sudoplatov, *Special Tasks,* 157–158; Bezymenskii, "Geine po imeni Maks," 42.

47. *Istorii Vneshnei Razvedki,* 4:113.

48. Sudoplatov, *Special Tasks,* 157–158; Bezymenskii, "Geine po imeni Maks," 42.

49. Sudoplatov, *Special Tasks,* 157.

50. *Istorii Vneshnei Razvedki,* 4:113–114; Sudoplatov, *Special Tasks,* 157. Sudoplatov's original suggestion was to allow the team to move about Moscow for approximately ten days so that Soviet counterintelligence could identify their contacts other than Dem'ianov. However, Beria did not want the team to commit any acts of sabotage while there. The compromise was to disarm the team. Sudoplatov does not provide any amplifying information on the team's activities or on what cover story (if any) the Soviets were to provide "Max" to explain away the fact that the team's weapons did not work.

51. Sudoplatov, *Special Tasks,* 158; *Liubianka II,* 246.

52. For an insightful description of the Abel case, see Robert Lamphere, *The FBI-KGB War,* 270–288; Romerstein and Levchenko, *The KGB against the Main Enemy,* 258–259; and Khenkin, "The Improbable Spy," unpublished manuscript in English, much of it concerning Rudolph Abel. According to Romerstein, Abel's true name came to light in 1972, when American journalists discovered a gravestone in a Moscow cemetery with the inscription "Fisher, William Genrykhovich" and, in small letters, "Abel, Rudolph Ivanovich." Fisher died in 1971, and an article was published in *Krasnaia Zvezda* on 17 November 1971 eulogizing him. The article stated that Abel had become an OGPU officer in 1927 and had served Soviet intelligence for forty-five years. Fisher's father, Genrykh Fisher, was a radical activist, had been an associate of Lenin's, emigrated to England in 1901, and returned to the USSR in 1921. Khenkin claims that the name Rudolph Abel was the name of Fisher's roommate when Fisher was undergoing intelligence training. Fisher used it as his ostensible real name when the FBI arrested him.

53. Sudoplatov, *Special Tasks,* 158; Glantz, "Red Mask," 245.

54. Sudoplatov, *Special Tasks,* 158–159.

55. Ibid.; Glantz, *Titans,* 295.

56. Glantz, *Soviet Military Deception,* 110–111; Thomas, "Foreign Armies East," 282–283.

57. Sudoplatov, *Special Tasks,* 159.

58. Glantz, *Soviet Military Deception,* 146–182.

59. Ibid.; Thomas, "Foreign Armies East," 285–286; Mulligan, "Spies, Ciphers, and Zitadelle," passim.

60. Kahn, *Hitler's Spies,* 316. For a more complete version of this message, see Gehlen, *The Service,* 57–58.

61. Glantz, *Titans,* 295.

62. Thomas, "The Legend of Agent Max," 5; Thomas, "Foreign Armies East," 286; Glantz, *Titans,* 203, 214–215, 298, 358.

63. Sudoplatov, *Special Tasks,* 155–159, 168–170; Bezymenskii, "Geine po imeni Maks," 42. The book *Liubianka II* claims that Heine was initially infiltrated behind German lines in February 1942; see 246.

64. Sudoplatov, *Special Tasks,* 155, 158. Sudoplatov discussed only the initial Abwehr suspicions of Dem'ianov and stated that the Germans took the Max material too much

on faith. He sheds no light on whether the Soviets received any indicators from Dem'ianov's post–December 1941 meetings (Dem'ianov's initial contact) with the Germans that the Germans suspected that Dem'ianov was, in reality, a Soviet double agent.

65. Ibid., 158–160; West, *The Crown Jewels,* 189; *Istorii Vneshnei Razvedki,* 4:117; Sudoplatov, *Special Tasks,* 158–160.

66. West, *The Crown Jewels,* 187–203, 218–220, 306.

67. Sudoplatov, *Special Tasks,* 155; *Top Secret History,* 383–389. Sudoplatov also said that, in training, agents' real names were not used, for security reasons.

68. Sudoplatov, *Special Tasks,* 155. Sudoplatov's gaps might also be the result of Schechter not having known enough about this case. If true, Schechter would have had difficulty in jarring Sudoplatov's memory enough to elicit more details on the operation.

69. CSDIC, SIR 1716; *Notes on Gruppe I Luft,* 21–22; Bezymenskii, "Geine po imeni Maks," 40.

70. Schellenberg, *Hitler's Secret Service,* 262–264.

71. Beevor, *Fall of Berlin,* 100. Rokosovskii had Polish relatives and was himself half Polish. Schellenberg, *Hitler's Secret Service,* 263–264; Sudoplatov, *Special Tasks,* 159; U.S. Army XE061758, *Interrogation of Lieutenant Colonel Wagner,* 4. Schellenberg makes no mention of either operation in his official postwar interrogation report.

72. Sudoplatov, *Special Tasks,* 155–159.

73. FHO, *Unternehmen Scherhorn,* 1–5; Sudoplatov, *Special Tasks,* 155–159.

74. Schellenberg, *Hitler's Secret Service,* 263–264.

75. West, *The Crown Jewels,* 198–200.

76. Ibid.

77. Ibid., 200.

78. Meyer, *Unternehmen Sieben,* 154–155.

79. West, *The Crown Jewels,* 197–198.

80. The three nondocumentary sources with the most detail on all the individuals involved in "Max South" are Kahn, *Hitler's Spies,* 312–317, 589–590; Silver, "Questions, Questions, Questions," 202–206; and West, *The Crown Jewels,* 187–203. In the spring of 1946 former U.S. Army CIC officer Arnold Silver interrogated Kauder, two of Kauder's associates — General Anton Turkul and Ira Longin — and Abwehr lieutenant colonel Otto Wagner, who was in charge of the Abwehr in Sofia. Kahn cites, among others sources, several letters and interviews with Wagner. The U.S. Army file on Anton Turkul cited above, XE061758, contains hundreds of pages of interrogations and investigative reports on the individuals (except Schultz) involved in passing the Max messages to the Abwehr. The primary document on Kauder's background is contained in XE061758, in an interrogation report conducted by SCI Unit A, Salzburg, Austria, *Interrogation Report No. 1: Richard Kauder, aka Klatt aka Karmany,* LSX 41, undated. While there are still numerous unanswered questions about the details of the Kauder-Klatt "Max South" organization, the four most reliable sources describing the mechanics of how the Kauder-Klatt wing of Operation Monastery worked are Arnold Silver's

account of his interrogations of the participants, the postwar Allied debriefing report of Abwehr major Brede (CSDIC, SIR 1716, *Notes on Gruppe I Luft*), the U.S. Army's investigative file on Anton Turkul, and West's chapter in his book *The Crown Jewels* on the "Klatt Affair." The file on Turkul reveals the extensive British and American effort over several years to try to determine exactly how the Max messages were forwarded from the USSR to Kauder's office in Sofia and whether the participants — primarily Richard Kauder, Ira Longin, and Anton Turkul — were knowingly working for the Soviet intelligence service. Much of Kahn's biographic information on Kauder is not contained in U.S. Army file XE061758.

81. Silver, "Questions, Questions, Questions," 202–206. Until the publication of Silver's article in 1993, Joseph Schultz's role had not been mentioned in any previous account of this operation. While Silver's account is not mutually exclusive, the interrogation report on Kauder indicates that Kauder was introduced to the Abwehr while in prison. Schultz is also not mentioned in the huge U.S. Army file on Turkul. However, many of Silver's interrogation reports are contained in the U.S. Army file on Turkul.

82. West, *The Crown Jewels,* 203. West, however, does not mention what, if anything, the Russians had in their files on Ira Longin. It is a curious omission by the Russians.

83. Ibid., 204–205. For extensive biographical data on Turkul, see CSDIC, SIR 1727, *Notes on Abwehr I Luft,* Appendix III, paragraph 15. This document is an Allied postwar interrogation report of Abwehr major Sandel, who had numerous air intelligence–related assignments within Abwehr. Sandel met both Kauder and Turkul in Budapest in the autumn of 1944. See also U.S. Army file XE061758, cited above, for detailed information on Turkul's background.

84. CSDIC, SIR 1727, *Notes on Abwehr I Luft,* Appendix III, paragraph 15; Thomas, "Foreign Armies East," 266–267, 295 n. 15; U.S. Army, *Anton Turkul,* XE061758, passim.

85. Kahn, *Hitler's Spies,* 314. Kauder worked for Abwehr I Luft. For Arnold Silver's interrogation of Wagner, see U.S. Army, XE061758, *Interrogation of Oberstleutnant Wagner aka Dr. Otto Delius on His Activities of the Klatt Meldekopf in Sofia,* 3 February 1947, NARS RG 319. Silver assessed Wagner at the time of the interrogation as a "forceful intelligent personality, with an exceptionally keen appreciation of intelligence problems and unlikely to be duped by sham and pretense."

86. CSDIC, SIR 1716, *Notes on Gruppe I Luft,* 20–21; U.S. Army, *GIS and the War,* 5; Sudoplatov, *Special Tasks,* 159; U.S. Army, XE061758, *Interrogation of Franz Bergler and Hilde Augusti,* 2 January 1947, 2; Sudoplatov, *Special Tasks,* 154; Silver, "Questions, Questions, Questions," 203–206. Oddly Silver did not mention the code name Max in his article either.

87. Bezymenskii, "Geine po imeni Maks," 40; Sudoplatov, *Special Tasks,* 155; Kahn, *Hitler's Spies,* 313; U.S. Army, *The GIS and the War,* 5; CSDIC, SIR 1716, *Notes on Gruppe I Luft,* 22; U.S. Army, XE061758, *Interrogation of Lieutenant Colonel Wagner,* 2–4.

88. CSDIC, SIR 1716, *Notes on Gruppe I Luft,* 20–21; Sudoplatov, *Special Tasks,* 159.

89. U.S. Army, *The GIS and the War,* 5.

90. U.S. Army, XE061758, *Interrogation of Franz Bergler and Hilde Augusti,* 2 January 1947, 2.

91. Bezymenskii, "Geine po imeni Maks," 40; Sudoplatov, *Special Tasks,* 155; Kahn, *Hitler's Spies,* 313; U.S. Army, *The GIS and the War,* 5; CSDIC, SIR 1716, *Notes on Gruppe I Luft,* 22; U.S. Army, XE061758, *Interrogation of Lieutenant Colonel Wagner,* 2–4.

92. U.S. Army, XE061758, *Interrogation of Lieutenant Colonel Wagner,* 2–4.

93. Ibid.

94. U.S. Army, XE061758, *File on General Anton Turkul;* untitled interrogation report by a "Mr. Johnson" and a British Intelligence (BIS) officer, dated 3 March 1947, 4.

95. Ibid.

96. U.S Army, XE067158, *Report on the Interrogation of George Leonidovitch Romanoff, 19th and 20th November 1946,* 6.

97. U.S Army, XE061758, *File on General Anton Turkul,* 4.

98. Kahn also cites former SD officer Wilhelm Hoettl as one of his sources on Kauder.

99. Silver, "Questions, Questions, Questions," 202–203. For details on the Soviet kidnapping attempt, see Harris Greene, "Rescue of Max," 1–3. Greene, a retired CIA officer, was then assigned to the 430th CIC Detachment in Salzburg, Austria. Greene participated in thwarting the Soviet attempt. The Soviets had disguised themselves in U.S. Army Military Police uniforms.

100. Kahn, *Hitler's Spies,* 312; CDSIC, 1716, *Notes on Gruppe I Luft,* 21; U.S. Army, XE061758, *Interrogation Report Number 1: Richard Kauder,* 1–2.

101. U.S. Army, XE061758, *Interrogation Report Number 1: Richard Kauder,* 2–4.

102. Ibid.

103. Ibid.; Kahn, *Hitler's Spies,* 317; CSDIC, SR 1716, *Notes on Gruppe I Luft,* 22.

104. U.S. Army, XE061758, *Interrogation Report Number 1: Richard Kauder,* 2–4; Kahn, *Hitler's Spies,* 317; CDSIC, SR 1716, *Notes on Gruppe I Luft,* 22.

105. U.S. Army, XE061758, *Interrogation Report Number 1: Richard Kauder,* 2–4; Kahn, *Hitler's Spies,* 312–313, 317; CDSIC, SR 1716, *Notes on Gruppe I Luft,* 22. Kahn gives a different account of Kauder's career. Although Kahn does not cite the U.S. Army file on Turkul, he states that, by the time Hitler came to power, Kauder found himself as a reporter in Hungary having made significant connections within high-official circles in Budapest. According to Kahn, Kauder came to the attention of the Abwehr in Budapest and carried out some minor assignments for them. One such assignment involved using a personal friendship with a U.S. diplomat to steal and copy documents for passage to the Abwehr and possibly the SD. Neither the U.S. Army file above nor Silver's article makes any mention of this incident.

106. U.S. Army, XE061758, *Interrogation Report Number 1: Richard Kauder,* 3.

107. Kahn, *Hitler's Spies,* 312–313; U.S. Army, XE061758, MISC, *Special Interrogation Report Number 2: Richard Kauder aka Klatt aka Karmany,* 7.

108. U.S. Army, XE061758, *Interrogation Report Number 1: Richard Kauder;* Kahn, *Hitler's Spies*, 312–313; U.S. Army XE061758, MISC, *Special Interrogation Report*

Number 2: Richard Kauder aka Klatt aka Karmany, 7; U.S. Army, *The GIS and the War,* 6.

109. Silver, "Questions, Questions, Questions," 203–204; Kahn, *Hitler's Spies,* 312–313; U.S. Army, XE061758, MISC, *Special Interrogation Report Number 2: Richard Kauder aka Klatt aka Karmany,* 7.

110. Silver, "Questions, Questions, Questions," 203–204; Kahn, *Hitler's Spies,* 312–314; U.S. Army, XE061758, MISC, *Special Interrogation Report Number 2: Richard Kauder aka Klatt aka Karmany,* 7. Kahn's version differs from Silver's. In Kahn's account, Turkul made an offer directly to the Germans, and the Abwehr assigned the task of running the operation to Marogna-Redwitz. Marogna-Redwitz eventually established a radio communications center in Sofia, having moved it from Vienna, to maintain contact with Turkul's sources because it was closer to the USSR. Silver infers that one of the reasons for the move may have been to keep the Gestapo away from Kauder. Kahn's and Silver's versions of how Kauder came into contact with the Abwehr in Vienna are not necessarily mutually exclusive, nor are they entirely in accord with what is contained in Kauder's two interrogation reports in the U.S. Army file on Turkul. While the massive file on Turkul contains numerous contradictions, and Kauder's own account of how he came into contact with the Abwehr appears to be the most coherent, Silver's memory cannot be dismissed lightly. He interrogated all the participants and was intimately familiar with their cases. The most logical explanations for the contradictions are that the sources themselves were of questionable character and not all the documentary evidence was available as of this writing.

111. U.S. Army, XE061758, *Interrogation of Oberstleutnant Wagner,* 2. To quote Wagner: "Almost immediately after the declaration of June 1941, however, a veritable surge of reports began to pour out of Klatt's *Meldekopf* (station)." At the beginning of 1941 Wagner learned from Lieutenant Colonel Rolf von Wahl-Welskirch, chief of Abwehr I Luft in Ast Vienna, that Kauder was connected with the Russian émigré movement and that he had sources in the Soviet High Command and was receiving messages from them. Wagner was not satisfied with this explanation and remained suspicious.

112. Ibid., 3.

113. Ibid.

114. Ibid. Wagner believed that at the beginning of the war Kauder may have been receiving his reports on a receiver belonging to, and operated by, the Bulgarian police. In a document in U.S. Army file XE061758 entitled "Conversation between Turkul and Ira" (undated), which appears to be the record of the U.S. Army counterintelligence monitoring of a conversation between the two men, Longin admits to Turkul that he received his information by radio in Sofia, Budapest, and Bratislava. He also said that at the beginning he did not receive any information by radio.

115. Leverkuehn, *German Military Intelligence,* 172.

116. U.S. Army, XE061758, *Interrogation of Oberstleutnant Wagner,* 2.

117. Ibid., 4.

118. Ibid.

119. *Istorii Vneshnei Razvedki,* 4:495.

120. Ibid., 505.

121. Ibid., 493–494, 502–505.

122. Ibid., 500–501.

123. U.S. Army, XE06178, "Summarization of M Notes on Kauder, Richard, alias Klatt," 15 July 1946; U.S. Army, XE06178, *Interrogation of Wilhelm Hoettel,* 1, 6 May 1946; Meyer, *Unternehmen Sieben,* 160; Leverkuehn, *German Military Intelligence,* 174–175.

124. West, *The Crown Jewels,* 199–200; U.S. Army, XE06178, *Interrogation of Klatt, No. 1,* 1.

125. U.S. Army, XE06178, *Interrogation of Klatt, No.1,* 7–8, 12.

126. U.S. Army, XE06178, 7707th MISC, "Answer to Kel-181, dated 17 February 1947."

127. U.S. Army, XE06178, *Interrogation of Rolf Wodarg,* 3.

128. U.S. Army, XE06178, "Westarp on Klatt," undated two-page memo in file, no addresses.

129. U.S. Army, XE06178, *Interrogation Report of Klatt aka Kauder,* by a Mr. Johnson, 2, 21 January 1947; U.S. Army, XE60178, Routing Sheet/Internal Memo, "Panda's Service in the Bulgarian I.S.," 21 January 1947.

130. U.S. Army, XE06178, MISC, *Report on Interrogation of Dr. Wilhelm Hoettel, SD,* 6 May 1946, 2.

131. U.S. Army, XE06178, *Interrogation of Oberstleutnant Wagner,* 4; Kahn, *Hitler's Spies,* 316–317; Silver, "Questions, Questions, Questions," 204; U.S. Army, *The GIS and the War,* 5.

132. Ibid.; Kahn, *Hitler's Spies,* 316–317; Silver, "Questions, Questions, Questions," 204; U.S. Army, *The GIS and the War,* 5.

133. CSDIC, SIR 1716, *Notes on Gruppe I Luft,* 22.

134. U.S. Army, XE061758, *Interrogation of Oberstleutnant Wagner,* 4.

135. Ibid.; Kahn, *Hitler's Spies,* 316–317; Silver, "Questions, Questions, Questions," 204; U.S. Army, *The GIS and the War,* 5; Leverkuehn, *German Military Intelligence,* 172–173; Weinberg, *World at Arms,* 706.

136. U.S. Army, XE061758, *Interrogation of Oberstleutnant Wagner,* 4. Nazi arrogance aside, the Germans believed that even if the Max material was controlled much of it was true, and therefore the operation should not be closed down. By implication, such reasoning would tend to indicate that the Germans — if they even thought that the Soviets were capable of strategic deception by giving up such an extraordinary amount of information — believed that they could recognize whatever disinformation the Soviets would potentially pass.

137. Ibid.

138. Silver, "Questions, Questions, Question," 205–206.

139. Ibid., 204–205; CSDIC, SIR 1716, *Notes on Gruppe I Luft,* 22. Although Silver does not mention it in his article, Kauder's mother had already been arrested twice by the Gestapo.

140. Silver, "Questions, Questions, Questions," 205–206. Kauder also said that Schultz tried to entice him into going into business in Vienna just after the war. Kauder, suspecting that Schultz was trying to lure him into Soviet hands, declined the offer.

141. Ibid.; Sudoplatov, *Special Tasks,* 156. Silver recounted that, when he met Kauder on a street in Salzburg in 1952, Kauder tried to sell Silver on the idea that he actually had a real network inside the USSR. As late as 1964 Kauder was still trying to sell the idea to the CIA. Silver's assessment that Kauder, Longin, and Turkul may not have been fully recruited Soviet agents is similar to Sudoplatov's experience with Dem'ianov. According to Sudoplatov, the Russian émigré leaders, who allegedly took credit with the Germans for finding such an impressive source of information in Moscow and in establishing Dem'ianov's bona fides, were not NKVD/NKGB double agents. The émigrés simply exploited an opportunity to verify a name for the Abwehr so that they could justify their financial support by the Germans. Sudoplatov also states that when the Americans analyzed Abwehr archives after the war, the Americans concluded that "Max" was planted in German intelligence by Russian émigrés. While Sudoplatov does not make clear which part of the "Max" operation he is talking about, his general minimalization of the Russian émigré role in Operation Monastery tends to be corroborated by the results of Silver's interrogation of Kauder, Turkul, and Longin.

142. Gehlen, *The Service,* 57–58; Thomas, "Foreign Armies East," 288–291.

143. Thomas, "Foreign Armies East," 288–291.

144. Glantz, "Red Mask," 243.

145. Ibid., 177. Glantz poses this question for Soviet military deception efforts.

146. Sudoplatov, *Special Tasks,* 140–143, 159–160; Bezymenskii, "Geine po imeni Maks," 42. Sudoplatov stated, even though he acknowledges that the British have not officially admitted it, that the British provided sanitized versions of their Ultra intercepts containing "Max"-originated information to a British double agent working in Red Orchestra. Sudoplatov implies, as does Bezymenskii, that an Abwehr lieutenant colonel by the name of Schmidt was working for the Soviets. Sudoplatov identifies Schmidt as "deputy director of the radio communications section of the Abwehr." According to Sudoplatov and Bezymenskii, Schmidt was recruited by members of a Soviet illegals network in France or at least passed "Max"-originated messages to those illegals. Schmidt was also working for the British, and in the beginning of the 1930s he apparently had also been recruited by French intelligence. The British may have passed some information gleaned from Schmidt to the Soviets, thereby disguising the fact that they were actually reading high-level German ciphers. The Germans eventually detected Schmidt's activities, and he disappeared without a trace. See also Waller, *Unseen War,* 22–25.

CHAPTER 7. Operations Berezino and Zeppelin

1. Sudoplatov, *Special Tasks,* 167.
2. Ibid.

3. Ibid.; Dieter Sevin, "Operation Scherhorn," in *Military Review* 46, no. 3 (March 1966): 43. Sevin stated that "it seems reasonable to assume that the game was for higher stakes than a few supplies."

4. Reshin, "Bez Grifa Sekretno," 7; Sevin, "Operation Scherhorn," 42–43; Sudoplatov, *Special Tasks,* 168–169; *Top Secret History,* 386–387. The Soviets released Scherhorn from captivity in 1948, and he returned to Germany. Reshin claims that a German intelligence officer along with Scherhorn and two radiomen who cooperated with the Soviets were also repatriated to Germany in 1948. All other agents dispatched by the Germans who parachuted behind Soviet lines in Operation Berezino were shot in October and November 1945. Sudoplatov's version differs slightly in that he stated that 1,500 German soldiers had been taken prisoner.

5. *Top Secret History,* 389; Reshin, "Bez Grifa Sekretno," 7; Sudoplatov, *Special Tasks,* 168–170. Sudoplatov called this operation "the most successful radio deception game of the war." Reshin attributed his information to an "evaluation that was drawn up after the war." Sudoplatov offers slightly different figures. He states that the Germans allocated sixty-seven transport aircraft in September 1944 to supply Scherhorn and that the Soviets captured twenty-five Abwehr agents and seized 10 million rubles.

6. *Top Secret History,* 389.

7. Reshin, "Bez Grifa Sekretno," 7; Sudoplatov, *Special Tasks,* 168–170.

8. *Top Secret History,* 389.

9. Sudoplatov, *Special Tasks,* 168.

10. Reshin, "Bez Grifa Sekretno," 7.

11. Ibid.

12. FHO, *Unternehmen Scherhorn,* 1–2.

13. Sevin, "Operation Scherhorn," 35–36; FHO, *Unternehmen Scherhorn,* 1–2; Reshin, "Bez Grifa Sekretno," 7; Guenther W. Gellermann, *Moskau ruft Heeres Gruppe Mitte* (Koblenz: Berbard und Graefe Verlag, 1988), 112–113.

14. FHO, *Unternehmen Scherhorn,* 1–2.

15. Sudoplatov, *Special Tasks,* 155.

16. FHO, *Unternehmen Scherhorn,* 1–2; Sevin, "Operation Scherhorn," 35–43; Sevin — probably basing his statement on the FHO report cited above — also mentions that an "Aleksandr" communicated through "Flamingo" to the Germans.

17. Hoehne and Zolling, *The General Was a Spy,* 17–20; Cookridge, *Spy of the Century,* 72–90, 370, 384.

18. Hoehne and Zolling, *The General Was a Spy,* 17–20, 318 n. 26; Cookridge, *Spy of the Century,* 72–90, 370, 384; Sevin, Operation Scherhorn, 35–36; FHO, *Unternehmen Scherhorn,* 1–2; Reshin, "Bez Grifa Sekretno," 7; Gellermann, *Moskau ruft Heeres Gruppe Mitte,* 112–113; Sudoplatov, *Special Tasks,* 168. Although Dem'ianov was known to the Germans as both Aleksandr and Max, there is no indication in the FHO document on Scherhorn that Aleksandr was referred to as Max. Though the data are sketchy, Dem'ianov and his Soviet controllers appear to have communicated Dem'ianov's information to the Germans via at least three different routes: directly from Moscow as a result of his initial contact with the Abwehr "volunteering" his services (no specifics

available); through the organization "Throne" via Flamingo to FAK 103 to Army Group Center in Operation Berezino; and possibly to the Germans via Flamingo relaying Minzhinskiy's information.

19. Sevin, "Operation Scherhorn," 35–36; FHO, *Unternehmen Scherhorn,* 1–2; Reshin, "Bez Grifa Sekretno," 7; Gellermann, *Moskau ruft Heeres Gruppe Mitte,* 112–113.

20. Sevin, "Operation Scherhorn," 35–36; FHO, *Unternehmen Scherhorn,* 1–2; Reshin, "Bez Grifa Sekretno," 7; Gellermann, *Moskau ruft Heeres Gruppe Mitte,* 112–113.

21. Sevin, "Operation Scherhorn," 35–36; FHO, *Unternehmen Scherhorn,* 1–2; Reshin, "Bez Grifa Sekretno," 7; Gellermann, *Moskau ruft Heeres Gruppe Mitte,* 112–113; Sudoplatov, *Special Tasks,* 168; Hoehne and Zolling, *The General Was a Spy,* 18–20, 318 n. 26; and E. H. Cookridge, *Spy of the Century,* 74–76. The Soviets have not made enough data public to determine exactly how "Aleksandr's" and "Max's" cover stories were presented to the Germans so as to reduce German suspicion. Hoehne, citing a précis of Cookridge's book that appeared in the 7 March 1969 edition of the *Daily Telegraph Magazine,* described "Aleksandr" as a captain in a Soviet reserve signals regiment who had access to Soviet military secrets. This description generally fits Sudoplatov's statement in his memoirs that Dem'ianov was assigned for cover purposes as a junior communications officer for the Red Army High Command in Moscow, as well as Sevin's description of Aleksandr's position as a "captain in the Soviet army working with communications detachments." Both Reshin's article and the FHO report on Scherhorn indicated that at some point during Operation Berezino Aleksandr had been assigned to either a sapper or to a road construction unit.

22. Sevin, "Operation Scherhorn," 35–36; FHO, *Unternehmen Scherhorn,* 1–2; Reshin, "Bez Grifa Sekretno," 7; Gellermann, *Moskau ruft Heeres Gruppe Mitte,* 112–113.

23. Sevin, "Operation Scherhorn," 35–36; FHO, *Unternehmen Scherhorn,* 1–2; Reshin, "Bez Grifa Sekretno," 7; Gellerman, *Moskau ruft Heeres Gruppe Mitte,* 112–113.

24. Sevin, "Operation Scherhorn," 35–36; FHO, *Unternehmen Scherhorn,* 1–2; Reshin, "Bez Grifa Sekretno," 7; Gellerman, *Moskau ruft Heeres Gruppe Mitte,* 112–113.

25. FHO, *Unternehmen Scherhorn,* 1–2; Cookridge, *Spy of the Century,* 72–90, 106–107. Cookridge praises Gehlen's handling of Operation Scherhorn and makes no mention of the questions raised by German officers handling Scherhorn's case about whether Scherhorn was under Soviet control — even though Cookridge claimed to have had access to original documentation. Dieter Sevin, who published his article on Scherhorn in an issue of *Military Review* in 1966, examined original German documents on the case and unequivocally concluded that the Scherhorn group was a Soviet ruse.

26. Ibid.

27. Sevin, "Operation Scherhorn," 36–37; FHO, *Unternehmen Scherhorn,* 3–4; Reshin, "Bez Grifa Sekretno," 7; Gellermann, *Moskau ruft Heeres Gruppe Mitte,* 113–114.

28. FHO, *Unternehmen Scherhorn,* 3–4. The 6 September 1944 message is interesting in that it alludes to the fact that Aleksandr's wife was a courier or messenger. The message stated that Aleksandr's wife came back to Moscow, would leave in a few days, and brought with her Scherhorn's reply. It is curious that the available German documents do not question the role of Aleksandr's wife. Sudoplatov does not discuss the

role of Aleksandr's wife in Operation Berezino, that is, how her role as a courier from the front lines to Moscow was justified to the Germans. However, Sudoplatov mentions that Dem'ianov's wife and father-in-law were briefed on every detail of Monastery (*Special Tasks,* 156–157).

29. Sudoplatov, *Special Tasks,* 68–79, 168; Reshin, "Bez Grifa Sekretno," 7.

30. FHO, *Unternehmen Scherhorn,* 3–4.

31. Sevin, "Operation Scherhorn," 37–38; Reshin, "Bez Grifa Sekretno," 7; FHO, *Unternehmen Scherhorn,* 4–6; Gellerman, *Moskau ruft Heeres Gruppe Mitte,* 114–117. German documents reflect that neither agent was heard from again.

32. Sevin, "Operation Scherhorn," 37–38; Reshin, "Bez Grifa Sekretno," 7; FHO, *Unternehmen Scherhorn,* 4–6; Gellerman, *Moskau ruft Heeres Gruppe Mitte,* 114–117.

33. Sevin, "Operation Scherhorn," 37–38; Reshin, "Bez Grifa Sekretno," 7; FHO, *Unternehmen Scherhorn,* 4–6; Gellerman, *Moskau ruft Heeres Gruppe Mitte,* 114–117.

34. Sevin, "Operation Scherhorn," 37–38; Reshin, "Bez Grifa Sekretno," 7; FHO, *Unternehmen Scherhorn,* 4–6; Gellerman, *Moskau ruft Heeres Gruppe Mitte,* 114–117.

35. Sevin, "Operation Scherhorn," 37–38; Reshin, "Bez Grifa Sekretno," 7; FHO, *Unternehmen Scherhorn,* 4–6; Gellerman, *Moskau ruft Heeres Gruppe Mitte,* 114–117.

36. Reshin, "Bez Grifa Sekretno," 7; FHO, *Unternehmen Scherhorn,* 8–10; Sevin, "Operation Scherhorn," 38–39; Gellerman, *Moskau ruft Herresgruppe Mitte,* 117–119.

37. Reshin, "Bez Grifa Sekretno," 7; Sevin, "Operation Scherhorn," 38; FHO, *Unternehmen Scherhorn,* 8–9; Gellerman, *Moskau ruft Herresgruppe Mitte,* 117–119.

38. Sevin, "Operation Scherhorn," 39–42.

39. Ibid.

40. Ibid.; Reshin, "Bez Grifa Sekretno," 7. For Skorzeny's unreliable account, see Otto Skorzeny, *My Commando Operations,* 387–395.

41. Reshin, "Bez Grifa Sekretno," 7.

42. Ibid.

43. Ibid.

44. *Istorii Vneshnei Razvedki,* 4:125.

45. Schellenberg, *Hitler's Secret Service,* 262–263; U.S. Army, *The Case of Walter Friedrich Schellenberg,* 32, Appendix III, 1.

46. Schellenberg, *Hitler's Secret Service,* 262–263; U.S. Army, *The Case of Walter Friedrich Schellenberg,* 32, Appendix III, 1.

47. Schellenberg, *Hitler's Secret Service,* 262–263.

48. Ibid.; U.S. Army, *The Case of Walter Friedrich Schellenberg,* 32, Appendix III, 1.

49. The major sources in English on Operation Zeppelin are Schellenberg, *Hitler's Secret Service,* 262–277; U.S. Army, *The Case of Walter Friedrich Schellenberg,* 32, Appendix III, 1–3; Kahn, *Hitler's Spies,* 273, 295, 360–361; U.S. Army, CI-SR/61, *Unternehmen (Operation) Zeppelin,* 1–10; CSDIC FR 31, *Dr. Willy Teich.* Histories of Soviet counterintelligence during World War II often describe specific cases in which SD agents were either caught, killed, or convinced to work for the Soviets. As yet, no detailed operational history solely devoted to Operation Zeppelin has been published. There is little information in the documents evaluated by this author, or in Soviet his-

tories, on the use of agents recruited for Zeppelin who were tasked to work specifically against Soviet partisans in the rear of the German army.

50. U.S. Army, CI-SR-61, *Interrogation of Heinrich Fenner,* 1–9; Schellenberg, *Hitler's Secret Service,* 271–273.

51. U.S. Army, CI-SR/61, *Interrogation of Heinrich Fenner,* 2.

52. Schellenberg, *Hitler's Secret Service,* 263–264.

53. Kahn, *Hitler's Spies,* 360–361; CI-SR/61, *Interrogation of Heinrich Fenner,* 4.

54. Kahn, *Hitler's Spies,* 360–361. See CSDIC, FR 31, *Dr. Willy Teich,* Appendix B, Annex 1, for a detailed organizational chart of how Operation Zeppelin was organized in the field. It bears a strong resemblance to Abwehr's FAK/FAT system.

55. Schellenberg, *Hitler's Secret Service,* 267–268.

56. Ibid.; U.S. Army, CI-SR/61, *Interrogation of Heinrich Fenner,* 4–6; Kahn, *Hitler's Spies,* 360.

57. Sergeev, *Tainye Operatsii,* 254.

58. U.S. Army, CI-SR/61, *Interrogation of Heinrich Fenner,* 4, 10; Schellenberg, *Hitler's Secret Service,* 264–265.

59. Schellenberg, *Hitler's Secret Service,* 269–272; CI-SR/61, *Interrogation of Heinrich Fenner,* 7; CSDIC, FR 31, *Dr. Willy Teich,* Appendix C.

60. Sergeev, *Tainye Operatsii,* 228–229.

61. Ostryakov, *Military Chekists,* 159.

62. Schellenberg, *Hitler's Secret Service,* 271–272.

63. U.S. Army, CI-SR/61, *Interrogation of Heinrich Fenner,* 7. Fenner said that some of the groups established contact with "persons of influence" (he did not elaborate). The context of his statement to his interrogators implies that he did not think that the operation produced anything of real value.

64. Schellenberg, *Hitler's Secret Service,* 264–265, 271–272. Schellenberg also stated that one of the main purposes of Zeppelin was to counter the effects of guerrilla warfare. A careful reading of his memoirs indicates that he envisioned these two objectives being accomplished in two ways: by establishing guerrilla movements in the Soviet rear, and by gathering information and infiltrating "Soviet partisan bands." Little information is available on how SD units assigned to Zeppelin infiltrated and gathered information on partisan bands.

65. Schellenberg, *Hitler's Secret Service,* 272–273; CIA, *Studies in Intelligence,* book review of Schellenberg's *Memoirs,* fall 1957, 125; CI-SR/61, *Interrogation of Heinrich Fenner,* 3. The unnamed intelligence officer who wrote the review of Schellenberg's memoirs, in *Studies in Intelligence,* strongly suspected that if the incident Schellenberg described were true, Rodionov probably had been a Soviet double agent from the beginning rather than a disaffected collaborator. Fenner's description of this incident is somewhat different from Schellenberg's; both agree, however, that Germans were murdered and that the Soviets escaped. Fenner stated that, although agents of the "Gil Troop" (named after its leader) had expressed themselves as anti-Soviet, they had not been thoroughly investigated by the Germans. Fenner said that a number of them turned

out to be either pro-Soviet or Soviet agents and that they escaped after murdering their German leaders.

66. Sergeev, *Tainye Operatsii,* 273.

67. Ostryakov, *Military Chekists,* 163–165.

68. Ibid.

69. Ibid.

70. The major sources on this operation are Ostryakov, *Military Chekists,* 183–191; Sergeev, *Tainye Operatsii,* 270–272; JPRS 55623, April 1972, "The Failure of Operation Zeppelin," 115–131; Gellerman, *Moskau ruft Heeresgruppe Mitte,* 86–92, 218–219; "Sovetskie Organy," 35–36. Gellerman's account is based on information obtained from interviews, reports, and diaries of mid-level and senior Luftwaffe aircrews who served in Kampfgeschwader 200 (KG 200) (bombardment wing) — one of the units assigned to drop German agents behind Soviet lines. Gellerman also relies heavily on the German version of Ostryakov's book, *Militaerchekisten* (Berlin-Ost, 1985), but is somewhat skeptical of Ostryakov's claims of success. Because of minor discrepancies in details, such as what type of aircraft was used to insert Politov-Tavrin behind Soviet lines (Ostryakov claimed it was an Arado 332 when the correct nomenclature was an Arado 232A and 232B) and a general reluctance to admit that Soviet counterintelligence may have actually doubled some of the German agents, Gellerman casts some doubt on Ostryakov. Gellerman, however, does not mention that the SD was the German intelligence organization directly responsible for this operation — a major oversight given that he used archival material. According to Gellerman, three aircrew members who were knowledgeable of this operation stated unequivocally that the target of the assassination was Stalin (88 n. 16) and that, according to Schellenberg, assassinating Stalin was discussed by Himmler, Hitler, and Ribbentrop in 1944. Schellenberg does not mention this operation in his memoirs, nor was it mentioned in his postwar interrogation report by the U.S. Army. An analysis of the Soviet sources shows that at least some of the accounts appear to have been based on the interrogation of Politov-Tavrin himself.

71. JPRS 55623, "The Failure of Operation Zeppelin," 115–131.

72. Ostryakov, *Military Chekists,* 190–191.

73. JPRS 55623, "The Failure of Operation Zeppelin," 131; "Sovetskie Organy," 35–36; Cookridge, *Spy of the Century,* 85–86, 370 n. 14. Cookridge's description of this operation is highly unreliable. In describing the Soviet version of this case, he cites as his source "Sovetskie Organy" (35–36). Cookridge claims that when the Soviets arrested Tavrin (Cookridge never used the name Politov and neither did the Soviet article on which he based some of his account), they discovered he had in his possession codes and ciphers written on cigarette paper that were sewn into his coat, that he was en route to a secret landing site to be picked up by an aircraft, and that he had been appointed to positions of high trust in the People's Commissariat of Defense. Cookridge also claims that this operation was run by Reinhard Gehlen, who singled out Tavrin for special training, and that Tavrin successfully infiltrated the higher levels of the Soviet military

but was caught while trying to return to German lines. A review of the original "Sovetskie Organy" cited by Cookridge does not confirm any of his claims. Three of the Soviet sources describing this case, which span the period from the early 1970s through 1992, consistently assert that the SD recruited, trained, and dispatched Politov-Tavrin (all use Politov's name) and that SS officers Grafe, Hengelhaupt, and Krauss took personal interest in supervising Politov-Tavrin's training. Archival documents substantiate Soviet claims. The Allied postwar debriefings of SD officers Gerhard Willy Teich and Heinrich Fenner, cited above, show that the SD officers Grafe, Krauss, and Hengelhaupt were all assigned to Operation Zeppelin.

74. JPRS 55623, "The Failure of Operation Zeppelin," 116; Sergeev, *Tainye Operatsii,* 270–271; Ostryakov, *Military Chekists,* 183. Politov used the names Shilo, Gavrin, and Serkov as aliases. The Soviet article cited here attributes much of the information on Politov to his file. However, it is unclear whether the Soviets were referring to a captured German file or to their own interrogation file on Politov.

75. Sergeev, *Tainye Operatsii,* 270–271.

76. Gellerman, *Moskau ruft Heeresgruppe Mitte,* 88 n. 17. Gellerman states that, according to Colonel Heinrich Heigl, who had been the commander of KG 200 for a time, Politov-Tavrin was trained in a house near Dresden.

77. Ostryakov, *Military Chekists,* 183–184; JPRS 55623, "The Failure of Operation Zeppelin," 117–120.

78. Ostryakov, *Military Chekists,* 183–184; JPRS 55623, "The Failure of Operation Zeppelin," 117–120.

79. There was little information in the source material evaluated on Shilova's background or on how the Germans recruited her.

80. Ostryakov, *Military Chekists,* 185–186.

81. Ibid., 184–185; JPRS 55623, "The Failure of Operation Zeppelin," 120–122.

82. Ostryakov, *Military Chekists,* 184–185; JPRS 55623, "The Failure of Operation Zeppelin," 120–122.

83. JPRS 55623, "The Failure of Operation Zeppelin," 126–128.

84. Ibid.

85. Ibid.

86. Ibid.

87. Ostryakov, *Military Chekists,* 186–188; Gellerman, *Moskau ruft Heeres Gruppe Mitte,* 90. Gellerman questions Ostryakov's version of this operation. Gellerman doubts that the Abwehr would have used such unreliable agents in such an important task as the assassination of Stalin when more reliable agents were available (90 n. 20). Because of the large-scale Soviet penetration of German agent training schools, the Germans probably had to use the agent groups that were completely trained and available for deployment regardless of any potential doubts about their reliability. This happened in Operation Scherhorn. In addition, since the agents were largely Soviet citizens, their motivations may have changed unbeknownst to the Germans, as it was clear by then that the Germans were going to lose the war. Gellerman rightly questions Ostryakov's version of this operation — specifically that a German airdrop took place in June 1944 —

by pointing out that a German airdrop could not have taken place at that time. Gellerman noted that the flight log of Master Sergeant Ewald Lange, who was assigned to KG 200, contained no entries indicating that KG 200 flew agent-insertion missions from Riga because there were no available aircraft. However, Gellerman goes on to say that Lange's flight log showed that he flew one mission on 14 August 1944, in which two German agents were dropped in an area not far from the location where Ostryakov claimed the June drop took place. Although Ostryakov strongly implies that the flight originated in Riga, he never unequivocally stated it. However, both Gellerman and Ostryakov agree that the radio playback was conducted with a German intelligence unit in Riga.

88. Ostryakov, *Military Chekists,* 186–188.

89. Ibid., 187.

90. Ibid.

91. Ibid., 188.

92. Ibid., 187.

93. Ibid.

94. Ibid., 189–191.

95. Ibid.

96. Ibid. The details and the results of this radio playback have not been made available.

97. U.S. Army, XE061758, *Interrogation of Oberstleutnant Wagner,* 4. Sometimes there were political reasons for the Germans to accept double agents as genuine. Wagner commented to Arnold Silver that Schellenberg once said that even if he had irrefutable evidence that an SD agent in Stockholm, by the name of Kraemer, was working for the British, Schellenberg would never have conceded that fact for fear of weakening his position vis-à-vis the chief of the Gestapo, Heinrich Mueller. When Schellenberg sided with the High Command on the validity of the "Max" traffic at a conference in the autumn of 1944, Wagner thought Schellenberg had done it for political reasons.

98. Peter Paret, ed., *Makers of Modern Strategy* (Princeton, N.J.: Princeton University Press, 1986), 299–300.

CHAPTER 8. The Sword and Shield

1. Glantz, "Red Mask," 177.

2. Ibid., 186, 243; Gehlen, *The Service,* 43–44.

3. *Germany in the Second World War,* 4:702.

4. Glantz, *Soviet Deception,* 47–48; Glantz, "Red Mask," 176, 245; Thomas, "Foreign Armies East," 280; *Germany in the Second World War,* 4:694.

5. Glantz, "Red Mask," 187.

6. Thomas, "Foreign Armies East," 282.

7. Gehlen, *The Service,* 57–59.

8. Krivosheev, *Soviet Casualties,* 126–127.

9. Ziemke and Bauer, *Moscow to Stalingrad,* 514; Ziemke, *Stalingrad to Berlin,* 141–143.

10. See Glantz, "Red Mask," passim, for figures on German losses during these offensives and for German assessments of Soviet intentions during these offensives.

11. Ziemke and Bauer, *Moscow to Stalingrad,* 514; Ziemke, *Stalingrad to Berlin,* 141–143.

12. Glantz, "Red Mask," 243–245; Erickson, "New Thinking about the Eastern Front," 287; Brian D. Dailey and Patrick J. Parker, eds., *Soviet Strategic Deception* (Lexington, Mass.: Lexington Books, 1987), 295–311. This concept is known as "reflexive control," briefly defined as the ability to orchestrate attempts to control the action of an opponent. See also M. D. Ionov, "On the Method of Influencing the Opponent's Decision," in *Selected Readings from Military Thought, 1963–1973,* vol. 5, part 2 (Washington, D.C.: U.S. Government Printing Office, 1982), 164–171.

13. Dziak, *Chekisty,* 124.

14. Bartov, *Hitler's Army*. Bartov provides an excellent well-researched account of the stress German units experienced when unit cohesion was decimated by sustained high casualty rates.

15. Michael I. Handel, ed., *Leaders and Intelligence* (London: Frank Cass, 1989), 2, 254–255.

16. Glantz, *Soviet Military Deception,* 470.

17. Thomas, "Foreign Armies East," 263–268, 288–289; Military Intelligence Division, *German Military Intelligence,* 1–35; Hoehne and Zolling, *The General Was a Spy,* 20–27; Kahn, *Hitler's Spies,* 428–432.

18. Thomas, "Foreign Armies East," 263–268, 288–289; Military Intelligence Division, *German Military Intelligence,* 1–35; Hoehne and Zolling, *The General Was a Spy,* 20–27; Kahn, *Hitler's Spies,* 428–432.

19. Kahn, *Hitler's Spies,* 428.

20. Thomas, "Foreign Armies East," 288–289.

21. Kahn, *Hitler's Spies,* 413.

22. Glantz, "Red Mask," 244–245.

23. Gehlen, *The Service,* 70–71.

24. Tarrant, *Red Orchestra,* 172, 159–161.

25. Erickson, "New Thinking about the Eastern Front," 290.

26. Kahn, *Hitler's Spies,* 439; Thomas, "Foreign Armies East," 291.

27. Kahn, *Hitler's Spies,* 460; Gerhard Reitlinger, *The House Built on Sand: The Conflicts of German Policy in Russia, 1939–1945* (London: Weidenfeld and Nicolson, 1960), 30.

28. Military Intelligence Division, *German Military Intelligence,* 8–9; Kahn, *Hitler's Spies,* 361.

29. Military Intelligence Division, *German Military Intelligence,* 5, 140, 283; Kahn, *Hitler's Spies,* 302–379.

30. U.S. Army, CI-SR/32, *FA III, OST,* 30, 32.

31. Ibid.

32. U.S. Army, CI-SR/42, *Counterintelligence Organization "Smersh,"* 30.

33. Military Intelligence Division, *German Military Intelligence,* 8–9; Schellenberg, *Hitler's Secret Service,* 265.

34. GSUSA, *Survey,* 15.

35. Ibid.; Cookridge, *Spy of the Century,* 86–89. The GSUSA study went so far as to say that the Germans penetrated some of the highest levels of the CPSU and the Soviet government. Cookridge, citing FHO files, describes in detail an operation Gehlen ran in which the Germans gave one Vassili Davidovich Skryabin, identified by Cookridge as the nephew of the Soviet foreign minister Vyacheslav Molotov, and an Albert Mueller false identities and dropped them behind Soviet lines to penetrate the headquarters staff of one General Koslov. According to Cookridge, the operation (German code name Drossel [Thrush]) succeeded so well that Skryabin was able to transmit military secrets obtained from Koslov's headquarters to FHO, and Mueller even obtained employment in an armaments factory and reported enormous quantities of information to the Germans. In October 1944, when Gehlen decided to recall the agents, Mueller successfully made it to the rescue plane; Skryabin did not. Given Cookridge's penchant for major factual errors, as demonstrated by his description of the Politov-Tavrin operation, Baun's statement that almost none of his operations were successful, and the demonstrated effectiveness of Soviet counterintelligence, Cookridge's description of Operation Drossel calls for considerable skepticism. A review of Gellerman's book, *Moskau ruft Heeresgruppe Mitte* — a history of Kampfgeschwader (bombardment wing) 200 — contains no references to this operation or to a rescue attempt.

36. Military Intelligence Division, *German Military Intelligence,* 8–9; Schellenberg, *Hitler's Secret Service,* 265.

37. Kahn, *Hitler's Spies,* 369. Kahn's point here is that, for an agent operating in enemy territory in wartime, the chances of being apprehended are high because of stricter controls.

38. Posdnjakoff, *German Counterintelligence,* 4.

39. For example, see Dziak, *Chekisty,* 42–103.

40. Glantz, "Red Mask," 237–239.

41. Kahn, *Hitler's Spies,* 453; Gehlen, *The Service,* 88–92.

42. Kahn, *Hitler's Spies,* 453; Knight, *Beria,* 126–129; Schellenberg, *Hitler's Secret Service,* 266–268.

Appendixes

1. For a description of the problems associated with estimating the number of personnel assigned to the Soviet intelligence and security services, see Dziak, *Chekisty,* 112. The estimate quoted here of 500,000 to 2 million includes only those personnel assigned to various NKVD/NKGB troop units and does not include personnel assigned to intelligence and counterespionage duties.

2. *Liubianka VChK-KGB,* 258–260; Dziak, *Chekisty,* 112.

3. See Wolin and Slusser, *The Soviet Secret Police;* Deriabin and Gibney, *Secret World;* Deriabin, *Watchdogs of Terror;* and GSUSA, *Survey,* for good organizational overviews of the Soviet security services.

4. Wolin and Slusser, *The Soviet Secret Police,* 65–152.

5. Ibid.

6. Ibid.

7. For an overview of the changes in the organization of the Soviet intelligence and security services, see Dziak, *Chekisty,* xvii–xx, 184–185.

8. Ibid. See also U.S. Department of the Army, Information Section, Counterintelligence Branch, Office of the Director of Intelligence, Headquarters U.S. Group C.C., *Russian Counterintelligence Organizations,* 14 August 1945, 1, NARS Record Group 319, Entry 85; see also Hingley, *The Russian Secret Police,* 188; Ostryakov, *Military Chekists,* 128; and *Top Secret History,* 341–343.

9. For detailed information on the organization (as well as operations) of the Soviet intelligence and security services, see A. N. Yakovlev, ed., *Rossiaya XX Vek: Liubianka: VCHK-OGPU-NKVD-NKB-MGB-MVD-KGB, 1917–1960, Spravochnik* (Moscow: Mezhdunarodnii Fond, 1997), 272–282; FSB, *Liubianka II,* 232; Oberkommando des Heeres/Fremde Heere Ost, Abteilung I, *Die sowjetische Agentenabwehr und Gegenspionage im Operationsgebiet der Ostfront (1943),* NARS Record Group 242, Microfilm Publication T78/Roll 562, Item No. H3/323; Oberkommando des Heeres/Fremde Heere Ost/Abteilung IIb, *Truppenverbaende und truppenaehnliche Organizationen des roten Volkskommissariats der Inneren (NKWD),* 16 January 1943, NARS Record Group 242, Microfilm Publication T78/Roll 563, Item H3/398, Frame 187; Oberkommando des Heeres/Generalstab/Hauptabteilung Fremde Heere Ost IIb, *Die Ueberwachungsorgane im sowjetischen Staat,* Merkblatt Geheim, 11/5, 1 December 1944, Annex 15, NARS Record Group 242; Department of the Army, Assistant Chief of Staff (ACS), G-2, *Intelligence and Counterintelligence Services of the USSR,* 9 October 1942, NARS Record Group 319, Entry 85, File ID No. 918441, declassified 6 February 1978; GSUSA, *Survey;* Department of the Army, Headquarters U.S. Forces European Theater, Office of the Assistant Chief of Staff G-2, Counterintelligence Division, *The Foreign Department and the Counterintelligence Department of the NKGB,* 15 July 1946, Counterintelligence Special Interrogation Report No. 4 (CI-SIR/4), 13 March 1978, NARS Record Group 84, Foreign Service Posts of the Department of State, Moscow Embassy, 1946, File No. 820.02 Box 117, Central File No. 861.20200/7–2346; ONI, *Espionage-Sabotage-Conspiracy;* Germany, Fremde Heere Ost, *Organisation und Aufgaben des Sowjetischen Geheimdienstes im Operationsgebiet der Ostfront,* October 1944, NARS Record Group 226; U.S. Department of the Army, Headquarters European Command, Office of the Deputy Director of Intelligence, Exploitation of German Archives, 258th Interrogation Team, *Organization and Mission of the Soviet Secret Service,* 15 August 1946, Record Group 319, File ID No. 960347. For exceptionally detailed nomenclature of the wartime Soviet services, see *Liubianka VChK-KGB,* passim.

10. *Liubianka VChK-KGB,* 272–280; FSB, *Liubianka II,* 11, 232.

11. The INU was essentially the forerunner of the postwar First Chief Directorate of the KGB. For organizational details of the INU, see FHO, *Organisation und Aufgaben,* 65–67; ONI, *Espionage-Sabotage-Conspiracy,* Appendix I, 12–15; CI-SIR/4, *Foreign Department of the NKGB,* 5–7; FHO, *Ueberwachungsorgane,* 12.

12. FHO, *Organisation und Aufgaben,* 65–67; ONI, *Espionage-Sabotage-Conspiracy,* Appendix I, 12–15; CI-SIR/4, *The Foreign Department of the NKGB,* 5–7; FHO, *Ueberwachungsorgane,* 12.

13. *Liubianka VChK-KGB,* 272.

14. 258th Interrogation Team, *Organization of the Soviet Secret Service,* 92–95. For information on INU organization for operations and contribution to the war effort, see CI-SIR/4, *Foreign Department of the NKGB,* 5–11.

15. GSUSA, *Survey,* 78.

16. For information on Fitin, see Andrew and Gordievsky, *KGB: The Inside Story,* 283, 649, 694 n. 38; Sudoplatov, *Special Tasks,* 138, 235. See also Knight, *Beria,* 133, 260 n. 5. The majority of the evidence appears to point to Fitin as chief of the INU. Gordievksy and Andrew cite an official U.S. government document that placed two American officers and Fitin at a meeting in Moscow in 1944 (694 n. 38). That an official FHO document as late as 1944 appears to have erroneously identified Titius as chief of the INU lends credence to the idea that the Germans had no high-level penetrations of the Soviet intelligence services.

17. *Liubianka VChK-KGB,* 26.

18. Ibid., 110, 272; For career highlights of Fedotov, see also FSB, *Nachalo,* vol. 2, book 2, 314; Parrish, *Lesser Terror,* 15–16; Parrish, *Soviet Intelligence Organizations,* 108.

19. For the most extensive description of the operations and organization of the KRU, see CI-SIR/4, *Foreign Department of the NKGB,* 22–33. See also 258th Interrogation Team, *Organization and Mission of the Soviet Secret Service,* 95–96; FHO, *Organisation und Aufgaben,* 67–68; FHO, *Ueberwachungsorgane,* 12; FHO, *Sowjetische Agentenabwehr,* passim; and GSUSA, *Survey,* chap. 6, 142–160. Analysis of German and CIC documents indicates that the SPU and KRU functions overlapped. To catch agents and dissidents requires a substantial informant network, and the security and reliability of those informant networks needs to be checked. Therefore the Soviet security system was, by design, highly redundant. The KRU headquarters in Moscow appears to have concentrated specifically on counterintelligence and counterespionage operations, whereas the SPU concentrated on political security. KRO offices in the republics appear to have concentrated less on these types of operations and more on running informant networks and monitoring Soviet citizen contact with foreigners, and so on. Both the KROs and the INOs in the republics ran operations abroad, albeit close to the borders. See also FSB, *Liubianka II,* 232; and *Top Secret History,* 347–348.

20. *Top Secret History,* 347–348; FSB, *Liubianka II,* 232.

21. CI-SIR/4, *Foreign Department of the NKGB,* 22–33; 258th Interrogation Team, *Organization and Mission of the Soviet Secret Service,* 95–96; FHO, *Organisation und Aufgaben,* 67–68; FHO, *Ueberwachungsorgane,* 12; FHO, *Sowjetische Agentenabwehr,* passim; and GSUSA, *Survey,* chap. 6, 142–160.

22. U.S. Army, CI-SIR/4, *Foreign Department of the NKGB,* 22–33; 258th Interrogation Team, *Organization and Mission of the Soviet Secret Service,* 95–96; FHO, *Organisation und Aufgaben,* 67–68; FHO, *Ueberwachungsorgane,* 12; FHO, *Sowjetische Agentenabwehr,* passim; and GSUSA, *Survey,* chap. 6, 142–160.

23. *Liubianka VChK-KGB,* 272–273.

24. Ibid.

25. Ibid.

26. U.S. Army, CI-SIR/4, *Foreign Department of the NKGB,* 22–33; 258th Interrogation Team, *Organization and Mission of the Soviet Secret Service,* 95–96; FHO, *Organisation und Aufgaben,* 67–68; FHO, *Ueberwachungsorgane,* 12; FHO, *Sowjetische Agentenabwehr,* passim; and GSUSA, *Survey,* chap. 6, 142–160. Robert Conquest, in *Inside Stalin's Secret Police,* mentions that in 1940 a major of State Security, A. S. Blinov, was assigned to Ivanovo Province in the RSFSR (94–95). He had an order of the Red Star on 19 December 1937 and apparently survived the purges. However, there is no definitive evidence that would make him identical with the commissar of State Security, Blinov, cited above. Parrish, in *Lesser Terror,* states that one A. S. Blinov was identified in 1942 as NKVD chief in Kuibyshev and, in July 1945, held the rank of Lieutenant General (302). In the postwar KGB, counterintelligence abroad was performed by Directorate K of the First Chief Directorate; counterintelligence within the USSR was performed by the Second Chief Directorate; and the SPU's function was performed by the Fifth Chief Directorate. For excellent studies of the postwar organization, missions, functions, and operations of the KGB, see Peter Deriabin and T. H. Bagley, *The KGB: Masters of the Soviet Union* (New York: Hippocrene, 1990); Dallin, *Soviet Espionage;* John Barron, *The KGB: The Secret Work of Soviet Secret Agents* (New York: Reader's Digest, 1974); John Barron, *The KGB Today: The Hidden Hand* (New York: Reader's Digest, 1983); Amy Knight, *The KGB: Police and Politics in the Soviet Union* (Boston: Unwin Hyman, 1988); Dziak, *Chekisty;* Andrew and Gordievsky, *KGB: Inside Story;* and Wolin and Slusser, *The Soviet Secret Police.*

27. *Liubianka VchK-KGB,* 109–110; For detailed career highlights of Gorlinksi, see also Parrish, *Lesser Terror,* 15–16, 60, 116, 119, 259; Parrish, *Soviet Intelligence Organizations,* 133; FSB, *Nachalo,* vol. 2, book 1, 167; and FSB, *Nachalo,* vol. 2, book 2, 314.

28. U.S. Army, CI-SIR/4, *Foreign Department of the NKGB,* 5; 258th Interrogation Team, *Organization and Mission of the Soviet Secret Service,* 94–95, ONI, *Espionage-Sabotage-Conspiracy,* Appendix I, 14. This directorate was the forerunner of the Fifth Chief Directorate of the KGB (dissidents). For functions of the former Fifth Chief Directorate, see Knight, *Police and Politics,* 123. A. I. Romanov, a former Soviet military counterintelligence officer who served in World War II, states, in *Nights Are Longest There,* that Lieutenant General Fedotov was head of the SPU (119). Sudoplatov stated, in *Special Tasks,* that General Viktor Ilyin was chief of the SPU during the war (162). In one case the SPU assigned its informant network the task of collecting information on the attitudes of "influential parts of the population" to the Anglo-Russian alliance against the Axis. According to the U.S. Army 258th Interrogation Team docu-

ment cited here, after the reoccupation of the western portion of the USSR, the Sixth Department of the SPU was responsible for seeking out all those who collaborated with the Germans. FHO believed that the commissar of State Security, Goryevskiy, may have headed this component of the NKGB.

29. *Liubianka VChK-KGB,* 273–274.

30. Ibid., 274–275.

31. Sudoplatov, *Special Tasks,* 126–129; ONI, *Espionage-Sabotage-Conspiracy,* Appendix I, 14; 258th Interrogation Team, *Organization and Mission of the Soviet Secret Service,* 96–97; FHO, *Organisation und Aufgaben,* 68–69; FHO, *Ueberwachungsorgane,* 12. Sudoplatov said, in October 1941, that the Directorate for Special Tasks was enlarged and reorganized into Independent Department Two of the NKVD, which was subordinate directly to Beria. However, Sudoplatov retained his position as a deputy chief of State Security. In February 1942 Independent Department Two became the Fourth Directorate, and in 1943 it was subordinated to the newly created NKGB. Many of these details are not reflected in German documents. Again, while the Germans were operating under combat conditions and undoubtedly missed numerous details on the organization of the Soviet intelligence and security services, such omissions of major facts as the resubordination of a main component of the NKVD/NKGB lends credence to the idea that the Germans had no high-level penetrations of the Soviet intelligence services.

32. FHO, *Organisation und Aufgaben,* 68–69.

33. Sudoplatov, *Special Tasks,* 126–129; ONI, *Espionage-Sabotage-Conspiracy,* Appendix I, 14; 258th Interrogation Team, *Organization and Mission of the Soviet Secret Service,* 96–97; FHO, *Organisation und Aufgaben,* 68–69; and FHO, *Ueberwachungsorgane,* 12.

34. Sudoplatov, *Special Tasks,* 126–129; ONI, *Espionage-Sabotage-Conspiracy,* Appendix I, 14; 258th Interrogation Team, *Organization and Mission of the Soviet Secret Service,* 96–97; FHO, *Organisation und Aufgaben,* 68–69; and FHO, *Ueberwachungsorgane,* 12.

35. Sudoplatov, *Special Tasks,* 126–129; ONI, *Espionage-Sabotage-Conspiracy,* Appendix I, 14–15; 258th Interrogation Team, *Organization and Mission of the Soviet Secret Service,* 96–97; FHO, *Organisation und Aufgaben*, 68–69; FHO, *Die Ueberwachungsorgane,* 12.

36. *Liubianka VChK-KGB,* 275–276.

37. FHO, *Organizationen und Aufgaben,* 70; ONI, *Espionage-Sabotage-Conspiracy,* Appendix I, 14–15; FHO, *Ueberwachungsorgane,* 12; and GSUSA, *Survey*, chap. 3, 55.

38. FHO, *Organizationen und Aufgaben,* 70; ONI, *Espionage-Sabotage-Conspiracy,* Appendix I, 14–15; FHO, *Ueberwachungsorgane,* 12; and GSUSA, *Survey*, chap. 3, 55.

39. *Liubianka VChK-KGB,* 278–279.

40. Ibid.

41. Ibid., 34; FSB, *Liubianka II*, 232.

42. *Liubianka VChK-KGB,* 34.

43. Ibid.; *Top Secret History,* 631.

44. *Liubianka VChK-KGB,* 280.

45. Ibid., 34; FSB, *Liubianka II,* 232.

46. *Liubianka VChK-KGB,* 280–281.

47. FHO, *Organisation und Aufgaben,* 58–61; 258th Interrogation Team, *Organization and Mission of the Soviet Secret Service,* 82–85. The FHO document refers to this entity as a directorate (*Verwaltung*) (66).

48. FHO, *Organisation und Aufgaben,* 58–61; 258th Interrogation Team, *Organization and Mission of the Soviet Secret Service,* 82–85.

49. FHO, *Organisation und Aufgaben,* 58–61; 258th Interrogation Team, *Organization and Mission of the Soviet Secret Service,* 82–85.

50. *Liubianka VChK-KGB,* 275–278; FSB, *Liubianka II,* 233; *Top Secret History,* 628–631.

51. FSB, *Liubianka II,* 233; *Top Secret History,* 630.

52. *Liubianka VChK-KGB,* 280–285; FSB, *Liubianka II,* 232; *Top Secret History,* 631.

53. ONI, *Espionage-Sabotage-Conspiracy,* Appendix I, 15–16; FHO, *Ueberwachungsorgane,* 13; GSUSA, Survey, chap. 3, 56–57; FHO, *Organisation und Aufgaben,* 70–71.

54. *Liubianka VChK-KGB,* 280.

55. Ibid., 292, 287, 272; FSB, *Liubianka II,* 233; *Top Secret History,* 630.

56. *Liubianka VChK-KGB,* 276.

57. For a further description of Smersh, see Stephan, "Death to Spies," 53–94; and Stephan, "Smersh," 585–613; *Top Secret History,* 346–348.

58. Stephan, "Death to Spies," 53–94.

59. Ibid.

60. GSUSA, *Survey,* 49–51; Romanov, *Nights Are Longest There,* 71–72; U.S. Army, *Russian Counterintelligence Organizations,* 2–9. For a detailed description of the operations and organization of Smersh, see U.S. Army, CI-SR/42, *Counterintelligence Organization "Smersh";* FHO, *Organisation und Aufgaben,* 31–46; 258th Interrogation Team, *Organization and Mission of the Soviet Secret Service,* 41–42, 61–64.

61. GSUSA, *Survey,* 49–51; Romanov, *Nights Are Longest There,* 71–72; U.S. Army, *Russian Counterintelligence Organizations*, 3; U.S. Army, CI-SR/42, *Counterintelligence Organization "Smersh,"* 19; 258th Interrogation Team, *Organization and Mission of the Soviet Secret Service,* 41. While all sources agree on the functions of Smersh, there are considerable contradictions among sources on the directorate/department numbering system, on which components are directorates or departments, and on the specific responsibilities for each directorate. The organizational description Romanov provides differs significantly from that of the GSUSA study, which was based on German documentation. The description given above largely relies on the GSUSA study and on a 258th Interrogation Team translation of the FHO document entitled *Organisation und Aufgaben des Sowjetischen Geheimdienstes im Operationsgebiet der Ostfront,* dated October 1944. While Romanov has unique insights into how Soviet military counterintelligence actually worked, information contained in German documents was often based on interrogations of multiple sources that were recorded and subsequently analyzed. Romanov wrote his book twenty-seven years after the end of the war and appears to have largely relied on his memory, as he did not claim to have based his account on any original Soviet documents.

62. GSUSA, *Survey,* 49–51; Romanov, *Nights Are Longest There,* 71–72; U.S. Army, *Russian Counterintelligence Organizations,* 3; U.S. Army, CI-SR/42, *Counterintelligence Organization "Smersh,"* 19; 258th Interrogation Team, *Organization and Mission of the Soviet Secret Service,* 41.

63. GSUSA, *Survey,* 49–51. See U.S. War Department, *Handbook on U.S.S.R Military Forces,* Technical Manual TM-30-430, November 1946, I, 26.

64. GSUSA, *Survey,* 49–51. See War Department, *Handbook,* I, 26.

65. FHO, *Truppenverbaende und truppenaehnliche Organisationen,* 7–9; FHO, *Die Sowjetische Agentenabwehr,* 7; U.S. Army, CI-SR/42, *Counterintelligence Organization "Smersh,"* 22; GSUSA *Survey,* 51; 258th Interrogation Team, *Organization and Mission of the Soviet Secret Service,* 48–51.

66. War Department, *Handbook,* IV, 4–6; Artemiev, "OKR," 30; James T. Reitz, "The Soviet Security Troops: The Kremlin's Other Armies," in David R. Jones, ed., *Soviet Armed Forces Review Annual* 6 (1982): 297–298; FHO, *Die sowjetische Agentenabwehr,* 11.

67. War Department, *Handbook,* IV, 4–6; Artemiev, "OKR," 30; Reitz, "The Kremlin's Other Armies," 297–298; FHO, *Die sowjetische Agentenabwehr,* 11.

68. War Department, *Handbook,* IV, 4–6; Reitz, "The Kremlin's Other Armies," 297–298.

69. War Department, *Handbook,* IV, 4–6.

70. U.S. Department of the Army, Headquarters 66th Counterintelligence Corps Detachment, *OO NKVD 45th Guards Infantry Division, 1942–1943 (Organization and Personalities),* November 7, 1949, 3; U.S. Army, *Russian Counterintelligence Organizations,* 3; Nosryev, *V poyedinke s abverom,* passim.

71. *Liubianka VChK-KGB,* 276–278; *Top Secret History,* 630; FSB, *Liubianka II,* 233.

72. FSB, *Liubianka II,* 232; *Top Secret History,* 630. The classified history identifies the Third Directorate as "combating parachutists."

73. *Liubianka VChK-KGB,* 276–278; *Top Secret History,* 628, 630.

74. *Liubianka VChK-KGB,* 275–276.

75. Ibid.

76. *Top Secret History,* 628.

77. For information on the organization, mission, size, and functions of the NKVD, see War Department, *Handbook,* IV, 1–12; Reitz, "The Kremlin's Other Armies," 279–327; FHO, *Ueberwachungsorgane* (trans. in ONI, *Espionage-Sabotage-Conspiracy,* Appendix I); FHO, *Die sowjetischen Agentenabwehr,* 3–48 (trans. in ONI, *Espionage-Sabotage-Conspiracy,* Appendix II); FHO, *Truppenverbaende und truppenaehnliche Organizationen;* Knight, *Beria,* 103–135; Wolin and Slusser, *The Soviet Secret Police,* 15–27, 96–152; GSUSA, *Survey,* 59–61; FHO, *Organisation und Aufgaben,* 72–75 (an edited translation of this document was done by the 258th Interrogation Team in *Organization and Mission of the Soviet Secret Service*).

78. Wolin and Slusser, *The Soviet Secret Police,* 135; GSUSA, *Survey,* 59; Reitz, "The Kremlin's Other Armies," 289. Wolin and Slusser estimated the size at 2 million and base their figure on estimates provided by former NKVD troop officers. The

GSUSA *Survey* estimated total NKVD troop strength at 850,000. Reitz estimates the strength of the Border Guards and the interior troops to have been about 700,000. The War Department *Handbook*, Reitz, Slusser, and the FHO study *Ueberwachungsorgane* provide the most detail on the organization of the NKVD.

79. Knight, *KGB*, 229.

80. War Department, *Handbook*, IV, 4–5; Knight, *Beria*, 119; ONI, *Espionage-Sabotage-Conspiracy*, 35, Appendix I, 7. In *KGB: Inside Story* (309), Gordievsky and Andrew, citing an article by V. F. Nekrasov in the *Military Historical Journal* (no. 9 [1985]: 698 n. 145), stated that NKVD troop strength was fifty-three divisions and twenty-eight brigades (not counting various independent units and border troops), totaling almost 750,000 men. If police units, border guards, militia, signal troops, construction troops, and troops assigned to the GULAG are added, the overall troop total would probably tend to support the Slusser figure of 2 million men, especially if there were 15,000 men assigned to an NKVD division (War Department, *Handbook*, IV, 5).

81. War Department, *Handbook*, IV, 4–5; Knight, *Beria*, 119; ONI, *Espionage-Sabotage-Conspiracy*, 35, Appendix I, 7. It appears that, even though the Directorate for Rear-Area Security was established in 1942, the Border Guards were not subsumed into this directorate until 1943; see also Knight, *KGB*, 229–239, 245.

82. *Liubianka VChK-KGB*, 110–112, 297–299.

83. War Department, *Handbook*, IV, 4–5; ONI, *Espionage- Sabotage-Conspiracy*, 35, Appendix I, 7.

84. Reitz, "Kremlin's Other Armies," 312–314; War Department, *Handbook*, IV–V.

85. *Liubianka VChK-KGB*, 110–111, 299.

86. Reitz, "Kremlin's Other Armies," 312–314; War Department, *Handbook*, IV, 5. For a more in-depth description of Border Guard intelligence and counterintelligence, see 258th Interrogation Team, *Organization and Mission of the Soviet Secret Service*, 100–103; FHO, *Organisation und Aufgaben*, 72–81; FHO, *Truppenverbaende und truppenaehnliche Organisationen*, 4–6; and FHO, *Sowjetische Agentenabwehr*, 12–13. In practice, the missions assigned to the Border Guards and the interior troops overlapped. See also Knight, *Beria*, 126–129.

87. Reitz, "Kremlin's Other Armies," 312–314.

88. Ibid.; ONI, *Espionage-Sabotage-Conspiracy*, Appendix I, 6–12. The functions and operations of the GULAG are well documented. See Aleksandr I. Solzhenitsyn, *GULAG Archipelago, 1918–1956: An Experiment in Literary Investigation*, parts 1 and 2, trans. Thomas P. Whitney (New York: Harper and Row, 1973; parts 3 and 4 [1975]); and Knight, *Beria*, 105–69, 106, 113–119; Levytsky, *Uses of Terror*, passim; Heller and Nekrich, *Utopia in Power*, 319–320; Wolin and Slusser, *Soviet Secret Police*, 322–337.

89. Vladimir Petrov and Evdokia Petrov, *Empire of Fear* (New York: Praeger, 1956), 101; *Liubianka VChK-KGB*, 260, 292.

90. War Department, *Handbook*, IV, 5–7. According to the War Department *Handbook*, NKVD signal troops consisted of fifteen regiments of about 1,000 men each.

91. ONI, *Espionage-Sabotage-Conspiracy*, Appendix I, 12; Yuri Modin, *My Five Cambridge Friends: Burgess, Maclean, Philby, Blunt, and Cairncross*, trans. Anthony

Roberts (New York: Farrar, Straus and Giroux, 1994), 30–33. Modin, who was the handler after the war for the British spies mentioned in the title, described his experience in the service of the NKVD during the war when he was assigned to the Leningrad Naval Academy. He was ineligible for frontline duty because he was too young; however, he was drafted into what appears to have been an NKVD liquidation squad. He describes his participation in a patrol in which he was with an "NKVD agent" when they found a German spy transmitting messages in an apartment.

92. Based on Barron, *KGB: Secret Work of Soviet Secret Agents,* 340–341; Hingley, *The Russian Secret Police,* 211–213; Dziak, *Chekisty,* 184–185; and Andrew and Gordievsky, *KGB: Inside Story,* 381–383, 416, 450.

93. Based on Dziak, *Chekisty,* 179; and Andrew and Gordievsky, *KGB: Inside Story,* 647–648.

94. Based on Stephan, "Death to Spies," 180–182.

95. On Nazi atrocities, see Christopher R. Browning, *Ordinary Men: Reserve Police Battalion 101 and the Final Solution in Poland* (New York: HarperCollins, 1992); Richard Breitman, *The Architect of Genocide: Himmler and the Final Solution* (New York: Knopf, 1991); Raul Hilberg, *The Destruction of the European Jews* (Chicago: Quadrangle, 1961); and Walter Laqueur, *The Terrible Secret: Suppression of the Truth about Hitler's Final Solution* (New York: Penguin, 1982). On the history of the SS and the Gestapo, see Heinz Hoehne, *The Order of the Death's Head: The Story of Hitler's SS,* trans. Richard Barry (New York: Ballantine, 1977); George H. Stein, *The Waffen SS* (Ithaca, N.Y.: Cornell University Press, 1966); Jacques Delarue, *The Gestapo: History of Horrors,* trans. Mervyn Savill (New York: Dell, 1964); and Edward Crankshaw, *The Gestapo* (London: Putnam, 1956). There are no good recent studies of the Gestapo in English.

96. Dziak, *Chekisty,* 2.

97. Kahn, *Hitler's Spies.* Kahn's book describes German operations in the West in considerable detail.

98. Since the end of World War II, hundreds of books, articles, monographs, and television documentaries, both in the United States and abroad, have been produced worldwide on the overall operations, mission, organization, and functions of the German intelligence services, especially those of the Abwehr. However, with the exception of certain books focusing on the career of former chief of FHO General Reinhard Gehlen (see below), little attention has been paid to German intelligence on the Eastern Front. The best published sources on German operations in the East include Hoehne, *Canaris;* Hoehne and Zolling, *The General Was a Spy;* Kahn, *Hitler's Spies;* and Military Intelligence Division, *German Military Intelligence.* Studies of the intelligence service of the SS — RSHA (SD/Ausland) — are virtually nonexistent. The only two books in English to describe any of the operations of SD/Ausland in the East are Walter Schellenberg, *Hitler's Secret Service: The Memoirs of Walter Schellenberg,* trans. Louis Hagen (New York: Harcourt Brace Jovanovich, 1977); and Otto Heilbrunn, *The Soviet Secret Services* (London: Allen and Unwin, 1957), specifically chap. 10 ("A Leaf Out of the German Book"), 147–167. The only other book in English to specifically

describe the clandestine collection operations of SD/Ausland worldwide is Wilhelm Hoettel, *The Secret Front* (New York: Praeger, 1954).

99. Hinsley, *British Intelligence in the Second World War,* 297–303. Appendix I gives a concise overview of the German services. The most comprehensive treatments of the *Abwehr* currently available in English are Kahn, *Hitler's Spies;* Hoehne, *Canaris;* and Military Intelligence Division, *German Military Intelligence.* For sources in German, see Oskar Reile, *Der Deutsche Geheimdienst im Zweiten Weltkrieg (Westfront)* (Muenchen: Weltbild Verlag, GmbH, 1990); and Gert Bucheit, *Der Deutsche Geheimdienst* (Muenchen: List Verlag, 1967). For a general overview of Abwehr organization, see Hoehne, *Canaris.* Inside the front cover is an excellent organizational chart on the Abwehr that corresponds closely with the organization of the Abwehr described in Hinsley, *British Intelligence in the Second World War,* 297. Hoehne, in *Order of the Death's Head,* provides a good organization chart of the SS and of the RSHA in particular (242–243). See also "The Abwehr and Its Kindred Organizations," undated, no author given, but found in OSS, Record Group 226, Entry 119, Box 23, Folder 176 (German Espionage), for a good documentary overview of the German services.

100. Hinsley, *British Intelligence in the Second World War,* 297–303.

101. Ibid.; Delarue, *The Gestapo;* Crankshaw, *The Gestapo;* Supreme Headquarters Allied Expeditionary Force, Counterintelligence War Room (London) Report, Situation Report No. 4, *Amt IV of the RSHA,* 19 February 1946, NARS Record Group 165, Entry 179, Box 707. While much of the literature on the Gestapo is subsumed in the general literature on the SS and the Holocaust, nothing in English has been published concerning Gestapo counterintelligence operations in the USSR. For a study of the Secret Field Police, see United States, Department of the Army, Military History Institute, Historical Division, Headquarters, U.S. Army Europe, Foreign Military Studies Branch, Wilhelm Kirchbaum, *The Secret Field Police,* No. MS-C-029, 18 May 1947. For a detailed description of the GFP in Army Group North, see United Kingdom, Combined Services Detailed Interrogation Center (CSDIC) S.I.R. (SIR) 1675 (U.K.), *Notes on the GFP and Other Security Services in the Area of Army Group Nord (Later Kurland) 1942–1 January 1945,* 24 May 1945, NARS RG 226, XL10664.

102. Hinsley, *British Intelligence in the Second World War,* 297–303; Military Intelligence Division, *German Military Intelligence,* 1–102. Books on the career of General Reinhard Gehlen include Hoehne and Zolling, *The General Was a Spy;* Gehlen, *The Service;* Cookridge, *Gehlen: Spy of the Century* (New York: Random House, 1971); and Mary Ellen Reese, *General Reinhard Gehlen.*

103. Hoehne, *Canaris,* inside front cover; and OSS, "Abwehr and Its Kindred Organizations." Abwehr I was divided into sections for Eastern and Western intelligence, sections for naval and air intelligence, technical and industrial intelligence, air force technical intelligence, and sections for administration of agents abroad, communicating with agents abroad, and a section that equipped agents with radios, false papers, secret writing systems, codes and ciphers, microdots, and cameras. Abwehr I was headed by Colonel Hans Piekenbrock from 1935 to 1943 and by Colonel Georg Hansen from 1943 to 1944. Abwehr II — which was divided geographically — was headed by Colonel Erwin Lahousen

from 1939 to 1943, and then by Colonel Wessel von Freytag-Loringhoven from 1943 to 1944. From 1939 to 1944 Colonel Franz-Eccard von Bentivengi headed Abwehr III. Abwehr III had several sections to cover most aspects of counterintelligence and counterespionage. Sections included liaison with the RSHA, industrial security, internal counterintelligence analysis, disinformation, liaison with the press, cinema, postal authorities and the post office, security in POW camps, assessment of treasonable acts, counterespionage in the armed forces (divided by army, navy, and air force), and a section for combating foreign intelligence services (often referred to as Abwehr III F).

104. Hoehne, *Canaris,* organization chart on inside front cover cited above. Abteilung Z was headed by Major General Hans Oster from 1938 to 1943 and by Colonel Jacobsen from 1943 to 1944, and was responsible for Abwehr archives and administration. Oster was suspected of having been a Soviet agent.

105. See Hinsley, *British Intelligence in the Second World War,* 295–298. See Kahn, *Hitler's Spies,* 238–250, for an in-depth discussion of Abwehr organization. The Abwehr also had Kriegsorganisationen (KOs) that were essentially Asts except they were located in embassies in neutral and Allied countries (Madrid, Lisbon, Ankara, Helsinki, Sofia, Zagreb, Shanghai, Casablanca, Bern, Stockholm, etc.). Operations conducted from these locations were primarily directed at Germany's enemies and conducted by officials or employees of German embassies who were in the armed forces but working as embassy civilians. They reported directly to Abwehr headquarters in Berlin. Many Asts conducted operations in areas covered by KOs; however, the cooperation and coordination between Asts and KOs were mixed.

106. Kahn, *Hitler's Spies,* 238–239.

107. For comprehensive treatments of the FAK/FAT system, see Military Intelligence Division, *German Military Intelligence,* 195–200; ONI, *Espionage-Sabotage-Conspiracy,* 8–12, 22–24; Kahn, *Hitler's Spies,* 249–250; Hinsley, *British Intelligence in the Second World War,* 298; and Bogdanov and Leonov, *Armeiskie Chekisty,* 160–161. Originally FAKs/FATs were referred to as Abwehrkommandos and Abwehrtruppen. When the Abwehr was amalgamated into the RSHA in 1944, the name of these mobile teams was changed to FAKs/FATs. For an organizational description of Abwehrkommandos and Abwehrtruppen, see Supreme Headquarters Allied Expeditionary Force, Counterintelligence War Room (London) Report SIR No. 195, *Leitstelle III Ost,* 18 December 1945, 1–9, NARS Record Group 319, XE013988. See also Seaton, *The Russo-German War,* 591, Appendix B. In Appendix B Seaton provides a detailed chart of the evolution of the various German army groups.

108. Kahn, *Hitler's Spies,* 249–250. For information on the Brandenburg Division, see ONI, *Espionage-Conspiracy-Sabotage,* 20–22; Hoehne, *Canaris,* 428–429, 458–461, 467–468. For FAK/FAT functions, see also OSS, "The Abwehr and Its Kindred Organizations," 13. There was considerable controversy during the war over the subordination of the Brandenburg Division and over how the regular army employed it.

109. For FAK/FAT strengths, see Military Intelligence Division, *German Military Intelligence,* 195–196.

110. Ibid.

111. Ibid.

112. Ibid. For example, by the end of the war Leitstelle III Ost (also known as Stab Walli III and Frontleitstelle III Ost) functioned as the de facto Abwehr regional controller for all Abwehr III (counterintelligence) activities on the Eastern Front and controlled approximately four FAKs. Each counterintelligence FAK in turn controlled approximately thirty-three subordinate FATs (whose three-digit numbering system also started with 3) for a total of 1,320 men. For the total number of personnel assigned to Abwehr III FAKs/FATs on the Eastern Front, see CIR/16, *German Methods,* 2. For a detailed breakdown of Walli III and the subordination of FAKs/FATs III on the Eastern Front, see SIR/195, *Leitstelle III Ost,* 1–8.

113. Kahn, *Hitler's Spies,* 250.

114. Ibid., 250; Hinsley and Simkins, *British Intelligence in the Second World War,* 297.

115. Thomas, "Foreign Armies East," 261–262.

116. Ibid.

117. Ibid.

118. Ibid. At the beginning of the war FHO did not have the charter to conduct clandestine collection and counterintelligence operations, as these operations were strictly the purview of the field organizations of Amt/Ausland Abwehr.

119. Military Intelligence Division, *German Military Intelligence,* 13–34. This section of the book gives a thorough description of FHO, the responsibilities of each Referat in each Gruppe and describes every kind of report FHO was known to have produced. For the organization of FHO in 1945, see United Kingdom, Combined Services Detailed Interrogation Center (U.K.), Special Interrogation Report (SIR) No. 1665, 5 June 1945, *Fremde Heere Ost: Information Obtained from Lieutenant Colonel I. G. Scheibe* (former chief of Gruppe I, Referat 1A of FHO), 5 June 1945, NARS RG 165, Entry 179, Box 704.

120. Military Intelligence Division, *German Military Intelligence,* 26.

121. Ibid., 28.

122. Ibid.

123. U.S. War Department, General and Special Staffs, Assistant Chief of Staff G-2, Intelligence Division, Captured Personnel and Material Branch, Enemy POW Interrogation File 1943–1945, *Report of Interrogation No. 5725: Preliminary Interrogation and Assessment of Brigadier General Reinhard Gehlen,* 28 August 1945, NARS Record Group 165, "G" Entry 179.

124. Hinsley and Simkins, *British Intelligence in the Second World War,* 299–300.

125. Ibid.

126. Ibid.

127. Ibid.; Hoehne, *The Order of the Death's Head,* 242–243; Schellenberg, *Hitler's Secret Service,* 208; U.S. Army, *Report on the Case of Walter Friedrich Schellenberg,* 14. Hoehne provides a good organization chart of the SS and the RSHA in particular. Three departments were responsible for budget, training, and ideological research, respectively. The other two departments supervised the criminal police (Amt V) and directed the activities of the Sicherheitsdienst within Germany (referred to as Amt III — SD/Inland).

See Crankshaw, *The Gestapo*, 16, 248 n. 2. No specific figures were available for SD/Ausland. In June 1942, at age thirty-two, Schellenberg was formally appointed head of SD/Ausland after having been acting chief for the previous year.

128. Kahn, *Hitler's Spies*, 266.

129. Counterintelligence War Room (London), *The Headquarters of Amt VI*, 1–2.

130. Ibid. It may have also been referred to as *Zwei* (two).

131. Schellenberg, *Hitler's Secret Service*, 262–277. Schellenberg discusses Zeppelin at length.

132. United Kingdom, Combined Services Detailed Interrogation Center (WEA) BAOR, Final Report (FR) No. 31, 20 February 1946, *Dr. Willi Teich*, ii–iii, NARS 165. This report is based on the British interrogation of SS *Hauptsturmfuehrer* Willi Teich, who served in Gruppe VI C of SD/Ausland. SD/Ausland mobile units were divided into Hauptkommandos and subordinate Aussenkommandos (much like the Abwehr's FAK/FAT system). Initially the Aussenkommandos consisted of two or three Russians led by a German NCO whose mission was to interrogate POWs and screen them for potential agent candidates. Reports were forwarded directly to SD/Ausland headquarters in Berlin.

133. CSDIC, FR-31, *Dr. Willi Teich*, i–vi, Appendix B, Annex 1.

134. Ibid. With the amalgamation of the Abwehr into the RSHA in 1944, Section C Zeppelin was upgraded to a department comprising four sections: schools and training, interrogation, operations, and administration.

135. Ibid.; Kahn *Hitler's Spies*, 265–266.

136. Kahn, *Hitler's Spies*, 265–266. For example, SS Colonels (*Standartenfuehrer*) Karl Tschiersky and Albert Rapp, both former chiefs of SD/Ausland's component responsible for training agents to collect intelligence on the USSR, advanced their careers by serving in the Einsatzkommandos. To quote Kahn: "Department VI was thus riddled with killers, and Nazi Germany depended for honest, unbiased information that alone can guarantee success in intelligence upon amoral compliant men."

137. Kahn, *Hitler's Spies*, 268–271. Kahn gives a good description of the amalgamation.

138. Ibid.

139. Ibid., 270–271; United States Forces European Theater, Military Intelligence Service Center, CI Final Interrogation Report (CI-FIR) No. 83, *Interrogation of Oberst Georg Buntrock*, 12 February 1946, 5–9, NARS RG 319. To fend off bureaucratic haggling for control of the remnants of the Abwehr, Colonel Georg Buntrock, newly appointed chief of Branch F, submitted a letter to Kaltenbrunner in late December 1944 asking Kaltenbrunner to issue an order clarifying the chain of command for the FAKs/FATs. Buntrock, with Kaltenbrunner's and Schellenberg's approval, issued an order, in February 1945, laying out the subordination and responsibilities of the chief of Milamt Branch F. The highlights were the following: chief of Branch F was to serve as chief of *Frontaufklaerung* (chief of the FAKs/FATs); chief of Branch F was administratively subordinate to OKW but operationally subordinate to the chief of Amt VI (Schellenberg) for matters relating to FAKs/FATs I and II and to the chief of the Gestapo (Mueller — Amt IV) for matters relating to FAK/FAT III (counterintelligence); only the chief of

Branch F, in his capacity as the chief of Frontaufklaerung, could issue orders to the FAKs/FATs. The FAKs/FATs in the field became operationally subordinate to the intelligence officer (also known as the 1c) assigned to the armies and army groups. Otto Skorzeny took over responsibility for the Abwehr's sabotage mission (nonmilitary) and continued his attempts to take over the operational control of FAK/FAT II. Despite Kaltenbrunner's order, organizational chaos and bureaucratic bickering continued unabated to the end of the war. Buntrock gives an excellent description of this bureaucratic infighting throughout his interrogation report. For more on the amalgamation of the RSHA and the Abwehr, see Heinz Hoehne, *Canaris,* 558–561.

140. Kahn, *Hitler's Spies,* 268–271.

141. Ibid., 270–271.

SELECTED BIBLIOGRAPHY

Documents

GERMANY

Abteilung Fremde Heere Ost. *Organisation und Aufgaben des Sowjetischen Geheimdienstes im Operationsgebiet der Ostfront: Heft 1: Oktober 1944*. NARS Record Group 226.

Abteilung Fremde Heere Ost (IIa). *Decknamenverzeichnis der Agenten Abwehr I.* 14 November 1944, NARS Record Group 242, T-78/673/825/H3/1510.

Abwehrabteilung III/Walli III: Abwehrstatistik: Operationsgebiet Ost, Folge 13. January 1944, T-311/7118109-7118110, NARS Record Group 242.

Abwehrkommando 304, Tagesbericht 1057, 8 Mai 1944. NARS Record Group 242, T-78.

Auswaertiges Amt. *Photocopies of Correspondence and Reports in Russian with Some Translations in German Pertaining to the Autobiography of Captured NKVD Lieutenant Tschigunow and His Exploitation by German Authorities, April 1941–April 1943*. NARS Record Group 242, T78/287/879, Item No. EAP-3-a-11/2.

Fremde Heere Ost. *Unternehmen Scherhorn: Entwurf.* NARS Record Group 242, T-78/479/H3/409.

Oberkommando des Heeres. Fremde Heere Ost. Abteilung I. *Die sowjetische Agentenabwehr und Gegenspionage im Operationsgebiet der Ostfront (1943)*. NARS Record Group 242, T78, Roll 562, Frame H3.323.

Oberkommando des Heeres. Fremde Heere Ost. Abteilung IIb. *Truppenverbaende und truppenaehnliche Organisationen des roten Volkskommissariats der Inneren (NKWD).* January 16, 1943. NARS Record Group 242, T78.563/H3/398.

Oberkommando des Heeres. Generalstab. Hauptabteilung Fremde Heere Ost IIb. *Die Ueberwachungsorgane im sowjetischen Staat.* Merkblatt Geheim, 11/5. 1 December 1945. Annex 15. NARS Record Group 242, OKH H3/753.

Oberkommando des Heeres. Abteilung 1c/A.O./Auswertung, Nr. 1231/44. *NKVD-Trupppen: Das Volkskommissariat fuer Innere Angelegenheiten.* 27 June 1944, T-78/567/891. NARS Record Group 242.

Panzerarmeeoberkommando 3 (Panzer A.O.K. 3), *Abteilung* 1c/AO. *Anlagenband A5, Taetigkeitsbericht-Nr. 11, 1 Januar-30 Juni 1944: Abwehrtrupp, Pz 113: 20 Marz 1944, Feindbild im Raum suedl.und nordwestl.Witebsk.* NARS Record Group 242, T-313/3098586-519–5.

Panzerarmeeoberkommando 3 (Panzer A.O.K. 3), *Abteilung* 1c/AO. *Anlagenband A5, Taetigkeitsbericht-Nr. 11, 1 Januar–30 Juni 1944: Abwehrtrupp, Pz 113: 12 Juni 1944, Vernehmungsbericht des V-Mann 2385*. NARS Record Group 242, T-313/3098586-519-5.

Panzerarmeeoberkommando 3 (Panzer A.O.K. 3), *Abteilung* 1c/AO. *Anlagenband A5, Taetigkeitsbericht-Nr. 11, 1 Januar–30 Juni 1944: Abwehrtrupp, Pz 113: 14 Marz 1944, Feindbild im Raum Janowitschi-Lisono.* NARS Record Group 242, T-313/3098586-519-5.

Panzerarmeekommando 3, *Abteilung* 1c/A.O. *Taetigskeitbericht Nr. 11 fuer die Zeite 1 Januar–30 Juni 1944, Betrieb Nr. 90, 9 Mai 1944, Feinbild im Raum Rudnja — Lisos; Quelle: V-Leute Smagin und Abdurhamet.* NARS Record Group 242, T-313/309/8586/519-5.

UNITED KINGDOM

Supreme Headquarters, Allied Expeditionary Force, Counterintelligence War Room (London). *Situation Report No. 4: Amt IV of the RSHA.* 19 February 1946, NARS Record Group 165, Entry 179, Box 707.

———. *Liquidation Report No. 183, FAK 202.* 23 November 1945. NARS Record Group 165, Entry 179, Box 705.

———. *Liquidation Report No. 187, FAK 203.* 22 November 1945. NARS Record Group, Entry 179, Box 705.

———. *The Headquarters of Amt VI (excluding VI S and Mil. Amt.* 23 April 1945. NARS Record Group 319, XE002666, Vol 5.

———. *Situation Report No. 143: FAK 301: Oberstleutnant Eric Suckow: June 1942 to End.* 11 December1945. NARS Record Group 165, Entry 179, Box 705.

———. *Situation Report No. 195, Leitstelle III Ost (Walli III).* 18 December 1945. NARS Record Group 319, XE013988.

Combined Services Detailed Interrogation Center. *S.I.R. 1665: Fremde Heere Ost: Lieutenant Colonel I.G. Scheibe, former Chief Gruppe I, Referat 1A of FHO.* 5 June 1945. NARS Record Group 165, Entry 179, Box 704.

———. *Special Interrogation Report, Notes on the GFP and Other Security Services in the Area of Army Group Nord (Later Kurland), 1942–1 January 1945.* 24 May 1945. NARS Record Group 226, OSS, XL 10664.

———. *Special Interrogation Report 1727, Notes on Abwehr I Luft, Interrogation of Major Sandel.* 16 September 1945. NARS, Record Group 165, Entry 179, Box 665.

———. *Special Interrogation Report No. 1716: Notes on Gruppe I Luft, Amt/Ausland Abwehr and on the Activities of Its Outlying Centers (March 1941–January 1943).* 9 August 1945. NARS Record Group 165, Entry 179, Box 665.

Combined Services Detailed Interrogation Center, (WEA) BAOR. *Final Report Number 31: Dr. Willi Teich,* 20 February 1946. NARS Record Group 165.

Combined Services Detailed Interrogation Center, BAOR, FR 53. *Final Report on Hauptmann Heinrich Otto Karl Soujon: Prisoner's W/T Activity on the Eastern Front (FULEI Ost),* 9 March 1946. NARS Record Group 165, Entry 179, Box 704.

UNITED STATES

Central Intelligence Agency. *Studies In Intelligence,* fall 1957, "The Labyrinth: The Memoirs of Hitler's Secret Service Chief." NARS Record Group 263, Box 1, Folder 2, Entry 8.

———. *Study of Intelligence and Counterintelligence Activities on the Eastern Front and in Adjacent Areas during World War II.* NARS Record Group 232, undated.

Department of the Army. Assistant Chief of Staff, G-2. *Intelligence and Counterintelligence Service of the USSR.* 9 October, 1942. NARS Record Group 319, Entry 85.

———. General Staff, United States Army (GSUSA). Intelligence Division. *Survey of Soviet Intelligence and Counterintelligence.* 9 January 1948. NARS Record Group 319, Records of the Army Staff. Declassified NND 770011.

———. Headquarters European Command. Office of the Deputy Director of Intelligence. Exploitation German Archives. 258th Interrogation Team. *Organization and Mission of the Soviet Secret Service.* 15 August 1946. Record Group 319.

———. Headquarters European Command. Office of the Military Government of Germany. Office of the Deputy Director of Intelligence. *Report on Soviet Military Espionage Activities.* 12 February 1946. Record Group 260, 7 21-3 15, Box 18, Folder 383, 4–1.

———. Headquarters 66th Counterintelligence Corps Detachment. *OO NKVD 45th Guards Infantry Division, 1942–1943 (Organization and Personalities)* 7 November 1949.

———. Headquarters, U.S. Forces European Theater. Military Intelligence Service Center. Office of the Assistant Chief of Staff G-2. *Special Report to Deputy AC of S G-2 USFET: The Secret Services of the USSR,* 3 November 1945.

———. Headquarters U.S. Forces European Theater. Military Intelligence Service Center. *German Methods of Combating the Soviet Intelligence Service.* September 9, 1945. Counterintelligence Consolidated Interrogation Report No. 16 (CI-CIR/16). NARS Record Group 238.

———. Center for Military History. *Effects of Climate on Combat in European Russia.* CMH-PUB 104-6. Washington D.C.: U.S. Government Printing Office, February 1952.

———. Headquarters U.S. Forces European Theater. Office of the Assistant Chief of Staff G-2. Counterintelligence Division. *The Foreign Department and the Counterintelligence Department of the NKGB.* 15 July 1946. Counterintelligence Special Interrogation Report No. 4 (CI-SIR/4). Declassified NND 765025. 13 March 1978. NARS Record Group 84. Foreign Service Posts of the Department of State, Moscow Embassy, 1946. File No. 820.02, Box 117. Central File No. 861.20200/7-2346.

———. Information Section, Counterintelligence Branch, Office of the Director of Intelligence. Headquarters U.S. Group C.C. *Russian Counterintelligence Organizations.* August 14, 1945. File ID No. 191047. Record Group 319. Entry 85, February 6, 1978.

———. Military History Institute. Historical Division. Headquarters U.S. Army Europe. Foreign Military Studies Branch. German Counterintelligence in Occupied Soviet Union, 1941–1945. By Wladimir Posdnjakoff. No. MS — P-122, 1952.

———. *Espionage Activities of the USSR,* by Wladimir Posdnjakoff. Edited by J. R. Robinson. No. MS-P-137.

———. *PW Project Number 5.* MSW-P-018e. 1950.

———. *Rear Area Security in Russia: The Soviet Second Front behind the German Lines.* No. MS-T-19. July 1950. Declassified 6 January 1954. (Also known as *German Report Series.*)

———. *The Secret Field Police*, by Wilhelm Kirchbaum. Edited by George C. Vanderstadt. Translated by M. Franke. No. MS-C-029, 18 May 1947.

———. 7707th Military Intelligence Service Center. *The Counterintelligence Organization "SMERSH" of the Red Army*. March 24, 1947. Counterintelligence Special Report No. 42 (CI-SR/42). June 5,1984. NARS Record Group 338.

———. *Operations and Experiences of Frontaufklaerung (FA) III OST during the Eastern Campaigns*. 27 January 1947. Counterintelligence Special Report No. 32 (CI-SR/32). NARS Record Group 319, XE013988.

Department of the Navy. Office of Naval Intelligence. *Espionage-Sabotage-Conspiracy: German and Russian Operations, 1941–1945: Excerpts from the Files of the German Naval Staff and Other Captured German Documents*. April 1947. NARS Record Group 226, Entry 120, Box 46.

Office of Strategic Services. *The Abwehr and its Kindred Organizations*. Undated. NARS Record Group 226, Entry 119, Box 23, Folder 176, German Espionage.

———. *Operational Methods of Security Units of the Red Army*. 12 September 1945. Report No. A-61642. NARS Record Group 226, XL 19175.

_________. *Soviet Activities in Estonia*. 31 January 1945. Report No. A-54556. Record Group 226, L555669.

United States Army, Bremen Interrogation Center Enclave Military District, Counterintelligence Annex. *Final Interrogation Report No. 68, Curdes, Richard*. 27 August 1945. NARS Record Group 319.

———. *File on Hermann Baun*. XE003134, Box 13, Project Number 871004. NARS Record Group 319.

———. Third U.S. Army Intelligence Center, Office of the Assistant Chief of Staff G-2, *Preliminary Interrogation Report: Baun, Hermann*. 30 August 1945. NARS Record Group 165, ACS G-2, Intelligence Division, Captured Personnel and Material Branch, Enemy POW Interrogation File (MI S4), 1943–1945, Entry 179, Box 708, Folder HTUSAIC PIR.

———. Records of the Army Staff. *Anton Turkul*. XE061758, NARS Record Group, 319.

———. Headquarters Third U.S. Army Interrogation Center (Provisional). *Interrogation Report No. 40: Frontaufklaerungskommandos*. 9 September 1945, NARS Record Group 238.

———. United States Forces European Theater, Military Intelligence Service Center. *CI Final Interrogation Report (CI-FIR) No. 83, Interrogation of Oberst Georg Buntrock*. 12 February 1946.

———. U.S. Forces European Theater, Military Intelligence Service Center. *CI Preliminary Interrogation Report (CI-PIR) 98: Heinrich von Westarp*. 31 January 1946.

———. *Report on the Case of Walter Friedrich Schellenberg*. NARS Record Group 319, XE001752, undated.

———. Seventh Army Interrogation Center, *Notes on the Red Army — Intelligence and Security: Interrogation and Assessment on P/W Brigadier General Reinhard Gehlen and Major Albert Scholler, Foreign Armies East,* SAIC/2/2, 24 June 1945, 5, NARS Record Group 238, Records of World War II War Crimes, Entry 160, Folder 87, Box 18.

———. United States Forces European Theater, Military Intelligence Service Center. *Counterintelligence Special Interrogation Report: Richard Kauder.* 15 July 1946. NARS Record Group 319, XE061758, Folder 2.

———. *Interrogation of Franz Bergler and Hilde Augusti,* 2 January 1947. XE061758, NARS Record Group 319.

———. SCI Unit A, Salzburg, Austria. *Interrogation Report No. 1: Richard Kauder aka Klatt aka Karmany.* LSX 41, undated. NARS Record Group 319, XE061758.

———. *Interrogation of Oberstleutnant Wagner aka Dr. Otto Delius on His Activities of the Klatt Meldekopf in Sofia.* 3 February 1947. XE061758, NARS Record Group 319.

———. Office of the Chief of Military History, Special Studies Division. *The German Campaign in Russia: Planning and Operations (1940–1942),* Department of Army Pamphlet No. 20–26a (Washington, D.C.: U.S. Government Printing Office, March 1955).

———. *Peter Report Number 576, Abwehr IG,* 10 December 1945. No other identifying data.

———. *The German Intelligence Service and the War.* 1 December 1945. NARS Record Group 319 XE003641, Box 5, Folders 1–3.

———. 7707th European Command Intelligence Center. *Counterintelligence Special Report No. 61 (CI-SR/61), Unternehmen (Operation) Zeppelin: Interrogation of Heinrich Fenner, Former Chief of Hauptkommando Sued.* 6 March 1948. XE003374, NARS Record Group 319.

———. Foreign Military Studies Program, No, D-407. 10 September 1954. Generalmajor Rudolph Langehaueser, "Studie ueber die Beschaffung von Feindnachrichten im deutschen Heer waehrend des 2.Weltkrieges an der Ostfront." Available, NARS, College Park, Md.

———. *Field Manual 34-60: Counterintelligence.* Washington, D.C. October 1995.

———. *Handbook on U.S.S.R. Military Forces.* November 1945. Technical Manual TM 30-430.

———. General and Special Staffs. Assistant Chief of Staff, G-2 Intelligence Division. Captured Personnel and Material Branch. Enemy POW Interrogation File, 1943–1945. *Report of Interrogation No. 5725: Preliminary Interrogation Report and Assessment of (Brigadier General Reinhard Gehlen).* 28 August 1945. WNRC 165, "G" Entry 179.

USSR

Komiteta Gosudarstvennoi Bezopasnosti pri Sovete Ministrov SSSR Vyshaia Krasnoznamennaia Shkola imeni F. Z. Dzerzhinskovo, Spetsial'naia Kafedra No. 9. *Istoriia Sovetskikh Organov Gosudarstvennoi Bezopasnosti,* Uchebnik, No. 12179, Sovershenno Sekretno, 2192, Moskva, 1977. Document available as of 31 August 2002 at http://www.fas.harvard.edu

Books and Articles

Ambrose, Stephen. *Ike's Spies: Eisenhower and the Espionage Establishment.* Jackson: University Press of Mississippi, 1999 [1981].

Andrew, Christopher. *Her Majesty's Secret Service: The Making of the British Intelligence Community.* New York: Viking, 1986.

Andrew, Christopher, and Oleg Gordievsky. *The KGB: The Inside Story of Its Foreign Operations from Lenin to Gorbachev.* New York: HarperCollins, 1990.

Armstrong, John A., ed. *Soviet Partisans in World War II.* Madison: University of Wisconsin Press, 1964.

Artemiev, Vyacheslav P. "OKR: State Security in the Soviet Armed Forces." *Military Review* 53 (September 1963).

Barron, John. *KGB: The Secret Work of Soviet Secret Agents.* New York: Reader's Digest, 1974.

———. *The KGB Today: The Hidden Hand.* New York: Reader's Digest, 1983.

Barros, James, and Richard Gregor. *Double Deception: Stalin, Hitler, and the Invasion of Russia.* De Kalb: Northern Illinois University Press, 1995.

Bartov, Omar. *Hitler's Army: Soldiers, Nazis, and War in the Third Reich.* New York: Oxford University Press, 1991.

Beevor, Anthony. *The Fall of Berlin, 1945.* New York: Viking, 2002.

———. *Stalingrad: The Fateful Siege.* New York: Viking, 1998.

Belousov, M. A. *Unreported at the Time: Memoirs of a Military Chekist* (Ob etom ne soobshchalos': Zapiski armeiskogo chekista). Translated by the Defense Intelligence Agency, LN 681-84. Moscow: Voennizdat', 1978.

Bentley, Elizabeth. *Out of Bondage.* New York: Ivy, 1990.

Bezymenskii, Lev. "Geine po imeni Maks, ili istoriya odnoi tainoi operatsii." *Novoe Vremia,* no. 41 (1993): 40–42.

Bialer, Seweryn, ed. *Stalin and His Generals: Soviet Military Memoirs of World War II.* New York: Pegasus, 1969.

Bogdanov, A. A., and I. Y. Leonov, eds. *Armeiskie Chekisty: Vospominaniia voennykh kontrrazvedchikov lenningradskovo, volkhovskovo i karel'skovo frontov.* Leningrad: Lenizdat', 1985.

Boog, Horst. "German Air Intelligence in the Second World War." In *Intelligence and Military Operations*, ed. Michael I. Handel, 350–425. London: Frank Cass, 1990.

Breitman, Richard. *The Architect of Genocide: Himmler and the Final Solution.* New York: Knopf, 1991.

Browning, Christopher R. *Ordinary Men: Reserve Police Battalion 101 and the Final Solution in Poland.* New York: HarperCollins, 1992.

Bucheit, Gert. *Der Deutsche Geheimdienst: Geschichte der militaerischen Abwehr.* Munich: List Verlag, 1966.

Bullock, Alan. *Hitler and Stalin: Parallel Lives.* New York: Knopf, 1992.

Burdick, Charles, and Hans-Adolph Jacobsen. *The Halder War Diary, 1939–1942.* Novato, Calif.: Presidio, 1988.

Carl, Leo D. *International Dictionary of Intelligence.* McLean, Va: International Defense Consultants, 1990.

Central Intelligence Agency, *Counterintelligence Briefs: The Hunt for "Gestapo Mueller"* (Directorate of Plans, Counterintelligence Staff, December 1971), NARS Record Group 263 (released under the Nazi War Crimes Disclosure Act, 2000).

Central Intelligence Agency. *The Rote Kapelle. The CIA's History of Soviet Intelligence and Espionage Networks in Western Europe 1936–1945.* Frederick, Md. University Publications of America, 1979.

Chernyavsky, Vitaly. "We Could Have Used Mueller." *New Times,* no. 36 (1991): 38.

Cookridge, E. H. *Gehlen: Spy of the Century.* London: Hodder and Stoughton, 1971.

Cooper, Matthew. *The German Army, 1933–1945: Its Political and Military Failure.* New York: Stein and Day, 1978.

Conquest, Robert. *The Great Terror: Stalin's Purge of the Thirties.* New York, Macmillan, 1968.

———. *Inside Stalin's Secret Police: NKVD Politics, 1936–1939.* Stanford: Hoover Institution Press, 1985.

———. *Stalin: Breaker of Nations.* New York: Viking, 1991.

Costello, John, and Oleg Tsarev. *Deadly Illusions.* New York: Crown, 1993.

Courtois, Stephanie; Nicholas Werth, Jan-Louis Panne, Andrzej Paczkowski, Karel Bartosek, and Jean-Louis Margolin. *The Black Book of Communism: Crimes, Terror, and Repression.* Cambridge, Mass.: Harvard University Press, 1999.

Crankshaw, Edward. *The Gestapo.* London: Putnam, 1956.

Dailey, Brian D., and Patrick J. Parker, eds. *Soviet Strategic Deception.* Lexington, Mass.: Lexington Books, 1987.

Dallin, Alexander. *German Rule in Russia, 1941–1945: A Study of Occupation Policies.* 2nd rev. ed. Boulder, Colo.: Westview, 1981.

Dallin, David J. *Soviet Espionage.* New Haven, Conn.: Yale University Press, 1955.

Defense Intelligence Agency, Defense Intelligence School. *Bibliography of Intelligence Literature.* 7th rev. ed. Washington, D.C.: Defense Intelligence Agency, August 1981.

Delarue, Jacques. *The Gestapo: A History of Horror.* Translated by Mervyn Savill. New York: Dell, 1964.

Deriabin, Peter. *Watchdogs of Terror: Russian Bodyguards from the Tsars to Commissars.* 2nd ed. Frederick, Md.: University Publications of America, 1984.

Deriabin, Peter, and T. H. Bagley. *The KGB: Masters of the Soviet Union.* New York: Hippocrene, 1990.

Deriabin, Peter, and Frank Gibney. *The Secret World.* New York: Ballantine, 1982.

Djakov, Yuri Y. and Bushuyeva, Tat'ana S. *The Red Army and the Wehrmacht: How the Soviets Militarized Germany, 1923–1933, and Paved the Way for Fascism.* New York: Prometheus, 1995.

Duffy, Christopher. *Red Storm on the Reich: The Soviet March on Germany, 1945.* New York: Macmillan, 1991.

———. *Russia's Military West: Origins and Nature of Russian Military Power, 1700–1800.* London: Routledge, 1981.

Dziak, John J. *Chekisty: A History of the KGB.* Lexington, Mass.: Lexington Books, 1988.

———. "Soviet Deception: The Organizational and Operational Tradition." In *Soviet Strategic Deception,* ed. Brian D. Dailey and Patrick J. Parker. Lexington, Mass.: Lexington Books, 1987.

———. "The Study of the Soviet Intelligence and Security System." In *Comparing Foreign Intelligence Services,* ed. Roy Godson, 65–88. London: Pergamon and Brassey's: 1988.

Dziak, John J., and Raymond G. Rocca. *Bibliography on Soviet Intelligence and Security Services.* Boulder, Colo: Westview, 1985.

Egorov, Viktor. *Zagovor pripriv Evriki* (Moscow: Sovetskaia Rossiia, 1968).

Erickson, John. "New Thinking about the Eastern Front in World War II." *Journal of Military History* 56 (April 1992): 283–292.

———. *The Road to Berlin: Continuing Stalin's War with Germany.* Boulder, Colo.: Westview, 1984.

———. *The Road to Stalingrad: Stalin's War with Germany.* Boulder, Colo.: Westview, 1975.

———. *The Soviet High Command: A Military-Political History.* New York: St. Martin's, 1962.

Federal'naia Sluzhba Kontrrazvedki Rossiiski Federatsii, Akademiia Federal'noi Sluzhby Kontrrazvedki Rossiiskoi Federatsii. *Organy Gosudarstvennoi Bezopasnosti SSSR v Velikoi Otechestvennoi Voine: Sbornik Dokumentov. Tom I, Nakanune, Kniga Pervaia, Noiabr' 1938 g.-Dekabr' 1940 g.: Kniga Vtoraia 1 Ianvaria–21 Iiunia 1941 g.* Moscow: Kniga i Biznes, 1995.

———. *Organy Gosudarstvennoi Bezopastnosti SSSR v Velikoi Otechestvennoi Voine: Sbornik Dokumentoi, Tom 2, Kniga Pervaia, Nachalo, 22 Iiunia–31 Avgusta 1941 goda, Kniga Dva, 1 Sentiabria–31 Dekabria 1941 goda.* Moscow: Izdatel'stvo Rus', 2000.

Federal'naia Sluzhba Bezopasnosti Rossiiskoi Federatsii i Moskovskoe Gorodskoe Obiedinennie Arkhivov. *Lubianka II: Iz Istorii Otechestvennoi Kontrrazvedki.* Moscow: Izdatel'stvo Obieedinennia Mosgorrkhiv, 1999.

Ferris, John. "Fortitude in Context: The Evolution of British Deception in the Second World War." Forthcoming.

Fischer, Klaus. *Nazi Germany: A New History.* New York: Continuum, 1995.

Gehlen, Reinhard. *The Service: The Memoirs of General Reinhard Gehlen.* Translated by David Irving. New York: World, 1972.

Gellermann, Guenther W. *Moskau ruft Heeres Gruppe Mitte.* Koblenz: Berbard und Graefe Verlag, 1988.

Geyer, Michael. "National Socialist Germany: The Politics of Information." In *Knowing One's Enemies: Intelligence Assessments before the Two World Wars,* ed. Ernest R. May, 310–347. Princeton, N.J.: Princeton University Press, 1984.

Glantz, David M. *Barbarossa: Hitler's Invasion of Russia, 1941*. Charleston, S.C.: Tempus, 2001.

———. *The Battle for Leningrad, 1941–1944*. Lawrence: University Press of Kansas, 2002.

———. "The Red Mask: The Nature and Legacy of Soviet Military Deception in the Second World War." *Intelligence and National Security* 2, no. 3 (July 1987): 175–259.

———. *The Role of Intelligence in Soviet Military Strategy*. Novato, Calif.: Presidio, 1990.

———. *Soviet Military Deception in the Second World War*. London: Frank Cass, 1989.

———. *Soviet Military Intelligence in War*. London: Frank Cass, 1990.

———. *Stumbling Colossus: The Red Army on the Eve of War*. Lawrence: University Press of Kansas, 1998.

———. *When Titans Clashed: How the Red Army Stopped Hitler*. Lawrence: University Press of Kansas, 1995.

———. *Zhukov's Greatest Defeat: The Red Army's Epic Disaster in Operation Mars, 1942*. Lawrence: University Press of Kansas, 1999.

Glantz, David M., and Jonathan M. House. *The Battle of Kursk*. Lawrence: University Press of Kansas, 1999.

Glees, Anthony. *The Secrets of Service: A Story of Soviet Subversion of Western Intelligence*. New York: Carroll and Graf, 1987.

Gorodetsky, Gabriel. *Grand Delusion: Stalin and the German Invasion of Russia*. New Haven, Conn.: Yale University Press, 1999.

Greene, Harris. "Rescue of Max." *Foreign Literary Intelligence Scene* 5, no. 3 (May/June 1986): 1–3.

Handel, Michael I., ed. *Leaders and Intelligence*. London: Frank Cass, 1989.

Haynes, John E., and Harvey Klehr. *Venona: Decoding Soviet Espionage in America*. New Haven, Conn.: Yale University Press, 1999.

Heilbrunn, Otto. *The Soviet Secret Services*. London: Allen and Unwin, 1957.

Heller, Mikhail, and Aleksandr N. Nekrich. *Utopia in Power: The History of the Soviet Union from 1917 to the Present*. Translated by Phyllis B. Carlos. New York: Summit, 1986.

Hilberg, Raul. *The Destruction of the European Jews*. Chicago: Quandrangle, 1961.

Hingley, Ronald. *The Russian Secret Police: Muscovite, Imperial Russian, and Soviet Political Security Operations*. New York: Simon and Schuster, 1970.

Hinsley F. H., and C. A. G. Simkins. *British Intelligence in the Second World War: Volume 4: Security and Counterintelligence*. London: Her Majesty's Stationery Office, 1990.

Hoehne, Heinz. *Canaris: Hitler's Master Spy*. Translated by J. Maxwell Brownjohn. Garden City, N.Y.: Doubleday, 1979.

———. *Codeword Direktor: The Story of the Red Orchestra*. Translated by Richard Barry. New York: Ballantine, 1982.

———. *Der Krieg im Dunkeln: Macht und Einfluss der Deutschen und Russischen Geheimdienste*. Munich: C. Bertelsmann Verlag GmbH, 1985.

———. *The Order of the Death's Head: The Story of Hitler's SS*. Translated by Richard Barry. New York: Ballantine, 1977.

Hoehne, Heinz, and Hermann Zolling. *The General Was a Spy: The Truth about General Reinhard Gehlen and His Spy Ring.* Translated by Richard Barry. New York: Coward, McCann, and Geoghegan, 1972.

Hoettel, Wilhelm. *The Secret Front: The Story of Nazi Political Espionage.* Translated by R. H. Stevens. New York: Praeger, 1954.

Hood, William. *Mole: The True Story of the First Russian Intelligence Officer Recruited by the CIA.* New York: Norton, 1982.

Iakovlev, A. N., ed. *Rossiia XX Vek: Dokumenty; Liubianka, VCHK-OGPU-NKVD-MGB-MVD-KGB 1917–1960, Spravochnik.* Moscow: Mezhdunarodnyi Fond, Demokratia, 1997.

Ionov, M. D. "On the Method of Influencing the Opponent's Decision." In *Selected Readings from Military Thought,* vol. 5, part 2 (Washington, D.C.: U.S. Government Printing Office, 1982), 164–171.

Istoriia velikoi otechestvennoi voiny Sovetskogo Soiuza 1941–1945, Volume 6. Moscow: Demokratia, 1960.

Kahn, David. *Hitler's Spies: German Military Intelligence in World War II.* New York: Macmillan, 1978.

Keegan, John. *The Second World War.* New York: Penguin, 1989.

Kerr, Sheila. "KGB Sources on the Cambridge Network of Soviet Agents: True or False?" *Intelligence and National Security* 11, no. 3 (July 1996): 561–585.

Khokhlov, Nikolai. *In the Name of Conscience.* Translated by Emily Kingsbery. New York: David McKay, 1959.

Korovin, V. V. *Sovetskaia razvedka i kontrrazvedka v gody Velikoi Otechestvennoi Voiny.* Moscow: Izdatel'stvo Rus', 1998.

Knight, Amy W. "The Alger Hiss Story: The Selling of the KGB." *Wilson Quarterly* (winter 2000): 1–10. Available from the journal's website.

———. *Beria: Stalin's First Lieutenant.* Princeton, N.J.: Princeton University Press, 1993.

———. *The KGB: Police and Politics in the Soviet Union.* Boston: Unwin Hyman, 1988.

———. "Russian Archives: Opportunities and Obstacles." *International Journal of Intelligence and Counterintelligence* 12, no. 3 (1999): 325–337.

Krivosheev, G. F., ed. *Soviet Casualties and Combat Losses in the Twentieth Century.* London: Greenhill, 1997.

Lamphere, Robert, and Tom Schachtman. *The FBI-KGB War: A Special Agent's Story.* New York: Random House, 1986.

Laqueur, Walter. *The Dream That Failed: Reflections on the Soviet Union.* Oxford: Oxford University Press, 1994.

———. *Stalin: The Glasnost Revelations.* New York: Scribner's, 1990.

———. *The Terrible Secret: Suppression of the Truth about Hitler's Final Solution.* New York: Penguin, 1982.

Lee, Bruce. *Marching Orders: The Untold Story of World War II.* New York: Da Capo, 2001.

Leverkuehn, Paul. *German Military Intelligence.* New York: Praeger, 1954.

Levytsky, Boris. *The Uses of Terror: The Soviet Secret Police, 1917–1970.* Translated by H. A. Piehler. New York: Coward, McCann, and Geoghegan, 1972.

Liddell Hart, B. H., ed. *The Red Army: The Red Army 1918 to 1945; The Soviet Army 1946 to the Present.* New York: Harcourt Brace, 1956.

Lucas, James. *War on the Eastern Front: The German Soldier in Russia, 1941–1945.* New York: Bonanza, 1982 [1979].

Lukin, A. "Zagovor ne sostoialsa." In *Front bez linii fronta* (Moscow: Moskovskiie Rabochii, 1970).

Malia, Martin. *The Soviet Tragedy: A History of Socialism in Russia, 1917–1991.* New York: Free Press, 1994.

Masterman, J. C. *The Double-Cross System in the War of 1939–1945.* New Haven, Conn.: Yale University Press, 1972.

Megargee, Geoffrey P. *Inside Hitler's High Command.* Lawrence: University Press of Kansas, 2000.

Meyer, Winfried. *Unternehmen Sieben: Eine Rettungsaktion vom Holocaust Bedrohte aus dem Amt/Ausland/Abwehr im Oberkommando der Wehrmacht.* Frankfurt-am-Main: Verlag Anton Hain GmbH, 1993.

Militaergeschichtliches Forschungsamt, ed. Boog, Horst, Juegern Foerster, Joachim Hoffmann, Ernst Klink, Rolf-Dieter Mueller, and Gerd R. Uebershcaer, *Germany and the Second World War.* Volume IV: *The Attack on the Soviet Union.* Translated by Dean S. McMurry, Ewald Osers, and Louise Willmont. New York: Oxford University Press, 1996.

Modin, Yuri. *My Five Cambridge Friends: Burgess, Maclean, Philby, Blunt, and Cairncross.* Translated by Anthony Roberts. New York: Farrar, Straus, and Giroux, 1994.

Moll, Wilhelm, Eric Waldman, and Earl Ziemke. *Project Cleopatra: Soviet Agent Operations in the German-Occupied Territories during World War II.* Bureau of Applied Social Research, Columbia University, on contract to the U.S. Government, May 1955.

Mueller, Rolf-Dieter, and Gerd R. Ueberschaer. *Hitler's War in the East, 1941–1945: A Critical Assessment.* Translated by Bruce D. Little. Providence, Oxford: Berghahn, 1997.

Mulligan, Timothy. *The Politics of Illusion and Empire: German Occupation Policy in the Soviet Union, 1942–1943.* New York: Praeger, 1988.

Murphy, David E., Sergei A. Kondrashev, and George Bailey. *Battleground Berlin: CIA vs. KGB in the Cold War.* New Haven, Conn.: Yale University Press, 1997.

———. "Spies, Ciphers, and Zitadelle: Intelligence and the Battle of Kursk, 1943." *Journal of Contemporary History* 22, no. 2 (1987): 235–260.

Naftali, Timothy. "Analysis of the Name File of Heinrich Mueller." In *Counterintelligence Briefs: The Hunt for "Gestapo Mueller"* (Directorate of Plans, Counterintelligence Staff, December 1971), NARS Record Group, 263 (released under Nazi War Crimes Disclosure Act, 2000).

———. "Pavel Sudoplatov Assassin's Tales." *Boston Book Review*, September 1994, 4, 31.

———. "Im Zerrspiegel: US-Gegenspionage in Deutschland, 1945–1948." In Wolfgang Krieger and Juergen Weber, *Spionage fuer den Frieden: Nachrichtendienste in Deutschland waehrend des Kalten Krieges*, Munich: Guenter Olzog Verland GmbH, 1997.

Nicolai, Walter. *The German Secret Service*. London: Stanley Paul, 1924.

Nosryev, D. P. *V poedinke s abverom. Dokumental'ny ocherk o chekistakh leningradskovo fronta, 1941–1945*. Moscow: Voennizdat', 1968.

Ostryakov. *Military Chekists (Voennye Chekisty)*. Translated by the Defense Intelligence Agency, LN-290-80. Moscow: Voennizdat', 1979.

Overy, Richard. *Russia's War: A History of the Soviet War Effort*. New York: Penguin, 1998.

Paret, Peter, ed. *Makers of Modern Strategy*. Princeton, N.J.: Princeton University Press, 1986.

Parrish, Michael. *The Lesser Terror: Soviet State Security, 1939–1953*. Westport, Conn.: Praeger, 1996.

———. *Soviet Security and Intelligence Organizations, 1917–1990: A Biographical Dictionary and Review of Literature in English*. New York, Westport, Conn.: Greenwood, 1992.

Perrault, Gilles. *The Red Orchestra*. Translated by Peter Wiles. New York: Schocken, 1969.

Petrov, Vladimir, and Evdokia Petrov. *Empire of Fear*. New York: Praeger, 1956.

Primakov, E. M., ed., *Ocherki Istorii Rossiiskoi Vneshnei Razavedki, Tom 3, 1933–1941*. Moscow: Mezhdunarodnnye Otonosheniia, 1999.

Radio Free Europe/Radio Liberty. "Declassified Documents Indicate Stalin Proposed Alliance with Hitler against U.S. and Britain." *Security and Terrorism Watch* 3, no. 37 (22 October 2002).

Reese, Mary Ellen. *General Reinhard Gehlen: The CIA Connection*. Fairfax, Va.: George Mason University Press, 1990.

Reitlinger, Gerhard. *The House Built on Sand: The Conflicts of German Policy in Russia, 1939–1945*. London: Weidenfeld and Nicolson, 1960.

Reitz, James T. "The Soviet Security Troops: The Kremlin's Other Armies." *Soviet Armed Forces Review Annual* 6 (1982): 297–298.

Reshin, Leonid. "Bez Grifa Sekretno: Skortseni, Sudoplatov porazhenie cheloveka so shramom: Vpervye rasskazyvaem o krupneishei v istorii vtoroi mirovoi voiny radioigre sovetskoi rasvedki s abverom." *Krasnaya Zvezda*, 23 September 1995.

Riasanovsky, Nicholas V. *A History of Russia:* 4th ed. New York: Oxford University Press, 1984.

Riele, Oskar. *Der Deutsche Geheimdienst im Zweiten Weltkrieg; Ostfront: Die Abwehr im Kampf mit den Geheimdiensten im Osten*. Munich: Weltbild Verlag GmbH, 1990.

Riha, Thomas. *Readings in Russian Civilization.* Volume 1: *Russia before Peter the Great, 900–1700.* 2nd ed. Chicago: University of Chicago Press, 1969.

Romanov, A. I. *Nights Are Longest There: A Memoir of the Soviet Security Services.* Translated by Gerald Brooke. Boston: Little, Brown, 1972.

Romerstein, Herbert, and Levchenko, Stanislav. *The KGB against the Main Enemy: How the Soviet Intelligence Service Operates in the United States.* Lexington, Mass.: Lexington Books, 1989.

Romerstein, Herbert, and Eric Breindel. *The Venona Secrets: Exposing Soviet Espionage and America's Traitor.* Washington, D.C.: Regnery, 2000.

Ruffner, Kevin. "CIC Records: A Valuable Tool for Researchers." Central Intelligence Agency, *Center for the Study of Intelligence Bulletin,* no. 11 (Summer 2000).

Ryan, Cornelius. *The Last Battle.* New York: Pocket Books, 1967.

Sayer, Ian, and Douglas Botting. *America's Secret Army: The Untold Story of the Counterintelligence Corps.* New York: Franklin Watts, 1989.

Schellenberg, Walter. *Hitler's Secret Service: The Memoirs of Walter Schellenberg.* Translated by Louis Hagen. New York: Harcourt Brace Jovanovich, 1977.

Seaton, Albert. *The Russo-German War, 1941–1945.* Novato, Calif.: Presidio, 1993 [1971].

Security and Intelligence Foundation. *The Trust.* Edited by Pamela K. Simkins and Leigh K. Dyer. Arlington, Va., 1989. Originally prepared by the Central Intelligence Agency, reprinted by SIF, and obtained under the FOIA.

Sergeev, F. *Tainye Operatsii Natsistskoi Razvedki, 1933–1945.* Moscow: Isdatel'stvo Politicheskoi Literatury, 1991.

Sevin, Dieter. "Operation Scherhorn." *Military Review* 46, no. 3 (March 1966): 35–43.

Silver, Arnold M. "Questions, Questions, Questions: Memories of Oberursel." *Intelligence and National Security* 8, no. 2 (April 1993): 199–213.

Smith, Bradley F. *Sharing Secrets with Stalin: How the Allies Traded Intelligence, 1941–1945.* Lawrence: University Press of Kansas, 1996.

Solzhenitsyn, Aleksandr I. *GULAG Archipelago: 1918–1956: An Experiment in Literary Investigation.* Parts 1 and 2. Translated by Thomas P. Whitney. New York: Harper and Row, 1973; Parts 3 and 4, 1975.

"Sovetskie Organy Gosudarstvennoi Bezopasnosti v Gody Velikoi Otechestvennoi Voiny." *Voprosii Istorii,* no. 5 (1965): 20–39.

Sovetskaia Voennaia Entsiklopediia 4 (1977); s.v. "Kontrrazvedka," 326.

Skorzeny, Otto. *My Commando Operations: The Memoirs of Hitler's Most Daring Commando.* Translated by David Johnston. Atglen, Pa.: Schiffer, 1995.

Stein, George H. *The Waffen SS.* Ithaca, N.Y.: Cornell University Press, 1966.

Stephan, Robert W. "Death to Spies: The Story of SMERSH: Soviet Military Counterintelligence during World War II." Master's thesis, American University, 1984.

________. "The Role and Effectiveness of Soviet Combat Counterintelligence during World War II." Ph.D. dissertation, George Washington University, 1997.

________. "Smersh: Soviet Military Counterintelligence during the Second World War." *Journal of Contemporary History* 22 (1987): 585–613.

Stolfi, R.H.S. *Hitler's Panzers East.* Norman: University of Oklahoma Press, 1993.

Strong, Sir Kenneth, W. D., *Men of Intelligence: A Study of the Roles and Decisions of Chiefs of Intelligence from World War I to the Present Day.* London: Cassell, 1970.

Sudoplatov, Pavel. *Spetsoperatsii: Liubianka i Kreml', 1930–1950 gody.* Moscow: Izdatel'stskaia Firma, Olma-Press, 1998.

Sudoplatov, Pavel, and Anatoli Sudoplatov, with Jerrold L. Schecter and Leona P. Schecter. *Special Tasks: The Memoirs of an Unwanted Witness — A Soviet Spymaster.* Boston: Little, Brown, 1994.

Tarasov, Dmitrii Petrovich. *Bol'shaia Igra (Dokumental'nii Obzor i Khudozhestvenno-dokumental'nii ocherk "Pamiatnaia duel'."* Moscow: Zhizn', 1997.

Tarrant, V. E. *The Red Orchestra: The Soviet Spy Network inside Nazi Europe.* London: Cassell Military Classics, 1998.

Thomas, David. "Foreign Armies East and German Military Intelligence in Russia, 1941–1945." *Journal of Contemporary History* 22 (1987): 261–301.

———. "The Legend of Agent Max." *Foreign Literary Intelligence Scene* 5, no. 1 (January 1986): 1–2, 5.

Trubnikov, V. I., ed. *Ocherki Istorii Rossiiskoi Vneshnei Razavedki, Tom 4, 1941–1945.* Moscow: Mezhdunarodnye Otonosheniia, 1999.

Tsinev, Georgi. "Na strazhe interesov vorruzhennykh sil SSSR." *Kommunist Vorruzhennykh Sil* 24 (December 1978): 26–31. Translated by U.S. Joint Publications Research Service No. 73037, *USSR Military Affairs,* no. 1421 (20 March 1979): 1–8.

Tsinev, G. K., ed. *Voenni Kontrrazvedchiki.* Moscow: Voyenizdat, 1978.

Ulam, Adam B. *Stalin: The Man and His Era.* New York: Viking, 1973.

United States Joint Publications Research Service, "Book on Military Counterintelligence Agents Reviewed," No. 1426, *Translations on USSR Military Affairs,* 133–135. Translation of a review by General of the Army A. Beloborodov of *Voennye Kontrrazvedchiki* (Moscow: Voyennizdat', 1978) in *Krasnaia Zvezda,* 21 February 179, 2.

United States, Joint Publications Research Service, No. 55623, April 1972, "The Failure of Operation Zeppelin." In *Collection of Articles on Soviet Intelligence and Security Operations,* 115–131. Translations of "Proval Aktsii Tseppelina," *Krasnaia Zvezda* 26, 28, 29, 30, December 1965, 4.

United States War Department, U.S. Army, Military Intelligence Division. *German Military Intelligence, 1939–1945.* Frederick, Md.: University Publications of America, 1984.

Volkogonov, Dmitri. *Stalin: Triumph and Tragedy.* Translated by Harold Shukman. New York: Grove Weidenfeld, 1991.

Vysshaia Krasnoznamennaia Shkola, Komitetea Gosudarstvennoi Bezopasnosti, pri Sovete Ministrov SSR imeni F. Z. Dzerzhinsogo, Sovershno Sekterno, *Kontrrazedyvatel'ni Slovar',* No. 10064, 1972.

Waller, John H. "The Double Life of Admiral Canaris," *Journal of Intelligence and Counterintelligence* 9, no. 3 (fall 1996): 271–289.

———. *The Unseen War in Europe: Espionage and Conspiracy in the Second World War.* New York: Random House, 1996.

Waller, Michael. "The Secret History of the KGB." *Insight Magazine* 15, no. 37, (4–11 October 1999): 1–7. Copy obtained from magazine's website.

Weinberg, Gerhard L. *A World at Arms: A Global History of World War II.* Cambridge: Cambridge University Press, 1994.

———. *Germany, Hitler, and World War II: Essays in Modern German and World History.* Cambridge: Cambridge University Press, 1995.

Weinstein, Allen, and Alexander Vassiliev. *The Haunted Wood: Soviet Espionage in America. The Stalin Era.* New York: Random House, 1999.

Werth, Alexander. *Russia at War, 1941–1945.* New York: E. P. Dutton, 1964.

West, Nigel, and Oleg Tsarev. *The Crown Jewels: The British Secrets at the Heart of the KGB Archives.* New Haven, Conn.: Yale University Press, 1999.

Whaley, Barton. *Codeword Barbarossa.* Cambridge: MIT Press, 1974.

Whiting, Charles. *The Hunt for Martin Bormann: The Truth.* Rev. ed. London: Leo Cooper, 1996.

Winterbotham, F. W. *The Ultra Secret.* New York: Dell, 1974.

Wolin, Simon, and Robert M. Slusser. *The Soviet Secret Police.* Westport, Conn.: Greenwood, 1964.

World Almanac and Book of Facts 2001. Mahwah, N.J.: World Almanac Books, 2001.

Ziemke, Earl F. "Operation Kreml: Deception, Strategy, and the Fortunes of War." *Parameters: U.S. Army War College Quarterly* 9, no. 1 (9 March 1979): 72–82.

Ziemke, Earl F., and Magna E. Bauer. *Moscow to Stalingrad: Decision in the East.* New York: Military Heritage, 1988.

———. *Stalingrad to Berlin: The German Defeat in the East.* Washington D.C.: Center for Military History, 1966.

INDEX

Numbers in italics are tables or figures.